C0-ATS-625

RE-MAKING POETRY

RE-MAKING POETRY

TED HUGHES AND A NEW CRITICAL PSYCHOLOGY

NICK BISHOP

———— • ————

St. Martin's Press
New York

All rights reserved. For information, write:
Scholarly and Reference Division,
St. Martin's Press, Inc., 175 Fifth Avenue, New York, NY 10010

First published in the United States of America in 1991

Printed in Great Britain

ISBN 0–312–07200–7

Library of Congress Cataloging-in-Publication Data

Bishop, Nick.
    Re-making poetry: Ted Hughes and a new critical psychology / by
Nick Bishop.
        p.   cm.
    Includes bibliographical references.
    ISBN 0–312–07200–7
    1. Hughes, Ted. 1930–   .   —Criticism and interpretation.
    2. Psychology and literature. I. Title. II. Title: Remaking
poetry.
    PR6058.U37Z59   1991
    821'.914—dc20   91–31179
                                                              CIP

To Samantha

No, don't go yet, don't lower your veil.
The fuel of crocuses has lit up the meadows.
That's what you are then, life, although you say:
– By desire, we add something. But love remains love.
(Vladimir Holan, 'No, don't go yet')

CONTENTS

ACKNOWLEDGEMENTS

I would like to thank Ted Hughes for his continual generosity in answering all my queries, conversationally and by letter. I am also indebted to Keith Sagar for his encouragement and sound advice, and to all those who provided help and assistance along the way – especially Professor Michael Wood, Ron Tamplin, Peter Faulkner and Ron Bedford from the English Department at Exeter University. Finally I would like to thank my parents for their constant loyalty and support throughout the past five years during the production of this book.

The author and publishers gratefully acknowledge permission granted to reprint material in copyright:

Faber and Faber Ltd and Harper and Row for lines from poems by Ted Hughes in the collections, *The Hawk in the Rain* (Faber, 1957), *Lupercal* (Faber, 1960), *Wodwo* (Faber, 1967), *The Life and Songs of Crow* (Faber, 1970), *Gaudete* (Faber, 1977), *Cave Birds: an alchemical cave drama* (Faber, 1978), *Remains of Elmet: A Pennine sequence* (Faber, 1979), *Moortown* (Faber, 1979) and *River* (Faber, 1983).

From *Post-war Polish Poetry* edited by Czeslaw Milosz (University of California, 1983). Copyright. Used by permission of Doubleday, a division of Bantam Doubleday Dell Publishing Group, Inc.

'No, Don't Go Yet' from *Vladimir Holan: Selected Poems* translated by Jarmila and Ian Milner (Penguin Books, 1971). Copyright © Vladimir Holan, 1971, translation copyright © Jarmila and Ian Milner, 1971.

3 poems from *Speaking of Siva* translated by A.K. Ramanujan (Penguin Classics, 1973). Copyright © A.K. Ramanujan, 1973.

From *East German Poetry*, edited and translated by Michael Hamburger (Carcanet Press, 1972).

From *Crater*, János Pilinszky, translated by Peter Jay (Anvil Press Poetry, 1978).

From *Conversation with the Prince and other poems*, Tadeusz Rozewicz, translated by Adam Czerniawski (Anvil Press Poetry, 1982).

From *The Desert of Love – Selected Poems*, János Pilinszky, translated by János Csokits and Ted Hughes (Anvil Press Poetry, 1989). A revised and enlarged edition of *Selected Poems* (Carcanet Press, 1976).

From *Selected Poems* Zbigniew Herbert, translated by J. and B. Carpenter (Oxford University Press, 1977). By permission of Oxford University Press.

Every effort has been made to trace copyright holders, but if any has been inadvertently overlooked the author and publishers will be pleased to make the necessary arrangement at the first opportunity.

CHAPTER 1

————— • —————

INTRODUCTION

What is above is like what is below. What is below is like what is above
. . . . Everything is formed from the contemplation of unity, and all
things come about from unity, by means of adaptation. . . . It was borne
by the wind and nurtured by the Earth. . . . Through wisdom it rises
slowly from the world to heaven. Then it descends to the world,
combining the power of the upper and lower. Thus you shall have the
illumination of all the world, and darkness will disappear. (Hermes
Trismegistos, *The Emerald Tablet*, quoted by Idries Shah, *The Sufis*, p. 198)

THE STRUCTURE OF SELF

The aim of this book, as the title suggests, is double: on the one hand, it
seeks to unearth a 'new' psychological basis for literary criticism; on the
other, it applies that criticism practically to the work of the current Poet
Laureate, Ted Hughes. As the 'method' follows the development of
Hughes, so its own underlying principles and motivation are both
illuminated and nourished. The idea of a psychologically based criticism
may not seem new at all, but there are some important differences
between this and previous versions. Its basis is neither Freudian nor even
primarily Jungian, but derives from a much older esoteric 'tradition' of
which Jung himself is one half-conscious modern offshoot; that tradition
includes G. I. Gurdjieff and his student P. D. Ouspensky, the various
teachers and teaching systems of Sufic origin (summarized by Idries Shah
in *The Sufis*) and more recent teachers such as Carlos Castaneda and
Simone Weil. Not only is the psychological 'origin' of this critical
method a departure from previous practice, its mode of application is
also different: it strives to locate the set of psychological and cultural
assumptions operating in both poet *and* reader during readership of a
poem, it 'deconstructs' its own multiple and often contradictory
interpretive impulses, and the interpretations of other readers, as
willingly as it deconstructs those operating in the poet; the result is a kind

of double-faced critical psychology, which looks both inwards and outwards at the same time.

This kind of double consciousness fixes the critical trajectory of the book and provides the basis for the idea of a 'moral readership' of poetry – a readership which generates and sustains psychological growth, rather than simply obeying a predefined set of abstract (and *external*) critical rules. It is here that the mutually reciprocal nature of the relationship between poetic and critical practice becomes relevant, because the major transition we will witness in Hughes' work is a shift from the 'aesthetic' centre of poetry to its 'moral' centre, from a too-exclusive preoccupation with language and linguistic effects towards the extra-literary effort to re-possess a deeper, more Essential Self. Poetic endeavour and critical method alike run parallel courses, striving to free themselves of External constraint in order to uncover a more Internal rationale for the writing/reading of literature. Hughes himself points out, in a strenuous combination of 'literary' and 'esoteric' terms, that the real poetry of the literary act happens below the surface of the words on the page, in a change of psychological understanding:

> All falsities in writing – and the consequent dry-rot that spreads into the whole fabric – come from the notion that there is a stylistic ideal which exists in the abstract, like a special language, to which all men might attain. But teachers of written English should have nothing to do with that, which belongs rather to the study of manners and group jargon. Their words should not be 'How to write' but 'How to say what you really mean' – *which is part of the search for self-knowledge and perhaps, in one form or another, grace.* (*Poetry in the Making*, p. 12; my italics)

Hughes gives ample demonstration of a conflict of directions in writing: on the one hand, the writer develops *externally* through a continuous refinement of verbal procedures towards a 'stylistic ideal which exists in the abstract', creating for himself an *acquired* 'Personality' composed entirely of psychological/linguistic/cultural stereotypes ('the study of manners and group jargon'); on the other, he tries to 'say what he really means', binding language to the endless series of adjustments and improvisations following from the imperative 'Know thyself.' In this case all aesthetic advances are simply the visible sparks thrown off by the engine of psychological transformation.

The reciprocal nature of the relationship between poetic and critical practice should become clearer within this frame of reference – Hughes is, after all, addressing all *writers*, not merely *poets*. Literary criticism, like Poetry, has to rediscover its 'inner life': 'aesthetic criticism', valuing language through an abstract set of critical standards, now has to subordinate itself voluntarily to the prior claim of 'psychological criticism', which values the internal process actually undergone. If it does not – even to a small extent – renounce its power, the 'story' it invents for the poet will be at least incomplete, at worst an outright fiction reinforcing the hypnotic tyranny of what Hughes calls the 'objective imagination', the fact-recording faculty which only peers *outwards*, thinking that what it sees, in a poem and elsewhere, is what is really there.

It is the loss of balance between 'subjective' and 'objective' imaginations in all areas that Hughes regularly laments in his prose writings, particularly his two 'Myth and education' essays.

> The word 'subjective' was invented for a good reason – but under that vaguest of general terms lies the most important half of our experience. (85)

> we solve the problem by never looking inward. We identify ourselves and all that is wakeful and intelligent with our objective eye, saying, 'Let's be Objective'. . . . All the urgent information coming towards us from that inner world sounds to us like a blank, or at best the occasional glint, or a twinge. Because we have no equipment to receive it and decode it . . . we are disconnected. The exclusiveness of the objective eye, the very strength and brilliance of our objective intelligence, suddenly turns into stupidity – of the most rigid and suicidal kind. (87)

> The whole inner world has become elemental, chaotic, continually more primitive and beyond our control. It has become a place of demons. But of course, insofar as we are disconnected anyway from that world, and lack the equipment to pick up its signals, we are not aware of it. All we register is the vast absence, the emptiness, the sterility, the meaninglessness, the loneliness. If we do manage to catch a glimpse of our inner selves, by some contraption of mirrors, we recognise it with horror – it is an animal crawling and decomposing in hell. We refuse to own it. (90) ('Myth and education' 2)

As I suggested at the start of this book, any writer who wishes to regain an internal rationale for Poetry – in its creation or criticism – and become conscious of the precise nature of his own 'subjectivity', can do so only by connecting with the worlds of modern psychology and esoteric science, and with religious mythologies as opposed to theologies. They provide the 'equipment' necessary to pick up the signals coming from the inner world. In Hughes' case, this is not only evident in his interest in the writings of Jung and Gurdjieff (and Ouspensky), Castaneda and Sufism;[1] but additionally in the whole wealth of world mythologies – of which Graves' *The White Goddess* and Paul Radin's collection of Winnebago Indian stories *The Trickster* are the most prominent examples. All these evince the collective will to organize the inner world into intelligent patterns, to recognize and value differing stages in the evolution of the self. As a first principle, they begin with the realization that everything which is experienced as an 'outside' must also be experienced as an 'inside', or as Hughes puts it 'What you find in the outside world is what has escaped from your own inner world.' Schopenhauer knew that the world is in a meaningful sense our *idea*, in continual subjection to the nature and level of the consciousness trying to grasp it; Castaneda not only attests a world inevitably conditioned by the subject, but one held fast in place by what Don Juan calls the 'Internal dialogue', his phrase for the false certainty of the 'objective imagination'. 'I've told you that the internal dialogue is what grounds us', Don Juan said. 'The world is such and such or so and so, only because we talk to ourselves about it being such and such or so and so.'

> 'To change our idea of the world is the crux of sorcery,' he said. 'And stopping the Internal dialogue is the only way to accomplish it . . . . Now you're in the position to know that nothing of what you've seen or done, with the exception of stopping the Internal dialogue, could by itself have changed anything in you, or in your idea of the world.' (Castaneda, *Tales of Power*, pp. 19–20)

The subject – including writer or reader – who is to some extent conscious of his own 'inner life' cannot simply attend to the apparently 'given' objectivity of experience, his prior concern is the psychological complex within that *receives* the experience on his behalf, which digests it into understanding *in his name*. He glances inwards, at his own subjective foundations, in order to clear a space in which the objective contents of his experience can manifest themselves more fully, without unconscious 'infection'. Substituting 'poem' for 'world' in the Castaneda quotation, one might say that the task of the contemporary critic is to dismantle *himself* as comprehensively as he takes to pieces the living '*text*' or reality that comes so convincingly from the 'outside'. This is particularly necessary in any study of Hughes' work, because his choice involves him in open warfare with the hypnotic powers of the 'objective imagination' in all its forms, whether it issues through a preoccupation with the false 'stylistic ideal in the abstract', or in an abstract picture of the self, or even in a corrupt image of the Divine Nature itself.

As Hughes' jolting conjunction of the words 'poetry' and 'grace' in the passage from *Poetry in the Making* indicates, the Internal direction in poetry is basically religious, although in our own time the passage between the two terms is increasingly uncertain, fraught with anxiety:

> When I ask myself 'Am I religious', I can only think of the other ages and situations in which I might willingly have been included in a group of believers. I don't think I could confidently describe myself as having a religious temperament – as distinct from a nostalgia for the religious temperament. On the other hand, it seems to me common enough that a slight change of circumstances produces the most unexpected changes of temperament. I think that the personalities of most people . . . are multiple enough to make any debate about these questions very provisional and

speculative. If you describe the attempt to write poetry as an attempt to integrate all the inner factors of one's awareness, which also means an attempt to integrate the deepest reaches of one's awareness, you probably end up using metaphors that draw on religious terminology. But I personally would hesitate to give them any theological definition. And the 'devotional' aspect of trying to produce poetry would be best described, I think (even with poems such as 'Ash Wednesday'), as a regular and persistent effort to grasp the deepest awareness more deeply, more precisely and more sensitively on its own terms. (personal communication, 10 October 1984)

The effort to integrate the deeper reaches of awareness not only cuts across its own internal obstacles – Gurdjieff's fractured, multiple Self – but founders more seriously on the absence of communal, cultural support, the besetting problem of *Gaudete*; the writer cannot centre himself in a group of believers, in the forms of Exoteric religion which no longer provide a meaningful framework for the experiences he encounters in the inner world: once the Art–Religion coupling begins to break up, the prevailing artistic condition could be termed 'creative distress'. According to Hughes, those individuals who invented the mythological blueprints of Religion

> would now be writers of some sort. But the communal carrier-wave took hold of it – the spiritual solidarity. Now the dream stays with the individual, doesn't it . . . . Maybe some few others – and does it come from the same place? What sort of assent does it win? On what level? (personal communication, 22 November 1983)

What is left to the writer now is a 'nostalgia for the "religious temperament" ', that single word *nostalgia* prescribing both the religious fulfilment of the Internal Direction in writing and the present distance from that ideal culmination.

The moral failure has a psychological explanation and a historical context. What Jung calls the 'spiritual catastrophe' of the Reformation exchanged the vertical development of the Gothic Age for 'the horizontal outlook of modern times' (*Modern Man in Search of a Soul*, pp. 200–1) with its emphasis on literal expansion and physical discoveries. The ideal of the vertical axis, self-development – which obtained its last stronghold in alchemy – was replaced by a stress on outer exploration, from which the subject could disconnect himself with apparent impunity. Such a wholesale commitment to the 'objective imagination' and the 'horizontal' future it engineers, had severe consequences on the psychological level. The subject's confidence in the 'objectivity' of his perceptions created a critically unbalanced situation within the psyche by giving birth to an imaginary *picture* of the self, a False Ego-Personality split off from its deeper roots just as surely as the abstract stylistic ideal (which Hughes suggested threatened the proper use of writing) was divorced from the endeavour to 'say what you really mean'. The chief feature of the Ego-Personality is a security in its own judgements which may suppress any meaningful dialogue with what Jung terms the 'shadowself', any exploration of the psychic origin of its own responses. Here is Jung's diagnosis of the situation:

> Western Man is in danger of losing his shadow altogether, of identifying himself with his fictive personality and of identifying the world with the abstract picture painted by scientific rationalism. His spiritual and moral opponent, who is just as real as he, no longer dwells in his own breast but beyond the geographical line of division, which no longer represents an outward political barrier but splits off the conscious from the unconscious man more and more menacingly. Thinking and feeling lose their inner polarity, and where religious orientation has grown ineffective, not even a god is at hand to check the sovereign sway of unleashed psychic functions . . . .
>
> The more power man had over nature, the more his knowledge and skill went to his head, and the deeper became his contempt for the merely natural and accidental, for that which is irrationally given – including the objective psyche, which is all that consciousness is not . . . . The individual psyche has become a mere accident, a 'random' phenomenon, while the unconscious, which can manifest itself only in the real, 'irrationally given' human being, has been ignored altogether. This was not the result of carelessness or lack of knowledge, but of downright resistance to the mere possibility of there being a second psychic authority besides the ego. It seems a positive menace to the ego that its monarchy can be doubted. (*The Undiscovered Self*, pp. 82–6)

Within this perspective, Hughes' poetry records the struggle with, and defeat of the Ego-Personality and the 'objective imagination' upon which its monarchy is based. The first three major volumes, *The Hawk in the Rain, Lupercal* and *Wodwo*, bear witness to the violence generated by the Personality's initial re-discovery of the primitive contents of the unconscious, mostly in the form of animals or the natural elements – its vibration between the poles of downright resistance and a broader acceptance of the need for transformation. This confrontation of the Ego-Personality with all the elements it excludes reaches its bottom-most point in *Crow, from the Life and Songs of Crow*, where Crow is both a savage embodiment of those elements and a frequent caricature of the Ego-Personality and its most typical attitudes. As this combination of functions within the single 'heroic' body suggests, Crow is at the point of crisis, or transformation. He is 'trying to become a man'. *Cave Birds, an Alchemical Cave Drama* – which is the second part of the *Crow* narrative – goes further to describe the 'death' of Personality and the re-birth of an expanded, more conscious self, although the structure of Hughes' 'spiritual story' is only intermittently or incompletely *fulfilled* in the experience of poet and reader; Hughes has to fight back over the same ground in sequences such as 'Earth-numb' and 'Seven dungeon songs' from *Moortown*, and it is perhaps only in *River* that we find poems written regularly and persistently from the perspective of that deepest awareness which has already been clearly grasped 'more deeply, more precisely, and more sensitively on its own terms'.

The writer's 'moral' endeavour to rediscover that 'deepest awareness' can only be sustained by a force which stands *outside* the straightforward collision of Ego-Personality and unconscious shadow-self as mutually exclusive opposites. In particular, once the provisionality of the Ego-Personality is recognized, it becomes simply a point on the circumference of a circle which has its centre in what Jung calls the *collective* nature of the psyche. Before this centring is achieved, every self will be an improvisation, always symbolically open-ended – open at one end to the possibilities thrown up by the Unconscious, embracing an ironic vigilance towards the abstract construction of false selves and the myth of purely 'objective' perception. This fundamentally ironic nature of the self Hughes discerns in both Central European poetry (see his introduction to Vasko Popa's *Selected Poems*) and Shakespeare:

> Everybody went to right or left. Or, if they were too deep in both worlds – the old medieval Goddess' world and the world of the new Jehovah – they could do something imaginative. They could create a provisional *persona*, an emergency self, to deal with the crisis. They could create a self who would somehow hang on to all the fragments as the newly-throned god and deposed goddess tore each other to pieces behind his face. (*A Choice of Shakespeare's Verse*, p. 188)

This is a sure description of the territory of Hughes' own struggle, as well as Shakespeare's. The creation of an 'emergency self' is a way of hanging on to all the fragments of the self, of sustaining the possibility of psychological wholeness. The persona does not identify with *either* pole of the opposition, the 'objective' Ego-Personality *or* the suppressed unconscious, the archaic instinctual nature seen by the Personality as 'a sort of refuse bin underneath the conscious mind . . . merely animal nature' (*The Undiscovered Self*, p. 91). As long as the artist goes 'to right or left' – as Hughes originally accuses Shakespeare of doing with the suppression of instinctual Caliban by the rationalistic trickery of Prospero in *The Tempest* – no resolution is possible, the horizontal movement guarantees an increase of tension, a widening of the psychic split, a maintenance of dualism. Only the creation of a psychological third term, a new moral centre outside the opposites, allows the potential for self-development by providing a neutral medium in which the dramatic collision of 'Force' (usually an aspect of Ego-Personality) and 'Resistance' (unconscious 'Matter') can be witnessed, rather than prematurely resolved.[2] The idea of 'persona' in poetry has from this vantage point a deeper significance than 'aesthetic criticism' appreciates: Hughes' emergency self is much more than a purely literary device, it shows that the flexible play of the poetic imagination has a definite psychological objective because the succession of provisional selves it sets up refine towards a centre in the 'deepest awareness' beyond the terms of the dualistic conflict. One could say that the very structure of poetic discourse – founded on the endless, purposeful play of improvised 'I's – affords these specific occasions for self-knowledge naturally, as a matter of course.

In his chapter on 'The psychology of Christian alchemical symbolism' from *Aion*, Jung makes an important connection between the psychological necessity of a third term and the use of symbolic language:

> What the separation of the two psychic halves means, the psychiatrist knows only too well. He knows it as the dissociation of personality, the root of neuroses; the conscious goes to the right and the unconscious to the left. As opposites never unite at their own level, a supraordinate 'third' is always required, in which the two parts can come together. And since the symbol derives as much from the conscious as the unconscious, it is able to unite them both, reconciling their conceptual polarity through its form and their emotional polarity through its numinosity. (p. 180)

This crucial dependence of self-exploration on the use of symbolic language will be examined more fully later in the chapter; for the moment it is sufficient to record Jung's acquiescence with Hughes and Gurdjieff in the necessity of a 'supraordinate third'. Hughes' own term for the point of consciousness separate from, and above the dualistic warfare that characterizes the life of Personality, is *Imagination* – the simple use of the upper case marking out a movement beyond both the 'objective imagination' we have already discussed, and the worst excesses of 'subjective imagination', for example nineteenth-century Romantic ideology's indiscriminate surrender to instinct and feeling and fractured dream–vision:

> [It] keeps faith, as Goethe says, with the world of things and the world of spirits equally . . . .
> The inner world, separated from the outer world, is a place of demons. The outer world, separated from the inner world, is a place of meaningless objects and machines. The faculty that makes the human being out of these two worlds is called divine. That is only a way of saying that it is the faculty without which humanity cannot really exist. It can be called religious or visionary. More essentially, it is imagination which embraces both outer and inner worlds in a creative spirit. ('Myth and education', 2 p. 92)

The human imagination becomes moral, and fulfils its divine aspect, by inclining neither to right nor left in an act equivalent to renunciation; particularly in a time which has identified the whole self so closely with the Ego-Personality, the truly creative action of the 'just imagination' will mean self-loss. Presumably this is the sense of renunciation Simone Weil had in mind when she pointed out that 'Creative attention means really giving our attention to what does not exist' ('Forms of the implicit love of God', *Waiting on God*, p. 105). The Imagination in this sense will always summon what does not exist – what is unconscious – through the point of access given by temporary selves: to all intents and purposes it '*dies*' to the forceful demands of the Personality, with its high-profile visibility. At several points in his prose writing, Hughes indicates his awareness of the necessity of this 'death'-of-Personality – his interest in *The Tibetan Book of the Dead*, Shamanistic experience and Sufism (see, for example, his double review of Idries Shah's *The Sufis* and Eliade's *Shamanism* in *The Listener*, 29 October 1964) all evince the same realization: whatever the surrounding cultural context, the fundamental psychological event remains the same, a 'central experience of a shattering of the self, and the labour of fitting it together again or finding a new one' ('Notes on the chronological order of Sylvia Plath's poems', p. 83). One could say that the material fact of death provides a complete image for the desired process of self-development. Matter, personified ultimately by death, is always a ready-made antidote to the Ego-Personality's illusions about its own autonomy, and its tendency to think of itself as an abstracted model of good. The Puritan fear of the material world in general, and of mortality in particular, simply evaporates within this psychological frame-of-reference:

> All religions speak about death during this life on earth. Death must come before rebirth. But what must die? False confidence in one's own knowledge, self-love and egoism. Our egoism must be broken. We must realise that we are very complicated machines, and so this process of breaking is bound to be a long and difficult task. Before real growth becomes possible, our Personality must die. (Gurdjieff, from *Views from the Real World*, p. 86)

This death-to-Personality is achieved by the gradual realization that it is at every moment subject to material reality in the form of Instinctual-animal Nature, temporarily driven down into the unconscious. Simone Weil knew that the Personality was mechanical rather than free, subordinate to a force called 'necessity': 'For us, matter is simply what is subjected to necessity. . . . Necessity is an enemy for man as long as he thinks in the first person' (*Intimations of Christianity among the Ancient Greeks*, pp. 179–80). Nothing terrorizes first-person thinking more than the idea of its own extinction; in the historical context provided by sixteenth-century Britain, one can see the civil war of the two disastrously split Puritan terms, 'Spirit' and 'Matter', as a psychological consequence of the False Personality's effort to disengage itself from its material roots in the unconscious whole, as in Marlowe's *Dr Faustus*. In the tragic theatre of the 'objective imagination', Spirit is good and Matter is evil, regardless of the psychological foundation of the attitude, and it is to the theological aspect of this crisis that we must now turn our attention.

THE *IMAGO DEI*

Hughes' struggle with false representations of the self finds a clear echo in his struggle with distorted conceptions of the divine nature; for, as he puts it in his appendix to *A Choice of Shakespeare's Verse*, 'How things are between man and his idea of the Divinity determines everything in his life, the quality and connectedness of every feeling and thought, and the meaning of every action' (pp. 184–5). Just as Hughes understood the structure of poetic discourse as an open-ended invitation to all 'I's within the self to re-combine, so the idea of the Divinity has a potential for establishing either connectedness or tragic division within the individual psyche – and it is quite clear from his essay on Shakespeare which of these alternatives Hughes sees as the historical consequence of the Reformation. There he describes a conflict between two versions of the Creator, the one 'who was the goddess of Catholicism, who was the goddess of Medieval and Pre-Christian England . . . who was the goddess of natural law and love, who was the goddess of all sensation and organic life' (p. 187), and identified in the Puritan mentality with the principle of Matter, and the other who was the purely all-good 'young Puritan Jehovah' and identified with Spirit. As early as 'Logos' from *Wodwo*, this conflict was surfacing directly in Hughes' poetry; that poem ends with the line 'God is a good fellow, but his Mother's against Him.' The title of Hughes' poem calls to mind Robert Graves' God of the Logos, who was also enthroned above Nature and Woman alike as the superior 'Universal Mind still premised by the most reputable modern philosophers' (*The White Goddess*, p. 465). The Logos-God of pure thought is really the perfect image of the 'objective imagination' crystallizing in the conventions of theology. And, in the same way as the emphasis on that imagination created a dangerously autonomous shadow of the animal nature, so the Logos-God creates the problem of Evil and Error, namely Satan: 'If the true God, the God of Logos, was, we thought, pure good, whence come evil and error? Two separate creations had to be assumed: the true spiritual creation and the false material creation' (*ibid.*). The Puritan perspective *invents* the distortion of the Goddess of Medieval Nature, the 'gigantic horrible female ogress' whom Crow confronts in Hughes' skeleton-fable to *The Life and Songs of Crow* (see Sagar, *The Art of Ted Hughes*, p. 235), and whom Crow confronts in *Gaudete* as a woman with 'a face as if sewn together from several faces/ A baboon beauty face,/ A crudely stitched patchwork of faces . . .' (p. 104). Only when that perspective has been weakened through the dramatic course of Hughes' poetry can she be re-assembled as an object of devotion in books like *Moortown* and *River*.

In *Aion*, Jung traces the history of theological oppression through Origen, Dionysus the Areopagite and Augustine, attributing it to the root-cause of 'the hybris of the speculative intellect' (p. 46). As the 'inner' basis of judgement became increasingly unconscious, Protestant theology was unhappily 'freed' to propagate the belief that perfect good could never have created evil – that 'God *can* only be good' – worsening the dualistic situation by attempting to resolve the opposition on its own level. Real evil does not reside in the formal situation ('Good' God versus 'Evil' Devil), but in the *deceived perception* 'that goodness does not exist merely *in relation to* evil but is, from everlasting, the very essence of God' (Alan Watts, *Myth and Ritual in Christianity*, p. 45).

The formal intellect has set up its abstract ideal immediately, and simply assumed its 'objective' validity. 'Objective imagination', which in Hughes' view is 'no more than a narrow mode of perception', has thus irresistibly staked its divisive claim in both the image of the self and the idea of the Creator within contemporary, post-Puritan culture. Just as it dictates our view of ourselves 'as the ego – a dissociated island of awareness, detached from the very body which it inhabits, let alone the environment. It follows then, that the Western God is likewise a discarnate ego . . . existing in total separation from his own body' (*ibid.*, p. 67). Such an abstract God cannot deliver his creatures from the disease with which he is himself afflicted.

As surely as the images of Jehovah or the Logos-God affirm the principles of isolation and self-sufficiency throughout their historical development, so the image of the Goddess seeks to encourage relationship, and mediation. But the cultural pressure of Puritanism and dualistic thinking suppressed her natural function, caricaturing her image as that of 'lower' Nature, 'leagued with everything occult, spiritualistic, devilish, over-emotional, bestial, mystical, feminine, crazy, revolution-ary and poetic' (Review of *The Environmental Revolution*, Faas, *Ted Hughes: The unaccommodated universe*, p. 187). As a result the pivotal idea of keeping a foot in both worlds associated with her has become inaccessible (which is why she has receded as a deity), effectively blanking answers to the riddle of the relationship between the spiritual and material creations – or indeed any terms that exist on the oppositional axis. However, as soon as a psychological basis for the *Imago Dei* is allowed, she appears: Jung formulates her ambivalence as 'the loving and terrible mother' – 'terrifying' when she is forced to connote what is dark or repressed within the psyche, 'loving' when the need for awareness and transformation of that state is acknowledged by the subject. In other words, she functions as a kind of barometer of the Ego-Personality's attitude to the Unconscious, or the extent of its abstraction or exclusivity or ignorance. Like Hughes' ogress or baboon-woman, she only *appears* as 'devouring' to the abstracted subject, so the centre of gravity shifts once more to the perceiver's consciousness: her devouring aspect is dependent upon our attitude to the process of death–rebirth, or self-development, of which she is the most complete personification. She *is* the necessity of Matter which confronts the Ego-Personality with its own unconscious 'original face', and offers its greatest challenge, one our culture conditions us to refuse. Within the programme of poetic development outlined by Hughes, however, the Goddess is the perfect object of devotion. She contains the need for consuming of false selves, deaths to certain types of consciousness, the regular and persistent return to an unconscious 'origin', all within herself. As Ovid said of Cardea, the Roman version of the Goddess, she is a creative hinge: 'Her power is to open what is shut; to shut what is open' (*The White Goddess*, p. 69) – demanding a provisional self free of identification with the absolute God, Personality.

Her flexibility as a psychological hinge is also a freedom from the absolutism of External morality. Nicoll – in his commentaries on Gurdjieff and Ouspensky – explains the psychological idea of morality as one in which 'whatever keeps you awake is right: whatever puts you to sleep is wrong' (III, p. 1025), an idea Hughes supports in his review, 'The genius of Isaac Bashevis Singer' (see Faas, *Ted Hughes*, p. 177) and his review of *The Selected Letters of Dylan Thomas*; in the latter he detects

> a vision of the *total* creation, where everything, man and atom, life and death, was equal, and nothing could be ugly or bad, where everything was a member of a single infinite being, which he sometimes called God. . . . It was a *morally undetermined, infinitely mothering creation*. He had no comments or interpretations or philosophisings to add to it. . . . But the vision included the hells as well as the 'faces of a noiseless million in the busyhood of heaven'. The hells were indeed a favoured part of the task. Poetry, he said, was to drag into 'the clean nakedness of the light more even of the hidden causes than Freud could realize'. (*New Statesman*, 25 November 1966, p. 783; my italics)

This kind of awakened perception needs an absence of formal moral points in order to thrive: only the disintegration of External morality paradoxically allows a moral purpose, the re-integration of self.

As soon as the Goddess is permitted to resume her natural psychological function, negotiations with what seemed 'beyond the pale' can begin as a first step in the *transformation* – rather than straight suppression – of evil. So in Hughes' story for children *The Iron Man*, the Dragon (Satan) is not destroyed as in the St George story; the little boy–hero 'includes the dragon in the world, he doesn't shut off and close the world back into a narrow prison. He keeps space open. In fact he invites space to take part in the life of the world and to completely envelop the world in the form of the dragon and his music' ('Myth and education', 1, p. 66). The tales of the heroic questers, in their endless struggles to rescue maidens and princesses (the transformed or developed female principle) from the threat of sea-monsters, dragons and serpents (nearly always primitive-female) can be understood as psychically healthy ways of preserving a creative breathing-space for unconscious elements within the self: the masculine Ego-Personality finds the positive aspect of those elements only when it begins to recognize and assimilate the 'lower' animal root–nature from which they grow. Theseus slays the Minotaur and finds his way out of the labyrinth of the Unconscious on its most primitive, animal level, only by means of the conscious 'thread' given him by Ariadne. She appears firstly as a creative hinge, engineering his liberation, and finally as the 'developed' object of his quest.

The Goddess–figure therefore keys within Hughes' critical prose psychological ideas such as 'keeping space open' and what he calls 'alert rationality', a vigorous re-definition of what we usually understand by rational thinking: 'The nearest we can come to rational thinking is to stand respectfully, hat in hand, before this creation, exceedingly alert for a new word' (Review of *Astrology*, *New Statesman*, 2 October 1964, p. 500). Hughes' terms all in a manner clean the mind of 'objective' thinking, leaving behind what Simone Weil calls 'attention':

> Attention consists of suspending our thought, leaving it detached, empty and ready to be penetrated by the object . . . our thought should be in relation to all particular and already-formulated thoughts, as a man on a mountain who, as he looks forward, sees also below him, without actually looking at them, a great many forests and plains. Above all our thought should be empty. Waiting, not seeking anything, but ready to perceive in its naked truth the object which is to penetrate it. ('Reflections on the right use of school studies', *Waiting on God*, p. 72)

We shall encounter several examples of this kind of imaginative attention in tracking the course of Hughes' development: through it the Goddess is embodied as a literary attitude, always attending towards the object as well as the Ego-Personality and its already formulated thoughts, striving for intermediacy, for relationship. And in her essay 'The three sons of Noah', Relationship or Mediation is exactly what Weil suggests is the original meaning of Logos – not 'thought' and not 'word'.

Hughes' most schematic guide to his own Creative Mythology is to be found in the mythic universe he constructed – or dreamed up – especially for the Orghast project in 1971. Its salient features are utterly consistent with the images of the Divine Nature discussed so far: the conjunction of Sun and Moa 'in a bliss of making and unmaking' – the one light and masculine, the other dark and feminine – is a clear reminder of the ambivalent Goddess who mediated between opposites; and the description of the Sun as a creative hinge, 'the door in created matter opening back on light', consolidates that initial identity. Furthermore, the Sun–Moa coupling is perceived as totally neutral – it has not yet resolved into the Reformation God–Satan dichotomy – and more akin to the complementary relationship in The Book of Job, which later theology found so disturbing because of the ambiguous idea of God's dialogue with Satan: in that book Satan is God's executor, obedient to his will, and the trials that Job undergoes promote his evolution.

Likewise, Krogon is a definitive model for the Logos-God who proclaims his own independence and self-sufficiency, resistant to his own 'death and replacement'. Krogon's false order and authority depends upon self-enclosure, the strength of his I-ness, and *darkness* – real evil – *comes from that*; his presence creates a false perspective which casts its shadow over all created beings. Darkness is not simply an absence of light, but rather the result of the intervention of an obstacle – a negative third force – between the light and the subject, it is brought into focus as his own delusion: the original meaning of 'sin', concealed in the Greek verb *Hamartanein*, was 'to miss the mark'.[3]

Within this created illusion, 'Moa, separated from the spiritualizing love of the Sun, sinks more and more into the chaotic and randomly productive fires of matter. Less and less of a divinity under Krogon's persecution, and more and more of a revengeful demon, suffering his rapes only to bear somehow a son who will destroy him' (Smith, *Orghast at Persepolis*, p. 93). In other words, this is the way Matter, or material nature looks once the illusion is given credence.

The need for a positive 'supraordinate third' above the lethal oppositional axis is as urgent here as it was in the structure of self determined by the 'objective' rationalistic Ego-Personality:

> There are two forms of good, of the same denomination; but radically different from each other: the one which is the opposite of evil, and one which is the absolute – the absolute which cannot be anything but the good. The absolute has no opposite. The relative is not the opposite of the absolute. . . . What we want is the absolute good. What is within our reach is the good which is correlated to evil. We mistakenly take it for what we want, like the prince who sets about making love to the maid instead of the mistress. (Weil, *The Notebooks of Simone Weil*, vol. II, p. 592–3)

When we fasten our mental grip onto the 'good' Logos-God that is within our reach, we unwittingly consolidate Krogon's point of view, multiplying the breadth and depth of his 'shadow'. It is necessary to realize that the Absolute is completely absent, or silent, *given our present moral location*. That is why Hughes begins by appealing to the God of Janos Pilinszky, 'A God of absences and negative attributes, quite comfortless', calling out in the darkness to an absent self, and an 'absent creator' equally: 'All we know is that somehow the great, precious thing is missing. And the real distress of our world begins there. The luminous spirit . . . that takes account of everything and gives everything its meaning is missing. Not missing, just incommunicado' ('Orghast: Talking without words', *Vogue*, December 1971).

THE IDEA OF LANGUAGE

The previous two sections have examined Hughes' perception of falsehoods in both ideas of the self and ideas of the Divine Nature. For the poet writing in language, this perception can be extended further, to the dimension of false styles. Hughes' suspicion of the tendency of words to build an abstract stylistic universe, filled with a certain disregard for the 'world of final reality' to which they are properly obedient, has already been noted; words continually stand in jeopardy of substituting a verbal or aesthetic centre for a moral centre, of 'trying to displace our experience. And in so far as they are stronger than the raw life of our experience, and full of themselves and all the dictionaries they have digested, they do displace it' (*Poetry in the Making*, p. 120). Just as the struggle to regain the 'totality of self' was frustrated by the intervention of the Ego-Personality and false gods, it is likewise obstructed by the nature of language, which could be described as the formal mechanism of that personality.

Historically, the combat over the fallen body of language begins with Plato and Aristotle's idea of a conceptual language in which words have an absolute significance. For Aristotle, for instance, words were 'spatial' and 'objective' and could be combined, like so many atoms in space, according to a linear model. But the Krogonish shadow in language falls with that word 'objective': the rational systemization of language creates a problem directly analogous to the psychological distress caused by the 'objective imagination', because the importance of words as registers of psychological states is thoroughly and disastrously omitted. So in his diagnosis of Orghast language, Tom Stoppard sieved an External from an Internal direction, the one designed to elicit 'semantic athleticism', the other an appeal to 'the instinctive recognition of a "mental state" within a

sound' (*Times Literary Supplement*, 1 October 1971). And the challenge
that Orghast language picks out for the actor is exactly the same as that
determined for the 'writer' or 'reader' of contemporary culture, not just
Hughes' own poetry: 'They can't short-circuit into the given meaning of
words and evade the real issue. The real issue is to confront their whole
response at the moment' (Hughes' notes, in Smith, *Orghast at Persepolis*,
p. 49). As long as words are imprisoned in their semantic dimension –
controlled by the 'objective imagination' – they cannot help the poet's act
of moral recovery. Language is then fictive in the same way that the
Personality invented by scientific rationalism is fictive.

The signs that this catastrophic descent into the absolutism of words
has indeed occurred in contemporary literature are numerous and
damning: Max Picard speaks of language as 'more than the sum total of
all things which it mediates and effects. It is something that exists on its
own, beyond all immediate purpose and effect. . . . Language is more
real than the reality by which it is confronted' (*Man and Language*, pp. 36
and 44), while Roland Barthes argues that the modern writer could now
lay claim only to the lexical basis of language; and in the absence of its
'spontaneously functional nature', the writer is capable of producing not
'an instance of reality' but rather, only 'an instance of discourse' (see
Barthes' essay 'Science versus literature'). Once words split off from
their mooring to a mental state – their psychological root in the speaking
subject – they acquire a 'pure' verbal logic of their own; to all intents and
purposes, they are a world unto themselves.

It is this subjection to the tyranny of the formal dimension of language
that Hughes observes variously in three writers who exhibit the
symptoms of the 'disintegrative phase of Christianity' in literature most
strongly, James Joyce, T. S. Eliot and Samuel Beckett. In this frame
Joyce's *Ulysses*, for example, is an epic dramatization of the poignant
failure to narrate reality 'objectively', while *Finnegan's Wake* marks a
fearful retreat from that knowledge into the book held together by the
'strength of it style' (Flaubert's ideal), its lexical interchangeability. Eliot
was victimized by the abstracting tendency of words in different manner:
in *The Waste Land*, he found himself appropriating a host of languages,
instances of religious or literary discourse – the fragments of a broken
voice, already beginning to fossilize into abstract knowledge (Eliot's
notes).

Perhaps Beckett suffers the predicament of the contemporary artist
called upon to resolve his Matter – either 'Self' or 'World' – in words in
its most painfully acute form:

> What I speak of, what I speak with, all comes from them. . . . It's of me I
> must now speak, even if I have to do it with their language, it will be a
> start, a step towards silence and the end of madness, the madness of having

to speak and not being able to, except of things that don't concern me, that don't count, that I don't believe, that they have crammed me full of to prevent me from saying who I am, where I am, and from doing what I have to do in the only way that can put an end to it. (*The Unnameable*, pp. 448–9)

Molloy's complaint 'All I know is what the words know' composes the futile entirety of the Unnameable's universe, and provides a compact reprise of the difficulties which beset Joyce and Eliot. *Their* language – an externally based language which has no 'inner' sanction – forms an impossible intervening wedge between the subject and his impulse to say what he really means, so that he can only tell the story of fictions to his real self, the story of False Personality. Having broken up irretrievably into discourses, it now only speaks for caricatures of the whole psyche, and there is nothing that Beckett and his surrogate narrators can do about it. Syntax, the very foundation of semantically-continuous utterance, fractures into 'bits and scraps' of speech, 'an image too of this voice ten words fifteen words long silence ten words fifteen words long silence long solitude' (*How It Is*, p. 126). In these circumstances words resemble the surviving fragments of some lost, unknown discourse which will never be re-discovered. But Beckett does not choose Joyce's path. Where Joyce, seeing the uselessness of 'objectivity', shrank from the laid-bare 'mess' of the self by taking refuge in a certainty of style, the hermetically sealed verbal structure of *Finnegan's Wake*, Beckett fixes his gaze on the given inadequacies of language directly, with no stylistic alternative to the situation and no hope of a fictive escape into false selves.[4]

Hughes' own counter-attack on the 'objective' hypnosis of language begins with the endeavour to find a poetic style – or styles – better aligned with the provisional nature of the self already examined, language 'for the whole mind, at its most wakeful, and in all situations. A utility general-purpose style, as, for instance, Shakespeare's was' (Introduction to Keith Douglas' *Selected Poems*, p. 14). Any aesthetic inflation – 'poetic breadth, a ritual intensity and music of an exceedingly high order' – is balanced by a 'colloquial prose readiness' which threatens at any moment to dissolve the formal structure (when it starts to supplant the perceived truth with its own autonomous mechanisms) back into casual speech. Hughes' language hopes to incline neither to 'right' nor 'left', refusing to identify with the 'objectivity' of any particular verbal or poetic discourse, its flexibility a way of keeping in touch with the speaking selves 'beneath'. Simone Weil makes a very interesting juxtaposition in this context:

In art, the equivalent of this reign of necessity is the resistance of matter and arbitrary rules. Rhyme imposes upon the poet a direction in his choice of words which is absolutely unrelated to the sequence of ideas. Its function in poetry is perhaps analogous to that of affliction in our lives. Affliction forces us to feel with all our souls the absence of finality. ('Forms of the implicit love of God', from *Waiting on God*, p. 131)

The arbitrary resistances of form in poetry are analogous to the effects of 'necessity' upon the self, maintaining our mechanical state of unconsciousness. The improvising, utility attitude of Hughes' 'casual speech' is working against this mechanical tyranny of form in the same way as his emergency selves are eroding that condition of unconsciousness, or acquiring a different point of view on Necessity. The utility general-purpose style is a poetic manoeuvre against the formal afflictions from which Beckett suffered, sustaining the 'presence of a whole human being – not just a lyrical or metaphysical or formal fragment of one' (*Listener*, 1069–71).

Elsewhere in his prose writings, Hughes has clearly indicated that the poet's confinement to the 'objective' dimension of language is not inevitable; that the 'audial–visceral–muscular' base of language – as opposed to its 'visual–conceptual' tendency – is indeed responsive to the presence of a whole human being, not just a rationalized abstract of one. It is 'more unified with total states of being and with the expressiveness of physical action' (Smith, *Orghast at Persepolis*, p. 45), opening a channel into those psychic contents normally unconscious to the Ego-Personality. More than that, re-entry into this suppressed inheritance is defined for Hughes as a recovery into the world of dialect and the Anglo-Saxon/Norse/Celtic linguistic ground 'where our real mental life has its roots' (Review of *Myth and Religion of the North*, *Listener*, 19 March 1964). The combination of the Greek–Roman branch, and the Anglo-Saxon/Norse/Celtic root of the English language 'is our wealth, but in the realm of mythologies, the realm of management between our ordinary minds and our deepest life, we've had no chance to make a similar combination' (*ibid.*). In Hughes' poetry, words have more opportunity to speak for the whole self when they are in an intermediate position, simultaneously hooked up to Graeco-Roman and Norse–Celtic vocabularies. Here is an example of what this act of linguistic re-possession means:

> This bird is the Sun's key-hole.
> The sun spies through her. Through her
> He ransacks the camouflage of hunger.
> Investigation
> by grapnel.
> Some angered righteous questions
> Agitate her craw.
>
> > ('The Interrogator', *Cave Birds*)

To summarize the prevailing situation briefly: the protagonist's False Personality is under scrutiny by the Vulture–Interrogator, who personifies the violence created by his attitudes, turned back on their source. On the verbal level, the true nature of that scrutiny is only brought home in the last four lines, in the seismic shift from the 'objective' collation of evidence, and the latinate passage between 'investigation . . . righteous . . . agitate' to the full-scale Norse violence of 'grapnel . . . angered . . . craw'. The protagonist's inner drama, his confrontation with his whole response at that moment, is registered by the brutal movement from the 'objectivity' of the latinate vocabulary – which only hints at the vaguest of disturbances – to the intimately physical, muscular violence of the Anglo-Saxon audial–visceral 'craw'. It is as if the breakdown in negotiations between our rational intelligence and animal–instinctual life can be witnessed completely as a linguistic event, on the 'third' bridge between those vocabularies.

This pincer movement, this breaking of latinisms on the wheel of Anglo-Saxon/Norse/Celtic, is a dialect instinct Hughes attributes to Shakespeare, the wrenching 'instinct to misuse latinisms, but in an inspired way' (*A Choice of Shakespeare's Verse*, p. 11), and it shows one aspect of the self's willingness to explore the vocabulary belonging to its real mental life. On the very same page of that essay, Hughes goes on to give a fascinating analysis of the word 'aggravate', in which it is the short-circuit to the Anglo-Saxon 'gr' core which gives a more powerful meaning, the psychological or dramatic depth of the word, rather than the 'Joycean fusion' of 'irritate, anger, exaggerate' and its abstract, lexical interchangeability of parts. According to Hughes, it is this wrenching misuse of latinisms which lends Shakespeare's language 'the air of being invented in a state of crisis, for a terribly urgent job, a homely spur-of-the-moment improvisation out of whatever verbal scrap happens to be lying around' (*ibid.*, p. 11). An Anglo-Saxon-based vocabulary appears particularly well suited to this improvisatory atmosphere: it works off an extremely distinct division between consonants and vowels, in which the four consonantal alliterations per line battle with the 'abundance and luxury and possible lasciviousness of the vowels' (Seamus Heaney in *Preoccupations: Selected prose 1968–78*, p. 154), a critical struggle which often appears more than a mere analogy for the primitive encounter of the authoritarian Ego-Personality and the undifferentiated, potentially chaotic flow of the Unconscious. The consonants are brutal (i.e. in the preponderance of 'kr', 'str' and 'gr' sounds) and violent because the Personality is always improvising on the frictional border of the Conscious–Unconscious, continually on the point of dissolution or re-creation. It is no accident that Anglo-Saxon is the language of epic poetry, of heroic action, of Beowulf's encounter with the she-monster Grendel. The heroic self in both Anglo-Saxon poetry and Hughes' work alike is always in contact with its own instinctual life, in the white heat of negotiation. And the coincidence of primary stresses with long quantities in the Anglo-Saxon line can only have intensified the astringency of the 'I's struggle with the monstrous archaisms of its own nature.[5]

Hughes followed the Anglo-Saxon lead when he constructed Orghast on a basis in which consonants were fixed but the vowels free, and open 'at every occurrence to a new and more essential kind of inspiration' (Smith, *Orghast at Persepolis*, p. 117). And one should perhaps add at this point a third 'accident': Robert Graves' potent suggestion in *The White Goddess* that the vowels A E I O U were sacred to the Goddess, and everything she represented (p. 468).

The re-combination of Anglo-Saxon and Latin-based vocabularies is only one feature of the literary effort to develop negotiations along the Conscious–Unconscious frontier. A *symbolic* language is necessary to resist the self-enclosure of the Ego-Personality and 'objective' verbal structures alike; in the New Testament, Jesus warned Nicodemus not to think carnally, or he would be in the flesh, but to think symbolically, in the spirit. The symbol speaks not only to the conscious mind but also to the deeper layers of the psyche 'lower down' because of its 'material' and 'collective' nature; indeed the possibility of the symbol's re-possession by the conscious Ego-Personality is a positive danger, as 'it runs the risk of becoming mere allegory which nowhere oversteps the bounds of conscious comprehension, and is thus exposed to all sorts of attempts at rationalistic and therefore inadequate explanation' (Jung, *The Archetypes of the Collective Unconscious*, p. 173). The intrusion of 'objective' thinking, in other words, converts a mode of understanding into merely a stylistic device:

> Meaning is completed, ended, and thus in a sense dead in allegory; it is active and living in the symbol. Here again, the difference between the symbol and allegory is fixed primarily by the task that one and the other impose on the mind of the receiver. (Todorov, *Theories of the Symbol*).

The symbol is paratactic, open-ended, and pliant to the moral activity of the self; because of its collective – and material – nature, it never submits wholly to 'unique' attempts at 'objective' explanation, its meaning remains to a large extent dependent upon the spiritual resonances the listener/reader is able to awaken in his own nature. It functions as a photographic exposure of the individual psyche responding to it, a natural tool in all psychological, transformative work. Symbolic stories, once read, are in 'continual private meditation on their own implications. New revelations of meaning open out of their images and patterns continually, stirred into reach by our own growth and changing circumstances' ('Myth and education', 2, p. 82). Symbols allow the material body or whole psyche to think and judge for itself, above or below the 'conscious' mind. It is no wonder, with this in view, that 'symbolic' has almost as bad a reputation as the word 'mythic' in our vocabulary – how can the Ego-Personality ever concede voluntarily to measurement by something outside itself? And yet it is precisely this action that is required, by reader or writer or initiate of any kind. As Gurdjieff points out, the study of symbols was an integral part of the preparation to receive real knowledge, and 'it was in itself a test because a literal or formal understanding of symbols at once made it impossible to receive further knowledge' (Ouspensky, *In Search of the Miraculous*, p. 280). Confronted by the fundamental action of the symbol, the reader is thrown back on the nature and motivation of his own responses, and literary criticism is invited to re-assess its orientation, 'Aesthetic' or 'psychological'. A circle closes, the end of the section returns to issues raised at the beginning of the chapter.

THE IDEA OF READERSHIP

Much of Hughes' first 'Myth and education' essay (see pp. 58–62) is devoted to the religious function of stories and the 'therapeutic effect of simple narratives'. Poems are transformed, in the course of this essay, from their 'formal being' as aesthetic objects towards their 'dynamic potential' for the simultaneous education of both writer and reader; the objective of a story or poem may be the acknowledgement of a demon or neurotic-making attitude, it may constitute a welcoming-back into conscious life of a 'devil' of suppressed energy. Fundamentally, it always *does* something to the reader–hearer, encouraging a consciousness of the psychological mechanics of the reading experience – especially the variable or unexpected element in that experience. Hughes appeals initially to the Sufi usage of stories, which show 'a much more sophisticated understanding of the effects upon the hearer . . . they claim to be able to bring a man to communion with his highest powers and abilities, to communion with God in fact' (*ibid.*, p. 62), an Internal sophistication attested by Idries Shah in his commentary on the function of the well-known Mulla Nasrudin stories of the Sufi teaching cycle: 'When a Nasrudin tale is read and digested, something is happening. It this consciousness of happening and continuity which is central to Sufism' (*The Sufis*, p. 87). The Nasrudin tales are only important in the context of conscious self-development, they have no ulterior or fixed aesthetic value. Their meaning is continuous as consciousness is continuous – and that is much more of an ambiguous or mutable quantity than we are prepared to admit.

Likewise, a poem is always open at one end, in our rapidly shifting sense of our experience of the words on the page. In his *London Magazine* interview, Hughes indicates many potential levels of interpretation of his poem 'The jaguar' and decides that 'it's the reader's own nature that selects. The tradition is, that energy of this sort once invoked will destroy an impure nature and serve a pure one' ('Ted Hughes and Crow', pp. 8–9). 'The poem' exists primarily as a yardstick of the hearer's moral condition, and the concern over what objectively belongs to the poem is of secondary importance. Before the reader ever moves 'outwards' to consider the merits of the poem as an aesthetic object, he moves 'inwards' in the struggle to re-possess *all* of his experience from the text. One practical consequence of this moral readership of Hughes' poetry is the realization of multiple readings, each derived from separate and often warring impulses within the reader's psyche. We could perhaps project a 'clever' reader, eager to avoid the premature fixation of his response and the suppression of contradictory or undesirable elements (i.e. elements which fall outside his critical/psychological range) – who follows Augustine's confessional willingness to 'confess what I know concerning myself; I will confess also what I know not concerning myself' (*Confessions*, x), prepared to confront the unconscious assumptions that motivate readings. As in Sufi practice, the reader/initiate completes the process of the poem himself, after the writer/teacher has deliberately 'broken away' – and his awareness of that act of completion is the poem's primary meaning, its concrete gain. Hughes' poetry has certainly provoked many curious acts of completion from his critical audience – for example, the accusation that the hawk in 'Hawk roosting' resembles 'some horrible totalitarian genocidal dictator', the general storm of critical abuse which greeted *Crow* and more universally, *Gaudete*: 'Hughes can't and won't think . . . *Gaudete*, simply, is a fantasy that has enslaved its creator' (Martin Dodsworth, *The Guardian*, 19 May 1977). Examples could be multiplied; the point is that the power of Hughes' poetry is partly derived from this disturbing ability to dissolve the 'objective' disguises of critical judgement and expose the often wildly subjective bases of assessment beneath. Frequently the reader of such criticism ends up paying more attention to the condition of the critic himself, rather than the poem or book of poetry under discussion.

In summary, in the reading of a poem it is the reader's suspension of disbelief in regard to the 'objectivity' of the text that is alone worthwhile. It runs parallel to the psychological thinker's intentional deafness to the Ego-Personality's certainties about Self and World, and parallel to the poetic aim of keeping space open, the openly rational stance which braces itself 'alert for a new word'.[6]

The theoretical problems raised by this discussion have been approached by Stanley Fish, in response to Wimsatt and Beardsley's article 'The affective fallacy', which attempted to elevate the poem 'as an object of specifically critical judgement' and criticized all efforts to 'derive the standards of criticism from the psychological effects of the poem . . . [which end] in impressionism and relativism' (*The Verbal Icon*, p. 21). Within the present frame of reference, it should be obvious that the affective fallacy is only a fallacy from a certain point of view on both text and external world. It assumes, for example, that the critic in his 'natural' condition can rise above impressionism and relativism towards the objectivity of the text with comparative ease. But in Hughes' terms, and Jung's and Gurdjieff's and a host of others – this is exactly what he cannot do. As he is fully immersed in the mechanisms of his own psychic life, the usefulness of the working hypothesis of the poem as 'an object of specifically critical judgement' is questionable; it tends to disappear under that internal pressure. What is left to the critic is a rigorous scrutiny of all those relativisms which make up his reading of a poem, the large set of cultural/psychological/verbal expectations he feeds into it. In order for the anxieties and uncertainties of the reading experience to emerge fully, the desire for an object of specifically critical judgement – which is nothing more than an outlet for the 'objective imagination' – must disappear.

The preceding argument is intended to offer a living cultural–psychological rationale for Fish's emphasis on considering meaning as an event which happens in the reader's mind, as opposed to the assumption that it is a formal function of the utterance. Within half-a-dozen lines of the 'theoretical' recognition that 'there is no direct relationship between the meaning of a sentence and what the words mean' he ends up assenting to the psychic dangers of the 'objective imagination' as it manifests itself through literary criticism:

> It is impossible to mean the same thing in two (or more) different ways, although we tend to think that it happens all the time. We do that by substituting for our immediate linguistic experience an interpretation or abstraction of it, in which 'it' is inevitably compromised. We contrive to forget what has happened to us in our life with language, removing ourselves as far as possible from the linguistic event before making a statement about it. (*Self-Consuming Artifacts*, p. 393)

The similarity between this tendency of readership and the psychological inclination of False Personality in Life hardly requires further comment; merely the erasure of 'with language' and 'linguistic' from that last sentence would be revealing enough – sufficient to show that the reading of a text can no longer be considered a separate or specialized function, because the concentrated attention on one's own experience is continuous at every moment with the cultivation of the same habits in Life situations. The reader can become a democratic, unifying force, if he so wishes: his attitude insists that the literary dimension is not a superior dimension to the world we actually have to live in; we need the same tools to examine both worlds because, as we have seen, in Hughes' view they are interdependent, they fit inside one another. A larger circle closes, we return to the epigraph at the very beginning of this chapter.

CHAPTER 2

THE POST-WAR POETIC ENVIRONMENTS: THE MOVEMENT AND CENTRAL/EAST EUROPEAN POETRY

It is possible to tighten the focus upon the cultural/literary contexts surrounding Hughes' creative endeavour by reference to two important poetic groupings which emerged in response to the events of the Second World War and the European holocaust – the so-called 'Movement' in Britain and the mass of Central European poetry (Hungarian, Czech, Polish and Yugoslav) which Hughes tends to see as a single imaginative unit. Both of these groupings are examined in isolated essays by Annie Schofield and Michael Parker incorporated in Keith Sagar's collection of articles *The Achievement of Ted Hughes*. But it is necessary to go further to flesh out the interconnection between the two contexts, their mirror-like reflection – or maybe anticipation – of both the problems and resolutions which are the moral possibilities of Hughes' own poetic world.

The post-war 'Movement' poets in Britain emerged as a conservative reaction to both the implications of wartime experience and the literary trends of the 1930s, particularly the group known as the Apocalyptic poets. Donald Davie was one of the first to formulate the new point of departure. He expressed the view that

> a poem is none the worse for being built around a structure of rational discourse, and that a poet's intelligence can be brought into play as effectively when he follows a rational argument as when he has recourse to witty metaphor or juxtaposition . . . healthy poetry today must find again a basis in rational philosophy. In general they [American poets whom Davie considered a model for their English counterparts] eschew free verse and write in strict metre and rhyme. . . . For the young English poet resentful of the tyranny of the 'image' in the restricted sense of 'metaphor' (whether inflated into symbols, worried into conceits, or compressed into 'striking' epithets), this American anthology points in a direction which may provide a wholesome alternative; i.e. it points to a renewed poetry of statement, openly didactic but saved by a sedulously noble diction, from prosiness. (*The Poet in the Imaginary Museum: Essays of two decades*, pp. 3–5)

As Davie indicates, the Movement posture was essentially one of retrenchment rather than exploration: on the stylistic level, a return to the rational orders of poetry, to 'strict metre and rhyme' corresponding on the psychological front to a consolidation of 'External' virtues – rational argument and openly didactic statement. There is in addition a notable fear of the image, and its tendency to 'inflate' or 'compress' aspects or levels of reality. The two terms, inflation and compression, themselves recall Hughes' paradigm of the self, in a mutable state of negotiation with the other, in exploratory flux. Didactic poetry always directs attention backwards, to what is already known, reinforcing the island of Personality. This confinement to familiar territory is a principle of conduct for poet and reader alike, the one preoccupied with the rapid closure of his argument or proposition, the other denied the opportunity to 'select' his reading – to manoeuvre against the opaqueness or possible hostilities of his own nature – the opportunity which symbolic language was especially liable to generate.

Robert Conquest, in his introduction to the *New Lines* anthology, actually went further than Davie in his claims for the Movement programme's rational–empirical base, becoming a strident spokesman for the 'objective imagination' itself, in a ghostly echo of Hughes' usage of the phrase: the Movement aesthetic, he announced, 'submits to no great systems of theoretical constructs nor agglomerations of unconscious commands. It is free from both mystical and logical compulsions and – like modern philosophy – is empirical in its attitude to all that comes' (p. xv). Both Conquest and Davie share this insistence on a steady reduction to the margins of the 'conscious' personality, and the fear of unconscious command in either the psychological or linguistic dimension (the inflating/compressive image), but the militant assertiveness of the attitude here virtually guarantees a resurgence of the 'compulsiveness' it thinks to leave behind. In her essay 'Hughes and the Movement' (in Sagar, *The Achievement of Ted Hughes*), Annie Schofield quotes the views of Robert Jay Lifton in his book *Death in Life: The survivors of Hiroshima* as one testimony to the dangers unconscious to the 'new' rationalistic posture. Lifton demonstrates that 'psychic numbness', the isolating recoil of the self from its own emotional/instinctual complexes, is often the result of the encounter with violent death; but when this encounter is as extreme and collective as in the Second World War, there is a danger that the natural, temporary act of human adaptation may become a permanent conscious attitude. It is possible to see this psychological movement in the space between Davie's comment and Conquest's invention or summary of a Movement *programme*. The 'objective imagination', working through Conquest, creates precisely the kind of theoretical construct he is at pains to condemn in others; worse still, Conquest's concretization of Davie's tendency imagines its own complete freedom from the 'unconscious command' which Lifton

analyses in his book. This hardening of attitude, this elevation of the
initial psychic numbness into a conscious value, is in Lifton's terms
nothing short of a pathological development; and it unwittingly makes
the Personality or culture vulnerable to those compulsions it supposes to
cancel.

Jung's re-assessment of Wilhelm Worringer's pair of opposites,
Abstraction and Empathy, is as helpful as Lifton's model in exploring the
underlying mechanics of the Movement's response. According to Jung,
the abstracting type *fixes* 'an abstract universal image' of Matter in order
to buffer himself from the bewildering chaos of the external world:

> This image has the magical significance of a defence against the chaotic flux
> of experience. The abstracting type becomes so lost and submerged in this
> image that finally its abstract truth is set above the reality of life; and
> because life might disturb the enjoyment of abstract beauty, it gets
> completely suppressed. . . . He divests himself of his real self and puts his
> whole life into his abstraction, in which he is, so to speak, crystallized.
> ('The type problem in aesthetics', in *Psychological Types*, p. 297)

The Second World War was, of course, the ultimate representation of the
chaotic flux of experience, and it provoked a correspondingly intense
counter-reaction on the part of the abstracting attitude. Hence Kingsley
Amis' strident demand – via a didactic imperative – for *'plain'* images,
'Warnings *clearly* said, shapes put down quite still/ *Within the fingers'*
reach, or else nowhere' ('Against Romanticism', in *Collected Poems 1944–*
1979). Everything beyond the fixed boundaries of the Ego–Personality is
shunned; technical proficiency is emphasized over against psychic exploration in an attempt to convert death from a 'smell' into a 'problem of
style':

> 'Alas, alas, who's injured by my love?'
> And recent history answers: half Japan!
> Not love, but hate? Well, both are versions of
> The 'feeling' you dare me to. Be dumb!
> Appear concerned only to make it scan!
> How dare we now be anything but numb?
> ('Rejoinder to a critic', in *Collected Poems 1950–1970*)

All the elements of the Jung–Worringer view are present here: the
unmanageable chaos of recent historical experience, the bewildered recoil
of the self from that flux, and the desire to replace it with an abstract
stylistic ideal (again note the use of the didactic imperative). The self
successfully 'crystallizes' in the logic of a rational proposition and the
order imposed by the technical requirements of rhyme-scheme. The
will-to-abstraction often involved Davie in some fairly contorted pro-
positions, of which a certain specialized mental or verbal ingenuity is the
most obvious characteristic:

If distance lends enchantment to the view,
Enormities should not be scrutinized . . . .

For fearsome issues, being squarely faced,
Grow fearsomely familiar. To name
Is to acknowledge. To acquire the taste
Comes on the heels of honouring the claim.
'Let nothing human be outside my range.'
Yet horrors named make exorcisms fail:

A thought once entertained is never strange,
But who forgets the face 'beyond the pale'?
('Eight years after', in *Collected Poems*)

The proposition depends on verbal relationships and a set of abstract assertions:

1. In the first conditional, the 'Unconscious command' which leads Davie/the reader to prefer enchanted distance to the horror of close-up reality is unacknowledged. The rational structure – 'If . . . , then . . .' – is *never fulfilled* by objective evidence. The pressurizing, didactic nature of the proposition makes the reader more aware, paradoxically, of its incompleteness. 'Why should we prefer enchantment to the direct view?' becomes a more, not less urgent question, in consequence.

2. The second sentence repeats the reader's discomfort: the hopeful, exploratory, forthright first line, with its suggestion of 'negotiation' with the source of 'inner uneasiness' (in 'squarely faced'), is then disappointed by 'Grow fearsomely familiar'. Just as the reader's responsive apparatus – his imagination – *opens out* onto the 'fearsome issue' with 'squarely faced', it is immediately contracted by the assertion that no understanding is possible, that the reality of the issue will be supplanted by the familiarity of an abstract idea of it. For both poetic persona and reader the mental movement is disheartening – truncating, contractive, with the origin of its strength located not in the authentic products of exploration but in the convictions of style: the verbal echo of 'fearsome . . . fearsomely' and the double alliteration of 'faced' and 'familiar'.

3. The last two sentences of the stanza repeat the same pattern. The positive-sounding 'To name/ Is to acknowledge' is defeated by another incomplete proposition, that acknowledgement of the issue is an inevitable step towards acquiring a taste for 'Enormity'. Again, the didactic stress of the three statements in the stanza lend them a 'disconnected' quality. They are hermetically sealed off even from one another, like little self-enclosed aphorisms.

4. Two further aphorisms follow in the final quoted stanza: 'Yet horrors named make exorcisms fail' and 'A thought once entertained is never strange'. Both again reduce the activity of the reader to nothing, or the bare agreement–disagreement polarity. This limiting of the reader's responsive activity is crucial; it corresponds in the extra-textual world to a resistance towards the idea that the effective scrutiny of 'Enormities' depends on the subject's own imagination or level of consciousness, more particularly his imagination of his own self. In contrast, the wartime Central European poets have managed constantly to confront and 'name' the horrors, but without in any way diminishing them. This is because their imagination of the self, conditioned as it is by the close-up experience of the war and its chaotic flux, simply does not allow the flight into a rationalized, fragment of the whole. So the Hungarian poet Janos Pilinszky points out that 'I did not live through, or endure, the war; *it became mine.*' And the deliberate vagueness of Davie's self-enchantment would cut no ice with Tadeusz Rozewicz; here he contrasts the archaeological discoveries of Renaissance Italy – sculpted master-pieces – with those of his own country Poland, in his poem 'Et in Arcadia ego' (in *Conversations with the Prince and Other Poems*): 'The objects excavated in my country have small black heads sealed in plaster and horrible grins.' In this context, Davie's set of abstract rules has rhyme, but is without reason; his view that the familiar 'naming' of the horror is reductive depends on his own contracted, contracting self-imagination in the poem.

The point about the confinement of the reader, or the reduction of his responsive activity, is an important one. In his excellent survey *The Movement*, Blake Morrison makes some perceptive comments on the last four lines of Philip Larkin's 'Dockery and son':

Life is first boredom, then fear.
Whether or not we use it, it goes,
And leaves what something hidden from us chose,
And age, and then the only end of age.

Such is the power of these and other concluding lines in Larkin's work, that it is easy to forget how closed they make the poem: beyond the response 'Yes' or 'How true' there is, as a Larkin poem of that title puts it, 'nothing to be said'. This is because Larkin's poetry minimizes the interpretative process by including it within the text: what is inferred by the reader is limited to what is inferred by the speaker, whose own struggle to 'discover meaning' is what the poem dramatizes. The reader is 'helped' (he cannot be confused as to what the poem means), but he is also restricted (the only meaning he takes away from the poem is the one found for him by the speaker). (*The Movement*, p. 143)

The reading experience of the lines, then, enacts the poignant fatalism of the progression from boredom to fear (and age), by disconnecting the reader's sense of his own inner activity. It is simply bracketed as irrelevant. In his 'Myth and education' essays, it was this bracketing of the inner world which Hughes suggested *does* produce boredom and fear, and worse. The pathos of the reader's condition is clear: he is confined, like one of Beckett's narrators, to someone else's words and the rigidity of *their* experience, because his own is absent, or rendered unavailable to him by the poem's attitude. The 'alienation of the reader' would not be too strong a phrase for it; he may agree or disagree, but either way he is subjected to the brutal 'objective' hypnosis of a poem's meaning entirely *included* in the text.

There is a direct connection, in summary, between the use of regular meter and rhyme and logical orders of syntax, and the preoccupation with a rational–'objective' philosophic base. The Ego-Personality's chronic fear of anything outside that range is attested by one tremendously ambitious passage from *The Purity of Diction in English Verse*, in which Davie goes so far as to assert – very nearly – that the abandonment of the logical order of syntax is equivalent to an invitation to Fascist thinking; he is talking here about Ezra Pound's version of Imagism:

> he pins his faith on individual words, grunts, broken phrases, half-uttered exclamations (as we find them in the *Cantos*), on speech atomized, all syllogistic and syntactical forms broken down. Hence his esteem of the definite lands him at last in yawning vagueness, the 'intuitive' welcome to Mussolini. . . .
>
> It would be too much to say that this is the logical end of abandoning prose syntax. But at least the development of imagism in poetry to fascism in politics is clear and unbroken. . . . It is impossible not to trace a connection between the laws of syntax and the laws of society, between bodies of usage in speech and in social life, between tearing a word from its context and choosing a leader out of the ruck. One could almost say, on this showing, that to dislocate syntax in poetry is to threaten the rule of law in the civilized community. (*Purity of Diction*, p. 99)

Whether it is the breaking of syntax, or rather the rigidity of abstract rational orders which constitutes a Fascist potential may only become apparent after comparison with the Central European response.

Another significant consequence of John Wain's desire for 'poise, coherence, and a logical *raison d'être* for every word, image and metaphor used' (my italics) is a reduction of the idea of symbolic language. Most Movement poets made a point of preferring the term 'emblem' to 'symbol'. In Davie's view, the difference between the two terms is that 'the symbol casts a shadow, where the emblem doesn't; the symbol aims to be suggestive, the emblem to be, even in its guise as riddle, ultimately explicit. Another difference might be that the emblem is made, fabricated, where the symbol is *found*' (*The Poet in the Imaginary Museum*, p. 77). So, for instance, for Larkin the moon is 'high, and preposterous and separate', useful only as 'a poetic property'. One could speak of the shift from 'symbol' to 'emblem' as the secularization of metaphor. The symbol was *religious* because it was *material* and *collective* in human terms – it organized the spiritual life of the community successfully into coherent patterns by that collectiveness, in the same way as the physiological bone-structure shapes the human body. Therefore the conscious personality 'finds' the symbol as it improvises towards its collective origin. The made/fabricated emblem is the result of that (rational) Personality remaining on its own apparently autonomous level. Its triumph is that of a self-sufficient fiction bodied over against the pressure of reality; by contrast, the symbol's triumph is that of a successful entry into, or discovery of, that reality. It is no wonder that the explicitness of the emblem wants to free itself of its symbolic shadow: recognizing it would be the equivalent of the man who identifies with the rational abstract image of himself admitting *his* own shadow.

One typical use of the explicit emblem is Larkin's 'No road', in which the road is directly descriptive of an emotional connection between the protagonist and the 'you' of the poem, and has no significance beyond this simple function. Some of Larkin's most effective poems, however, appear to include a pathetic realization of the inadequacy of emblem and the way of thinking it represents. In 'An Arundel tomb', for instance, the emblem of the earl and countess's mutual devotion in effigy – 'His hand withdrawn, holding her hand' – is shadowed in the final stanza by a sense of invalidity, so that its explicitness appears simultaneously as its incompleteness:

> Time has transfigured them into
> untruth. The stone fidelity
> They hardly meant has come to be
> Their final blazon, and to prove
> Our almost–instinct almost true:
> What will survive of us is love.
>   (*The Whitsun Weddings*)

In the last line the emblem is unequivocally *stated*, though Larkin makes the reader fully aware of the cost of that statement. The surrounding context is the shadow the emblem never manages to cast out: belief in the emblem's explicit, but fabricated statement entails 'looking' rather than 'reading', and the preference for an 'attitude' rather than their 'identity'. One senses in the poem a barely concealed nostalgia for the symbolic language which could comprehend that identity more fully, yet Larkin stubbornly dramatizes the solidity of that fiction over against the 'chaotic flux' of other possible interpretations, in other stanzas. One could almost say that the extreme poignancy of the poem is derived partly from the failure of the emblem to become a symbol.

The most effective and subtly handled Movement poems usually involve the persona's awareness, in some measure, of the limitations and insufficiency of his conscious attitude. It is interesting that William Empson's poetic personality possesses none of the confident sophistication of his critical personality:

> It is this deep blankness is the real thing strange.
> The more things happen to you the more you can't
> Tell or remember even what they were.
>
> The contradictions cover such a range.
> The talk would talk and go so far aslant.
> You don't want madhouse and the whole thing there.
> ('Let it go', quoted in Morrison, *The Movement*, p. 103)

The severity of this condition is even more marked in some of Larkin's poetry. In his famous poem, 'Church going', the protagonist is ordinary, fallible and completely incapable of fathoming the Church's religious significance:

> Once I am sure there's nothing going on
> I step inside, letting the door thud shut . . .
>
> . . . Hatless, I take off
> My cycle-clips in awkward reverence,
> Move forward, run my hand around the font.
> From where I stand, the roof looks almost new –
> Cleaned, or restored? Someone would know: I don't.
>
> . . . Bored, uninformed, knowing the ghostly silt
> Dispersed, yet tending to this cross of ground . . .
>
> . . . though I've no idea
> What this accoutred frowsty barn is worth,
> It pleases me to stand in silence here.
> (*The Less Deceived*)

The whole encounter is evaluated by an ignorant, self-parodying persona, and the poem develops by directing its ironic force increasingly against his own attitude, rather than the Church itself. It is like this in other poems, too: Larkin's alienated speakers endure the tragedy of the 'objective imagination' from which there seems no escape:

> Strange to know nothing, never to be sure
> Of what is true or right or real
> But forced to qualify *or so I feel*,
> Or *well, it does seem so:*
> *Someone must know.*
> ('Ignorance', *Whitsun Weddings*)

When Ted Hughes made his comment about Eliot, Joyce and Beckett representing the 'disintegrative phase of Christianity', perhaps he had in mind Larkin as well; for Hughes, Larkin's assertion later in the same poem that 'our flesh/ Surrounds us with its own decisions –/ And yet [we] spend all our life on imprecisions' is a new beginning, not a necessarily futile end.[1] Larkin's self-qualifying scepticism is negative, the irony of the moral vacuum in which the self knows nothing and will continue to know nothing – the linear irony of a closed situation, distinct from the Central European poets' usage of irony as an 'open' instrument of reconstruction and exploration.

The failure of the prototypical Movement attitude dramatized by Larkin was later acknowledged by Davie, standing on the bridge between abstracting Ego and flexible, exploratory 'emergency self':

> Hardly ever did we seem to write our poems out of an idea of poetry as a way of knowing the world we were in, apprehending it, learning it. The most obvious register of this is the striking absence from 'Movement' poetry of outward and non-human things apprehended crisply for their own sakes. I'm not asking for 'nature poetry', but simply for an end to attitudinising. (*The Poet in the Imaginary Museum*, p. 74)

In his *London Magazine* interview, 'Ted Hughes and Crow', Hughes found himself standing on the same bridge as Davie, retrospectively noting both the oppressiveness and temporary strength of the *New Lines* poets' careful retreat into the rational Ego, yet witnessing in himself the unmistakeable new possibilities for 'negotiation':

> One of the things these poets had in common I think was the post-war mood of having had enough . . . enough rhetoric, enough overweening push of any kind, enough of the dark gods, enough of the id, enough of the Angelic powers and the heroic efforts to make new worlds. They'd seen it all turn into death-camps and atomic bombs. All they wanted was to get back into civvies and get home to the wife and kids and for the rest of their lives; not a thing was going to interfere with a nice cigarette and a nice view of the park. The second war after all was a colossal negative revelation. In a sense it meant they recoiled to some essential English strengths. But it set them dead against negotiation with anything outside the cosiest arrangement of society. They wanted it cosy. It was an heroic position. They were like eskimos in their igloo, with a difference. They'd had enough sleeping out. Now I came a bit later. I hadn't had enough. I was all for opening negotiations with whatever happened to be out there. (pp. 10–11)

It is chiefly this attitude which brackets Hughes firmly with the Central European poets' response to the 'colossal negative revelation' of the war. In that response nothing is put out of bounds because nothing can be put out of bounds: remembering Pilinszky's statement that 'the war *became mine*', it is clear that the pressures of the immediate experience of 'Enormity' – of the ruthless demands of objective reality, inner and outer

– have staked an irresistible claim in their idea of the world so that no heroic, Movement-type recoil is possible. Instead, the model of self stays open to the collective nature of its experience. Here is Tadeusz Rozewicz's poem 'The new man':

> The new man
> that's him there
> yes it's that
> sewage pipe
> which lets through
> everything
> (*Conversation with the Prince and other Poems*)

In such a context, the backward-looking, didactic bent of poetry is clearly not feasible. The Movement's emphasis on rational order dissolves in the indiscriminateness of those last three lines, and even the poem's syntax 'lets through everything' – the complete absence of punctuation an intuitive assault upon what Donald Davie saw as the linguistic cornerstone of West European culture. The New Man admits waste products, the 'filth' that the abstract ideal excludes; he does not imagine himself to be free of unconscious commands, although his essential passivity in the face of what Simone Weil calls 'the mechanical brutality of circumstances' is seen as a moral positive, something akin to Hughes' idea of 'alert rationality':

> I am
> stubborn
> and submissive in my stubbornness
> like wax
> only thus can I
> impress the world[2]
>
>   (*ibid.*)

In this paradoxical situation – and we must think that such ambiguity is anathema to the Movement style of direct statement – the protagonist finds the true contours of the self through his obedience to the impression the world makes on him. Rozewicz's attitude is typical of the Central European response to their experience of the war. One of the most prominent post-war Hungarian poets, Sandor Csoori, re-phrased that response in terms that recall Holloway's 'Warning to a guest': 'The ocean would come up to my window in vain if I, its host, no longer knew anything about myself', compared with 'Do not demand a walk tonight/ down to the sea. It makes no place for those/ Like you and me who, to sustain our pose,/ Need wine and conversation, colour and light.' Where Holloway refuses a walk down to the sea in favour of a return to the laws of society and the rule of civilized community, Csoori's impulse is to negotiate with whatever the 'ocean' represents, and that impulse is reflexive – it depends on self-knowledge. In addition, the process implicitly demands engagement with the issue of just why those laws and that rule actually enabled, or even generated the two Holocausts. Instead of Holloway's monologue of abstracted cultural conventions, we get a continuous dialogue in which the self plays host to the ocean, as the individual plays host to collective nature–Nature.

The encounter with death in all its forms, which Hughes saw as a necessary aesthetic experience for the poet, was unavoidable, and the task – as Hughes points out in his Introduction to Vasko Popa's *Collected Poems* – is thus to unearth a poetry which is adequate speech 'for life in a world where people actually do die'. Again Csoori's experience is representative. He narrates how, at the age of thirteen or fourteen, he was initiated into adulthood, or 'let me say bitterly rather – modernity, universality. I arrived in the vicinity of physical catastrophes from alongside oxen. Within the period of three and one-half months, my village changed hands seventeen times. After the front passed by, we spent two weeks burying human beings and animals' (in Tezla (ed.), *Ocean at the Window: Hungarian prose and poetry since 1945*, p. 277). Western Europe's accidental freedom from the finality of such experience enabled the theoretical construction of multiple 'freedoms' in both art and society as a whole, despite Robert Conquest's claims. But these poets have been thrown by the blindness of circumstances into a position not unlike that Hughes discerned in Shakespeare, i.e. the frenzied creation of emergency selves on which to hang all the fragments exploding out of a rational–irrational collision. They exist on the flux of a continual dialectic between theory and experience; like Hughes' own Crow, they have acquired a position at a moral border, a third position which pays homage to both elements of the opposition equally. Hughes calls it 'an endless scrupulous alertness on the frontiers of false and true. In effect, it is an intensely bracing moral vigilance' (Introduction to Vasko Popa, *Collected Poems*, p. 3). So Zbigniew Herbert's poem 'To the Hungarians' concludes,

> the wounded stones beseech
> the dead water beseeches
> we stand at the border
> we stand at the border
>
> we stand at the border
> called reason
> and we look into the fire
> and admire death
> (*Selected Poems*, 1977)

The well-known Hungarian poet Agnes Nemes Nagy has expressed this conflict as an aesthetic problem, 'the duel of the unequivocal word and the unarticulated general condition', and it is interesting to note Janos Pilinszky's observation that Western European literature has imposed a false resolution of this dilemma when it chose 'the assailing intensity of the moment and irredeemably left behind the street's disproportionately more monstrous possibilities' (from a speech delivered at the International Conference on Poetic Imagination, Poigny, 1970). Pilinszky goes on to relate the story of Rilke's death, in which the great German poet dismissed with a single sweep of his hand all that his pen had created, and refused attention from all but an illiterate peasant girl, who had not the slightest idea of whom she was tending in his last agony. For Pilinszky, this story

> exemplifies the constantly recurring trial and encounter of (in Rilke) consciousness and (in the peasant girl) unconsciousness, [and] for me also somehow represents the two Europes.
>   While one half of our continent has for centuries been writing the drama of the individual, of freedom, and of complexity, the other has been testifying through the ages to the hardships of community, of oppression, and of the simple human fate. I shall give but one example. Western Art left behind the potential world of motionlessness in the thirteenth and fourteenth Centuries and through the Renaissance and the Baroque's storm of movement painted canvases full of the problematics of freedom, while in the East the icons remained motionless, and only the ebb and flow of their intensity testified to all they found inexpressible in time. (in Tezla (ed.), *Ocean at the Window*, pp. 146–7)

On the historical level, Central Europe is the third Europe, or the setting for the dramatic collision of these two forces, it is their battleground. Amongst contemporary British poets, one can think of only Hughes and Seamus Heaney who have dared, as individuals, to occupy this territory in spirit.

If anything, the immediate post-war years have intensified the dichotomy of 'theoretical construct' and the violent reality of experience. Movements like Schematism in Hungary (1949–52) attempted the reimposition of political ideology in as ruthless a manner as Nazism – on all levels of cultural life. The problem of synthesis in poetry became both more urgent and more problematic. Ferenc Santa was not the only poet to see that 'shelves are lined with books containing the thoughts of humanists, yet the generation stepping into our place is being taught to shoot down human beings, the mother what to do when her child is incinerated by a radioactive ray' (Interview in *Life and Literature*, 6 May 1967). The political showing of the abstract picture of the world painted by scientific rationalism had to be reconciled with the negative revelation of the war, that everything in nature, including psychological nature, is entirely subject to Necessity – a force as brutal, as pitilessly directed downward as gravity itself. 'The monster of Mr. Cogito' (Zbigniew

Herbert, *Selected Poems*, 1977), because it is everything in nature, is not as easily dealt with as St George's dragon

> the monster of Mr. Cogito
> doesn't really have measurements . . .
>
> you can't touch it
> with a pen
> or with a spear
>
> were it not for its suffocating weight
> and the death it sends down
> one would think
> it is an abstraction
> of the type *informel* . . .
>
> the proof of the existence of the monster
> is its victims
> it is not direct proof
> but sufficient

This acknowledgement that the 'objective imagination' can understand the situation only on its own level – as a formal abstraction – is followed in the second part of the poem by an explicit declaration of the need for a new perspective:

> reasonable people say
> we can live together
> with the monster
>
> we have only to avoid
> sudden movements
> sudden speech
>
> to breathe lightly
> to pretend we are not there
>
> Mr. Cogito however
> does not want a life of make-believe
>
> he would like to come to grips
> with the monster on firm ground

Rozewicz's poem 'Head in a void' (*Conversation with the Prince*) is an even more aggressive attack on the intellectual hubris which thinks to dissociate itself from 'a motionless trunk/ which sinks in earth/ blood and cow-dung . . . the grunting bustling/ and lip-smacking mob'.[3] The conscious attitude is of necessity – or Necessity – in a process of constant modification. The moral meaning of the encounter with death (the shattering and re-constitution of self) which I observed in Hughes' 'theory' is an essential part of Central European practice. Their opposition to totalitarianism is not just to its two obvious political faces,

the extremities of Nazism and Marxism. As Herbert's 'The monster of
Mr. Cogito' (Part II, lines 1–8) demonstrates, they are also wary of the
danger of *liberal totalitarianism*, in so far as it paints another – only
apparently more harmless – abstract picture of the world. The
combination of those two words must appear startling, but it is
supported by Santa's comment on humanism and an equally jolting
assertion by Simone Weil that 'Totalitarianism is an ersatz form of
Christianity. Christianity became a totalitarian, conquering and destroy-
ing agent because it failed to develop the notion of the absence and non-
action of God here below' (*The Notebooks of Simone Weil*, vol. II, p. 505).
That is, both liberal and Christian thought failed to develop the notion
that humanity, on the showing of the war, is totally responsive to the
field of influence of the Necessary, and instead promulgated the idea that
it was responding to an abstract 'good' (the political ideal of democratic
freedoms etc.). As Herbert recognizes, such an attitude fails to come to
grips with the real problem. The danger of totalitarian thinking processes
is described in a poem by the Polish poet Tymoteusz Karpowicz entitled
'The pencil's dream':

> When the pencil undresses for sleep
> he firmly decides
> to sleep stiffly
> and blackly
>
> he is helped in it
> by the inborn inflexibility
> of all the piths of the world
> the spinal pith of the pencil
> will break but cannot be bent
>
> he will never dream of
> waves of hair
> only of a soldier standing at attention
> or coffins
>
> what finds its place in him
> is straight
> what is beyond is crooked
> good night
> (C. Milosz (ed.), in *Post-War Polish Poetry*)

The animalistic obliqueness of the poem consolidates the lesson of
Herbert's and Rozewicz's poems. It keeps interpretative space open, so
that more than one reading is available, according to a decision made by
the reader's nature. The double emphasis on the colour black and
militaristic stiffness, in addition to the dualism of the final stanza, *may*
persuade the reader to confine the poem's meaning to an indictment of
Fascism; in this case, the colour is a reminder of Mussolini's black-shirted
supporters, the stiffness and militarism recalls (say) the 'elite' German SS

Corps, and the dualism becomes that of Aryan and Jew or Slav. But the poem is non-explicit – and here we should be conscious of Davie's demand for explanatory statement – and the virtue of that suggestive openness becomes apparent in the existence of a second reading: the pencil's decision to sleep 'stiffly' and 'blackly' was helped 'by the inborn inflexibility/ of all the piths of the world', suggesting that the rigidity of the abstracting attitude is an original psychological menace *within* (human) nature. The purity or goodness of its own self-image ('straight') is so accentuated that everything 'beyond' appears unspeakably 'crooked' or evil in those last four lines. The second reading ironizes the first, because it is exactly this identification with an abstract image of our own 'good' which characterizes the first reading; *we name* the pencil's dream-attitude 'Fascist' and immediately shrink its reality or horror; the name gives us independence of, or superiority to, the bare fact, only the second reading presumes something of the experienced reality of evil, of what Ferenc Juhasz calls 'conscious horror', by allowing the realization that the mental movement described in the poem is one of which we are all guilty. In other words, we experience the first reading – and I think it is almost impossible to be innocent of those initial associations – in order to recognize subsequently that we have performed a 'totalitarian' mental action which is similar or even identical to the one that is the poem's subject. By attending to the origins of our response as well as the 'objective' poem, we get an opportunity to defuse one of the chief delusions of the liberal acquired Personality, though that open-plan 'opportunity' is directly resistant to the Movement's demand for the didactic and explicit.

The speech of the poetic self is 'suggestive as reality is suggestive', deprived of the prejudicial aspect of 'explanation'. Such a broadening vocal range of the self necessarily involves – as we have just witnessed in Karpowicz's poem – an ironic decreation of the False Personalities, for both poet and reader alike. They are only too ready to 'explain', and construct entire worlds in their own image:

I build

I tread on a pane
on a mirror
that cracks

I tread on Yorick's
skull
I tread on this brittle
world

and build a house
a castle in the air
within all's ready
for a siege

only I
remain surprised
outside
the walls
(Tadeusz Rozewicz, *Conversation with the Prince*)

As soon as he breaks the fragile world which is his own true reflection
the protagonist is free to construct his own version of it, resilient with its
fortifying explanations. Only in the last four lines is this 'I' revealed as a
fiction, merely an abstract empty shell. This self-qualifying irony is not
the same as Larkin's, which is the negative irony of all the ignorances and
imprecisions that come with the closure of the world by rational
scepticism. It is rather the positive irony of moral development,
improvising its way through a process of mistake and correction to the
totality of the self, and *striking down false selves* and constructions of the
world wherever it finds them. As a final example, here is a poem in
which one false self is quite literally struck down:

My Jacobean fatigues

My Jacobs of tiredness

Higher
clarion calls of form,
habitations of touch,
all serenities of senses.

Lowest of all, I.
From my breast they grow
stairs of reality.

And I feel nothing.
Nothing of juiciness.
Nothing of colour.
Not only am I not
one of the Testament heroes
but worse than a flounder
glued to the bottom to die
with balloons of breath
bubbling up in bundles,
worse than a potato mother
who put forth
enormous antlers of tubes
and herself is shrinking
up to disappearance.

Strike me
construction of my world!
(Miron Bialoszewski, in Milosz (ed.), *Post-War Polish Poetry*)

The poem condenses many of the salient possibilities of post-war poetry:
there seems to be resistance to Romantic ideology – 'serenities of senses'

– similar to the Movement's response, though the similarities end there. Bialoszewski, unlike Davie and others, does not take up the invitation made by 'Higher/ clarion calls of form', the aesthetic possibility of poetry; like Lifton, he uncovers a self which is psychically numb, and like Jung he recognizes that self as 'Lowest down' – amongst the 'autonomous functional systems', and material, particularly in the 'potato mother' analogy. But he has gained, it is clear, a radically different perspective on it. There is no attempt to cover that condition (the 'experienced self') 'theoretically' with the loud chord of rationalist discourse or the purity of aesthetics; rather, a simultaneous awareness of the fictive personality (which is always generating those theories) and the perfectly silent, unresponsive self 'Lowest of all'. The space between the two is filled – permanently – by irony. In the poem, one species of that irony lies in the fact that the advertisements of that personality – clarion calls, balloons of breath, 'enormous antlers of tubes' – which are termed 'reality', only occupy five lines of the poem. The invisible self which is 'glued to the bottom to die' and is 'shrinking up to disappearance' occupies sixteen lines, and perhaps in this we can see Bialoszewski fulfilling Simone Weil's demand that the creative artist pays attention to what does not exist. Thus it would seem more accurate to call the process by which this self produces 'stairs of reality' not so much an evolution as an involution, a growth into potentially delusory 'freedoms',[4] or abstractions only interested in preserving themselves. It is this idea of the world which the poetic persona realizes must be 'stopped': 'Strike me/ construction of my world!' One cannot imagine any British poet of a comparable generation speaking these lines, or achieving such a radical examination of human consciousness.

One could paraphrase this ironic process as creative silencing of false conscious attitudes or False Personality. This silencing must be performed in order that the 'real' may take place, and a poet be an objective witness to that reality. 'I would like to write', Pilinszky has said, 'as if I had remained silent.' The lack of language, the speech which disturbs the silence only minimally, is a way of keeping in touch with our origins, or checking the hubris of a conscious addition, or the possible inflations of style. What is collective is of primary importance, the merely individualistic is of merely secondary value: 'Every work is a prototype of the world. A message derived from the Whole' (Pilinszky, quoted in Tezla (ed.), *Ocean at the Window*, p. 119). And this is the crux of these writers' human improvement on Adorno's notorious, though sensational edict 'No poetry after Auschwitz', their method of keeping their humanity intact without a complete surrender of consciousness to the animal cells. Pilinszky himself sees the silence in the same way as Simone Weil, as the capacity to 'listen', the approach to divine nature:

He who is capable not only of crying out but also of listening will hear the answer. Silence is the answer. This is the eternal silence for which Vigny bitterly reproached God; but Vigny had no right to say how the just man should reply to the silence, for he was not one of the just. . . .

The speech of created beings is with sounds. The word of God is silence. God's secret word of love can be nothing else but silence. (Weil, 'Additional pages on the love of God and affliction', from *Gateway to God*, p. 101)

We will see in Hughes' own work an increasingly systematic silencing of false consciousness – particularly from *Crow* onwards – and a growing recognition of the religious context of that process, culminating in *River*.

Positioning oneself outside self–fictions also means – as some of the poems have already hinted – that these poets cannot have the same attitude to aesthetics and language that is characteristic of the Movement, for instance (or Joyce, for that matter). Zbigniew Herbert, at the end of his poem, 'On the road to Delphi' (*Selected Poems*), makes the statement that 'A craftsman must probe to the very bottom of cruelty.' Both the free play of styles and the added emphasis on the purely technical craftsmanship and organization of the poem came to an end with the Second World War. Craft is at the mercy of cruelty. Apollo – despite his formally given victory – at the mercy of Marsyas. In 'Apollo and Marsyas' (*Selected Poems*) Herbert describes the confrontation as that of 'absolute ear/ versus immense range'. While Apollo cleans his instrument, the entire landscape resounds to the howling of Marsyas:

> only seemingly
> is the voice of Marsyas
> monotonous
> and composed of a single-vowel
> Aaa
>
> in reality
> Marsyas relates
> the inexhaustible wealth
> of his body . . .

That howling does indeed result in a new 'concrete' art at the end of the poem, in which every item of the natural environment 'is white/ completely'. And this eventuality is of course, 'beyond the endurance/ of the god with nerves of artificial fibre'.

Tadeusz Rozewicz, like Hughes himself in *Crow*, consciously began to give up the aesthetic privileges enjoyed by poetry, and the beauties and formalities of language, in favour of the truth of language 'really used by men'. His 'growing contempt for aesthetic values', which he shares with the majority of Central European writers of the period, constitutes the mandatory 'death of poetry' which I indicated earlier: death, that is, as a preface to the re-making of poetry, its shift from an *aesthetic* to a *moral* centre. He goes on to cite the dictum of the great Polish poet Mickiewicz that 'it is more difficult to spend a day well than to write a book.' The following commentary, however, is perhaps his most comprehensive summary of the effects of the Second World War upon the world of aesthetics:

> The dance of poetry came to an end during the Second World War in concentration camps created by totalitarian systems. . . . The departure in such *Grenzsituationen* from the 'special' poetic language has produced those poems which I call stripped of masks and costumes. Our critics talked of the 'prosaicization' of poetry. This was a simplified and mistaken view. It is precisely the poems written in *Grenzsituationen*, in ultimate situations, 'prosaicized' works, which created the conditions for poetry's subsistence and even survival. In the works of every writer, even the greatest, such poems are very rare . . . of course, there are poets who perform their 'poetry dance' resolutely to the end without reference to the state of humanity, their country or even their own condition. (from Adam Czerniawski's Introduction to Rozewicz, *Conversation with the Prince*, p. 13)

The impact of such statements upon the free play of aestheticism is self-evident, and perhaps should be borne in mind in an examination of contemporary literary trends such as Martianism. But if Rozewicz's comments could be taken as an attack on Romanticism in poetry, then they are equally resistant to Davie's view of the necessity of a traditional formal organization in the poem. A complete abandonment of punctuation and the logical orders of prose syntax, along with metrical patterns and regular stanzaic forms, characterizes the vast bulk of post-war Czech, Polish and Yugoslavian poetry. Furthermore, it is sufficiently evident that the Fascist potential which Davie observes in the breaking of rationally ordered syntax is not at all supported by the practice of this poetry; even his assertion about the direct relation between Imagism and Fascism is contradicted by a poem like Karpowicz's 'The pencil's dream'. This irony directed against the formal structures of language, the 'refusal to surrender themselves to any mechanical progression imposed on them by the tyranny of their own words or images' (Hughes' introduction to Vasko Popa's *Collected Poems*, p. 3), goes hand in hand with the moral vigilance against false assumptions about the self and the world. Even within an individual poem, we witness constant ironic shifts of gaze, re-inventions, changes of course, derived from this restless moral preoccupation with truth rather than beauty, and the satisfying completeness of the artistic product. This habit of mind describes an exploratory, open-ended self, sensitive to its own errors but not helpless in the collision of forces that play through it. It is not the collapse of rule and order in language that invites Fascism, but the very rigidity and abstraction of formal structures on all levels, whether in the dimension of the self, or

aesthetics, or politics: the biggest delusion is in the apparent completeness of the abstraction, and the fundamental belief in the 'given'
adequacy of language.

It is these poets – in whose footsteps Hughes keenly follows – who
have given the lie to Jung's pessimistic view of the current state of the
arts:

> The pleasingness of the artistic product is replaced by chill abstractions of
> the most subjective nature which brusquely slam the door on the naive and
> romantic delight in the senses and their obligatory love for the object. This
> tells us, in plain and universal language, that the prophetic spirit of art has
> turned away from the old object relationship and towards the – for the time
> being – dark chaos of subjectivisms. (*The Undiscovered Self*, pp. 109–10)

Although Central European literature, like its Western counterpart, has
indeed shut the door on the naivety of Romantic object – love, it cannot
be said to have turned its face towards the 'dark chaos of subjectivisms'.
In Herbert's 'Study of the object' (Parts 5–6),[5] the poet rejects both the
Romantic possibility of art (Part 5) and the movement towards an
abstracting attitude with which that section ends, 'obey the counsels of
the inner eye/ admit no-one'. Tentatively, ironically, he extracts 'from
the stern reveries of the inner eye/ a chair', and when the individualistic
'creative imperative' 'let it be' is in danger of making something
'beautiful and useless/ like a cathedral in the wilderness', the possibility
of a new sort of creation emerges, based on the collective, submissive
beggary of the 'we':

> we ask reveal o chair
> the depths of the inner eye
> the iris of necessity
> the pupil of death

It is difficult not to sense that this attitude of submissiveness, and the
need to maintain a poetic, though inarticulate space in the face of
necessity leads writing inevitably into the religious dimension. That
dimension, with its point of reference always outside the immediate
visibility of both the world and the self, by its nature undermines the
desire for aesthetic completeness:

> One must give up stories that can be pursued. One must give up the stories
> that can be told. Stories and tales are contrived by affection and wisdom,
> because affection and wisdom believe in them. They believe that the joy
> and sorrow of a good story may bring someone comfort. What pious
> credulity! What fraudulence! In a world where the news of a single
> morning can overshadow Dante and all his hell, the stories, too, are
> obscure. One knows neither where they begin, nor where they end. And
> who, finally, dares to call his story his own? To call it finished, complete?
> Who dares to oppose the almost universal fate . . . that hangs over us now?

(Csoori, 'Approaching words', in Tezla (ed.), *Ocean at the Window*, p. 298–9)

Likewise Janos Pilinszky – the most obviously religious Hungarian poet – says that the dents and scratches to be found on various objects in the Auschwitz Museum were 'written' by those who never managed to compose their sentences, only to be transcribed later into the literary 'achievements' of others: 'In the context of the divine: it is usually one person who lives out the value and someone else who may write it up. Does it matter? It is God and God alone who writes, on the fabric of actions or on paper' (Poigny Speech, 1970). The poet's contribution to the unfinished nature of the tale, it could be added, is reminiscent of Hughes' vision of the artist as a kind of universal instrument, redressing a lost balance. For Pilinszky, all art becomes fundamentally religious once the artist acquires the knowledge that every creative act is a *passive act*:

> There is no such thing, in a literal sense, as artistic creation. But the obedient imagination may find it possible to establish contact with that absolute freedom, love, immanence and familiarity with which God chose the world.
>
> In short, what we call 'creative imagination' is nothing else than the sacrifice of the imagination: it is *passive creation* (by comparison, fancy is imagination's venial sin, its chronic childhood disease). (Poigny Speech, in Tezla (ed.), *Ocean at the Window*, p. 143)

Pilinszky interprets the imagination's morality as its willing obedience to the collective reality which it inhabits, and it is that submissiveness which puts it in contact with God. Once the imagination accepts this moral basis, the Yeatsian choice between the perfection of the individual life and the perfection of art simply ceases to exist, because poetry has no other context than the process of self-development. From this point of view, undivided attention to style or technique – the isolated perfection of one's art – is just the alienation of art from its proper function. This is the direction Pilinszky speaks of in perhaps the most lucid and damning account of the fate of the imagination at the present time:

> If we now consider our own time, we find that the fate of our imagination is rather disquieting and tragic. I would not go so far as to say that it has renounced its arduous mission for good, but it has undoubtedly strayed onto heretical paths, taking the wrong turning. It succumbed to its original weakness when it began to covet the *certainty* of the Sciences. Imagination has since then led a mirror-existence, striving to experience in the certainty of style that which should be attainable only in the self-forgetfulness of obedience, only 'with eyes downcast'. Whether it meant to do so or not, scientific thought in art has in a curious way inaugurated a mirror-age, an age of narcissistic elements. It is since then that we speak of good stylists. A new epoch dawned, an epoch that places the stylistic certainty of appearances before the self-forgetful incarnating of the world. We have

striven to remove into the mirror all the virtues of the great literatures, from carefully-controlled beauty to carefully-controlled ecstasy. We see and know all, what's more we see and know better since then; but would that we were blind and alive – with our backs to the mirror. ('Creative imagination in our time', Poigny 1970, quoted in Tezla (ed.), *Ocean at the Window*, p. 144)

Donald Davie's faith in rationalist discourse and philosophy is perceived as just that – subjective belief – under this sort of pressure. It is possible to use Pilinszky's paradigm as one conclusive description of Hughes' entire development, from the aesthetics of the mirror to the submissive 'incarnating of the world'. In his second interview with Ekbert Faas (1977; see Faas, *Ted Hughes*, pp. 208–9), Hughes explains the difficulty of the transition between two poems in *Lupercal*, 'To paint a water-lily' and 'View of a pig'; the writing of the former was like 'squeezing language out at the end of this long, remote process' (p. 208), whilst the latter 'had nothing to do with the way in which I thought I ought to be writing' (p. 209), in a moment of impatience. Confronted by Faas' assertion that 'To paint a waterlily' is one of the most beautiful poems in the volume, Hughes replies 'but it isn't as interesting to me' (p. 209). What Hughes was evidently impatient to break up was the self-admiring mirror of a beautiful style and its flattering certainty of appearance. 'View of a pig' and 'Hawk roosting' metaphorically turn Hughes' back to the mirror, engaging the realities of the outside world and his own experience more directly; the shift between poems, moreover, is one illustration of Hughes' developing preoccupation with a body of experience rather than a body of language. In this context, all his poems are 'invocations to writing'.

The importance of Hughes' imaginative endeavour should be clearer by now, mindful of the literary–cultural perspectives provided in the current chapter. I should leave the final words to Pilinszky, here re-establishing the value of the *literary* imagination in its true proportion:

In reality the drama of the imagination is one and indivisible. And although on the surface – with the postponing of salvation – there is a welter of the most diverse variations and improvisations of errings and errors in the interplay of the mirror and our daily life, deep down the unity is unbroken, the burden is carried, justice is loved, the continuity of awe and obedience remains. It is true that this unity and continuity is only occasionally called art, only occasionally literature. Does it matter? In the true history of the imagination silence is sometimes more important than all the sentences that have ever been written.

And here – finally – I have in mind that imageless imagination, that ultimate and inexhaustible source, that brotherly stillness of imagination, which no sort of noise can silence. ('Creative imagination in our time', in Tezla (ed.), *Ocean at the Window*, p. 147)

CHAPTER 3

———————— • ————————

THE HAWK IN THE RAIN

Ted Hughes' first three major volumes of published poetry, *The Hawk in the Rain*, *Lupercal* and *Wodwo* have frequently been characterized as 'the poetry of violence' in critical response (cf. the Rawson–Hainsworth controversy over whether Hughes celebrates violence for its own sake, to which Faas draws attention in his *London Magazine* interview 'Ted Hughes and Crow', p. 8), and the several contextual shadings of the phrase do indeed provide a decisive entry-point into Hughes' imaginative world. Hughes himself illuminated one such context in the same interview:

> Any form of violence – any form of vehement activity – invokes the bigger energy, the elemental power-circuit of the universe. Once the contact has been made – it becomes difficult to control. Something from beyond ordinary human activity enters. When the wise men know how to create rituals and dogma, the energy can be contained. When the old rituals and dogma have lost credit, and disintegrated, and no new ones have been formed, the energy cannot be contained, and so its effect is destructive – and that is the position with us. And that is why force of any kind frightens our rationalist, humanist style of outlook. . . . We have settled for the minimum practical energy and illumination – anything bigger introduces problems, the demons get hold of it. That is the psychological stupidity, the ineptitude, of the rigidly rationalist outlook – it's a form of hubris, and we're paying the traditional price. (*ibid.*, pp. 9–10)

In this synopsis, elemental 'energy' only becomes 'violence' when it is given no role to play in the subject's conscious outlook. The narrowness or rigidity of the rationalist point of view actively determines the nature and intensity of the violence encountered in the outside world. 'Violence', in short, is the visibility of the world or self beyond the limited range of the Ego-Personality – or the residue of the dramatic confrontation between the two forces. In this sense Hughes is resuscitating the dilemma which afflicted the Movement poets, whose temporary solution only re-emphasized the 'External' attitude, and kept poetry's 'act' going by formal tricks, and the repetition of words and motifs. This understanding of violence shadows somewhat grimly the critical debate, which concerns itself with discussion of the term as a moral absolute, whether or not violence has a 'justification' (gratuitous or not gratuitous?). Hughes fully exploits both 'readings' of the word – and their underpinning presuppositions about the nature of reality – in the course of his early poems. Two of the best illustrative examples of the embracing nature of this debate on 'violence' are, suitably enough, the title poem of Hughes' first volume and 'The jaguar'. An examination in depth of these two poems takes us into virtually every corner of Hughes' characteristic territory; they provide what could be called a 'gate to readership' of contemporary poetry in general.

'The hawk in the rain' works through a dialectical presentation, in which fragmentary perceptions of the hawk's perfect balance counter-point the images of ever-increasing violence that afflict the persona of the poem. Not only do they 'counterpoint' those images, they actually *provoke* them – as if the poet's identification with the hawk actually triggers, with a kind of metronomic regularity and a burgeoning intensity – the violence that Nature does to the protagonist.

At the beginning of the poem, however, the violence seems to be 'contained'. The poet reaches for control through the classic Anglo-Saxon line, with four major stresses (two in each half-line) three of which are picked out by alliteration: 'I drówn in the drúmming ploughland, I drág úp . . .'. The 'I', the 'commanding self' strains to exert a conscious, consonantal grip upon the structureless, possibly chaotic flux and opulence of the vowels: 'Heel after heel from the swallowing of the earth's mouth . . .'. The 'heroic' tendency of Anglo-Saxon syntax and diction which was examined in the Introduction is clearly in evidence: both magnetically attract the condition of the self at a moral border – in Rozewicz's terms a *Grenzsituation* – in which the conscious personality is continually engaged in an abrasive struggle with its own unconscious material contents; armed with consonants, it confronts, in Graves' terms, a 'devouring' image of the Goddess, and the vowels which are sacred to her.[1] The stringent intellectual effort of the combat with the 'dogged grave' is interrupted by the appearance of a third term, which carries the struggle over into the fresh possibilities of a new stanza: '. . . but the hawk/ Effortlessly at height hangs his still eye.' Both the protagonist and the reader come with relief to what Keith Sagar calls the hawk's 'centrality and poise'. He goes on to say that, far from being an hallucination, the hawk is 'the only reality' and quotes Mircea Eliade in *The Sacred and the Profane*:

> For it is the break effected in space that allows the world to be constituted, because it reveals the fixed point, the Central axis for all future orientation. . . . In the homogeneous and infinite expanse, in which no

point of reference is possible and hence no *orientation* can be established, the hierophany reveals an absolute fixed point, a centre. (p. 21, from *The Art of Ted Hughes*, p. 15)

The psychological trend, for persona and reader alike, is away from both the raw fluctuating struggle with material contents and language whose density – in the friction of the consonant–vowel fight – requires a conscious physical effort, and towards the 'fixed centre' and the effortless formal beauty of the hawk's lines. One tempting critical reaction would be to claim that those lines pivot on the word 'hangs' in exactly the same way as the violence of the natural environment is balanced out in the hawk's 'master-fulcrum': 'The word "hangs" suspends itself in the exact centre of the line just as the hawk is suspended, timeless, at the centre of reality.' In this case, the aesthetic satisfaction afforded by the poised symmetry of this and the following lines ('wings . . . creation . . . weightless/ Steady . . . hallucination . . . streaming'), and the portable meaning supplied by Eliade encourage our assumption that the hawk's freedom is already within the range of the I's authoritarian voice: to write the perfect line is, after all, the poetic equivalent of mastering reality, giving the reader the comfort of a stable world-view; to adapt a saying of Schopenhauer's 'our personality, our will with its constant pain, disappears, so long as the pure aesthetic pleasure lasts' ('The world as idea' (2nd Aspect), in Mann (ed.), *The Living Thoughts of Schopenhauer*, p. 71).

In a secondary reading, we may feel some reservations about this 'flight': we may become aware that alliteration – which rivets the formal beauty of the whole sense-unit together – is a mechanism which *belongs* to the poem's 'masculine', commanding persona who wants to preserve *his* organization of the world inside and outside the poem. A further disturbing recognition is possible: not only does the poem use Gerard Manley Hopkins' 'The windhover' as its general model, it also imitates Dylan Thomas' predator in 'Over Sir John's hill' rather more immediately:

Over Sir John's hill,
The hawk on fire hangs still . . .
Flash, and the plumes crack,
And a black cap of jack-
Daws Sir John's just hill dons, and again the gulled birds hare

To the hawk on fire, the halter height, over Towy's fins,
In a whack of wind.
  (in D. Jones (ed.), *Dylan Thomas, The Poems*, pp. 201–2)

We only come to the hawk at two removes, as a purely literary convention. In this sense, Hughes is repeating what Ferenc Juhasz calls a 'recorded text', and the direct participation of his image in a conscious literary tradition – which Hughes himself has unflatteringly referred to as the 'maternal octopus of English Literary tradition' – may limit its moral currency in the poem.[2]

Gurdjieff's definition of the basic difference between *Essence* and *Personality* is very revealing here:

> Essence in man is what is *his own*. Personality in man is what is 'not his own'. 'Not his own' means what has come from the outside, what he has learned, or reflects . . . all words and movements that have been learned, all feelings created by imitation – all this is 'not his own', all this is personality. (Ouspensky, *In Search of the Miraculous*, p. 161)

Hughes' hawk is a fabrication 'not his own' but exists in the literary abstract, as part of the personality's speech set against a vital awareness of the continuum outside itself. Not until 'The risen' from *Cave Birds* do we encounter the hawk's meaning as a triumph of original re-discovery, rather than as a literary trophy.

The 'aesthetic' image recurs, with minor variations, in the next two stanzas:

> . . . the hawk hangs
> The diamond point of will that polestars
> the sea-drowner's endurance . . .

> . . . [I] strain towards the master-
> Fulcrum of violence where the hawk hangs still.

By the third repetition, the strain and tension of the effort to cling to the image is indeed beginning to show. Unlike the hawk, the poet proves quite unable to hold his own creation in a weightless quiet. When the poet turns, in the spaces between his contemplations of the hawk, to confront the natural environment, and tries to impose the same formal authority which comprised the 'beauty' of the hawk's description, he receives quite a shock: the ritual intensity of style fails completely to put its finger on an elegant formula to contain the violence of the elements, but gives us instead its own shadow-side in the worst hyperbolic excesses of language. The more the authoritarian voice struggles for a controlling 'word', the more desperately the poet/persona flounders in an exaggerated quagmire of language; and the reader becomes proportionately more aware of the limitations of the vocal range of that 'commanding self'; so the marginal strain and awkwardness of:

> While banging wind kills these stubborn hedges,
> Thumbs my eyes, throws my breath, tackles my heart,
> And rain hacks my head to the bone . . .

gives way to a full-scale rhetorical or 'aesthetic' disaster: 'Bloodily grabbed dazed last móment-counting/ Mórsel in the earth's mouth . . .'

in which the alliteration is really a risible parody of the vigilant control exemplified in lines 1–4.

What it is vital for the reader to realize, however, is that these lines are nothing more than the negative aspect of the same rhetorical mode of language – and the same conscious attitude – which produced the hawk's mastery. It is a language and an attitude ill-equipped to deal with a world in which people actually do die, or are at least threatened with annihilation – although that incompatibility does not stop both from 'trumpeting the ear dead' (to modify a phrase from 'Egg-head') with the vehemence of the attempt. It is as if the prevailing style of the poem tries to resist its central dramatic event, the conversion of the protagonist from active subject to humbled, passive object in lines 9–10, 13–14. It is the language of verbal ascent, a rhetorical straining for the heights, but it has to give up in the face of the anonymous materialisms of Nature which are 'lowest down'. Even the final, clenched effort to renew the image in lines 14–15 ends in a thoroughly anachronistic full-stop, which utterly fails in its task of keeping the lofty perception of the hawk discretely isolated from the surrounding chaos:

> *That* maybe in his own time meets the weather
>
> Coming the wrong way, suffers the air, hurled upside down,
> Fall from his eye, the ponderous shires crash on him,
> The horizon trap him; the round angelic eye
> Smashed, mix his heart's blood with the mire of the land.
>
> (my italics)

The masculine endeavour to erect an image of its own order disintegrates, and language at the same time assumes its most self-effacing attitude within the poem. For the most part it is content to describe the hawk's death simply, only drawing attention to itself in the relatively minor excesses of 'ponderous shires' and 'the round angelic eye'. And the dramatic experience of the conclusion forces the reader to feel that the symbol of the hawk as an exact centre of reality is beyond him, 'not his own'. The violence of the poem subsists in the wrenching knowledge that such a centring is not to be attained by the ego's wilful effort to escape from the collective and material nature of the unconscious. Therefore, in terms of moral development, *the image must collapse* at the end of the poem.

Instead of being permitted to gaze more or less serenely *upwards*, the conclusion forces the reader *downwards*, in the opposite direction. According to esoteric and psychological practice, this downward mobility is an absolute necessity, without which no further progress is possible. Jung says that the tree which grows to the heights of heaven has its roots in the deepest hell. In *The Archetypes of the Collective Unconscious*, he expands this statement with reference to the dreams of a Protestant theologian.[3] Maurice Nicoll, in his commentaries on the teachings of Gurdjieff and Ouspensky, points out that a man can never 'do' from an Imaginary 'I' or False Personality, 'but only from what is lowest in this respect – from what is most simple and genuinely sincere. *So to go up he must go down*' (III, p. 826; my italics).

The impulse to 'descend', however, is exactly what the reader, along with the poet and his persona, has been resisting during the course of the poem, setting up a dualistic situation within the text: where the persona is trying to drag himself clear of the chaos of matter towards the abstract model of the hawk's 'aloof' self, the poet 'strains' rhetorically to quell the violent elements – and bring them within the range of his commanding 'I' – through the formal strength of his language; and the reader performs the same action when he prefers (in the 'primary' reading) the certainty of an aesthetic appreciation to the dramatic – i.e. moral – context in which that appreciation is involved. By elevating the aesthetic critical positive – cf. Gifford and Roberts' reading – and finding the pleasurable height of that linguistic moment enhanced rather than undermined by the continuity with poetic tradition (Hopkins and Thomas), the reader is *not* making an independent judgement about an artistic object, but expressing a dangerous psychological preference. He wants to go straight *upwards*, or soar over the depths like Jung's theologian, separating off the 'beautiful' language from the 'ugly' diction of lines 8–10 and 13–14, which may be judged as the understandably inferior productions of a 'promising', linguistically ambitious poet. This acquired aesthetic sensibility is the visible evidence of False Personality in literary criticism, threatening to fabricate the poem's verbal triumphs and cast the poet's future in its image; its omission of any psychological understanding of the relationship between the persona's movement 'up' and 'down' actually reinforces the violence of the poem, preventing any healing of the dramatized psychic split through a divisive act of readership. The violence of the poem's ending only appears 'gratuitous' – i.e. beyond understanding – when the critic's own attitude makes it so, when the literary response has effectively released 'craftsmanship' from its obligation to 'probe to the bottom of cruelty'.[4]

The psychological and verbal processes of 'The jaguar' are remarkably similar to those of the title poem of the volume. The initial situation in the first eight lines is only apparently inert:

> The apes yawn and adore their fleas in the sun.
> The parrots shriek as if they were on fire, or strut
> Like cheap tarts to attract the stroller with the nut.
> Fatigued with indolence, tiger and lion

Lie still as the sun. The boa-constrictor's coil
Is a fossil. Cage after cage seems empty, or
Stínks of sléepers from the breathing stráw.
It might be painted on a nursery wall.

What Alvarez would term the 'gentility' of latinate diction – 'Fatigued
with indolence' – and the regular rhyme-scheme is shadowed more
disturbingly by the direct engagement of the Anglo-Saxon line with
concealed and possibly hostile contents in line 7. One can sense, in that
sudden tensing of the alliterative grip, the hardening of the conscious
attitude itself in response to the violent onset of those contents. They
duly emerge in the form of a jaguar 'hurrying enraged/ Through prison
darkness after the drills of his eyes// On a short fierce fuse.' The image of
mechanicalness the jaguar presents comes from 'below', and has the same
effect on the protagonist as the natural elements in the previous poem,
converting him from subject to passive object. Like the rest of the
crowd, the Poem's 'I' shrinks 'mesmerized/ As a child at a dream', at this
vision of the mechanical–instinctual body, described by that pounding,
equally machine-like coincidence of stress and quantity which is the
living centre of the Anglo-Saxon line: 'On a short fierce fuse'. As in 'The
hawk in the rain', the poetic persona's response to the 'opening' created
by Anglo-Saxon forms is to explain, and hence abstract the image:

> . . . Not in boredom –
> The eye satisfied to be blind in fire,
> By the báng of blóod in the bráin deaf the ear –
> He spins from the bars, but there's no cage to him
>
> More than to the visionary his cell . . .

It is in those last two lines that the jaguar most nearly resembles the
hawk's image of detached freedom in the title poem. But that resemblance brings with it all the difficulties attendant on the hawk's
abstraction: the stiffening of alliterative control in 'By the bang of blood
in the brain deaf the ear' is a rather sinister echo of the parallel
authoritarian effort to control the 'enraged' elements in lines 9–10 and
13–14 of the first poem. Moreover, the bang of blood conspicuously fails
to deafen the poet's *conceptualizing* ear in the next two lines. The
conscious attitude not only survives the jaguar's 'violence', it appropriates the meaning all too easily. The explicitness of the equivalence 'jaguar
= visionary' suggests a reduction of the symbol to the status of emblem,
in Davie's understanding of the two terms. Such a forcible abstraction of
jaguar-material threatens to deprive the symbol of the openness with
which Hughes credits it in his *London Magazine* commentary:

> I prefer to think of them [the present poem and 'Second glance at a jaguar']
> as first, descriptions of a jaguar, second . . . invocations of the Goddess,

third . . . invocations of a jaguar-like body of elemental force, demonic force.

It's my belief that symbols of this sort work. . . . The way it works depends on that mind [which receives it] . . . on the nature of that mind. I'm not at all sure how much direction, how much of a desirable aim and moral trajectory you can fix onto a symbol by associated paraphernalia. A jaguar after all can be received in several different aspects . . . he is a beautiful, powerful nature spirit, he is a homicidal maniac, he is a super-charged piece of cosmic machinery, he is a symbol of man's baser nature shaved down into the id and growing cannibal murderous with deprivation, he is an ancient symbol of Dionysus since he is a leopard raised to the ninth power . . . . Or he is simply a demon . . . a lump of ectoplasm. A lump of astral energy.

The symbol opens all these things . . . it's the reader's own nature that selects. ('Ted Hughes and Crow', *London Magazine*, p. 8)

The persona's own nature selects a limited conscious meaning which tends to make all the other meanings invisible: the point is that the reference to the visionary in his cell *does* fix a trajectory and 'desirable aim' onto the symbol, which also crucially limits the reader's responsive activity. Instead of being encouraged to make his own selection from the symbolic matter – and hence to further the moral purpose of readership – he is forced to assume a position of inert passivity, something akin to the animals' condition in the first eight lines. Like Krogon in *Orghast*, the conscious interpretative bias of Hughes' poetic persona casts its shadow over the reader's response, so that it splits in the struggle to reconcile the deaf-and-blind instinctuality of the jaguar and its conceptualization as visionary; the reader becomes aware of the enormous irony involved in the straddling of that psychological gap. He is being pulled in two directions at once – like the protagonist of 'The hawk in the rain' from 'below' by the evidence of mechanical life, from 'above' by the urge for a cleansing abstraction of the symbol in more palatable human terms. Like Crow in 'Crow blacker than ever', Hughes' poetic persona has 'nailed Heaven and Earth together', and it becomes essential, to paraphrase Gurdjieff, that the 'crystallization' of the struggle in the last three lines of the poem does not take place on a 'wrong foundation':

His stride is wildernesses of freedom:
The world rolls under the long thrust of his heel.
Over the cage floor the horizons come.

If the reader crystallizes on the basis of the conceptualization (the primary reading), these lines are read as a direct image of superior, conscious control, in which the Mind chooses its own path among a multiplicity of possible freedoms. From another vantage point (the secondary reading), this is the wrong foundation, the poem's tragic event, fully dramatized; the reader does not have to give priority to the 'human' element of the analogy – its visible or 'phenomenal' face. He can free the jaguar-symbol from the explicitness of the human assumption about it in order to regain all the other hidden meanings which belong to it – its suggestive *shadow-side*. In concrete terms, in the last three lines that shadow-side immediately gives a darker shading to 'wildernesses', suggesting a confused lack of direction, the original blindness/deafness of the jaguar, a clear warning against complacency. Furthermore, the jaguar becomes an ideal representative of the World-as-Will (Schopenhauer) which under-scores all our ideas, which makes Reason its mouthpiece, there 'to justify it, to provide it with "moral" motivations and in short to rationalize our instincts' (Mann's Introduction to *The Living Thoughts of Schopenhauer*, p. 8): so 'The wórld rólls under the lóng thrúst of his hèel.'

More and more of Hughes' interview-meanings may make a sudden re-appearance: the jaguar is indeed a 'super-charged piece of cosmic machinery' and a symbol of man's lower nature growing murderous with its suppression by the autonomous visionary-image. In the jaguar the reader re-discovers the wilful, subjective nature of *his* construction of the 'world': and this realization of the World-as-Will is filtered majestically through the language in the stressed, and therefore dominant, long vowels, for the first time liberated from their confine-ment by alliterating consonants. By 'crystallizing' on this interpretative foundation, the reader once again *finds* the symbol and maintains an ironic distance against those more assertive shapings of it by the fictive personality. Whether the dramatic context of the poem fully allows this 'crystallization' is another matter: the two readings remain split, they co-exist side by side in the poem – painfully – at the point of maximum friction for both poet and reader. The *violence* of the poem inheres in this, the difficulty of reconciling 'jaguar-like elementals' – once invoked from the unconscious – with the conscious interpretation of them, the corrupt container represented by the visionary-image.

Other poems in the volume indicate Hughes' *apparent awareness* of the 'ethical danger' present in both 'The jaguar' and 'The hawk in the rain', the hubris of the conscious personality which thinks to contain jaguarish or 'chaotic' elementals so readily. 'The man seeking experience enquires his way of a drop of water', for instance, offers the skeletal, structural outline of the dilemma which is dramatized – so to speak, fleshed out – by the first two poems. The protagonist first demands an *explicit* lesson of the water-drop's experience, never realizing that what he sees will be a reflection of his 'idea of the world', the narcissistic mirror; the protagonist listens unconsciously 'for *himself* to speak for the drop's self'. This arrogance of the 'commanding self' characterized Hughes' poetic personae in 'The hawk in the rain' and 'The jaguar', and it is baffled by a similarly silent, unresponsive Reality (cf. the 'chaotic' nature of the swallowing earth, and the 'blindness–deafness' of the jaguar):

> This droplet was clear water still.
> It no more responded than the hour-old child
>
> Does to finger-toy or coy baby-talk,
> But who lies long, long and frowningly
> Unconscious under the shock of its own quick
> After that first alone-in-creation cry
> When into the mesh of sense, out of the dark
> Blundered the world-shouldering monstrous 'I'.

In Gurdjieff's frame of reference, the False Personality is 'active' in the first four stanzas while the water-drop is the 'passive' Essence, childlike and unconscious 'under the shock of its own quick'. In fact the over-emphasis of the False Personality guarantees the unresponsiveness or under-developed nature of Essence:

> Essence is the truth in man; personality is the false. But in proportion as personality grows, essence manifests itself more and more rarely and more and more feebly and it very often happens that essence stops in its growth at a very early age and grows no further. It happens very often that the essence of a grown-up man, even that of a very intellectual, and, in the accepted meaning of word, highly 'educated' man, stops on the level of a child of five or six. This means that everything we see in this man is in reality 'not his own'. What is his own in man, that is, his essence, is usually only manifested in his instincts and in his simplest emotions. . . . As a rule a man's essence is either primitive, savage, and childish, or else simply stupid. (Ouspensky, *In Search of the Miraculous*, pp. 162–3)

Unless the situation is reversed, and Essence becomes active and the Personality passive, no development is possible.

This at least is the 'objective' critical response elicited by the poem. The didactic tendency of 'A man seeking experience', and poems like it, has clearly been inherited from 'Movement' practice, and brings with it the same effects upon readership: the reader is condemned by the simple, oppositional structure of the poem to inertia, passivity – he is engaged in 'objective' observation in which all judgements are made for him. Likewise the sense of the poet's struggle with language and the composition of his poem, which was the mirror-image of the persona's struggle with chaotic elementals, is simply absent. Both the 'aesthetic' drama of poetic creation and the drama of readership are bracketed by the poem's explicitness. The poem gives us the abstract outline of the dilemma, not its 'inner life'. As a result, it fails to generate the 'shock' which would allow an act of self-discovery within the text by both 'combatants' (poet and reader).

'The man seeking experience' is typical of the several structural accounts of the psychological dualism within the volume ('Meeting',

'Law in the country of cats', 'Bayonet charge', 'The conversion of Reverend Skinner', 'Phaetons', 'Six young men') which is elsewhere fully dramatized in the active experience of poet and reader. The crucial point is that the distinction between 'structural' and 'dramatic' accounts stands in jeopardy of repeating the same dualism in a higher octave. As Thomas West puts it,

> One senses a problem often in the relationship between lesser self and the superior or visionary self, because the poet appears to align himself more with the superior self than with the inferior self. Instead of a psychodrama, the imbalance between the two voices turns some poems into caricatures of the ordinary self. The vision then weighs heavily, like a badge of achievement, and the poetry begins to be argumentative and approaches rhetorical posturing. (*Ted Hughes*, p. 54)

The explicit or didactic versions of the situation – whole poems which demand the poet's remote or 'objective' attitude – are a symptom of the same hubris which drove his effort to sustain the hawk-image by the strength of his style, or contain jaguar-type elementals in an analogy of his own making. The difference is this: in the hawk and jaguar poems, the impulse towards explicitness, the aspiration towards verbal command of the elements, is only one-half of the drama. The poet voluntarily submitted that impulse to 'ascend' to the ironic challenge of 'elementals', and the hawk hardly survived the experience of the poem, the visionary-metaphor in 'The jaguar' only ambiguously – without freeing itself from the animal's shadow-meaning as pure, blind instinctuality. It is paramount for the reader to recognize that although the formal *content* of the poems like 'Meeting' appears to accuse the abstract Ego, Hughes' *attitude* of superiority to his subject consolidates it. The poet holds himself aloof, and 'descends' in only a minority of poems into the world of primitive violence he sees so readily in the outside world.

On occasion, a 'structural' account becomes 'dramatic' imperceptibly, unconsciously. 'Egg-head', for instance, starts out as a didactic warning against the abstracting attitude and its attendant dangers, and ends by struggling unsuccessfully to maintain the 'outside' view of the externals and surfaces of the dilemma. By the end it is looking from the 'inside', and manifests the falsity of self it purports to condemn in its own falsity of style.

> Spurn it muck under
> His foot-clutch, and opposing his flea-red
> Fly-catching fervency to the whelm of the sun,
> Trumpet his own ear dead.

The only thing which trumpets the reader's ear dead is the rhetorical posturing of the language and its own stupefying 'juggleries of

benumbing'. What began as 'objective' detailing of a certain psychological condition turns into a dramatic enactment of it: the double failure of
the self and poetic language to hover, as it were, at a convenient distance
above its subject. The same rhetorical assertiveness surfaced in 'The
hawk in the rain', when the 'I' was in danger of being swallowed by the
chaos below.

Language raises its voice or becomes hyper-extended when it finds
itself at the moral border, where consciousness is aware of the immediate
threat of unconscious 'elementals'. The 'militant pride' of language re-
establishes the same pride in the Ego. This is a modification of West's
statement, in that the posturing and argumentativeness of language is
only visible in the situation I have described; in another set of poems the
preoccupation with the formal details and effects of language is sufficient
in itself to overwhelm the violent character of Matter, the poem's
content. In 'Parlour-piece', for example, the lovers suppress the
elemental 'fire and flood' of their love – 'they dared not/ Let out a trickle
lest the whole crack . . .' – only in so far as the style stays clear of
Grenzsituationen, in the comfort of a gentility of diction and the regular
syllabic lines of the first stanza. The poet holds to a superiority of style – a
further facet of Pilinszky's stylistic certainty – in the face of the violent
potentialities of his subject-matter. In 'A modest proposal', the chaos of
sexual desire which features in 'Incompatibilities' is contained within an
ideal or ceremonial stylism which the reader feels is slightly artificial. The
'Slavering rush' of the two wolves in which 'Neither can make die/ The
painful burning of the coal its heart', is simply replaced by the final
stanza:

> And there rides by
> The great lord from hunting. His embroidered
> Cloak floats, the tail of his horse pours,
> And at his stirrup the two great-eyed greyhounds
> That day after day bring down the towering stag
> Leap like one, making delighted sounds.

As Keith Sagar suggests, these lines are beautiful in themselves 'with all
the stateliness of a medieval tapestry brought to life', but they are
undercut by the dramatic context of the poem. They are so absolutely
self-contained that they might have come from another poem, and they
cannot resolve the preceding seventeen lines because they fail to engage
the violent materials there. Style, suspicious of the darker forces in the
self and the explosive compressions and excuses of language that attend
the encounter with those forces, keeps itself entirely separate, creating
two worlds in the poem. It provides an aesthetic false conclusion which
is a symptom of the disease of dualism, not a resolution of it.

A third 'dramatic' group of poems is written on the bridge between
the dominant 'I'-fiction and the primitive Essence or 'elementals': this
group includes 'The hawk in the rain', 'The jaguar', 'The thought-fox',
'Wind' and 'October dawn'; and they temporarily accomplish the moral
function set down in 'Fair choice', the equal development of Personality
and Essence, conscious and unconscious:

> . . . you must bend your dilemma-feebled spine
> Under – as if nobly and under tons –
> Rearing both fairly. The spilt blood be your own!
> Your every glance shall see one of your twins
> An Abel to the other's bloody Cain.

Almost every other poem witnesses the violent imbalance of the two
terms, the hopeless split between a domineering 'I'-fiction and the
archaisms of instinct, desire, animal nature, etc. made murderous or
chaotic by suppression – although the blood spilt is 'not the poet's own'.

In order for the two terms to receive equal imaginative attention in
these poems, the 'death', or voluntary loss of power of the domineering
'I' is necessary. Psychologically – if not sequentially – we come to that
third group through poems that explicitly deal with violent death: 'The
casualty', 'Bayonet charge', 'Six young men' and 'Griefs for dead
soldiers'. 'The casualty', for example, reads like a summary of possible
poetic attitudes to the burned man who 'Bulks closer greater flesh and
blood than their [the spectators'] own . . .', the final image of the
elemental world. Both poet and reader may insist on maintaining their
distance, like the mourners' 'Holding close complacency its most dear/
Unscratchable diamond', or they can accept the loss of self-will inherent
in the lesson that 'the truth of a man is the doomed man in him or his
dead body', in which case 'Sympathies/ Fasten to the blood like flies.'
These two split directions decided the fate of hawk and jaguar between
them.

> . . . [they] start to the edge
> Of such horror close as mourners can,
> Greedy to share all that is undergone,
> Grimace, gasp, gesture of death. Till they look down
> On the handkerchief at which his eye stares up.

The mourners' perspective, looking down from above at a voyeuristic
distance, is the perspective of the 'objective imagination'. To 'descend',
and assume the position of the dead man staring up from below, is
nothing less than the death of that point of view, which in turn
guarantees the authenticity of 'The thought-fox'.

'Griefs for dead soldiers', though debilitated by the didactic patterning
of its three sections – 'Mightiest . . . Secretest . . . Truest' – also
communicates 'knowledge' about the responses of the imagination to

death. Within the present frame of reference, the first section might be
described as a public or collectivized grief, the face of death turned
towards the 'objective imagination'. In the illusory freedom of that
imagination, death can be manipulated into 'permanent stupendous
victory'. The second section, in contrast, gives us the 'subjective
imagination' through the private response of the widow, which, though
poignant, is in its own way no less extreme, or imbalanced: the 'hawsers
of love' sheared by the telegram's news blind and sever the material
'lesson' of death. The emotional identification with personal loss
becomes a new kind of egoism:

> Closer than thinking
> The dead man hangs around her neck, but never
> Close enough to be touched, or thanked even,
> For being all that remains in a world smashed.

Although the possibility of attachment to either pole of imagination is
purged in these two sections, the misfortune of the didactic patterning
persists, buffering the poet from the psychological commitment to
'death' implied by the 'truest' imagination:

> . . . the dead wait like brides
> To surrender their limbs; thud of another body flung
> down, the jolted shape of a face, earth into the mouth –
> Moment that could annihilate a watcher!

The moment *could* annihilate a watcher, either poet or reader, but it does
not in the present poem. The conditional remains a conditional, the
structural posture awaits animation by the dramatic 'descent' of the 'The
thought-fox' and 'Wind'.

A similar last-stanza didacticism,

> That man's not more alive whom you confront
> And shake by the hand, see hale, hear speak loud,
> Than any of these six celluloid smiles are . . .

and the same conditional gesturing – 'To regard this photograph might
well dement' – characterizes 'Six young men'. The poet's contemplation
of the still photograph becomes an exact metaphor for the inert distance
between the reader and the imaginary picture of death the poem presents.
Only in the last three lines does the poem begin to justify its 'theoretical'
claims:

> Such contradictory permanent horrors here
> Smile from the single exposure and shoulder out
> One's own body from its instant and heat.

The single verb 'shoulder' is enough to puncture the didactic, contemplative veil of the poem, somewhat like a nail suddenly piercing

the palm of the man to be crucified. The complacent overview from above (cf. 'Here see . . . see bundled in it . . . see fall war's worst . . .' in the previous stanza, as a further example of the superior, voyeuristic attitude the poet encourages both himself and the reader to adopt) is shattered by the physicality of the verb from 'below': the long, accented vowels not only ironize the poet 'sitting considering possibilities' (Introduction to Keith Douglas' *Selected Poems*, p. 12) in didactic–contemplative ease, they threaten to break up the 'I', and the brittleness of its consonants in the last line, completely. It is a pity that this genuine 'moment of consciousness' (Gurdjieff) should, like the penultimate line of 'Meeting', be diminished rather than amplified by its conscious environment.

'The thought-fox' offers neither contemplative ease nor 'objective' judgements, but gives instead a passive, inviting persona, consciously 'within' his experience, not thinking it out through a limited didacticism, but preparing an 'opening' for perception by the virtue of his dialect, the 'heroic' readiness of the Anglo-Saxon line for contact with elementals, primitive materialisms:

> I imágine this mídnight móment's fórest:
> something else is alive
> Beside the clock's loneliness
> And this blank page where the fingers move.

The line contains four stresses, three of which are bound together by alliteration. Despite what Seamus Heaney calls 'a hush achieved by the quelling, battening-down of the m's and d's and t's' ('Englands of the mind', an essay collected in *Seamus Heaney: Preoccupations: Selected prose 1968–78*, p. 154), it is not without its subversive elements for the reader. The rhythmic stress on 'forest' and its placement at the end of the line initially encourage a reading of the word as the object of the poet's imagining. That reading gives us the solidity of the visible, external world of physical appearances, but the sudden untangling – on second reading – of 'midnight moment' as the true object is breath-taking: the realist solidity dissolves in a perception of the rather more tenuous world of the psyche, the half-lit border of the conscious-unconscious. The line dramatizes a momentary loss of control for the reader, confusing the clarity of formal syntax upon which his discursive 'pattern thinking' (Shah) and its world-view depend. It is this loss of control – anticipated by the fluid sibilants and vowels of the second line – which the poet consciously prepares for in the rest of the stanza.

The same pattern repeats itself in the second quatrain: the cerebral experience of everything as an outside is supplanted by the sympathetic nervous-system, which experiences everything as an inside:

Through the window I see no star:

Something more near
Though deeper within darkness
Is entering the loneliness

As Heaney points out, the presence conjured by this shift of perspective
is 'granted its full vowel music as its epiphany' (*Preoccupations*, p. 154)
within these lines; at the same time, the reader's impulse to spatialize
reality and apprehend only surfaces and externals is banished from the
poem forever – the possibility of either the poet or the reader following
the remote externality of the 'star', or the hawk in the title-poem, is
simple excluded.

The fox dominates the next fourteen lines of the poem, in one
complete sentence:

Cold, delicately as the dark snow,
A fox's nose touches a twig, leaf;
Two eyes serve a movement, that now
And again now, and now, and now

Set neat prints into the snow
Between tress, as warily a lame
Shadow lags by stump and in hollow
Of a body that is bold to come

Across clearings, an eye,
A widening deepening greenness,
Brilliantly, concentratedly,
Coming about in its business

Till, with a sudden sharp hot stink of fox
It enters the dark hole of the head.

In marked contrast to 'The hawk in the rain', the contact with elementals
does not stimulate language to resound at an even higher rhetorical pitch
than before; neither does it respond to the menacing world of archaic
instinctuality by inventing an aesthetic world of its own which
consolidates the dualism, as in 'A modest proposal'. In her essay 'Forms
of the implicit love of God', Simone Weil notes that:

There are people who try to raise their souls like a man continually taking
standing jumps in the hope that, if he jumps higher every day, a time may
come when he will no longer fall back but will go right up to the sky. Thus
occupied he cannot look at the sky. We cannot take a single step towards
heaven. It is not in our power to travel in a vertical direction. If however
we look heavenwards for a long time, God comes and takes us up. (*Waiting
on God*, p. 147)

In 'The thought-fox', Hughes' language, which throughout the volume
attempts to jump higher at every turn in the belief that it can 'ascend' of
its own accord, makes the same sign of renunciation. It accomplishes the

same triumph Hughes attributes to Keith Douglas, the discovery of a speech for the whole mind: 'he renews the simplicity of ordinary talk and he does this by infusing every word with a burning exploratory freshness of mind' (Introduction to *Selected Poems*, pp. 12–13). The capacity to renovate language in exactly this way depends on the provisional attitude of the speaking self to its own nature, the unconditional obedience of the imagination to 'the reality of creation' (Pilinszky). We see that obedience directly in the third stanza: the firm, though under-stated grip of the 'd' and 't' consonants in the first three lines voluntarily submits to an evocation of the fox's physical movements, until *it* appears as the commanding subject – in that fourfold repetition of 'now' – setting its neat prints into the snow and on paper alike. This is poetry pursuing its moral function, the opposite of the modernist dream-world of the absolutism of words, of language speaking about itself: Hughes would agree with Pilinszky when he claims that 'poetry is not an ultra-linguistic phenomenon; it is, rather infra-linguistic or sub-linguistic, just as life itself remains under the surface of the entirety of the universe' ('An autobiography', in Tezla (ed.), *Ocean at the Window*, p. 148).

One consequence of this emphasis is that the incidental aesthetic felicities, such as the adjective 'lame' dragging itself over from one line-ending to the beginning of the next in order to re-unite with its noun, and the fox literally coming across the open 'clearing' between the fourth and fifth stanzas, are 'naturalized' – neither as disruptive nor escapist as the hawk's appearances in the title poem. This infra-linguistic nature of poetry creates a third opening for the 'specimen of life outside [it's] own' (*Poetry in the Making*, p. 17), after due consonantal 'preparation': 'Of a bódy that is bóld to cóme/ Acróss cléarings', giving way to the 'eye/ A widening deepening greenness'. The brief checking movement of the next two lines is followed by the most intense resurgence of that vowelling reality, barely contained: 'Till, with a súdden shãrp hót stĭnk of fŏx/ It enters the dark hole of the head.' The poet who had claimed that 'This is hunting and the poem is a new species of creature' (*Poetry in the Making*, p. 17), and whose fingers thought to move so command-ingly over the blank page at the end of the first stanza, has either been seeing the true situation upside down, or denied its paradoxical, interdependent nature. The ideal of language in which words displace experiences with their own meanings *as* words, and the poet's assump-tion of his absolute control over the process of literary creation, the act of writing, are both humbled. 'Creation' is passive creation: 'The window is starless still; the clock ticks,/ *The page is printed*' (my italics). This recognition is only made available by a change in the structure of the self. The persona's attitude closely resembles Simone Weil's state of 'Atten-tion' which I described in the Introduction (p. 13), the suspension of thought, 'leaving it detached, empty and ready to be penetrated by the object'. The voluntary renunciation of the impulse to 'command' – wherever one has the power to do so – extends from poet to critic, who also needs to jettison his 'acquired aesthetic sensibility'. The reader of the poem who was surprised by the forcible removal of 'visible' co-ordinates in the first two stanzas, misses the mark when he pays more attention to the mechanical details of the poem's effects – its incidental felicities in stanzas 3–5 – to the cost of the moral process in which the poem participates, which is always open-ended and pointing beyond itself. The reader has to give up the poem as a self-contained artifact, though even the conclusion of the poem tempts the illusion by offering the satisfaction of a neat, compact block of print which fits the dimensions of the page exactly.

This fulfilment of the Sufi demand that the hearer complete the action of the poem/story with reference to *his own* experience is sufficient to indicate the presence of the one totally successful symbol in the volume. The symbol is found *only* when the poet's emergency self stands outside the conflict of the opposites – Independent Ego versus blind-elemental nature in all its variations (sexual desire, natural elements, instinct-drives, animals, mechanical War-death, etc.) – as a third party, an action it signally fails to perform elsewhere in *The Hawk in the Rain*. Then the will (Jung's 'Libido') decides for the totality of self, and a symbolic language becomes natural: the freed libido

> sinks into the unconscious,
> where it automatically takes possession of the
> waiting fantasy material, which it thereupon
> activates and forces to the surface.
> ('Schiller's ideas on the Type problem', from *Psychological Types*, pp. 114–15)

The symbol is not artificially reduced to the deviancy of Emblem by the poet's conscious attempt to explain it as in 'The jaguar', instead it re-discovers its capacity to identify fully the permanent, mirror-like interdependence of the 'inner' and 'outer' worlds without unduly constraining the interpretative activity of the reader. The poem extends the 'psychological invitation' to criticism I spoke of in the Introduction – 'it's the reader's own nature that selects' his meaning, and it is the reader who must witness the origin of that response without Egoistic interference from the poem's 'guiding fiction'.

'The thought-fox' shows the Ego voluntarily keeping space open for the reader and its own unconscious contents in equal measure, but the essential 'preparation' for the poem consists in the two poems 'Wind' and 'October dawn'. These two poems could be called the immediate predecessors of 'The thought-fox' in the moral imagination. 'October dawn' is the more obvious of the two:

. . . Mammoth and Sabre-tooth celebrate

Reunion while a fist of cold
Squēezĕs thĕ fire ăt thĕ cōre ŏf thĕ wōrld,
Squēezĕs thĕ fire ăt thĕ cōre ŏf thĕ hēart,
Ánd nów it is abóut to stárt.

Here the Ego is wiped clean by a sort of expurgation of its chief features in poetic language. The controlled regularity of the anapaestic rhythms in the two penultimate lines suggests lawful territory already mapped out by the conscious intelligence. The pressure exerted by the 'fist of cold' is only confirmed in the last line, where the process breaks out of both formal discipline and rational containment and into the thudding, primary life of stress. The full couplet-rhyme of the last two lines is an ironic delusion, fulfilling none of the conventional functions of the couplet: it is neither witty, nor compressive, nor in any sense a resolution of the previous eighteen lines. As the tense shifts disturbingly from past to an open future the brutally abbreviated rhythm and the ironic denial of couplet sufficiency combine to shove the reader out into empty space, both typographic and psychological, beyond the poem.

'Wind' gives a more complex account of this shrinkage of the Ego-Personality. The poem appears to begin as a final example – in the present study – of what Jung names the 'empathizing' tendency of the artist, following in Worringer's footsteps. 'Empathy' is the apparent opposite of 'Abstraction' – the urge to create one's own hermetic world to neutralize the terrifying chaos of objects and events – which we examined in relation to the Movement poets in the last chapter:

> through feeling some essential psychic contact is projected into the object, so that the object is assimilated to the subject and coalesces with him to such an extent that he feels himself, as it were, in the object. This happens when the projected content is associated to a higher degree with the subject than with the object . . . the 'empathized' object appears animated to him, as though it were speaking to him of its own accord. ('The Type problem in aesthetics', *Psychological Types*, p. 290)

The empathizing attitude, Jung adds, has the (unconscious) effect of devaluing or 'depotentiating' the object, 'empathy gives the object a permanently lower value, *as in the case of abstraction*' (p. 295; my italics) The two apparently contradictory attitudes have a common root in 'self-alienation', to use Worringer's phrase. We have already seen the worst effects of Empathy in the hawk and jaguar poems, in the poet's attempt to dominate the object with his own interpretations of it. In this frame, the release from the abstracting attitude of 'A modest proposal' and 'Parlour-piece' and the structural accounts of dualism must be paralleled by a release from the empathizing impulses within 'The hawk in the rain' and 'The jaguar' and 'The horses'. 'Wind' gives us a violently animated landscape, with the apparent suggestion at the end of the second stanza that the violence is a projection of inner disturbance:

> This house has been far out at sea all night,
> The woods crashing through darkness, the booming hills,
> Winds stampeding the fields under the window
> Floundering black astride and blinding wet
>
> Till day rose; then under an orange sky
> The hills had new places, and wind wielded
> Blade-light, luminous black and emerald,
> Flexing like the lens of a mad eye.

It is clear that Empathy is not carried through to its logical conclusion: the poet 'improves' on the title-poem by refusing to invent the ultimate empathetic image of the hawk representing his urge to escape from the unstable environment. The relationship between the description of the material landscape and the psychic content is more one of interdependence, in accordance with the symbolic structure of 'The thought-fox'; the poem opens out on to subjective and objective contents in equal measure, avoiding the aesthetic dualism Empathy–Abstraction, and the deeper ethical dualism of which it is itself a member. That is the poet's relationship to his composition, and the emergency self it creates in the poem's realist situation keeps a tenuous balance between the conflicting opposites:

> . . . I dared once to look up –
> Through the brunt wind that dented the balls of my eyes
> The tent of the hills drummed and strained its guy rope,
>
> The fields quivering, the skyline a grimace,
> At any second to bang and vanish with a flap . . .
>
> . . . The house
> Rang like some fine green goblet in the note
> That any second would shatter it.

Neither the poet nor his 'guiding fiction' within the poem, attempt to solidify the unstable natural environment by the certainty of their view of it. Both are in a state of suspension, a detached or empty *agnosia*, in the verbs of the last eight lines:

> Now deep
> In chairs, in front of the great fire, we grip
> Our hearts and cannot entertain book, thought,
> or each other. We watch the fire blazing,
> And feel the roots of the house move in, but sit on,
> Seeing the window tremble to come in,
> Hearing the stones cry out under the horizons.

Keith Sagar (*The Art of Ted Hughes*, p. 227) quotes a very apt passage from Castaneda's *Tales of Power* in his discussion of the poem, in which the wind is a collective force outside the *tonal* (Don Juan's term for the Ego) which may threaten it with extinction – 'no metaphor. A wind that can blow one's own life away. In fact . . . the wind that blows all living things on this earth.' It becomes the subject of a poem when the *tonal* no longer imposes its own fixed order on an unstable world (which incorporates all the excluded or misfitting elements). So the last seven verbs of Hughes' poem accomplish Don Juan's talks of 'shrinking the *tonal*', allowing the wind to blow the psychic surface clean:

> It is the *tonal* that has to relinquish control. But it should be made to do so gladly. . . . The task then is to convince the *tonal* to become free and fluid. That's what a sorcerer needs before anything else, a strong, free *tonal*. The stronger it gets the less it clings to its doings and the easier it is to shrink it. (*ibid*. p. 153)

> You call it explaining. I call it a sterile and boring insistence of the *tonal* to have everything under its control . . . . The island of the *tonal* has to be swept clean and maintained clean. That's the only alternative that a warrior has. A clean island offers no resistance; it is as if there were nothing there. (p. 171)

Where Holloway's 'Warning to a guest' emphasized the *tonal*'s control – in 'wine and conversation, colour and light' – Hughes sweeps it clean by denying the usual buttresses – book, thought, the 'other person'. Once the 'tonal' relinquishes control, the possibility of dualism – aesthetic or psychological – vanishes also.[5] But a new difficulty arises 'not to let the *tonal* itself out of the picture' (*ibid.*, p. 173), and Hughes' poem graphically demonstrates this problem of maintaining balance: in the last two lines, only a fragile window seems to stand between the ego and total extinction. One final comment from Don Juan adequately illustrates the development between 'Wind' and 'The thought-fox':

> A grave issue for the warrior is to know exactly when to allow his *tonal* to shrink and when to stop it. . . . A warrior must struggle like a demon to shrink his *tonal*; and yet at the very moment the *tonal* shrinks, the warrior must reverse all that struggle to immediately halt that shrinking. (*ibid.*, p. 173)

In 'Wind' the violent imbalance of the sudden contraction is still evident, in 'The thought-fox' the *nagual* emerges more smoothly in response to the fluid *tonal*, and there is a greater sense of a controlled 'summoning'.

In conclusion, it is necessary to return to the question of violence in the book. The violence appears to be generated by the magnetic proximity of several of the poems in the volume to situations from 'life at its most severe' which confront the rationalistic world-view with all that it excludes. If the poet, or his persona, or the reader happens to hold that view, he must also experience the violence. The poet frequently does

hold versions of that view, and justifies Calvin Bedient's accusation that
he is a 'voyeur of violence' ('On Ted Hughes'), dispensing 'objective'
judgements from a safe, self-protective distance. But that is balanced by a
number of poems which voluntarily break down the distance, enduring
in dramatic form the violence attendant on the disturbance of that view.
The volume as a whole subsists on the working-out of that dualism. It
promotes the moral activity of poetry, needfully exposed to its own
errors. That Hughes is a 'voyeur of a violence' is a positive thing – as
one-half of the whole drama; friction is necessary for further development, not the complacent illusion of stability. In poetry, this means that
we should expect not aesthetically final results (as Bedient does) but
living accounts of an imagination endeavouring to *find its way home*, only
accidentally, secondarily, through language.

CHAPTER 4

——————— • ———————

LUPERCAL

> Almost all the poems in *Lupercal* were written as *invocations to writing*. My main consciousness in those days was that it was impossible to write. So these invocations were just attempts to crack the apparent impossibility of producing anything. (Faas, *Ted Hughes: The unaccommodated universe*, p. 209; my italics)

That is how Hughes describes the objectives of his second volume to Ekbert Faas in their 1977 interview. The statement is initially characterized by the poet's vigilant, though passive approach to his materials – 'with eyes downcast' – followed by an overwhelming sense of aesthetic insufficiency and limitation, in the final synopsis. Both elements of the statement consolidate psychological and linguistic lessons of *The Hawk in the Rain*. On the one hand, it was the art of invocation, of passive creation, which achieved 'The thought-fox'; on the other, the 'apparent impossibility' of the writer's position is a swingeing counter-reaction from the 'titanic extravagance', the strident effort to master reality of the first volume, it comes with all the force of rebound. The rhetorical posturing is notably absent from *Lupercal*, and so is the 'empathetic' tendency with which it was often allied. It is replaced by a kind of poetic entrenchment, a careful rounding-off of verbal edges, or a deliberate working within a consciously narrowed linguistic environment. The formal features of poetic discourse begin to surface again: nineteen poems contain rhymes or half-rhymes, a syllabic count becomes increasingly prominent in the organization of the line. Self-limitation is the governing principle of *Lupercal* in all except a handful of poems. 'Hawk roosting', 'View of a pig', 'Pike', 'The bull Moses', and 'Bullfrog':

> it [*Lupercal*] culminated a deliberate effort to find a simple concrete language with no words in it over which I didn't have complete ownership: a limited language, but authentic to me. So in my ordinary exercise of writing I felt that the *Lupercal* style simply excluded too much of what I wanted to say. But the 'Hawk Roosting' style offered infinite expansion and flexibility. It was just too difficult a road, in my

circumstances. It needed a state of concentration which I was evidently
unable to sustain. (Faas, *Ted Hughes*, p. 209)

This intentional confinement to known horizons, in terms of both the
self and language, is double-faced: it clarifies the 'authentic' situation of
the self by stripping away the illusions conjured by hyperbole but it is
exposed to dangers we have seen before: the possible closure of the world
by style; the negative will set dead against the image of alert; flexible
exploration 'summoned' by 'The thought-fox'. As one *modus operandi* of
the 'superego stylist' is denied – the 'empathetic' impulse – the other
'abstracting' attitude becomes correspondingly more active. It is as if the
rigorous, Movement-type repudiation of the worst excesses of Romantic
Individualist ideology brings with it, unavoidably, Movement-type
evils.

The most obvious invocation in writing in the volume is 'Crag Jack's
apostasy'; the poet calls on

> . . . you, god or not god, who
> Come to my sleeping body through
> The world under the world; pray
> That I may see more than your eyes
> In an animal's dreamed head; that I shall
> Waking, dragged suddenly
> From a choir-shaken height . . .
> Keep more than the memory
> Of a wolf's head, of eagles' feet.

This could be used as a summary of the poet's development so far, and an
indication of the potential difficulties ahead: the experience of poems
such as 'Wind', 'October dawn' and 'The thought-fox' did indeed drag
the poet's primary 'I' (the dominant-explosive stylist) from its 'choir-
shaken height'. Now he passively 'invokes' the secondary imagination of
the self (Essence, the Unconscious, etc.), the 'world under the world',
afraid that it has already been abstracted into a memory, the property of
the limited, fixed consciousness. To keep hold of merely the externals
(the 'eyes') is self-alienation by another name, and it finds its own image
in the tramp who is continually at the mercy of elemental forces beyond
his control: 'Both my power and my luck since/ Have kicked at the
world and slept in ditches.'

In 'Things present', the poet imagines himself as a beggarly outcast,
'pagan' in the original meaning of the word and dispossessed of his
psycho-spiritual inheritance, the moral opportunity given to his ances-
tors. When the tramp image does make contact with elementals, it is
immediately heroified as a model of self almost in desperation, as in
'Dick Straightup':

His upright walk,
His strong back, I commemorate now,
And his white blown head going out between a sky and an earth
That were bundled into placeless blackness, the one
Company of his mind.

Dick Straightup is an example of 'Essence' in the raw; in the episode the poem narrates, he is discovered quite literally 'lowest down' – in a frozen ditch – at home in the world of instinct and animal nature so that the ice preserves rather than threatens his well-being. But this turns out to be only another violent swing on the dualistic axis, rather than a psychological movement into the neutral 'third' position which alone allows the equal and harmonious development of *both* terms (Conscious–Unconscious, Personality–Essence) on that axis. Such a judgement is only available, however, by cross-reference to the group of poems, clustered around 'Hawk roosting', which *do* 'negotiate' from that position – further evidence of the necessity of the reader's attention to the 'whole' process of the volume, rather than the discrete, isolatable elements of it. The valuing of the tramp-image in the poem really is a 'placeless' vocal fragment, a disconnected voice in the multiple poetic personality *Lupercal* presents.

The last idea, that of the book containing a multiple poetic personality, has to be formulated before examination can proceed. Although the analysis of *The Hawk in the Rain* defined an underpinning *dualism*, we became aware that *more than two voices* participated in that dualism. In fact, four distinct voices are identifiable: (1) the voice of the 'abstracting' stylist (cf. 'Secretary', 'A modest proposal', 'Parlour-piece') who was concerned with suppressing a violent subject-matter with the strength and integrity of his style; (2) the voice of the 'empathizer' of the title poem, 'The dove breeder', 'The horses', and 'The jaguar', characterized by his identification with the 'virtues' of his creatures; (3) the voice of the 'objective' or didactic commentator on human hubris and ignorance ('A man seeking experience', Law in the country of the cats', 'Griefs for dead soldiers', etc.). In addition to these three voices, which belonged in varying degrees to the False Personality, there was a fourth; that of the clairvoyant artist in his successful premonitions or 'summonings' of elementals ('Wind', 'October dawn', 'The thought-fox') belonging generically to the self. The existence of these distinct voices is connected with one of Gurdjieff's major theses:

> *Man has no permanent and unchangeable I.* Every thought, every mood, every desire, every sensation, says 'I'. And in each case it seems to be taken for granted that this I belongs to the *Whole*, to the whole man. . . . In actual fact there is no foundation whatsoever for this assumption. Man's every thought and desire appears and lives quite separately and independently of the Whole. And the Whole never expresses itself, for the simple reason that

it exists, as such, only . . . in the abstract as a concept. Man has no
individual I. But there are, hundreds and thousands of separate small I's,
very often entirely unknown to one another, never coming into contact,
or, on the contrary, hostile to each other, mutually exclusive and
incompatible. . . . *Man is a plurality*. Man's name is legion. (Ouspensky,
In Search of the Miraculous, p. 59)

This plurality of voices exists in *Lupercal* also. We have already heard the
empathetic admiration of Dick Straightup, 'exclusive' within the
volume; more prominent is the voice of 'Crag Jack's apostasy', conscious
of its alienation from the roots of the self and the limitations of language
alike:

> . . . These [the Wolf's] feet, deprived,
> Disdaining all that is caged, or storied, or pictured,
> Through and throughout the true world search
> For their vanished head, for the world
> Vanished with the head, the teeth, the quick eyes –
> Now, lest they choose his head,
> Under severe moons he sits making
> Wolf-masks, mouths clamped well onto the world.
>
> ('February')

This response is the opposite of the poet's claim to embody elementals in
'The jaguar'; the elementals exist, but they frustrate all the attempts of
the Ego-intelligence to assimilate them in words or concepts. The line
'Disdaining all that are caged, or storied, or pictured' reads like an
acknowledgement by the poet of the inadequate 'containers' he invented
in *The Hawk in the Rain*. In the last stanza, the poetic persona appears to
retreat fearfully – Movement-style – before the possibility that the
elemental body may 'choose his head', recalling Lifton's analysis of
'psychic numbness' and Davie's amplification of it into a deliberate
conscious attitude. The last two lines, however, remain ambiguous: the
logically consistent reading, that the poet constructs imaginary pictures
('wolf-masks') to keep securely to his fixed description of the world, fails
to shake off completely its 'shadow' reading – that 'wolf-masks' bring
the violent energies into play rather than resist them, that the 'world' is
not the arbitrary idea of it but the 'world under the world', or the 'world
of final reality'. Equally, the making of the wolf-masks can have two
meanings: it may suggest either the type of perception which sees the
visible surface rather than the reality beneath, or that which sees the
creation of provisional, ironic personae as the only long-term resolution
of the poetic dilemma. It would not be too much to say that the rest of
Lupercal witnesses the struggle between these options, the limited self
which clings to the 'memory' or abstract idea of elementals, treating
them as counters in a stylistic game, and the improvising self which
confronts them head-on, *through* the mediation of hawk, dead pig, otter,

etc.; for this secondary self, words are the same as the 'I', a disposable utility to be shed like a skin once they have achieved their purpose.

The explicitness which featured in *The Hawk in the Rain* is echoed in 'Fourth of July' and in 'Esther's tomcat', which is based on the second-hand re-telling of the Barnborough Knight legend, although the loud-voiced didacticism is carefully subdued. Both the empathizing ('Dick Straightup', 'A dream of horses') and the didactic voices tend to operate in a minor key in *Lupercal*, as centre stage is increasingly dominated by the third voice, that of the abstracting stylist. His efforts received comparatively minor emphasis amid the explosive torrents of language in the first volume, but in the given psychological circumstances – the ego's sudden awareness of its alienated condition – it becomes the primary mode of speech. To re-phrase the final line of 'Historian', the 'live brain's envying to *master*' may have been expurgated, but its will to 'last' in its artistic products is unimpaired: the maintenance of stylistic appearances amounts, as before, to an act of self-preservation by the fictive personality. The basics of the situation are laid open in 'Urn burial':

> An improvement on the eagle's hook,
> The witty spider competitor,
> Sets his word's strength against the rock,
> No foot wrong in the dance figure –
>
> So by manners, by music, to abash
> The wretch of death that stands in his shoes:
> The aping shape of earth – sure
> Of its weight now as in the future.

The experience of *The Hawk in the Rain* denied the poet the full-blooded 'intensity' of language, and now he falls back upon the 'rituals' of form in a dramatic fulfilment of Hughes' phrased desire for a 'ritual intensity of music'. But the fulfilment is fractured, and the guiding 'I' fiction shifts 'mechanically', so to speak, between intensity and ritual, ignorant of the versatile, ruthless 'colloquial prose readiness' which would make of it a language suitable for the whole human being, not just a formal fragment of one. In the last two lines the poet carries out his programme to set his word's strength, and the measured harmony of the dance figure, against the rock of material reality. In the event, the 'wretch of death' – the self which participates in collective reality – is not at all displaced by his 'witty competitor', the stylist; the stress-rhythm of Middle English totally over-runs the metrical demands of the couplet-rhyme, so that the reader is *only* aware of the rhyme as a visible appearance on the page, *not* as a 'material' component of spoken utterance: 'The áping shápe of èarth – súre/ Of its wèight nów as in the fùture.' The impact of two chief stresses, 'sure' and 'now', exposes the optical illusion of the end-rhyme

as just that, a fiction, a superfluous bit of artifice. And because there is a
direct connection in the poem between stylistic artifice and psychological
artifice, the guiding fiction is recognized as superfluous too; it hardly
seems to weigh in any balance with the 'sure weight' of collective Man.
In the face of those long stresses, the certainty of the stylist and that of the
'I' fiction could 'bang and vanish with a flap' at any moment, one senses.
The poem thus takes up more overtly the implicit direction at the end of
'October dawn'. The poet does not seek to overpower the elements with
his own intensity, but attempts a craftsmanlike shaping of his poetic (and
real-world!) matter 'by manners, by music', though reality still proves
resistant, constantly threatening to break out of its new container. As a
result, the principle of self-alienation is affirmed rather than eroded.

The insistent pressuring of stylism by material reality characterizes the
progression of 'Relic'. The poem begins as a contemplation of a jawbone
thrown up by the incoming tide, and much of the first stanza is written in
the 'casual speech' which is such an important part of Hughes' model
language: 'Nothing touches but, clutching, devours. And the jaws./
Before they are satisfied or their stretched purpose/ Slacken, go down
jaws.' The shape of living reality is rapidly marked out by the passage
from the frenchified 'touch' to the Anglo-Saxon 'clutching' and the
prosaic 'go down', but the effect is somewhat diluted by the ritual music
of the intended echo 'go gnawn bare' which follows, and the rhyme
which immediately precedes the lines: 'The deeps are cold:/ In that
darkness camaraderie does not hold.' The insight may be authentically
Hughesian, but both the abstract 'wisdom' of the rhyme and the
unnecessarily musical echo have the effect of blurring the stark
definiteness of outline the poet carves out in the middle phrase; they
surround, and as it were suppress the reality that phrase points towards.
Something similar happens in the last five lines:

> Time in the sea eats its tail, thrives, casts these
> Indigestibles, the spars of purposes
> That failed far from the surface. None grow rich
> In the sea. This curved jawbone did not laugh
> But gripped, gripped and is now a cenotaph.

The awesome suggestion of the mechanicalness of Nature is there in the
first half-line, and it is brought into the rational light by the formulation
'None grow rich/ In the sea.' But if we get a sense of the limited, but
authentic language over which the poet has complete ownership in these
lines, then we receive, in equal measure, the negative consequences of
that certainty in the final couplet. For a moment the poem tenses to hang
on to the fragments of the life of 'final reality' in the repetition of the
Anglo-Saxon 'gr-' root ('gripped, gripped . . .') before giving way to the
inevitable completion of the rhyme; and in that musical completion, in

that formal fulfilment, the reality is converted into a 'cenotaph' – a dead monument, an abstract, contemplated memory of the elementals, just as the persona of 'Crag Jack's apostasy' had feared.

Simone Weil's intuition that the mechanical 'necessity' of rhyme excludes the energies tapped by the self at the point of improvisation is confirmed by the development of 'Relic'. It is tempting to go further and say that in the prevailing cultural circumstances, the use of rhyme or formal meter is by definition anachronistic. As Hughes indicates in his *London Magazine* interview ('Ted Hughes and Crow', p. 20), the 'muscially deeper' world which formal patterning *may* enter depends on the writer's total awareness of the solidity and range of his experience at the moment of writing. In terms of the present poem, 'Relic' clearly does not exhibit the 'perfectly pure grasp' of mechanical nature/Nature shown by 'Hawk roosting' or 'View of a pig', for instance. It does so only intermittently, and as a consequence formal patterning is relegated to the status of a mere device or technique, not so much transparent to the experiential reality as in conflict with it, constraining its possibly violent irruption into the world of the poem. Ted Hughes offered a psychological explanation of these possibilities for the poet in a letter to me:

> I have a theory that for most poems there are two basic versions – the version which 'interprets' the impulse, using all the machinery of the conscious mind, and another, quite different version, which is attracted towards the first version from the unconscious mind . . . the conscious mind gets busy from its side and the unconscious from its side, separately.
>
> Ideally, (Z) the two should work as one. In practice – you usually get (A) the conscious efforts which have a dim awareness but a certain disregard for what the unconscious is offering, (B) the unconscious effort (very rare) which often seems irrelevant, (C) after a gruesome struggle of redrafting, the battletorn fragments of (A) carrying scraps and rags and bits lost from (B) . . . .
>
> The prevailing mood of (A) & (C) is aesthetic distress. (26 April 1987)

'Relic' would appear to follow Hughes' model (C), in which the conscious mind has got its formal machinery to work and preserved only 'scraps and rags' of the 'unconscious effort'. Presumably, the world of formal patterning and its deeper music only becomes available – in its correct usage – in the ideal version (Z), where the conscious mind stays perfectly free and fluid, like Don Juan's *tonal*, both utterly open to the offerings of the unconscious, and utterly competent to organize them in the forms of language.

The ultimate achievement of the abstract stylist in *Lupercal* is 'To paint a water-lily'. Once again formal machinery is prominent in the regular syllabic line and the consistent rhyme or half-rhyme endings. Moreover, another patterning is superimposed over that of the formal machinery: the entire poem is 'framed' by the imperatives of the painter's eye, 'Study

. . . Observe . . . Think . . . Now Paint', it declares itself as a self-conscious aesthetic product. This reflexive stance repeats the stress on 'limitation'; it *knows* that what it produces will be a fiction, looking across a wide, self-manufactured gulf at objective reality, but it is determined to maintain that *structural* integrity. It is no wonder that Hughes 'felt very constricted fiddling around with it. It was somehow like writing through a long winding tube, like squeezing language out at the end of this long, remote process' (Faas, *Ted Hughes*, p. 208). Nearly all the brushstrokes in the 'painting' derive from the superego stylist who is capable of 'music of an exceedingly high order' (Introduction to Keith Douglas' *Selected Poems*, p. 14):

> Others as dangerous *comb the hum*
>
> Under the trees. There are battle-shouts
> And death-cries everywhere hereabouts
>
> But inaudible, so the eyes praise
> to see the colours of these flies
>
> *Rainbow their arcs*, or settle
> Cooling like beads of molten metal
>
> Through the spectrum
>   (my italics)

The musical reverberation of the two phrases in italics has the literal effect of deafening the reader's ear to the 'battle-shouts' and 'death-cries' which are the unrealized substance of the picture. The exclusive praise of the phenomenal 'eye' is only possible on the premise of psychic imbalance, once the 'ear' which is equipped to hear the brutality of animal Nature is repressed into the unconscious. The poem thus enacts the process by which the 'I' separates off into its own aesthetic fiction, cleansing itself of the filth of the undesirable elements, which are 'inaudible' but also collective, 'everywhere'. It also demands a certain effort from the reader: If he acquiesces in the formal beauty of the words – 'the eyes' praise' – he mimics the dualistic action of the poet, and opens himself to the danger of equating 'inaudible' with 'unreal'. But if he perceives the psychological root of the reading, he endeavours to pay attention to what is *unemphasized*, or the reality which is inaudible, and keeps his distance from poem's immediate musical effects. The poem contains a kind of 'morality of stylistics', and the ritual music is nothing less than an ethical peril for the reader: he stands in jeopardy of being recreated in the image of an abstract 'I' addicted to 'beauty' and 'form' in the poem. The danger is scarcely lessened in the description of the elements below the pond surface: 'Prehistoric *bedragonned* times/ Crawl that darkness with Latin names', in which the archaism 'bedragonned' stylizes the lurking horrors in much the same way as the Latin names

which the poet himself points out. When the poet-stylist finally comes to
'paint' the water-lily in the final five lines, the divisiveness of the reading
experience – the reader's 'split response' – is fully apparent.

Now paint the long-necked Lily-flower

Which, deep in both worlds, can be still
As a painting, trembling hardly at all

Though the dragonfly alight,
Whatever horror nudge her root.

The lily, 'deep in both worlds', seems to provide a point of balance
between the two, though there is the ominous implication, in the 'double
take' effect of 'Now paint . . . can be still/ as a painting', that the stillness
only exists in the terms of a self-referential world of art. The water-lily
can only be as 'still as a painting' because *it has been painted* by the poet
already, and what is offered as an analogy of the lily's stillness is actually
its cause! It is the reader's option either to elevate the artistic world above
the reality which also includes 'horrors', or to understand it as an illusory
re-birth, a puritanical urge to hear no evil and see only beauty in the
surrounding world – only *he* completes the process of the poem.[1]

It is clear from a poem like 'Strawberry Hill' that Hughes will not
eventually follow the first path; he 'invokes' the stoat which bites
through 'grammar and corset' and is its own lesson to art: 'its red
unmanageable life/ Has licked the stylist out of their skulls.' The
exploration of that red, unmanageable life is concentrated into the most
important group of poems in *Lupercal*, which includes 'Hawk roosting',
'View of a pig', 'Pike', 'An otter' and 'The bull Moses'. Here is the first
of those poems in its entirety:

Hawk roosting

I sit in the top of the wood, my eyes closed.
Inaction, no falsifying dream
Between my hooked head and hooked feet:
Or in sleep rehearse perfect kills and eat.

The convenience of the high trees!
The air's buoyancy and the sun's ray
Are of advantage to me;
And the earth's face upward for my inspection.

My feet are locked upon the rough bark.
It took the whole of Creation
To produce my foot, my each feather:
Now I hold Creation in my foot

Or fly up, and revolve it all slowly –
I kill where I please because it is all mine.
There is no sophistry in my body:
My manners are tearing off heads –

The allotment of death.
For the one path of my flight is direct
Through the bones of the living.
No arguments assert my right:

The sun is behind me.
Nothing has changed since I began.
My eye has permitted no change.
I am going to keep things like this.

The exploratory nature of the poem, its full engagement with the 'other' is immediately – even shockingly – evident in the use of the nominative 'I', which simply abolishes the subject–object relationship, and the 'empathetic' – 'abstracting' polarity at a stroke! At least for the duration of the poem, the 'guiding fiction' can neither draw off from a fearsome universe of objects into the exclusive world of style, nor can it pour into the object only those characteristics with which it feels most comfortable: the poem is an act of suspension, and the poet extinguishes his illusion of detachment of his own accord – testing the reader's willingness to perform the same action.

It is possible to paraphrase the challenge the poem presents by reference to Hughes' own comments about it: 'Actually what I had in mind was that in this hawk Nature is thinking. Simply Nature' ('Ted Hughes and Crow', *London Magazine*, p. 8). The juxtaposition of 'Nature' and 'thinking' may rest uneasily with the reader who has been exposed to the cultural influence of Descartes' famous maxim 'Cogito ergo sum', and who is accustomed to believe that the power of independent Thought is exactly what makes the human world superior to Nature. In this case, the whole impact of the poem centres on the reader's perception of the fundamental unity, or fundamental separateness of these two terms. For the first three and a half stanzas, the hawk possesses precisely that contemplative superiority and detachment which the 'guiding fiction' usually attributes to itself. It even appropriates its verbal discourse, the heavily latinized vocabulary which we tend to equate with the civilized, or educated intelligence: 'Inaction . . . falsifying . . . convenience . . . buoyancy . . . advantage . . . inspection'. This vocabulary composes the 'verbal centre' of the poem, locking each stanza to the next like vertebrae; the poem has a kind of 'spinal column' of language drawn from an 'objective' context which has its own moral bent, re-creating the reader in its own image. Under pressure from this language, the reader initially interprets the 'Inaction', of the second line as the power of the intellect to comprehend reality in the secluded calm of its own mental 'rehearsal', and 'the earth's face upward for my inspection' (line 8) as the experimenter's impersonal position outside his experience, his 'objective' distance from the world under 'inspection'. This interpretative impulse reaches its climax in the third stanza, in which the hawk's literal 'My feet are locked upon the rough bark' is intellectualized as an assertion of the human conquest of Nature: 'Now I hold Creation in my foot'. The invitation made by the poem's 'verbal centre' to establish a human context is irresistible, although the band of evidence excluded by this interpretive construction becomes increasingly difficult to ignore: the first reading of 'Inaction' is immediately ironized by the demonstration that it is *not* an opportunity for the self-sufficient intellect to get to work, but for a blind, mechanical rehearsal of 'perfect kills and eat'. This realization filters into the second stanza, in the knowledge that the advantage afforded by the environment are all devoted to the same single 'automatic purpose' ('Thrushes'). And, of course, the double-statement 'Now I hold Creation in my foot// Or fly up, and revolve it all slowly' is literally consistent with the hawk's subjectivity. This band of evidence could be called the 'material centre' of the poem; and the existence of those two centres side by side in the text is severely problematic for the reader, for he can maintain the interpretation derived from the verbal centre only at the cost of the complete denial of the other 'material' reading. The structure of the poem invites the reader to re-enact the archetypal perceptual crime: the assertion of a 'rational' or 'objective' Ego-Personality somehow independent of, somehow purer than its underpinning animal–mechanical nature:

> I kill where I please because it is all mine.
> There is no sophistry in my body:
> My manners are tearing off heads.

The reader 'suffers' the traumatic exposure of the illusion in these lines exactly to the extent he has silently 'agreed' with it in himself.

From this point of view, it is easier to understand the tirade of critical abuse which greeted the 'violence' of the poem, in which the hawk 'is accused of being a Fascist . . . the symbol of some horrible genocidal dictator' ('Ted Hughes and Crow', *London Magazine*, p. 8). Those critics obviously recognized the savage self-irony involved in the poem's reading experience, and they reacted with disgust when the mechanically brutal undertext was revealed as the truth behind the rational–humane fiction and its language, infesting the pure ideal with all the 'filth' it thought to exclude. Lacking that flexible, ironic attitude to their own fictions which characterized the Central European response to similar revelations, the only way the critics could at the same time acknowledge the human context and yet 'separate off' from its negative implications (the consistent development from 'objectivity' to militant Egoism) was to brand it as 'Fascist', irredeemably evil, 'beyond the pale'.

The poem, meanwhile, goes on doing away with the deceptive surfaces of the 'verbal centre', including 'sophistry', 'manners' and 'arguments'. The 'material' organization of the poem perfects its irony in a phrase like 'the allotment of death', in which the democratic even-handedness of the (Latin-based) *word* is replaced by its grim consequences in *reality*. The counter-attack on language's capacity for the 'mystification of experience' (the term is R. D. Laing's) is an extension of the poet's counter-attack on his superego-stylist self, which he also accomplishes in the present poem through a forefronting of 'colloquial prose readiness' in the last three stanzas in particular.

That this is poetry pursuing its moral function should by now be sufficiently obvious: not only does it strike down the falsity of an abstract–rational picture of the self and the narrowly 'pure' vocabulary that goes with it, it even goes so far as to offer, as a tentative background, an older *Imago Dei* than the Christian Logos-God.

> I intended some Creator like the Jehovah in Job but more feminine. When Christianity kicked the Devil out of Job what they actually kicked out was Nature . . . and Nature became the devil. He doesn't sound like Isis, mother of the gods, which he is. ('Ted Hughes and Crow', *London Magazine*, p. 8)

In the Introduction, we noted that the feminine aspect of the Creator represented the more 'material' elements of Nature. As Hughes also suggests, there is a line in the poem quoted almost verbatim from the Book of Job: 'I kill where I please because it is all mine', cf. 'Whatsoever is under the whole heaven is mine' (Job, 41: 11). The images of Jehovah in Job, or the feminine Isis, are the 'material' centre of the poem on its broadest, most collective level. The highest point of development of this image, which is almost totally invisible as a reading of the poem except, one would assume, to high-grade spiritual disciplinarians, is indicated by the Brhadāranyaka Upanishad:

> As a hawk, or other great bird, soaring in space, becomes weary and, bending its wings, glides down to its place of rest, even so does Purusha, the human spirit, glide to that *state in sleep* where no desire whatever stirs and *no dream is seen*. . . . And when it there feels itself to be a God as it were, a King as it were, thinking 'I am this, I am all', that is its own best world. . . . As a man embraced fully by a living woman knows no distinction of other and self, so too this human spirit, embraced fully by that wisdom of absolute being knows no distinction of other and self. (4.3.19–21)

'Hawk roosting' holds out this vision as a remote possibility, but the poem's basic objectives are identical to those of 'View of a pig', which Hughes contrasts directly with 'To paint a water-lily' in his 1977 interview with Faas: ' "View of a Pig" was just an impatient effort to break that [the "remote process" of the artful poem] and write in absolutely the opposite way' (pp. 208–9). The critical point is the same – the essential transition from the aesthetic centre of poetry to its moral centre. So 'View of a pig' begins with a 'material' renewal of ordinary speech:

> The píg láy on a bárrow déad.
> It weighed, they said, as much as three men.
> Its eyes closed, pink white eyelashes.
> Its trótters stúck stráight óut.
>
> Such wéight and thíck pínk búlk
> Set in death seemed not just dead.
> It was less than lifeless, further off.
> It was like a sack of wheat.

Whatever potential exists in these stanzas for 'music of an exceedingly high order' is shattered by the 'deadly factual' spondaic rhythms. The musical generosity of lyrical or elegiac cadences is simply not possible in a situation where every word has an emphatic, monosyllabic dead weight. The consonantal diction, which was at the service of the domineering 'I' in *The Hawk in the Rain*, has changed proprietorship. It belongs to the open-ended self intent upon preserving a space in which his experience can speak without interpretative distortion. Here the labials and aspirates of the second stanza – culminating in 'set' – figure the unresponsiveness of the dead body; they resist the interpretative impulse of the conscious mind to accommodate the bare, material fact with its own fictions. In *The Hawk in the Rain*, in contrast, they did exactly the opposite. Language becomes truly 'material' not by attempting to rival the 'fullness' of the object with the show of its processes, but by collapsing its own will into that of the object, becoming pure function, not a world unto itself. The functional aspect of language is there in final simile, too: in order to communicate the body's less-than-lifeless quality, metaphor forgoes its usual privilege of perceiving similarity in apparent dissimilarity, giving us two terms which hardly have anything at all in common, except the bare fact that both are totally inanimate. It enacts 'lifelessness' by pointing towards its own dissociation, and its utter inadequacy to reveal any compact 'meaning' to the reader's understanding.

The renewal of ordinary speech, a general-purpose style, dominates much of the poem.

> I thumped it without feeling remorse.
>
> Just so much
> A poundage of lard and pork.

    Its weight
    Oppressed me – how could it be moved?
    And the trouble of cutting it up!

The flexibility of such prosaic language is attuned to the 'everywhere' which the selective eye's 'praise' in 'To paint a water-lily' was so eager to suppress. It resists the stylist's prejudicial perception of the surrounding environment in much the same way as the poetic persona (in stanzas 3–6) rules out the conscious interpretations which conventionally buffer us from the grim material fact of death. Within twelve lines 'remorse', 'guilt', 'pity', nostalgic 'remembrance', 'dignity', 'pathos' and 'comedy' are all repudiated as viable human responses or accommodations of that fact. The poem makes a ritual of excluding the 'human readings' the reader is likely to entertain, putting its subject-matter so far outside the conventional range of thought and feeling that it appears to be about Nothing at all, a poem composed entirely of negative attributes, 'quite comfortless'. It refuses to 'cut up' the reality for any kind of instant semantic consumption, leaving us with the oppressive, irreducible bulk of the simple collective fate, the doomed body which humanity shares with all organic life.[2]

    The poem's resistance to these different and contradictory impulses to 'contain' the material reality is one aspect of the Hughes' endeavour to diminish the Ego-Personality's capacity to defend itself against the idea of its own 'death', on the psychological level. For the reader, the challenge is concentrated into a potent ambiguity in the final couplet: 'They were going to scald it,/ Scald it and scour it like a doorstep.' 'They' refers to much more than simply an anonymous group of pork-curers, it relates to all the 'distinctions and admirations', the separate little 'I's and their mechanical formulations of death which would 'scald' and scour the material evidence clean into abstraction! The reader who recognizes that it is all those intellectual and emotional responses that are doing the false 'scouring' in the poem takes a positive psychological step forward. By striking down his immediate interpretative impulses, the contradictory 'wills' which change so easily and radically, he keeps faith with the real self 'lowest down', he extends an invitation to Gurdjieff's single, permanent centre of gravity concealed behind the Personality's potent apparition of multiplicity.

    As Hughes himself suggests in his second interview with Faas, both 'Hawk roosting' and 'View of a pig' appear to pick out the 'thought-fox'-type passive, 'inviting' self and its flexible, stripped-away speech more cleanly than the other poem in the group, 'Pike', which 'immediately became much more charged with particular memories and a specific obsession' ('Ted Hughes and *Gaudete*' (1977), Faas, *Ted Hughes*, p. 209).

That poem combines the ruthless–versatile speech with more of the stylist's verbal elements (lines 4–7), and an anecdotal voice which bears more than a passing resemblance to the explicit commentator of 'Fourth of July' (lines 29–34). The final nine lines of the poem clarify the third imagination of the self, fighting back over the same ground as the persona of 'The thought-fox':

> past nightfall I dared not cast
> But silently cast and fished
> With the hair frozen on my head
> For what might move, for what eye might move.
> The still splashes on the dark pond,
>
> Owls hushing the floating woods
> Frail on my ear against the dream
> Darkness beneath night's darkness had freed,
> That rose slowly towards me, watching.

The generally apprehensive 'attention' to the other, the shocking audial conflation of 'eye' and the emergent, deeper 'I', the sudden displacement of the objective environment by 'dream darkness', and the ironic inversion of the original hunter–hunted relationship, all this is familiar territory. Interestingly, the deeper self which is summoned in the last two stanzas 'rises' to the textual surface of the poem in a phrase almost identical to Simone Weil's image of its activity: 'watching', itself an echo of the earlier 'Watching upwards'. But because we come to this self-imagination through the dramatization – however muted – of the two major voices in the volume, it cannot help but function as a resolution of those voices, as if the poet 'tries out' each language and attitude in turn on the matter of his experience, gravitating towards the 'thought-fox' style as the truest, most embracing account of it.

Hughes' intuition that his poems are written by 'three separate characteristic states of mind' ('The poet speaks', XVI) – his increasingly lucid perception of a multiple, inchoate self – is confirmed by the progression of 'Pike', and the nature and motivation of each state of mind becomes clearer as that awareness grows. The two halves of 'An otter', for instance, embody a *conscious* shift from one state of mind to another: in the first part, the apparently 'objective' awareness of the otter's alienation ('neither fish nor beast is the otter') is actually a projection of the poet's alienation from his subject-matter, his inability to bring the otter's elusive double nature within the hard grasp of semantic formulation. *Because* the poetic 'I' strives to define aspects of the otter's nature with a kind of epigrammatic force in almost every sense-unit of this section of the poem, it discovers only the otter's elusiveness. Reader and poet alike go 'without answer': 'Till *light and birdsong* come/

Walloping up roads with the milk-wagon' (my italics). Both suffer under
the paradox that any clear statement about the otter's land-nature is likely
to be confounded by the contrary truth of its water-nature.

The 'mechanical' paradox does not vanish in the second part of the
poem, but the 'direction' into the paradox has been transformed. It starts
with an act of self-abandonment, a surrender of the self dependent on
definitive meanings: 'The hunt's lost him.' To seek an abstract definition
only increases the mechanical force of the paradox, insulating us from
any possibility of inheritance of the whole meaning:

> So the self under the eye lies,
> Attendant and withdrawn. The otter belongs
> In double robbery and concealment –
> From water that nourishes and drowns, and from land
> That gave him his length and the mouth of the hound.

All the 'material' elements of the otter's world are the same as in Part i, in
themselves unchangeable, but the interpretative impulse is solidly
founded on an acceptance of that dual reality, not on the alienating urge
to dominate it by means of a fixed, abstract definition. The lesson is
really contiguous with those of 'Hawk roosting' and 'View of a pig':
'Blood is the belly of logic; he will lick/ The fishbone bare.' So 'logic' –
the construction of the conscious mind – does not misuse its apparent
freedom by establishing alternative contexts to that of 'Blood' or Matter.
In this case, a provisional 'third' position is re-discovered, a point of
orientation or moral centre which hangs on to the fragments of the
duality, rather than confirming their irreconcilable opposition, as in the
first part. The last two lines of Part ii, visually similar to those of Part i,
are in fact completely transfigured by the conditional: '*Yanked above
hounds*, reverts to nothing at all, to this long pelt over the back of the
chair' (my italics). The otter 'reverts to nothing', and self-alienation
becomes a real thing, only when a land-locked conscious 'I' thinks to
appropriate it by force, and carry it off as a mere trophy, the tendency of
so many of the poems in *The Hawk in the Rain*.

The shift from the 'polluted' state of mind of Part i to the psychological consciousness of Part ii is corroborated by Hughes' difficulties with
the composition of the poem:

> Hughes wrote Part i with great labour over a long period and was not
> really satisfied with it. The second part virtually wrote itself and seemed to
> Hughes to be the Ouija spirit's revision of the first part – and very much
> better. (Sagar, *The Art of Ted Hughes*, p. 39)

The poem was clearly as much of a challenge to the poet as it is to the
reader, demanding that he complete its process by recognizing the

distinction in forms of consciousness between the two parts – particularly the crucial change of 'direction' or perspective on the otter's semantic elusiveness in the final two lines of each part. Not for the first time, the reader's responsive choice, which 'selects' the meaning of the image, determines his own moral status.

The same is true of the fine poem 'The bull Moses', in which two readings of the poem are two versions of consciousness, engaged in a kind of lethal internal warfare. The readings are first compressed together in the description of the protagonist's gaze into the 'byre's blaze of darkness' as a 'sudden shut-eyed look/ Backward into the head'. What is an 'objective' blindness at the end of the first line re-appears as the secondary, 'thought-fox'-type consciousness by the end of the sentence. This secondary consciousness gains in strength through the succeeding six lines, only to be confronted by a resurgence of the primary consciousness of self-alienation, the bull's reality

> too deep in itself to be called to,
> [Stood] in sleep. He would swing his muzzle at a fly
> But the square of sky where I hung, shouting, waving,
> Was nothing to him; nothing of our light
> Found any reflection in him.

The illusory temptation of that consciousness – the same as in 'An otter' (i) – is there in the last phrase, in the interpretative impulse to moralize 'light' which finds no reflection in the 'Other' reality, as evidence of its (own) superiority. The semantic clarity of this illusory re-birth opposes the 'material' reading of the poem, both the audial-muscular properties of the bull's verbal 'body' in lines 7–9 and the protagonist's merely literal positioning in the light outside the byre. Indeed, it might not be too fanciful to suggest that the opportunity to de-moralize the 'light–darkness' duality in these lines is a chance for the reader to rid himself of the legacy of more than fifteen hundred years of Christian theological dualism! From yet another point of view, the contest between the voices could be seen as a struggle between 'The thought-fox' (the secondary consciousness of lines 7–12) attitude and that of 'The hawk in the rain' (particularly in the reference to 'the square of sky where I hung', and its abstract image of the self).

The primary consciousness goes on to dominate the next nine lines of the poem with its anecdotal facility, just as the abstract Personality subjugates the bull-like 'Essence' which alone possesses a potential for development: 'the weight of the sun and the moon and the world hammered/ To a ring of brass through his nostrils.' The situation detailed in the poem precludes the 'moral opportunity' of artist and reader, at least in the terms offered by the primary consciousness:

But the grasses whispered nothing awake, the fetch
Of the distance drew nothing to momentum
In the locked black of his powers.

The following four lines – in addition to the earlier reference of the bull
swinging his muzzle at flies, in ignorance of the watching human
presence – directly recall an important suggestion of Gurdjieff's:

He came strolling gently back,
Paused neither toward the pig-pens on his right,
Nor toward the cow-byres on the left: Something
Deliberate in his leisure, some beheld future
Founding in his quiet.

Substituting bull for 'horse' and remembering that the horse is
Gurdjieff's image for 'Essence', here is his statement:

first of all you must learn the language of the horse, its psychology, in
order to be able to talk to it. Then you will be able to do what the mind,
what logic, wishes. But if you try to teach it now, you will not be able to
teach it or change anything in a hundred years; it will remain an empty
wish. At present you have only two words at your disposal: 'right' and
'left' . . . if you start telling it something it will only keep on driving away
flies with its tail, and you may imagine that it understands you. (*Views from
the Real World*, p. 144)

The bull appears obedient to the farmer's will, but his powers remain
locked up, he does not move on the horizontal axis – the primary
consciousness' organization of the world.

The full-scale drama of engagement of 'Hawk roosting' and 'View of a
pig' is thus foreshortened to a collision of 'directions', a quarrel between
versions of consciousness: 'I kept the door wide,/ Closed it after him and
pushed the bolt.' For a moment the secondary consciousness keeps the
door onto the experience of lines 7–12 open – the door that leads towards
'Hawk roosting' – only to be supplanted by the primary awareness of self
in the last line, which opens its own door – backwards – onto the stylistic
certainty so much in evidence throughout *Lupercal*. Despite the humility
of the final acknowledgement (a clear advance from the egotistical
appropriation of elementals in 'The jaguar'), the door *is* closed, the bolt *is*
pushed, confirming Hughes' bleak admission to Faas that 'It was just too
difficult a road, in my circumstances.' Enshrouded by the dual/multiple
character of mechanical consciousness, and the chaos of interpretations *in
potentia*, poet and reader alike are deprived of 'the emotional intuition
that the will is the same in the one and the all: [which] is the *beginning and
essence of ethics*' (Thomas Mann's introduction to *The Living Thoughts of
Schopenhauer*, p. 17). *Lupercal* moves further along the road towards that

intuition than most poets ever get, but for Hughes it is the start, and the most severe and extreme Stations lie before him in the disintegrative experiences of *Wodwo* and, more especially, *Crow* – though they *are* Stations of the Self, stages in development towards that ethical centre which Christianity intuits in the symbol of a Crucifying Cross.

CHAPTER 5

———— • ————

WODWO

Hughes' next major volume, *Wodwo*, appeared four years after Sylvia Plath's death in 1963, and it is not a surprise to find that, in his *London Magazine* interview with Faas, 'Ted Hughes and Crow', Hughes defined its theme as 'a descent into destruction of some sort' (p. 15). But the descent is circumscribed by what Hughes, seven years later, called the limitations of his 'equipment': '*Wodwo* was one way of looking for the new ground with the old "equipment"' (Ted Hughes and *Gaudete*, (1977), in Faas, *Ted Hughes: The unaccommodated universe*, p. 209). That is to say, what the reader tends to discover in *Wodwo* is not so much a sustaining of the 'state of concentration' which opened the new territory of 'Hawk roosting' and 'View of a pig', as a return to the high-pitched 'art of explosive compression' of *The Hawk in the Rain*. This regression to the psychological and linguistic stance of the earlier volume generates, if it is possible, even greater violence than before. It is as if the poet inaugurates a desperate effort to regain the dominating heights of *The Hawk in the Rain* in circumstances – the shattering revelations of the 'new ground' (both linguistic and psychological) have already happened – which utterly disallow that effort. To explore the new territory with old equipment is itself dualistic, the exploration *requires* the new equipment – an ironic emergency self and a radical 'idea of style' – which erupts with *The Life and Songs of Crow*.

The 'old equipment' surfaces most visibly in the return of some of Hughes' most characteristic prosodic methods:

> Hère is the férn's frónd, unfúrling a gèsture,
> Like a conductor whose music will now be pause
> And the one note of silence
> To which the whole earth dances gravely.

The Anglo-Saxon line is echoed later in lines 7–8, 'And the retina/ Reins the creation with a bridle of water'; as Seamus Heaney points out, 'although the frosty grip of those f' s thaws out, the fern is still subsumed into images of control and discipline and regal authority' ('Englands of the mind', in *Preoccupations: Selected prose 1968–78*, p. 155). The conductor's 'reining' of Creation, the adjustment of the world to *his own* music, governs the entire poem. The poet signally fails to establish that promised musical pause, that 'note of silence' in which the whole earth – as envisaged in 'Hawk roosting' or 'View of a pig' or 'Pike' – is permitted to sing its own tune. 'Music of an exceedingly high order' artificially smoothes over the warrior's passage into his own birthright in the final four lines:

> And, among them, the fern
> Dances gravely, like the plume
> Of a warrior returning, under the low hills,
> Into his Kingdom.

The pervasive music of the poem's 'guiding fiction' in line 1 quite effaces the endeavour of a second voice (lines 2–4) to 'say what [it] really means'. But the undeniable formal beauty of this poem only exists in isolation, as an object of aesthetic contemplation, when the reader forcibly dissociates it from other, more insistently 'violent' voices in the volume. The return of questing warriors is not always etched so harmoniously as in 'Fern': 'The Warriors of the North' bring themselves

> To no end
> But this timely expenditure of themselves,
> A cash-down, beforehand revenge, with extra,
> For the gruelling relapse and prolongueur of their blood
>
> Into the iron arteries of Calvin.

The ritual intensity of the first eight lines, epitomized by 'the elaborate, patient gold of the Gaels', breaks up into the ready-to-hand verbal scraps of idiom, and the crushing subversion of the latinism 'prolongueur' by the Anglo-Saxon 'gr' root in 'gruelling'. The apparent harmony of 'timely expenditure' is eventually declared as a 'revenge', the skull beneath the skin of the puritanical, repressive Calvinist body.

'The Warriors of the North' themselves graduate into the 'Thistles' of the volume's opening poem:

> Every one a revengeful burst
> Of resurrection, a grasped fistful
> Of splintered weapons and Icelandic frost thrust up
>
> From the underground stain of a decayed Viking.
> They are like pale hair and the gutturals of dialects.
> Every one manages a plume of blood.
>
> Then they grow grey, like men.
> Mown down, it is a feud. Their sons appear,
> Stiff with weapons, fighting back over the same ground.

We have returned to the original situation of *The Hawk in the Rain*, the primitive contact with elementals made by the 'Viking', or the Anglo-Saxon literary hero. The poet himself is fighting back over the same ground, not least in the dimension of language, where the thistles represent 'images of a fundamental speech, uttering itself in gutturals from behind the sloped arms of consonants' (*Preoccupations*, p. 155). When the 'new' territory unearthed and brought out into the light by *Lupercal* makes its appearance, however, the warrior-self tends to assume its deadly–abstracted look, 'like St. George in his armour, you see, this innocent, virginal being inside this mechanized protective, aggressive, defensive case' ('Myth and education', 1, p. 65). That is, the legacy of the 'old equipment' – the heroic self which belongs naturally to Old and Middle English tradition and the attendant 'heroic' structuring of the Anglo-Saxon line and diction – which only intermittently exploited its opportunity for 'negotiation' on the Conscious–Unconscious border in Hughes' first volume, now shows its negative aspect, creating an invulnerable St George-type warrior-self and a dominant, formalistic mode of proceeding in language.

A classic example is the three-part poem 'Gog'. The first poem re-opens the 'new territory' of 'Hawk roosting', describing the same brutal animal underself from its own point of view, within the same nominative usage. Gog is woken by the shout of the demiurge, Graves' Logos-God who claims that: 'I am Alpha and Omega.' The psychological reflex is the same as in the earlier poem too – the grotesque assertion of this *Imago Dei* runs parallel to that made by the 'objective' vocabulary of 'Hawk roosting', and both summon their opposite: Gog is accompanied by an 'absence', he becomes 'darkness. Darkness that all night sings and circles stamping.' He is the essential natural compensation for the self-advertisements of the Ego-Personality (and its derivatives in language and theology), just like the Dragon in Revelation: 'And it was given unto him [the dragon] to make war with the saints, and to overcome them; and power was given to him over all kindreds, and tongues, and nations' (Revelation, 14:7). But any further exploration of Gog-elementals/materialisms is crucially circumscribed by the following two parts of the poem, which have a problematic and divisive relationship to the first: indeed, Hughes actually wrote the first part five years before the third, in 1961, salvaging it from a verse play called 'Difficulties of a bridegroom' – itself based on Andreae's *The Chymical Wedding of Christian Rosencreutz*. Part (ii) is a dimly recognizable 'invocation' (in lines 13–16) of the Goddess which forms a distinctly uneasy hinge between the warring factions of the poem, parts (I) and (iii). In that third part, we get the psychically extreme version of the Anglo-Saxon hero, the abstracted warrior-self of Reformed Christianity,

St George. He is based squarely upon the horseman 'called Faithful and True' (Revelation, 19:11) of the final book of the New Testament, who is also a Red-Cross Knight, armed with a 'sharp sword, that with it he should smite the nations' (19:15). In the second half of the poem he is also Coriolanus, following his weapons towards the light:

> when he walks, he moves like an engine, and the ground shrinks before his treading: he is able to pierce a corslet with his eye; talks like a knell, and his hum is a battery. . . . He wants nothing more of a god but eternity and a heaven to throne in. (Menenius, from *Coriolanus*, IV, iv, lines 20–7)

Coriolanus wanted to establish his own range of moral values as something superior to the tidal mutability of the mob, so that he even 'disdain[ed] the shadow which he treads on at noon' (I, i, lines 266–7). Likewise, the 'Holy Warrior' tries to free himself from

> The grooved kiss that swamps the eyes with darkness.
> Bring him to the ruled slab, the octaves of order,
> The law and mercy of number.

At the end of the chapter *The Hawk in the Rain*, I recorded Castaneda's suggestion that as soon as the *tonal* created a prepared space into which the *nagual* could successfully emerge, it had to reverse all its previous effort to avoid its own complete extinction. The third part of 'Gog' clearly embodies that reversal of effort, but it does so in terms of the 'old equipment', the ego's aggressive, self-insulating attitude which was proved inadequate. The empathizing 'I' was solidly encased within the apparent invulnerability of his own interpretative impulses (cf. 'more than to the visionary his cell'), the abstracting 'I' within the elegant armour of stylistic certainty, and in the third part of the present poem the persona struggles visibly against the mechanical rhythms and repetitive line-structure which threaten to overwhelm him: in the first four lines the single-word imperative 'Out' shoves the Holy Warrior clear of four versions of the 'blood-dark womb'; the variations of the womb's 'smile' in lines 22–9 are all wound up together and suppressed by the doubly corrective 'That is illusion'; and the animal reality contained within the last six lines is surrounded and controlled by the movement outwards which comes immediately before and after those mechanical/repetitive lines. Finally, attention might also be drawn to the poem's symmetrical poise, both beginning (within four lines) and ending with the phrase 'Out under the blood-dark archway, gallops the horse-man of iron.' In all these cases, the specialized tunnel vision of a limited consciousness is steadfastly resisting the intensification of galloping rhythms that foreshadow the stylistics and preoccupation of *Crow*, narrowing through 'slits of iron' against its perceived enemy.

There is no sense of flexible negotiation with the 'enraged' matter of

Part I, the two antagonistic elements of the dialogue have to be segregated or realized in separate poems, or through the inadequate 'hinge' of Part II. Thus the poem as a whole ends by dramatizing the inherent difficulty of negotiating one's way through new territory with old equipment – that equipment will have to be abandoned on all levels, whether it is the idea of self, language or the Creator, before progress is possible in *Crow*. I might add that it is surely a sign of Hughes' development that, in both the US edition of *Wodwo* and the 1982 *Selected Poems* version of 'Gog', he felt sufficiently confident to let Part I stand by itself, without further interference from II and III.

Other poems evince this undeniable strain in fitting the language of the 'old' self to the new ground under examination. The triumph of 'Gnat-psalm', for example, exists within a linguistic 'crucible of magic prohibitions' (*A Choice of Shakespeare's Verse*, p. 198), to adapt one of Hughes' own criticisms of *The Tempest*. The reading experience is painfully ambiguous, even dualistic in response to the poem's own double vision, simultaneously celebrating the gnats' activity and increasing the reader's awareness of the machinery which made that celebration possible. For example, the opening lines (particularly lines 1–5 and 10–14) offer an accurate mimesis of the gnat's physical activity, but it is the sort of accuracy that tends to project the masculine capability and athleticism of language and provoke a disturbing consciousness of *words as words*. The early use of alliteration and repetition hint at it, but it is there for all to see in the self-referentiality of 'Writing on the air, rubbing out everything they write/Jerking their letters into knots, into tangles . . .', reinforcing the sense – evident even in the surplus of 'crazy' consonants in the title – that the persona is playing with his poetic lexicon within easy hearing distance of the reader. Such self-consciousness could be considered simply playful, were it not for lines 6–9, with the darker suggestion that words, like gnats, possess 'frail and crepuscular temperaments', and their dance is sustained by artistic self-enclosure, an exclusion of the 'broad thrusts of the sun'. The reader may begin to feel some discomfort as the poet's own poetry-dance tenses itself to resist the 'sun which blasts their [his] song'. The fragile ingenuity of a conceit transforms the Crucifixion-image by its 'magical' sleight of hand: 'they are the nails/ In the dancing hands and feet of the gnat-god', and the serious effects of the wind's 'death-dance', 'Plunging into marshes and undergrowth/ And cities like cowdroppings huddling to dust', are restrained by a further access of the ritual stylization – in the vertical arrangement of the lines – which cushions the gnats from that reality:

    and hangs them a little above the claws of the grass
    Dancing

Dancing
In the glove shadows of the sycamore

As the gnat-dance approaches the possibility of extinction more closely, so the ritualized music steels itself to preserve it: 'Shaken in the air, shaken, shaken/ And their feet dangling like the feet of victims.' The threefold repetition ensures that the simile keeps its distance, that 'like' does not come to mean 'the same as'.

The deliberative effort of the language reaches its climax in the last twelve lines of the poem; from the archaic romanticism of the initial appeal 'O little Hasids' – for which Crow, incidentally, will be severely reprimanded in 'A glimpse' – and the triple 'exclamatio', to the programmatic identification of subject and object and the contrived suspense of the final three lines, the rhetorical labours of language and its ability to strike poses occupy the foreground of the reader's attention. As an authentic experience of the 'new ground' is translated into conscious-ness – which for the poet means its translation into language – it is victimized by the 'old equipment' belonging to the limited self. The personality, it becomes painfully obvious, knows only one language, the 'ritual intensity' of formal music and patterning; when that language attempts to embrace fully the 'ecstatic' experience contained in the poem, it proves too inflexible and threatens self-parody, splitting off into its own reflexive world to complete its rituals, so that the reader is forced to observe – with a certain amount of anguish – both the 'dazzling' experience and the inadequate 'translation' of it side by side, without relief from either, in an echo of the first two poems of *The Hawk in the Rain*. Not one line of the poem evidences the 'colloquial prose readiness' which Hughes sees as an essential component of his ideal language for the Whole Mind, 'at its most wakeful', and which the subject of the poem – the gnat's provisional–crazy dance – singularly appears to invite. Because of the presence of 'old equipment', the poem's 'ecstatic experience' does not obtain the validity with which Scigaj credits it in his article 'Oriental mythology in *Wodwo*' (in Sagar (ed.), *The Achievement of Ted Hughes*, pp. 143–5). I prefer the following 'theory', which seems to keep more in touch with the difficulties the poem presents:

> The ecstatic condition, when the human being feels himself at one with creation, or a Creator, rapture, something like intoxication . . . when all senses interchange or become one sense – these can be the inability to accept and participate in *tajalli* ['irradiation']. What is considered by the individual to be a blessing is in fact a flooding-out of potentiality. It is as if a flood of light has been shone into the eyes of someone who was until recently blind. It has a glory and fascination. But it is no use, because it dazzles.
>
> . . . There is the illusion of *tajalli*, sometimes a foretaste, sometimes a reflection, which is useful for artistic creativity or self-indulgence, but is –

for a Sufi – a fictitious state. This can be easily discerned because it is not
accompanied by an access of knowledge. (Idries Shah, *The Sufis*, p. 297)

Only when the personality – and its language – are 'wakeful and versatile
enough to accept *tajalli*' does it become of permanent use. In the
companion-piece 'Skylarks', we get that versatility of attitude and
language, and an 'access of knowledge' which permits the ecstatic dazzle
to be put to use in the concrete scheme of self-development.

The mesmeric process of 'Gnat-psalm' might also be seen as part of an
attempt to surrender to the 'surrealistic or therapeutic torrent . . . the
delicate cerebral disaster that demolishes the old self for good, with all its
crushing fortifications, and leaves the atman a clear field' (Review of *The
Selected Letters of Dylan Thomas*, p. 783). Unfortunately, the poem
articulates the impulse to 'build' a visionary potential long before that
permanent demolition has finished. 'Magniloquence' is a negative in
Hughes' critical vocabulary (cf. his comments on Wallace Stevens in
'Ted Hughes and *Gaudete*', in Faas, *Ted Hughes*, p. 210), and when the
protagonist of *Cave Birds* attempts a similarly elevated act of praise in
'The scream' he is crushed by irony:

> Then I, too, opened my mouth to praise –
> But a silence wedged my gullet.
>
> Like an obsidian dagger, dry, jag-edged,
> A silent lump of volcanic glass,
>
> The scream
> Vomited itself.

'Gnat-psalm' provides the most complex and dramatic example of the
use of magniloquence within *Wodwo*. The same 'old equipment'
inherited from *The Hawk in the Rain* commands other poems in the
volume more straightforwardly – 'Ludwig's death-mask', 'Bowled
over', 'Out (III)', 'Mountains' and 'You drive in a circle'. It is hardly a
surprise to find that the linguistic bent is often combined with the
hubristic attitude of the 'objective commentator' also bequeathed by the
first volume, in three of these poems ('Ludwig's death-mask', 'Bowled
over', 'You drive in a circle'). That voice achieves its purest release in
another group of poems, including 'Vegetarian' from Part I and
'Kreutzer sonata', 'Karma' and 'Wings' (I, II and III) from Part III. The
last-mentioned poem is fairly typical of the group, in its outright
suppression of the dynamic stimulus – for both poet and reader – gained
from persistent contact with 'new territory', in favour of outwardly
directed derision against three others whose answers were also incomplete: Jean-Paul Sartre, Franz Kafka and Albert Einstein. Each 'objective'
criticism is the eerie projection of an error that the poet has himself made,
not so long ago; imagine the abstract stylist of 'To paint a water-lily'

with reference to these lines: 'Humped, at his huge broken wing of shadow,/ He regrows the world inside his skull, like the spectre of a flower' (I, 'M. Sartre considers current affairs'). Imagine the following poem as a critique of 'Stations' (III and IV):

> And he is an owl
> He is an owl, 'Man' tattooed in his armpit
> Under the broken wing
> (Stunned by the glare, he fell here)
> Under the broken wing of huge shadow that twitches across the floor.
>
> He is a man in hopeless feathers.
>
> (II, 'Kafka writes')

Imagine the 'fall' of the domineering self in *The Hawk in the Rain* to the chastened, alienated persona of *Lupercal* in conjunction with these lines:

> And finally he has fallen. And the great shattered wing
> Of shadow is across the floor,
> this memory is lifting what it can manage
> Of the two worlds, and a few words.
>
> (III, 'Einstein plays Bach')

One could look at all of Hughes' explicit–didactic poems as a self-contained critique of the poet's 'guiding fiction' from the point of view of the unconscious shadow-self.

To return to Hughes' comment in his review of Dylan Thomas, published less than a year before the appearance of *Wodwo*: the 'surrealistic or therapeutic torrent' may be regarded as the most overtly violent effort to destroy the old self and its equipment in the volume. The extreme nature of this 'liberation' is itself a sure indication of the oppressiveness and resilience of the ego's 'crushing fortifications', within poems as apparently diverse as 'Gnat-psalm' and 'Gog'. 'Cadenza', 'Ghost crabs', 'Wino', 'The green wolf' and 'The bear' are all prominent in the uninhibited release of unconscious fantasy directed against the superego and its stylism. It is this moral purpose which, according to Hughes, distinguishes folktale surrealism from literary surrealism; where the latter seeks to escape the struggle with circumstances by surrendering to 'the arbitrary imagery of the dream-flow',

> Folktale surrealism, on the other hand, is always urgently connected with the business of trying to manage practical difficulties so great that they have forced the sufferer temporarily out of the dimension of coherent reality into that depth of imagination where understanding has its roots and stores its X-rays. There is no sense of surrender to the dream flow for its own sake or of relaxation from the outer battle. (Introduction to Vasko Popa's *Collected Poems*, pp. 6–7)

Such a description casts doubt upon the term as a conventional label for a purely aesthetic style, itself 'above' or 'more than' reality (the literal semantic of 'surrealism'). The aesthetic superiority of the Literary Ego is precisely what surrealism intends to cancel, so in 'Cadenza' the fortifying 'Artist' is intentionally banished, in the form of the violinist: 'The Violinist's shadow vanishes.' The poet is forced temporarily out of 'the dimension of coherent reality' into dream-flow images, unified by their shared emphasis upon the truth of the doomed body within the self-sufficient superego artist. When the artist threatens a literary relaxation into ritual music (i.e. lines 11–16), his influence is brusquely terminated by a surrealistic gesture which is only apparently arbitrary:

> Till the whole sky dives shut like a burned land back to its spark –
> A bat with a ghost in its mouth
> Struck at by lightnings of silence –
> Blue with sweat, the violinist
> Crashes into the orchestra, which explodes.

In the last couplet, the individual violinist or 'creator' is consumed by a collective music to which he plays host, the 'set of sounds I can hear going on in the bottom of my mind, that's not quite English but not quite music. It's probably some sort of forgotten inherited language' ('The poet speaks', XVI), to the same extent that the conscious personality is deliberately flooded by the contents of the unconscious.

The moral inflection of surrealism, and the defeat of the superego's 'objective' eye characterizes the longest poem in this group, 'Ghost crabs'. Within the first ten lines, the comfortable 'realism' of the landscape is seen to be its least important feature: what look like 'rocks uncovering' from the retreating tide turn into 'a packed trench of helmets', graduating magically into ghost crabs. This is creative fantasy in full swing, although the free play of the unconscious remains for the time being on the purely literary level of 'arbitrary dream-flow'. The conclusion of the poem attests the transition from literary surrealism to folktale surrealism, from aesthetic play to purposive play:

> These crabs own this world
> All night, around us or through us
> They stalk each other, they fasten on to each other,
> They mount each other, they tear each other to pieces,
> They utterly exhaust each other.
> They are the powers of this world.
> We are their bacteria,
> Dying their lives and living their deaths.

Schopenhauer's World-as-Will is in the background here, as well as the terrifying visions of predatory beasts and sexual activity encountered by the Initiate in the *Sidpa Bardo of The Tibetan Book of the Dead*, which provoke a complete surrender of 'the supremacy of egohood', a capitulation into 'uninhibited imagination' and thence into the 'objective powers of the psyche' (see Jung's 'Psychological commentary' to Evans-Wentz (ed.), *The Tibetan Book of the Dead*, p. xivi).

The surrealist method becomes a responsible act, an act of artistic conscience in such poems. It breaks through the deficiencies of the 'old machinery' to a renewed discovery of 'the convulsion/ In the roots of the blood', and the new ground which Hughes neglects elsewhere in *Wodwo*. Moreover, the realization that such artistic 'play' is fundamentally serious and meaningful connects directly with the 'outward' recognition at the end of the poem that these crabs 'are *God's only toys*'. The distancing from egoism prescribed by the free 'play' of surrealistic fantasy is the exact, self-same distance between the Creator and his mechanical creation. In his essay 'Schiller's ideas on the Type problem', Jung notes that for the artist, it is not

> a matter of *wanting* to play, but of *having* to play; a playful manifestation of fantasy from inner necessity. . . . *It is serious play*. And yet it is certainly play in its outward aspect, as seen from the standpoint of consciousness and collective opinion. . . . Out of a playful movement of elements whose interrelations are not immediately apparent, patterns arise which an observant and critical intellect can only evaluate *afterwards*. The creation of something new is not accomplished by the intellect, but by the play instinct acting from inner necessity. *The creative mind plays with the object it loves*. (*Psychological Types*, pp. 122–3).

An idea of style, Hughes' surrealism, recreates on the poetic level the original relationship – 'in illo tempore' – between God and his world,

> The mechanism of necessity can be transposed on to any level while still remaining true to itself. . . . Seen from our present stand-point, and in human perspective, it is quite blind. If, however, we transport our hearts beyond ourselves, beyond the universe, beyond space and time to where our Father dwells, and if from there we behold this mechanism, it appears quite different. What seemed to be necessity becomes obedience. Matter is entirely passive and in consequence entirely obedient to God's will. It is a perfect model for us. ('The love of God and affliction', in Weil, *Waiting on God*, p. 87)

Egoism only gives the illusion of detachment from material necessity, the illusion of the vocabulary of 'Hawk roosting' which was so savagely subverted. When, however, that illusion is extinguished and we recognize that the crabs 'are the powers of this world. [and] We are their bacteria', the religious attitude of necessary 'Play' becomes primary in the modes of art and as a 'direction' of the self.

Surrealism is one version of a 'new machinery' which Hughes starts to unearth in order to keep in touch with the new range of perceptions generated by *Lupercal*. In one poem, 'Second glance at a jaguar', the infinitely clear, ruthless–direct *Lupercal*-style, which embraced the new range of perceptions so readily, makes a re-appearance – without an accompanying St George-poem to 'control' it, as in 'Gog'. It unpacks the disturbing vision of the jaguar in Hughes' earlier poem 'hurrying enraged/ Through prison darkness after the drills of his eyes' without interference, furthermore, from the empathetic 'controlling' analogy 'there's no cage to him/ More than to the visionary his cell'. The first twenty-two lines of the poem compose only three sentences, the jaguar's heedless energy continually renews itself through descriptive embodiments, wearing out each successive verbal 'container' just as we think its force must be spent. The jaguar's energy sheds every aesthetic skin the poet gives it, forcing him towards moment-to-moment provisional, and therefore 'attentive', formulations of it. But the destruction of fixed, conscious interpretations by this constant renewal of ordinary talk is only the prelude to a much bigger act of subversion:

> At every stride he has to turn a corner
> In himself and correct it . . .
>   club-tail lumped along behind gracelessly,
> He's wearing himself to heavy ovals,
> Muttering some mantrah, some drum-song of murder
> To keep his rage brightening, making his skin
> Intolerable, spurred by the rosettes, the cain-brands,
> Wearing the spots off from the inside,
> Rounding some revenge. Going like a prayer-wheel.

In these lines the jaguar is consumed, so to speak, by religious imagery, and an entire structure of human moral evaluation becomes suddenly accessible: the jaguar is in a state of prayer, attempting to 'correct' a nature which is graceless, expurgating his blood-guilt. The availability of this moralistic context is underscored by Gifford and Roberts in their commentary on the poem, in which they claim that the poem's very achievement is to express

> the animal's unyielding ferocity yet carries a rhythmic embodiment of his tragic loss of grace in every line. As in Milton's devils, traces of his angelic nature remain, filling the reader with awe, but emphasizing the calamity of his fall. (*Ted Hughes: A critical study*, p. 65)

This is in fact where the division of soul and body begins for the reader, to adapt a phrase Hughes uses about his childhood in 'Scout rock' (1957). The conscious interpretative impulse gains a foothold in the imagination only when it separates off from the 'material' reading which threatens to subvert it: the *literal* reading in which the jaguar is physically changing direction, in which he moves inelegantly rather than immorally, in which the prayer is for a perfection of the predatory nature and the tokens of guilt are there to be worn off by a 'brightening' rather than a suppression of the animal energy. One reading only subsists at the expense of the other, though this does not mean that all readings are equal. The moralistic context is quite superfluous to the material necessity of giving the jaguar a verbal body in language. To fix the judgement, and the absolutism of its vocabulary, in place entails the desertion of the open-ended, crisis-torn self, and its use of words as merely a set of provisional conventions to pierce reality. In other words, the moralistic context in which the jaguar is tragically 'fallen' can only be maintained in the knowledge that it is purely incidental to the 'material' need for exploration of jaguar-type elementals, which shoves on under it, regardless. The poet could easily have found other words to do the same *literal* job, after all. The interpretative impulse is entertained, then crushed, in contrast to 'A jaguar', where both poet and reader struggled valiantly to contain the elementals via a conceptualization until the very end of the poem. It is a sign of the poet's advance that an ironic perspective on that struggle should be offered the reader in the last three lines:

> He coils, he flourishes
> The blackjack tail as if looking for a target,
> Hurrying through the underworld, soundless.

Here is the most painful cost of the 'Christian'-moralistic reading: when we rejected Nature or Matter as sinful we actually rejected our own 'underworld', which is only 'soundless' because our construction of reality was deaf to it. This deafness is partly a deafness to symbolic language; for it is when the jaguar is *found* as a symbol that the irony becomes impossible to avoid. The symbol's authenticity is guaranteed by the fact that it pays respect to the world of 'things' (it confirms the physical motions of the animal described in lines 1–6) and the world of 'spirits' (here 'man's baser nature shoved down into the id and growing cannibal murderous with deprivation') equally. By this route, the reader is condemned out of his own mouth, or interpretative attitude. However, unlike Hughes' earlier poem, it really is 'the reader's own nature that selects', and if he *received* the jaguar as, say, 'a beautiful powerful nature spirit' or 'a supercharged piece of cosmic machinery' the traumatic reading, of human moralism and its ironic defeat, simply ceases to exist. Jaguarish elementals are freed to enter his understanding – for better or worse – with as few 'controls' as possible from the conscious standpoint, which is consistent with Hughes' use of surrealism in *Wodwo*. Where Blake, in his poem 'Tyger! Tyger!' framed the tiger-energy by yoking it to a companion-piece 'The lamb', and Yeats could still control it by offering an ironic direction at the end of 'The second coming' (as Hughes suggests in 'Ted Hughes and Crow', *London Magazine*, p. 9), 'And what rough beast, its hour come round at last/ Slouches *towards Bethlehem* to be born?' (my italics), the extremity of cultural circumstances now dictates that the elementals must be released either without 'controls', or with those that are dramatically swept away in the course of the poem. Evidently, the 'spiritless materialism' of civilization and the self-conceit of the Ego (on the individual level) have reached such colossal proportions that only a precipitate, torrential release of elementals can break down those crushing barriers: the symbol *must* be unqualified for it to succeed in the given circumstances.

'Stations', like 'Second glance at a jaguar' – though in a radically different manner – chronicles the clearing-out of the old self and its linguistic equipment. The title refers to the series of pictures which image the successive stages of Christ's Passion, each one demanding a separate devotional exercise or prayer. The first poem gives the spareness of a meditation, describing the pathos of a residual emotionalism which offers to fill, however precariously, the *absence* of 'reality' – that is, the tear in the habitual idea of the world – caused by the suddenness of death. III goes further, magnifying that emotionalism – via the ritual high music of the a first quatrain – into a cenotape-type consecration of the dead. Both elegiac and militant–oratorical impulses to 'renew the dead' are, however, annihilated by disintegrating punctuation and an echo of the surrealistic dream-flow:

> [They] are nowhere they are not here I know nothing
> Cries the poulterer's hare hanging
> Upside down above the pavement
> Staring into the bloody bag Not here
>
> Cry the eyes from the depths
> Of the mirror's seemless sand.

The undifferentiated nature of the syntax is a premonition of the 'death of poetry' in *Crow*, and more immediately prepares for the fourth poem, where 'Absence' becomes a dominating factor, slowly erasing the awareness of the personal pronouns, whether 'you' or 'they' or 'he'. All are given definition only by the collective 'emptiness' that surrounds them:

> You are a wild look – out of an egg
> Laid by your absence.
>
> In the great emptiness you sit complacent,
> Blackbird in wet snow.

The attempts at emotionalist 'construction' and ritual-musical 'rejoicing' all fail in the knowledge of this subjection, preparing the way for a new sense of self and a new language:

Absence. It is your own
Absence

Weeps its respite through your accomplished music,
Wraps its cloak dark about your feeding.

From this point of view, 'accomplished music' only gives further
evidence of its poignant – and Beckettian – inadequacy to make contact
with its own origins, and those of the self.

This built-in corrective to 'Gnat-psalm' and other poems cast in the
image of that musically intense voice is taken up in the concluding poem:

Whether you say it, think it, know it
Or not, it happens, it happens, as
Over rails over
The neck the wheels leave
The head with its vocabulary useless,
Among the flogged plantains.

This is a summarizing reprise of 'View of a pig' and its religious
divestiture of thought, feeling and words as proper grounds of response.
The formal mechanisms of each are superfluous – as in 'Second glance at
a jaguar' – to the implacable reality of *dramatic process*. That truth was
applied consistently to the argumentative interpretative impulses that
both the reader and the poets' own personae brought forward in order to
dominate the poem's Matter. So even in the present poem, the word
'vocabulary' is *dramatically* out of place in the rhythmic structure of the
line in the same way that the polysyllabic light of the head and its
discourse is 'useless', by itself, to any scrutiny of experience or natural
relations. The invisible drama of experience must be liberated from its
'controls' before it can be understood, in Simone Weil's attitude of
Obedience. The unavoidability of the 'simple human fate' – as opposed
to the problematics of freedom – brings the Central European response
back into view, in particular a poem by the East German poet Gunter
Kunert entitled 'Oral declaration':

The whole problem is
since it's the only one
it's unreal and simple at once
like dreams:
one foot wedged into the steel points
to see the train come at you.

The engine was open to talk:
its nature is full understanding
but it can't choose to stop.
Serious words, too, were exchanged
with the rail which on its own initiative

never
will trap a foot.
We all agree about one thing
that our situation is hopeless

True, better
the boiler had never been stoked.
True, better the points had been switched.
True, never to have taken
the old railway track
would have been better.
(Hamburger (ed. and trans.), *East German Poetry*, pp. 107–9).

Both the surrealist voice of poems such as 'Cadenza' and 'Ghost-crabs'
and the *Lupercal*-style voice of 'Second glance at a jaguar' are written
from the standpoint of the Unconscious/Essence. In terms of the
compositional model I quoted in the discussion of *Lupercal*, the surrealist
poems are basically Hughes' (B) version modulating into (C), while
'Second glance at a jaguar', like 'Hawk roosting' comes close to the ideal
(Z), though again (necessarily) biased on the side of (B). But perhaps the
most interesting poem in the book, 'Skylarks', dramatizes the encounter
of conscious and unconscious versions ((A) and (B)), just about
managing to hang on to the antipathetic fragments of both. In other
words, it actually tries to modify its 'controls' fluidly to fit the material
experience of the poem *as it occurs, in the course of* the poem.[1] As such, it is
unique – with the exception of 'Full moon and little Frieda' – within the
book.

Once again there are two separate editions of the poem in *Wodwo* and
Selected Poems, of which I shall refer to the latter, which contains two
extra parts. 'Skylarks' claims direct antecedents in Shelley's 'To a
skylark', and Wordsworth's poem of the same title, although the
relationship between those pieces and Hughes' poem is one of ironic
contrast. Wordsworth's bird is an 'Ethereal minstrel! pilgrim of the sky!',
and offers – not surprisingly – an affirmative answer to the poet's
question 'Dost thou despise the earth where cares abound?': it sings 'All
independent of the leafy Spring.' Shelley's perception of the skylark is
virtually identical, as a 'scorner of the ground', an 'unbodied joy'.
Hughes' bird, however, only reaches such exalted spiritual heights by
descending more fully into Matter. The poem hinges on the interpretation of the word 'leaden' in the last twelve lines:

But leaden
With muscle
For the struggle
Against
Earth's centre.
And leaden

For ballast
In the rocketing storms of the breath.

Leaden
Like a bullet
To supplant
Life from its centre.

In the first stanza, the Shelleyan upward surge of spiritual aspiration
tends to overwhelm the adjective which makes it possible; the immediate
invitation to defy gravity, or soar over the depths seems to occur
'naturally', rather like the identification with the hawk-image in 'The
hawk in the rain'. The next three make acceptance of that invitation
considerably more problematic: the adjective has become more insistent,
the body is the necessary foundation of the 'rocketing storms of the
breath', the height-seeking spirit. The 'materialization' of the idea of
Ascent is completed in those last four lines, where the concept of an
'unbodied joy' is shattered by the ultimate meaning of 'leaden'. Death,
the most incontrovertible evidence of Matter, is also the final reality of
the adjective: as its gravitational pull increases with each repetition, so
the Shelleyan–Wordsworthian perception recedes as a viable response to
the skylark. The first poem keeps faith with the world of things and the
world of spirits equally by showing that no flight is possible without
prior acknowledgement of the absolute, pitiless tyranny of Matter, and
submission to the death of any 'independent' point of view on the world,
the illusory freedom of 'I'-ness. The challenge for the reader is to
supplant one reading of nature – full of literary preconceptions – with a
secondary consciousness that is non-dualistic, to move 'downwards'
before he tries to 'soar upwards'.

So, in the second section, the romantic impulse embodied in the
rhythm built by the dramatic line-spacing of 'climb . . . climb . . . Sing'
is resolved by the revelation that the lark is 'only' following through its
own mechanical nature obediently, 'obedient as to death a dead thing'.
To expand into the terms in which I introduced the poem, the disclosures
of poems written from the Unconscious/material standpoint are now the
foundation-stone (literally, the bottom line) of the present poem and the
conscious appreciation has to accommodate that knowledge. More
concretely, the ritual intensity of poetic language now has to admit the
more flexible, alert – and colloquial – elements:

III
I suppose you just gape and let your gaspings
Rip in and out through your voicebox
                                    O lark
And sing inwards as well as outwards
Like a breaker of ocean milling the shingle
                                    O lark

O song, incomprehensibly both ways –
Joy! Help! Joy! Help!

                                      O lark

In 'Gnat-psalm' the ritual music – what I called the formal mechanism of
the Personality, 'false' if left to its own devices – could never have
allowed, by its own efforts, the purely *animal* realization that begins and
concludes this poem. The music, the act of aesthetic praise, here in the
literary appeal 'O lark' and the middle couplet, has to prove its moral
fitness as well, its openness to the material evidence of 'Hawk roosting'
and 'Second glance at a jaguar'. The poet's own formidable, soaring
imagination, with its dangerous potential for rootless 'fancy' –
Pilinszky's 'venial sin' – has to be forced down into obedience.

   With this in mind, the attitude of Hughes' surrogate 'I' in Section v is
quite consistent, because it involves a voluntary loss of the verbal
imagination's power to soar as effortlessly as the beautiful objects it
pursues: losing sight of the bird in the sun was scarcely an obstacle to
Shelley's musical evocation,

> We hardly see, we feel that it is there.

> All the earth and air
> With thy voice is loud,
> As, when the night is bare,
> From one lonely cloud
> The moon rains out her beams, and heaven is overflow'd

But Hughes is less concerned with the assailing intensity of the 'visionary
moment' than with what endures of the unconscious, or material,
offering after the rituals die away. In fact, the understanding of the lark's
physical nearness to death engineered by the homespun, crisis-ready
language, utterly subdues any possibility of exalted verbal activity
following the bird's flight upward:

> Its feathers thrash, its heart must be drumming like a motor,
> As if it were too late, too late . . .
> . . . my eye's gossamer snaps
>   and my hearing floats back widely to earth

> After which the sky lies blank open
> Without wings, and the earth is a folded clod.

As soon as the normally unconscious meaning makes its mark in the first
two lines, all of Hughes' 'old machinery' (high-music, domineering 'I') is
disconnected, freeing consciousness to grasp a more collective truth:
'Only the sun goes silently and endlessly on with the lark's song.' If we
go deeply enough into the collectiveness of Matter, we find ourselves on
the spiritual plane in which the lark's song is being sung at the very

centre of the universe, or as Hughes puts it in 'Root, stem, leaf' (III): 'Everything is inheriting everything.' From this vantage-point, religious terminology becomes first speech, and in VI the larks are 'Like sacrifices set floating/ The cruel earth's offerings// The mad earth's missionaries.'

The process of Poem VII, which concludes the sequence in *Wodwo*, is almost identical with that of Poem V. There is the death of a verbal machinery, and a sense of self, which has exerted a powerful grip on Hughes' first three volumes; in its most reprehensible form, it condoned the suppressive violence of 'Gog' (III), and it was responsible for the musical illusion of 'Gnat-psalm', as hermetically sealed-up as Shelley's lark, 'Like a high-born maiden/ In a palace tower'. The high music in the first five lines of VII, however, is so much less than the whole point of the poem. The central issue clarifies only as the ritual strivings of that voice begin to break up into an idiom flexible enough to cope with a much wider range of situations. Where the surrealist poems simply wiped out the possibility of formal controls in the torrential dream-flow, VII projects a language taking steps towards the ideal of wakeful readiness Hughes sees in Keith Douglas. The new set of controls is adept at following the larks' every movement, not merely their exalted upward flight and song: it improvises its mimesis through their 'Dip and float, not quite sure if they may/ Then they are sure and they stoop', to the 'plummeting dead drop', and the sudden, carving 'flare and glide off low over grass'. The material inclusiveness of the larks' description – embracing its passage through 'ultimate-situation' intensity, death and recovery – holds up an image of self-development, and of the necessary 'direction' of poetic language, as a matter of course:

Weightless,
Paid-up,
Alert,

Conscience perfect.

The protagonist – in accordance with Don Juan's demand of Castaneda – appears to 'reverse his effort' successfully in the last four lines, so that the conscious standpoint is expanded, rather than totally extinguished. The reading of 'conscience' is crucial: if the reader confines the word to its customary moralistic inflection it will indeed seem absurdly irrelevant to the world of the larks' activity. But another reading is available: 'conscience' means 'consciousness', an act of knowing, and on the inner level the value of the larks' contribution is undiminished, it offers a model of development. The single word is established as a yardstick of the reader's fitness, it is his choice which isolates the natural world even more conclusively from the human context, or observes the identity of 'outer' and inner' dimensions within the text – 'If any man have an ear, let him hear' (13:9) is a condition which applies to Hughes' poetry as much as the Book of Revelation.

The final poem Hughes appends in the *Selected Poems* suggests a fear that even this conclusion may be dangerously open to 'sentimental reading', as Sagar puts it (p. 93). As close as the poem swoops to the fact of death, the satisfaction of its final image may still be misused for the heroic preservation of the 'old self', a Cuchulain-style resistance to any awareness of his own material or mechanical allegiances. So now the lark's song is guided by another bird, a crow, to emphasize the realities that demand 'obedience and self-abandonment' (*ibid.*),

> '*That some sorry little wight more feeble and misguided than thyself*
> *Take thy head*
> *Thine ear*
> *And thy life's career from thee.*'

This is the bridge Hughes builds between 'Skylarks' and *Crow*: the gesture of balance with which Poem VII terminates is still only a fragmentary 'moment of consciousness' (Gurdjieff), which needs to be consolidated by an even more systematic descent into the darkness of the Self with new equipment. The poem in fact provides the equipment for that descent by re-discovering a language outside the purity of the ritual–intense range. Despite its obvious difference in style and tone from the other poems in the sequence, VIII plays the important role of pointing us away from the immediate satisfaction of the final image of VII towards the new, relentlessly material 'exploratory body' supplied by Crow himself.

The beautiful poem 'Full moon and little Frieda' works, like the seventh part of 'Skylarks', off a Conscious–Unconscious balance reminiscent of 'The thought-fox':

> A cool small evening shrunk to a dog bark and the clank of a bucket –
> And you listening.
> A spider's web, tense for the dew's touch.
> A pail lifted, still and brimming – mirror
> To tempt a first star to a tremor.

The world-idea shrinks, and the passive, alert subject simply waits in a typographic emptiness: the technical evidence of 'Skylarks', that Hughes' use of syntax and line-arrangement is proving increasing transparent to its subject-matter, is here confirmed. This is the self-effacing attitude Alan Watts detects in the Sung Chinese landscape painters:

> the secret lies in knowing how to balance form and emptiness. . . . For Zen spoils neither the aesthetic shock nor the *satori* shock by filling in, by explanation, second thoughts, and intellectual commentary. Furthermore, the figure so integrally related to the empty space gives the feeling of the

'Marvellous Void' from which the event suddenly appears. (*The Way of Zen*, p. 198)

Hughes' prosodic and psychological orientation alike deliberately avoids 'filling in' reality with the second-hand versions of consciousness; he strives for freedom not only from his own commanding voice, potent in *The Hawk in the Rain* and *Lupercal*, but also the widespread Western European idea of the forms of art as a kind of superior intelligent energy imposed from above on the inert matter of Nature, as in Malraux's conception of the artist perennially *conquering* his medium. That is nothing less than the philosophical division of Spirit and Matter, translated into literature.

The results of this humble, mirror-like consciousness are condensed into the astonishment of the last three lines:

'Moon!' you cry suddenly, 'Moon! Moon!'
The moon has stepped back like an artist gazing amazed at a work
That points at him amazed.

From such a perspective the dualities of subject–object, and Spirit– Matter can hardly be said to exist; if the terms have to be used, it is possible to say that the end of the poem takes up an implicit suggestion of 'Skylarks', that Spirit is a *refinement of Matter*, the subject a refinement of collective elements – a Sufi idea that becomes increasingly prominent in Hughes' later work. The speed at which apparently diverse fields of reference collapse into one another is quite breathtaking: the moon is first object, then subject, then object to the child, and utterly reflects the moral state of the artist's relationship with his creation, not so much conquest as fluid surrender.

The same proviso incorporated in the final poem of 'Skylarks' applies to 'Full moon and little Frieda'; but the ironic shadow of Crow will hang over this poem only if the reader is prepared to exalt the 'visionary moment' above the testament of a fractured poetic self which *Wodwo as a whole* affords – i.e. its invisible, 'continuous' process. The choice of the individual beauty over the more 'monstrous' evidence of the collective statement is a tragic preference. We ourselves – who, as Hughes suggests in 'Ludwig's death-mask', are all too ready with our 'marzipan amazement' – should not grasp that beauty, but avert our eyes, because what really matters is the creation of a *permanent* centre of gravity within the self, which is *regularly* open to this kind of perception. It is to this end that the unifying mythic machinery of *Crow* is set in motion.

We actually get the prototype of Crow himself in the title-poem of the volume, 'Wodwo'. This bewildered, questioning 'half-man half-animal spirit of the forests' (*Poetry in the Making*, p. 62) is the very obverse of the St George warrior-self who battles with it in the excerpt from *Sir*

Gawayne and the Grene Knight that prefaces the book; it is as if Hughes really shifts across the psychological spectrum, from one self-fiction to the other, the extremist 'Warrior of light' to its goblin-like shadow-self, in the course of *Wodwo*. Both are potential developments – towards abstraction or negotiation – of the basic Middle English 'heroic condition'. On the linguistic level, the wodwo's no-holds-barred approach is reflected in the complete absence of any sort of syntactical organization within the poem, and its prosaicization which, as Rozewicz indicated, *creates the conditions for poetry's subsistence*. The run-over of a 'whole string of thoughts' into one another is a survival technique, evading the fixed stare of the all-powerful *idea* by an adjustment of form to the rapidly flickering perspectives of a *plural* self. As in the Central European response, the omission of punctuation and the prosaic nature of poetry are naturally transparent to the full range of multiple I's and the unconscious elements of the psyche. The self is a provisional fiction, so that the instinctive movement towards Egoism is observed within the ironic perspective of 'seem' and 'suppose' and the immediate formal overrun into 'Other' evidence:

> I suppose I am the exact centre
> but there's all this what is it roots
> roots roots roots and here's the water
> again very queer but I'll go on looking.

The impulse to place oneself at the exact centre of the universe may only be 'touching one wall of me', it has to be fitted to the material recognition that 'all this' is rooted in the collective, not the merely personal. Only when Wodwo is transformed into the ruthlessly direct exploratory body of Crow does this elemental conflict assume its most harrowing, savagely ironic aspect.

CHAPTER 6

— • —

CROW

Every writer if he develops at all develops either outwards into society and history, using wider and more material of that sort, or he develops inward into imagination and beyond that into spirit, using perhaps no more external material than before and maybe even less, but deepening it and making it operate in many different inner dimensions until it opens up perhaps the religious or holy basis of the whole thing. . . . Developing inwardly, of course, means organizing the inner world or at least searching out the patterns there and that is a mythology. It may be an original mythology. Or you may uncover the Cross – as Eliot did. ('Ted Hughes and Crow' *London Magazine*, pp. 14–15)

Crow, published in 1972, is the first of Hughes' books to deepen the inward exploration far enough that it begins to take on the structural hardness of a mythology. The 'Author's note' at the start of *Wodwo* expressed, somewhat desperately, a desire that the play, stories and poems be read together, 'as chapters of a single adventure'; but the clear lens of that hope diffused within the fractured voices of individual lyrics. This was equally true of *The Hawk in the Rain* and *Lupercal*, but by the time of *Crow* the fragmentary patterns of the inner life have become sufficiently familiar to compose their own story, the solidity of a mythological 'map'. Moreover, a mythological language not only realizes the fundamental patterns of the psychic 'whole', it also inaugurates the effort to integrate all the voices within the self which are artificially isolated from one another as a formal consequence of the lyric. That is to say, the imagination takes another step forward in the fulfilment of its 'arduous mission for good' when it begins to connect all the I's – the rags and scraps of an alienated self – within the concentrated focus of a unifying *Narrative*. Hughes had already started to exploit this opportunity in his re-working of Seneca's *Oedipus*, and the moral 'momentum' and 'fitness' he derived from this exercise was an excellent preparation for *Crow*; as he points out: 'Poems come to you much more naturally and accumulate more life when they are part of a connected flow of real narrative that you've got yourself involved in' (Faas, *Ted*

Hughes: The unaccommodated universe, p. 213). This concentrated 'atten-tion' is also reflected in a much greater uniformity and ruthless clarity of style than before, as we shall see later in the chapter.

Hughes' use of mythic machinery in *Crow* defines even more comprehensively than *Wodwo* a transition from what Jung calls the 'psychological' to the 'visionary' mode of artistic creation. Of the first, Jung says

> Countless literary works belong to this class: the many novels dealing with love, the environment, the family, crime and society, as well as *didactic poetry*, the larger number of *lyrics*, and the drama, both tragic and comic. Whatever its particular form may be, the psychological work of art always takes its materials from the vast realm of conscious human experience – from the vivid foreground of life, we might say. I have called this mode of artistic creation psychological because its activity nowhere transcends the bounds of psychological intelligibility. ('Psychology and literature', in *Modern Man in Search of a Soul*, p. 180; my italics)

In Hughes' first three books, the tendency to break off into a didactic, 'lyrical or metaphysical or formal fragment' of a 'whole human being' was constantly observable: as a result, several poems never escaped the 'phenomenal' grip of the preoccupation with 'the vivid foreground of life'. But the mythic machinery of *Crow* puts this mode of artistic creation permanently out of range, the book remains quite invisible when the vast realm of conscious experience is forefronted: 'If a reader has no instinct for folklore, Myth etc. . . . I don't know what *Crow* can offer. I kept the immediate world out of it – the external immediate world. I'm sure to some it's an invisible book' (Personal Communication, 22 November 1983). Where the Movement poetry invokes the psychological mode of creation, poets like Hughes, Vasko Popa and Miroslav Holub assuredly summon the visionary approach:

> The experience that furnishes the material for artistic expression is no longer familiar. It is a strange something that derives its existence from the hinterland of man's mind – that suggests the abyss of time separating us from pre-human ages, or evokes a *super-human world of contrasting light and darkness*. . . . The value and force of the experience are given by its *enormity*. It arises from timeless depths; it is *foreign and cold, many-sided, demonic and grotesque*. A *grimly ridiculous sample* of the external chaos . . . it bursts asunder our *human standards of value and of aesthetic form*. The disturbing vision of monstrous and meaningless happenings that in every way exceed the grasp of human feeling and comprehension makes quite other demands upon the powers of the artist than do the experiences of the foreground of life. . . .
> We are astonished, taken aback, confused, put on our guard or even disgusted – and we demand commentaries and explanations. . . . The reading public for the most part repudiates this kind of writing – unless, indeed, it is coarsely sensational – and even the literary critic feels embarrassed by it. (*Modern Man in Search of a Soul*, pp. 180–2; my italics)

As the proliferation of italics indicates, Jung's commentary is applicable to *Crow* in every particular, even down to a common critical reaction to the volume. Whether we assess the shift as one between the 'psychological' and 'visionary' modes of artistic creation, or between the dislocation of individual lyrics and the coherence of mythic narrative, the psychological action is the same: the exploration of the unconscious, the 'deepest awareness' which dominates only a handful of poems in each of the previous three volumes, is now a disciplined, consistent and therefore decisive imaginative endeavour.

The following summary compresses the substance of the narrative, the account of Crow's creation Hughes usually gives at readings:

> Having created the world, God has recurring nightmare. A huge hand comes from deep space, takes him by the throat, half-throttles him, drags him through space, ploughs the earth with him then throws him back to heaven in a cold sweat. God cannot imagine what in his own created universe can have such power over him. And repeated attempts to make the nightmare show itself fail until God finally manages to make it speak. But its voice simply mocks God and his creation, particularly Man, who has completely mismanaged his gifts and destroyed himself and the world. And God doesn't seem to be able to do anything about it. He becomes enraged and challenges the nightmare to prove what it is saying. In reply, the nightmare simply points to man in the gates of heaven, who has come to ask God to take life back. The nightmare is jubilant and God mortified. So God challenges the nightmare to do better and this is exactly what the nightmare has been waiting for. It plunges down into matter and creates Crow. God puts Crow through all kinds of ordeals involving his annihilation, dismemberment or transformation, but Crow survives them all. Meanwhile he interferes in God's activities, sometimes trying to learn or help, at other times openly opposing God's will.

The God of this narrative is the Gnostic demiurge of 'Gog' who claimed to be Alpha and Omega, and who is called Krogon in Hughes' *Orghast* mythology. He is the 'young Puritan Jehovah' whom Hughes castigates in his appendix to *A Choice of Shakespeare's Verse* and who survives as a contemporary cultural legacy, 'the man-created, broken-down, corrupt despot of a ramshackle religion' (*Crow* record sleeve). He holds a 'mysterious, powerful, invisible prisoner' (*ibid.*) who is variously Gog himself, Moa in *Orghast* and the medieval Goddess in Shakespeare's canon; she is the Mother of this God in the poem 'Logos', turned into a nightmare by suppression: 'Crow's whole quest aims to locate and release his own creator, God's nameless hidden prisoner, whom he encounters repeatedly but always in some unrecognisable form' (*ibid.*). It is a further tribute to the unifying force of Hughes' mythic machinery that the undertext of poems like 'Hawk roosting', 'Gog' and the two jaguar poems – which narrated the replacement of one idea of the Creator with another, much larger image – should now itself be located and released, given a conscious freedom by *Crow*'s structural breadth and flexibility. Once a 'mythic perspective' is established, it becomes clear that no single dimension of the struggle – against falsities of self, style and the Creator-image – can be foregrounded without summoning all the other aspects into view simultaneously, with an instant, concentrated force.

Crow's own mythological ancestry is extensive: it includes the Celtic Crow-God Bran and the Pelasgian hero Aesculapius, the Greek God of healing. Bran was credited by the bards – in particular the poet Gwion-ap-Don – with the invention of their art and the ownership of the cauldron of Cerridwen (a version of Graves' 'White Goddess') from which the Triple Muse had been born. He acquired the ability to prophesy by borrowing the crow of the Goddess, and continued to do so even after decapitation. As final proof of his allegiance in the combat between the two rival Images of the Creator, he fought on her side in the prolonged battle against the masculine god Beli, or immortal Apollo. Crow draws the psychological aspect of that struggle even more lucidly, through his significant relationship to the Trickster of North American Indian mythology, a resemblance noted variously by Sagar, Gifford and Roberts and Graham Bradshaw in his essay 'Ted Hughes' Crow as Trickster–hero':

> Nobody knows quite how he was created, or how he appeared. He was created by God's nightmare. . . .
> It's something outside God, outside the God that created Man, or the men we know, so the Crow is a sort of extra-man, a shadow-man. He's a man to correct man but . . . he never does quite become a man – Maybe his ambition is to become a man, which he never quite manages. ('Ted Hughes' *Crow*', from 'Poetry Now', in *The Listener*, p. 149)

Hughes' description of Crow and his function has a clear affinity with Radin's understanding of the Trickster Wakdjunkaga in the Winnebago story-cycle, and Jung's psychological commentary on him (see Radin, 'On the psychology of the Trickster-figure', *The Trickster*, pp. 195–211). Both Crow and Trickster figure the shadow-side of the psyche, epito-mizing those 'black' elements which are judged negative or inferior, and therefore suppressed by the Ego-Personality. The shadow functions as an 'autonomous complex', free both to oppose the intentions of consciousness, and to come and go as it pleases; Crow and Trickster alike are faithful copies of 'an absolutely undifferentiated human conscious-ness, corresponding to a psyche that has hardly left the animal level' (*The Trickster*, p. 200), dominated by primitive biological instincts like sex and hunger, and radically hostile to the processes of conceptual formulation. Kerenyi, in his essay 'The Trickster in relation to Greek mythology' (in Radin, *The Trickster*), calls him by turns ' "phallic", "voracious", "sly", "stupid" – *the spirit of disorder, the enemy of boundaries'* (*ibid.*, p. 185; my italics).

But if Crow/Trickster is capable of the most atrocious things through 'sheer animal unconsciousness and unrelatedness', he is also capable of the very opposite, due to his nature as a 'cosmic' being of *divine-animal* nature, on the one hand superior to man because of his superhuman qualities, and on the other hand inferior to him 'because of his unreason and unconsciousness' (*ibid.*, p. 204). As the survivor of unimaginable tortures, he 'approximates the saviour' (Jung's terms), confirming the mythological truth that 'the wounded wounder is the agent of healing, and that the sufferer takes away suffering' (*ibid.*, p. 196). Crow/Trickster has a double potential, he is a symbol *waiting to be fulfilled*, what Radin terms the 'undifferentiated present' within every generation and every individual: 'before good and evil, denier, affirmer, destroyer and Creator. If we laugh at him, he grins at us. What happens to him happens to us' (Radin, 'The Wadkjunkaga Cycle', *ibid.*, p. 169). More relentlessly than jaguar, hawk, fox, dead pig, otter and pike, Crow simply plays back the conscious attitude of the perceiving subject to its own unconscious elements or 'Essence'. The suppression of Crow/Trickster as Satan, engineered by Reformation theology, unhappily ensured that the Trickster-figure is realized only on the primitive, animal level, imprisoned in its most basic material form. This attitude – which we carry with us as a cultural legacy into the readership of the poems – is tragically self-defeating, for in its suppression of the 'negative' side of Crow/Trickster it simultaneously rids itself of the 'divine' potential contained within the symbol. Crow/Trickster is a primitive version of the 'creative hinge' embodied in the Goddess-image, undeveloped: destructive when you see him as destructive, creative when you see him as creative. So in the twentieth episode of the cycle, Wakdjunkaga – in an echo of the three-personed Goddess who is all of mother, lover and daughter – contrives to become both bride and mother at a wedding feast, while the poem 'Crow's undersong' expresses the developmental potential or creative underswell of the entire book:

> Only out of disaster can the longing for a saviour arise – in other words, the recognition and unavoidable integration of the shadow create such a harrowing situation that nobody but a saviour can undo the tangled web of fate. In the case of the individual, the *problem constellated by the shadow is answered on the plane of the anima* [the collective shadow], that is, through relatedness. In the history of the collective as in the history of the individual, everything depends on the development of consciousness. ('On the psychology of the Trickster-figure', in *The Trickster*, p. 211; my italics)

It is no wonder that Crow's quest aims to 'locate and release' his own Creator, because she represents an image of the highest pitch of his own consciousness. The bridge between the two is his 'eagerness to learn', and his essential character as an ironic fiction, an emergency self liable to be blown up, mutilated or transformed at any given moment in the sequence. One might say that Crow is Hughes' most appropriate poetic persona to date, breaking the possibility of egoism by his natural engagement with the shadow-self and animal nature, presenting a succession of provisional 'conscious' perspectives in a self which is scarcely more than a compact, explodable mass.

But *Crow* first began as an 'idea of style'. In his *London Magazine* interview, 'Ted Hughes and Crow', Hughes indicates that the psychological casting-out of 'beautiful horses' in favour of the 'dirty, scabby little foal', of the eagles in favour of the crow, required the creation of a shadow-language appropriate to the task – 'songs with no music whatsoever . . . a super-simple and super-ugly language which would in a way shed everything except just what he wanted to say without any other consideration and that's the basis of the style of the whole thing' (p. 20). Two poems from *Wodwo*, 'Logos' and 'Theology', already contain the germ of this new linguistic possibility, discovered in the uproar of Hughes' increasingly desperate struggle against the formal fortifications of the Ego-Personality.

In 'Crow and the birds', Hughes makes the prototype gesture, throwing out the eagles and choosing the crow – discarding the angelic use of language upon finding its super-simple, super-ugly 'shadow'.

> When the eagle soared clear through a dawn distilling of emerald
> When the curlew trawled in sea dusk through a chime of wineglasses
> When the swallow swooped through a woman's song in a cavern
> And the swift flicked through the breath of a violet . . .

These, the first four lines of the poem, are a good example of Poetry's implicit offer (in the words of one of Wallace Stevens' 'Adagia') to create 'a fictitious existence on an exquisite plane'. On closer inspection, they may create far more problems than they resolve as the reader becomes aware that every line in the stanza is, in effect, a 'divided line'. Each verb concentrates the focus on the birds' material reality: perhaps the finest is 'trawled', an exact evocation of the curlew's flight, hauling its legs behind as if dragging some great weight through water. But as surely as that concentration is achieved, it is diffused by the gratuitously aesthetic contexts which compose every second half-line. All four contexts are virtually interchangeable, the half-line break immediately starts to dramatize the tragic literary situation examined in the third part of the Introduction: a certain 'material' accuracy in language gives way to the 'hermetic' freedom to create its own world, to crystallize in an alluring certainty of style. The reader thus has the option of experiencing, in the

line-structure of the stanza, the poetic trauma Roland Barthes understood so well – the shift from a language capable of reproducing an
'instance of reality' to a language which can draw only an 'instance of
discourse'. I say 'the reader thus has the option' because if he give
priority to what Graham Bradshaw terms 'the expressive resources of
poetic language', or 'the significance of language, which shapes and
recreates an autonomous human world' ('Ted Hughes' Crow as trickster-
hero', in Williams (ed.), *The Fool and the Trickster, a Festschrift for Enid
Welsford*; my italics), the lines will not seem traumatic at all.

That attitude is, however, significantly discomfited in the second
stanza, where the verbs if anything intensify ('zipped . . . drummed . . .
tumbled'), and the birds are actively engaged in an effort to shed their
containing human contexts; both moral and materialist discourse fall
away into comic inappropriateness: 'the owl sailed clear of tomorrow's
conscience . . ./ the peewit tumbled clear of the laundromat.' The
various enclosed worlds of cultural discourse are not transparent to
matter, they collide with it ironically. Even the third stanza which is
ostensibly the most 'natural' in the poem, has its own prejudice: it never
escapes the hypnotic hold of a static, imagistic *idea* about the birds. The
angelic or aesthetic voice creates a distance between the verb and its
environment which the reader cannot close down into a concrete *meaning*
by his own efforts, however strenuous. It is only in the last line that the
'expressive resources of language' (embodied in the verb) find their true
moral foundation, and the poetic imagination *finds its way home*: 'Crow
spraddled head-down in the beach-garbage, guzzling a dropped ice-
cream.' 'Spraddled' is the first verb not to be crippled by its context,
because that context is wholly – even grossly – *material*. Crow's
connection with the human world is not at all aesthetic, but it is
unquestionable: he thrives on human leavings direct, just as the crow in
Eat Crow (1964) waits for a single man in the desert to die, and become
carrion. At this, the lowest point possible – when the spotlight falls on
Crow, and the confrontation with Matter can no longer be avoided –
language suddenly gives birth not to an instance of discourse (in any
meaningful sense) but an instance of reality. The overall impression
really is of an emergence from the general lifelessness, from an
undifferentiated welter of arbitrary connections onto solid ground. The
line allows us to make a more accurate judgement about the 'ethical
potential' of the two readings noted earlier: however 'ugly' it may
appear, the language clustered around Crow emphasizes a relatedness to
the material creation which is lacking in the more 'aesthetic' previous
fourteen lines, which slipped into technical instances of discourse as a
consequence. If we continue to praise the 'expressive resources of poetic

language' – which are simply its *mechanical* capacities – as an ideal detached from everything else, we stand in jeopardy of finding ourselves in the same position as the typical Beckettian narrator, whom words could not liberate, despite his imperious command of their expressive abilities. As surely as the relative clauses of lines 1–14 are subordinate to the main clause of line 15, that response has to recognize that the aesthetic possibility of words, their true expressiveness, depends on their *moral fitness* – their submission to the poet's religious activity. For Hughes, the descent into the 'Matter' of our suppressed natures is an individual and cultural necessity, which *demands* a corresponding 'super-simple, super-ugly' language; criticism of the effort, therefore, has to take place in full consciousness of the psychological bias of its own vantage-point.

So 'Crow and the birds' testifies to a seminal moment in Hughes' imaginative progress: the final replacement of natural images and a language 'from above' with a bird, and a style culled 'from below'. Crow, who exists literally at the bottom-most point of the poem, is the foundation-stone from which re-construction can begin; both the dance of poetry's ritual music, and the dance of the false self associated with it, come to an end in the realization of this moment. It is not too difficult to see Hughes in this poem exorcising the demons of his own past, attempting to throw off the prejudices of attitudes to the self and poetic language, and some large-scale cultural relativisms, all at once. When the 'attentive' man begins to feel that reality has been converted defensively into discourses 'not his own', and that the whole psyche has started to fossilize into a false personality, he needs a figure as explosive as Crow to shed those 'containers', that machinery.

Hughes' descent into a new idea of style in *Crow* not only highlights the suspect double-nature of language he singled out so lucidly in *Poetry in the Making*, it casts the linguistic problem in its most encompassing, and yet concise form: Hughes goes straight to the heart of the matter when he claims that the God of *Crow* – the 'man-created, broken-down, corrupt despot of a ramshackle religion' – '*bears about the same relationship to the Creator as, say, ordinary English does to reality*' (Crow record-sleeve notes; my italics). Only here do we see the poet's struggle with language in its true dimensions – that the assault on the abstract ideal of conceptual language is the same as the psychological, or the Metaphysical, assault. Thus several poems in the volume image this assault directly. The 'word' in 'A disaster', for example, makes the same claims as the 'Word' of the Logos-God in 'Gog' – it consumes the earth's people within its own illusion, its instance of discourse. 'Crow and the birds' presented the world of words as a dramatic challenge to the poet and reader, and 'A disaster' substantializes the perspective which alone enable us to evade those false 'instances' of language successfully: in order to keep our ethical vigilance, to 'fly clear and peer', we have to assume the same point of view as Crow himself – entailing recognition of our material allegiances, acceptance of the shadow-truth which he embodies. Aesthetic language failed when it 'tried its great lips' on the bulk of the birds' material character, though the failure only becomes obvious when the reader, so to speak, finds his own Crow-like body. At that point, consciousness is widened to the fullest impact of the irony of a poem like 'Crow's first lesson'; here the word 'love', lying at the exact centre of modern theological discourse on the New Testament, fails dismally to appropriate Crow's own utterly mechanical nature. A verbal concept – and the poem revolves around its first statement: 'God tried to teach Crow how to *talk*' – cannot by itself educate primitive 'Matter', and if it makes the attempt it produces a nightmare of violent sexuality:

'A final try', said God. 'Now, LOVE.'. . .
And Crow retched again, before God could stop him.
And woman's vulva dropped over man's neck and tightened.
The two struggled together on the grass.
God struggled to part them, cursed, wept –

Crow flew guiltily off.

Likewise, in 'The Battle of Osfrontalis' words try to digest Crow of their own volition, only to be proved superfluous to one of his primary biological instincts, hunger – although the 'lesson' of this poem does not deter Crow from 'trying' words in one notable poem, 'Crow goes hunting', none the less. As Sagar points out, the poem re-interprets the shape-changing formula of *The Romance of Taliesin* to suggest the inadequacy of language. And as in 'A disaster', the physical universe proves totally impervious to words, or any kind of semantic container; when Crow turns literary creator, he naturally exposes the shadow-side of poetry, its innate deficiency. At the end of the poem he is left '*Speechless* with admiration'. But it is just at this point that the reader may feel most uncomfortable, and the repetitive, formulaic pattern of the poem – which is typical of a great many others in the book – has attracted much adverse critical comment; the most eloquent spokesman is Graham Bradshaw, who compares 'Crow goes hunting' unfavourably with 'The thought-fox', arguing that it depends on the poet's willingness 'to replace creative exploration with the [formally arbitrary] gesture' (see 'Ted Hughes' Crow as Trickster–Hero', pp. 89–91). He accuses Hughes of

too readily capitulating to the Post-Romantic feeling that, since the most vital kinds of experience resist articulation, what matters most is whatever cannot be expressed. This may be proper in Zen, but the master Kitano Gempo knew that it entailed giving up poetry. (*ibid.*)

Significantly, he also suggests that the repetitive structure of the poem shows 'little evidence of the *expressive control over intonation* that distinguishes verse from prose' (*ibid.*; my italics), or verbal play from slapstick. These criticisms, as I understand them, thoroughly omit any idea of poetry as a developing or continuous *process*: the desire for 'expressive control over intonation' hardens too readily, it seems to me, into a set of 'objective' critical standards and an 'objective' model for the Hughesian poem, 'The thought-fox' and its 'raid on the inexpressible'. The point is that once that model and those standards are fixed as a critical 'conscious standpoint', any poem which appears to be outside the prevailing aesthetic and *psychological* range must be judged unacceptable. The critic demands the finished aesthetic product in language *regardless of the current 'state of negotiations'*.[1] So, for example, the value placed on 'expressive intonation', the elevation of verse above prose, puts out of bounds Rozewicz's revelation – most appropriate to *Crow* – that it is just these 'prosaicized' works 'which create the conditions for poetry's subsistence and even survival', and the ethical necessity which underpinned Witold Gombrowicz's attack on 'excess of poetry, excess of poetical words, excess of metaphor, excess of sublimation, excess of condensation, and the elimination of all anti-poetic elements' (*Dziennik 1953–1956*, p. 317). Moreover, the giving-up of 'poetry', which Bradshaw considers a requirement in Zen, is in Sufism merely the preface to the unearthing of a new poetry, but shifted to its proper ground. Gurdjieff terms it the passage between 'subjective' and 'objective Art', in which the 'exquisite' mechanisms of language are thrown out temporarily, until the user is fit to exploit their 'resources'.

Within the psychological frame of reference, 'Crow goes hunting' *does* participate in the creative exploration inaugurated by 'The thought-fox', though the development may be invisible to the critic's 'aesthetic Personality'. *Crow* is undoubtedly the most abrasive challenge to the assumption of the 'objectivity' of the text, and the customary critical separation of aesthetic and moral judgement, in Hughes' entire canon. In more concrete terms, the poem – and others like it – is indeed repetitive and formulaic, devoid of all 'interesting' qualities. Aestheticism must have been one of the 'tabus' Hughes saw himself breaking in his *London Magazine* interview ('Ted Hughes and Crow', p. 18), the reduction to a purely mechanical language is a positive achievement: only this mechanical patterning, this vision of language as 'nothing' beyond a functional capacity, could rid Hughes of the deviances of the superego stylist and his ventriloquisms – Empathy, Abstraction, Didacticism, etc. The formulaic design of the poem – as much as the hare's elusiveness – resists *any* conscious articulation of 'the inexpressible', imposes an absolute silence at the end of the poem. It abjures 'expressive intonation' and 'verbal play' to evade the falsity of self which has mastered those devices; it keeps touch with the functional–material nature of words as surely as Crow prescribes the shadow-reality of our material natures. In the religious perspective, the acknowledgement that *language is nothing more than a machine*, constitutes for the poet a step towards grace.

Hughes' reduction of language to its mechanical base – which dominates roughly one-third of the poems – is not only rigorous, it has some 'natural' purposes in the book: in 'Examination at the womb door', the repetitive structure enforces the inescapability of the material answer, 'Death', to each question, and carries through much the same lesson in 'A kill', and 'Oedipus crow'. In the latter poem, Crow's repeated effort to escape re-absorption by Nature gives the impression of renewing the mechanical force of the rhythmic pattern all by itself. Only when that force is spent, 'Crow dangled from his one claw – corrected./ A warning.' The repetitive formula always has the effect of concentrating attention remorselessly on Matter, without any possibility of alternative, verbally created realities. In 'Crow's song of himself', the Logos-God's attempts to destroy Crow only succeed in re-emphasizing what he represents, the 'world of final reality', the material universe itself; and it is almost as if the poet, as a kind of 'co-creator' with God, is likewise helpless in a mechanical flow of words, which cannot choose but to face Matter, whichever way they turn:

> When God hammered Crow
> He made gold
> When God roasted Crow in the sun
> He made diamond
> When God crushed Crow under weights
> He made alcohol
> When God tore Crow to pieces
> He made money
> When God blew Crow up
> He made day
> When God hung Crow on a tree
> He made fruit
> When God buried Crow in the earth
> He made Man
> When God tried to chop Crow in two
> He made woman
> When God said: 'You win, Crow',
> He made the Redeemer.
>
> When God went off in despair
> Crow stropped his beak and started in on the two thieves.

The process of readership is as reductive as the process of composition: there is a tacit invitation – a reading potential – to moralize Crow as Satan in the first eight lines, where he is equated with the materialistic evils of

gold, diamond, alcohol and money. But if the reader tries to fulfil this
potential in the next octet he soon finds himself repudiating the whole
world of Nature, from which Man and Woman themselves grow. The
mechanical structure makes of the reading experience a merciless irony:
in the penultimate couplet, the reader is told that his initial response has
denied the possibility of the Redeemer, who is nothing more than Crow-
nature, developed. And if, like God in the last two lines, he goes
pridefully off in despair – refusing to make that gesture of renunciation,
'You win, Crow' – it is *he* who returns Crow to his most basic animal
level who endorses unwittingly the final savage image. The poem's
machine-like construction has the virtue of forcing the reader towards a
more brutally direct realization of the consequences of his interpretative
acts, and their origins in psychological dualism.

Elsewhere, the mechanical language focuses the equally mechanical
force of sexuality ('Lovesong'), and Crow's unalterable connection with
his true Creator, 'God's nameless hidden prisoner, whom he encounters
repeatedly but always in some unrecognisable form' ('Crow and Mama',
'Magical dangers', 'Revenge fable'). As before, any perception of an
independent human freedom outside the range of mechanical affinities is
a most serious lapse:

> 'He tried a step, then a step, and again a step –
> Every one scarred her face for ever . . .
>
> He jumped into the rocket and its trajectory
> Drilled clean through her heart he kept on.'
>
> ('Crow and Mama')

> 'Crow thought of intelligence –
> It turned the key against him and he tore at its fruitless bars.
> Crow thought of nature's stupor –
> And an oak tree grew out of his ear.
>
> ('Magical dangers')

> 'With all her babes in her arms, in ghostly weepings,
> She died.
>
> His head fell off like a leaf.'
>
> ('Revenge Fable')

Like the highly non-theological Christian God Hughes observes in Janos
Pilinszky's poems, this is a comfortless language, composed almost
entirely of negative attributes; denying the illusory freedoms and re-
births offered by 'poetic' language – Pilinszky's stylistic manipulations
falling within the domain of 'the Mirror' – it shows an absolute
determination not to yield to any possibilities beyond the materially
founded, the materially proven. So the return of language to its most
primitive, functional origins enforces the subject's confrontation of
Matter, of his own 'Essence'. The uncovering of its mechanical 'root'

refuses the flight into a formal fragment of the self (a literary personality), paradoxically forces that self to examine 'Reality' – 'inner' and 'outer' – as a set of fictions which have a provisional, potentially ironic, relationship with the material evidence. Poetic language in this case refines towards the 'open-ended' discourse Hughes ascribes to Vasko Popa

> The air of trial and error exploration, of an improvised language, the attempt to get near something for which he is almost having to invent the words in a total disregard for poetry or the normal conventions of discourse, goes with his habit of working in cycles of poems. He will trust no phrase with his meaning for more than six or seven words at a time before he corrects his tack with another phrase from a different direction. In the same way, he will trust no poem with his meaning for more than fifteen or so lines, before he tries again from a totally different direction with another poem. (Introduction to Vasko Popa's *Collected Poems*, p. 7)

The insufficiency of 'poetry' and 'the normal conventions of discourse', of art which 'remains stuck in aesthetics – [in which] the ugly is also "beautiful", even beastliness and evil shine forth enticingly in the false glamour of aesthetic beauty' (Jung, 'The Apollinian and the Dionysian', *Psychological Types*, p. 141), should be sufficiently obvious by now. But once a mechanical 'core' has been fully established, in language which cannot avert its gaze from Matter, the self can begin to improvise 'directions' into that unquestionable Reality, testing out conscious attitudes which may be more, or less, organic to it.

Two poems in particular provide a kind of threshold to the main body of investigation; 'Glimpse' and 'Owl's song':

Glimpse

'O leaves', Crow sang, trembling, 'O leaves –'

The touch of a leaf's edge at his throat
Guillotined further comment.
Nevertheless
Speechless he continued to stare at the leaves
Through the god's head instantly substituted.

The rhetorical indulgence of the invocation recalls a similar appeal in 'Gnat-psalm'. This 'aesthetic' addition to Matter is ironically reduced in the third line, but even then the illusion fostered by consciousness persists: the creative 'silencing' of the personality – a dominant strand of Central European poetry – apparent in 'Speechless', only occurs on the surface of consciousness. Any precipitate inflation of the self and language beyond the material roots is deliberately restrained in the phrase 'Through the god's head *instantly substituted*' (my italics). The reader is left in a typographic emptiness, a real silence created by the pitiless doubling of the poem's irony.

The same silence and the same emptiness follow the conclusion of 'Owl's song', where Owl is finally confronted by the resurgent echo of his *own* singing, and the 'experience of a world that he has defensively filled with himself' (in Gifford and Roberts, *Ted Hughes: A critical study*, p. 108). The poem expresses the type of silence Simone Weil perceived as the essential preface to any contact with divinity. 'He who is capable not only of crying out but also of listening will hear the answer' and the reader forced to 'obey' that recognition finds the tightly packed print of the 'song' fragmenting into empty space, until in the last line Owl's singing appears to be surrounded – without even the formal comfort of a full-stop – by blank silence, and the depth of the unprinted page. Instead of attempting to rival the clamour of the words with our own critical 'noise', we start *listening* to the anti-aesthetic silence beyond them. As the French poet Mallarmé says,

> in the tiniest and most scattered stopping points on the page, when the lines of chance have been vanquished word by word, the blanks unfailingly return; before they were gratuitous; now they are essential; and now at last it is clear that nothing lies beyond; now silence is genuine and just.
> (*Oeuvres*, p. 387)

Such poems possess an almost talismanic quality within the book, affording a charm-like protection against the fictions invented by 'poetry': they enable the poet to establish an ironic perspective on the aestheticism of 'Crow and the birds' and the emotional pathos of 'That moment', which threaten to 'close' the world 'forever' into either the exquisite realm of aesthetics, or the indulged futility of a Beckettian, or Sartrean landscape. In the latter case, Crow's super-simple, super-ugly activity – 'Crow had to start searching for something to eat' – puts a stop to the false, though intoxicating, glamour of the elegiac impulse, bringing up a 'shadow'-instinct – the urge to eat, and thus survive – which contradicts that limited 'I' and its world-idea. For any reader who has clung too hard to that idea (in either poem) in true dualistic fashion, the message from 'below' will be proportionately more savage, more apparently 'inhuman'.

Five seminal poems, 'Crow Tyrannosaurus', 'Crow on the beach', 'Crow's nerve fails', 'Crow and the sea' and 'Crow's account of the battle', centre on Crow's developing endeavour to become a Man, and witness the transformation of super-simple, super-ugly language from a mechanical register of our material origins (language as a machine, 'lowest down') into an instrument of exploration, continually sensitive to its own peculiar errors – the sprawling mass of stylistic certainties, illusory re-births, aesthetic possibilities of the 'Word', etc. – at every verbal stride. 'Crow on the beach' may be used as a starting-point:

Hearing the shingle explode, seeing it skip,
Crow sucked his tongue.
Seeing sea-grey mash a mountain of itself
Crow tightened his goose-pimples.
Feeling spray from the sea's root nothinged on his crest
Crow's toes gripped the wet pebbles.
When the smell of the whale's den, the gulfing of the crab's last prayer,
Gimletted in his nostril
He grasped he was on earth.

That final statement lies at the exact midpoint of the poem, syntactically and psychologically. Before that break, the sea's effects on Crow's senses (hearing, sight, sensation, smell) are focused in four 'materially' disciplined sentences. Here language does not have to keep to its bare mechanical foundation, because Crow's responses are not discordant with the 'Matter' of the poem: he keeps faith with the collective 'world of things' rather than trying to escape relatedness with them, gesturing towards his potential status as a complete human being – in Gurdjieff's terms, primitive 'Essence' (Crow's usual condition) developing towards 'Individuality'. It is this success of the creative exploration, improvising its way forward through Crow, that encourages a richer, more confident music to push up from the simple–ugly root. Some of Hughes' most characteristic techniques re-surface without any sign of distress, in the four-beat Anglo-Saxon line (line 1), the alliterative latticing of the natural experience and the accent upon the audial-muscular properties of language – for example, the fluid 's' consonants literally 'break' explosively over the labials of 'skip' and 'explode' – indicating that relations on the Conscious–Unconscious border are harmonious, that one is fully receptive to the other. But the moment of satisfactory negotiation begins to lose its transparency with the final, ominous verb 'grasped':

> He knew he grasped
> Something fleeting
> Of the sea's ogreish outcry and convulsion.
> He knew he was the wrong listener unwanted
> To understand or help –
>
> His utmost gaping of brain in his tiny skull
> Was just enough to wonder, about the sea,
>
> What could be hurting so much?

The passage from the physiological 'gripped' to the ambiguous 'grasped' suggests a growth of the abstract awareness which becomes fatally self-important with the insurgence of 'He *knew* he grasped . . .' (my italics). Crow's Tricksterish 'eagerness to learn' is brusquely cut off by the

movement outwards to the seemingly autonomous world of conceptualization, the fictive personality, which may have been anticipated by the
increasingly obtrusive presence of 'Poetry' in lines 7–8. In the second half
of the poem, the mind is 'conscious' only of alienation from the natural
world, and its possible hostility. It is, however, a crucial, if 'invisible',
advance on Hughes' earlier practice that language should return
modestly – in the given psychological conditions – to its much simpler,
uglier base with the last three lines, rather than re-double its strident
efforts to hold the original vision intact. Crow is again exposing the
negative print of 'consciousness' in the poem: Gurdjieff's 'impetus of
knowledge' is only accessible to the primitive awareness of lines 1–8,
which lies outside the normal range of the personality, and if the reader
finds that range inevitable (as Gifford and Roberts do) he ensures that the
alienated condition of lines 9–16 becomes a tragic, unalterable condition.
He has to read experience 'upside down', as it were, reversing the force
of all his usual, self-protective conscious interpretations of it. In those
circumstances, Crow's Trickster-like *dual image* appears in view: *both* his
embodiment of all the negative consequences of 'consciousness' we tend
to ignore, *and* his potential image of the divine nature, his redeeming
aspect as Saviour.

'Crow and the sea' is a companion-piece to 'Crow on the beach'; it also
narrates his encounter with the most alien, least formulated element on
earth. Up until three lines from the end of the poem, we are given a
conclusive account of the defeat of all the distinctively human 'directions'
Crow tries out as containing formulations of the sea. 'Ignorance', 'Talk',
'Sympathy', 'Hatred' and 'Co-existence', all serve only to intensify the
sheer opaqueness or density of the material world, readily engaged by
the 'mechanical' reflexes of the super-simple, super-ugly diction. Crow
explores the ultimate 'freedom' of the fictive personality in the penultimate line, the same freedom invoked by Kingsley Amis and John
Holloway in the Movement response to Nature: 'Finally/ He turned his
back and he marched away from the sea'; but it is exactly at this point
that the image of spiritual self-sufficiency is challenged by its 'shadow'
material image, also at its further point of development – 'when the iron
nails remain fixed in the wounds, with an eternal iron fixity, and neither
hands nor feet can move' (Janos Pilinsky, *Selected Poems*, Introduction
p. 10): 'As a crucified man cannot move.'

The reader himself is spreadeagled on the stark irreconcilable polarity
of the opposite images, one apparently from 'Spirit', the other from
'Matter', and he must choose between them: the choice is concentrated in
the reading of the last line, as either (1) 'He is free to march away from
the sea as a crucified man isn't' or (2) 'He turned his back and marched

away from the sea to the same extent that a crucified man is capable of performing the same action.' The first reading has some ferocious consequences. Identification with that 'freedom' really strips the crucifixion-image of its last vestiges of human relevance, it dramatizes the pathology of the symbol within the living fabric of the poem and our response to it. The symbol – which is capable of miraculously reconciling us to the blind mechanisms of Nature–nature – is doomed, foreclosed into another version of its 'senseless' condition at the end of 'The contender'. Crow is condemned to his most primitive, animal value 'Flying the black flag of himself' ('Crow blacker than ever'), and to the most unconscious state of self-will.

In the second reading, however, Crow's action is ironic, and performed in full consciousness. We have already observed signs of that consciousness in Crow's growing awareness of his own inadequacy in lines 7–12. In the space between lines 14 and 15, Crow does become a Man, holding to his biological allegiances and reclaiming the living force of the crucifixion-symbol. Only in that symbol does he approximate his potential, 'developed' image as Saviour: virtually the entire process of the poem – and much of *Crow* as a whole – is anticipated by the comments Simone Weil makes in her essay 'Additional pages on the love of God and affliction' (from *On Science, Necessity and the Love of God*). Here is her description of the effects of Affliction, which represents acceptance of the knowledge that all natural and psychological life is ruled by a blind mechanism, Necessity, a force as brutal, 'as rigorous as that of gravity' (*Intimations of Christianity among the Ancient Greeks*, p. 194):

> Affliction is essentially a destruction of personality, a lapse into anonymity . . . it is the pulverization of the soul by the mechanical brutality of circumstances. . . . Affliction is something which imposes itself upon a man quite against his will. Its essence, the whole thing it is defined by, is the horror, the revulsion of the whole being, which it inspires in its victim. . . . So long as the play of circumstance around us leaves our being almost intact, or only half impaired, we more or less believe that the world is created and controlled by ourselves. It is affliction that reveals, suddenly and to our very great surprise, that we are totally mistaken. ('Additional pages on the love of God and affliction', pp. 94–6)

Because of his proximity to Matter, Crow is continually being 'corrected' by Affliction throughout the book, being shown that – as in the present poem – the soul 'is a dead thing, something analogous to matter . . . the thing we believe to be our self is as ephemeral and automatic a product of external circumstances as the form of a sea-wave' (*ibid.*). As surely as Simone Weil defines the sea's effects on Crow in the term 'Affliction', so she goes on to predict the 'first reading' with equal accuracy:

Thought is so revolted by affliction that it is as incapable of bringing itself voluntarily to conceive it as an animal, generally speaking, is incapable of suicide. Thought never knows affliction except by constraint. Unless constrained by experience, it is impossible to believe that everything in the soul – all its thoughts and feelings, its every attitude towards ideas, people and the universe, and, above all, the most intimate attitude of the being towards itself – that all this is entirely at the mercy of circumstances. . . . Thought can never really be constrained; evasion by falsehood is always open to it. When thought finds itself, through the force of circumstance, brought face to face with affliction, it takes immediate refuge in lies, like an animal dashing for cover. (*ibid.*, p. 91)

If the reader is able to uphold the Crucifixion-image at the end of the poem as a desirable conclusion, he must be able to do so in terms similar to those proposed by Weil:

There is only one cross; it is the whole of that necessity by which the infinity of space and time is filled and which, in given circumstances, can be concentrated upon the atom that any one of us is, and totally pulverize it. To bear one's cross is to bear the knowledge that one is entirely subject to this blind necessity in every part of one's being, except for one point in the soul which is so secret that it is inaccessible to consciousness. However cruelly a man suffers, if there is some part of his being still intact and if he is not fully conscious that it has escaped only by chance and remains at every moment at the mercy of chance, he has no part in the Cross. (*ibid.*, p. 89)

As clearly as in any other poem in the volume, Crow is a mirror to our own response: if we find him heroically 'free' in the action of the penultimate line, he mocks us in its successor; if we acquiesce in the motionlessness of the final line – into which the 'problematics of freedom' do not obtrude – he shows us the way forward, and the religious termination of the quest. Again, within these contradictory frames of reference, he may be perceived as either the destroyer or creator of value.

This quarrel in the perception of Matter – and in the perception of the image that Crow presents – is taken up in 'Crow Tyrannosaurus'. In the first five stanzas of the poem, both the mechanical core of Nature and its consideration in language – the repetitive structure – are prominent. Nature is a 'cortege/ Of mourning and lament',

And the dog was a bulging filterbag
Of all the deaths it had gulped for the flesh and the bones.
It could not digest their screeching finales.
Its shapeless cry was a blort of all those voices.

The descent into the super-simple, super-ugly ground of language is here conducted through an inspired subversion of latinate diction; the dog's inability to disguise the material horror of the 'outcry' of its victims is precisely enacted as a failure of language, for the genteel 'digest' and the theatrical 'finales' tend to shrink the horror that the super-ugly 'blort' cannot even pretend to 'contain'. Beastliness has pierced the veil of language, and there is nothing that false 'poetic' glamour can do to restore its cosmetic unity. Crow's initial response is a variation on his 'marching away from the sea' in 'Crow and the sea':

> Crow thought 'Alas
> Alas ought I
> To stop eating
> And try to become the light?'
>
> But his eye saw a grub. And his head, trapsprung, stabbed.
> And he listened
> And he heard
> Weeping
>
> Grubs grubs He stabbed He stabbed
> Weeping
> Weeping
>
> Weeping he walked and stabbed
>
> Thus came the eye's
>   roundness
>   the ear's
>   deafness.

Revolted by the realization of Necessity, thought takes evasive action, attempting to escape into the dualistic falsehood of the rationalization – though once again, the false option opened by the need to explore is checked by *Crow*'s self-regulating irony. The 'Glimpse'-like lyrical potential of 'Alas/ Alas', the pathos of the concretization of Crow's 'sympathizing' impulse in a kind of vertical axis, giving each repetition ('And he listened/ And he heard . . . Weeping/ Weeping') a particular emotional weight, is annihilated by syntax that works like a 'mechanical' tripwire: the third, climactic 'Weeping' triggers, so to speak, the material response of the verb ('he walked and stabbed') and only ever exists in utter subjection to it. The whole construction recalls the movement of 'Thrushes' from *Lupercal*:

> No indolent procrastinations and no yawning stares,
> No sighs or head-scratchings. Nothing but bounce and stab
> And a ravening second.

Unlike 'Thrushes', however, in the present poem no further autonomous 'human' activity is permitted after this revelation. It finishes with a 'fateful, step-by-step evolution' (Gifford and Roberts, *Ted Hughes: A critical study*, p. 144) in the last line which evokes the simple, undeveloped human fate Gurdjieff describes in Ouspensky's *In Search of the Miraculous*, his realization that

> Man is a machine. All his deeds, actions, words, thoughts, feelings, convictions, opinions, and habits are the results of external influences,

external impressions. Out of himself a man cannot produce a single
thought, a single action. (p. 21)

And as Crow discovers in 'Crow Tyrannosaurus', 'it is one thing to
understand with the mind and another thing to feel it with one's "whole
mass", to be really convinced that it is so and never forget it' (*ibid.*).

That conviction deepens, if anything, in the poem 'Crow's nerve fails',
which seems to 'improve' 'The black beast' in much the same way that
'Crow and the sea' was an improvement of the Crucifixion-image first
encountered in 'The contender'; Crow's consciousness in the 'The black
beast' confined him to the typical mechanical contours of language when
he projected the Black Beast as an external enemy, the primitive action of
a dualistic consciousness. It is imperative that the reader detects a
development between this illusion and Crow's assumption of responsibility in 'Crow's nerve fails', locating the Black Beast within himself:

> Crow, feeling his brain slip,
> Finds his every feather the fossil of a murder . . .
>
> Is he the archive of their accusations?
> Or their ghostly purpose, their pining vengeance?
>   Or their unforgiven prisoner?

But the reader – like the poet – has to remain continually sensitive to his
own errors, interpreting without disturbing the silence, in order to
identify the 'failure of nerve' which occurs in the final four lines:

> He cannot be forgiven.
>
> His prison is the earth. Clothed in his conviction,
> Trying to remember his crimes
>
> Heavily he flies.

It is here, as the flexible, pragmatic questioning – the energy of
exploration – is exchanged for the fixed attitude of consciousness, that
Crow's error becomes serious; he presumes to answer his own questions
too readily, and only succeeds in inventing a Kafkaesque existential
situation, another false 'objectivity' of the world. Crow has to sustain his
'eagerness to learn' and keep space open for the 'collective' revelation
permanently: Gurdjieff's assertion is not a cynical, summarizing
reduction of the nature of Reality, but the necessary foundation for
further self-development.

Two poems, 'Crow's account of the battle', and 'Crow's account of St
George', distil the educational force of Matter dramatized within this
group of poems. In both instances, Crow's narrative detachment has
been earned by the ruthlessness of his contact with raw 'elementals' in
'Crow and the beach', 'Crow and the sea' and 'Crow Tyrannosaurus',
particularly. 'Crow's account of St. George' is the more straightforward

of the two, disallowing the negative emphasis of the Manichaean 'Holy Warrior' once and for all in Hughes' praxis – when the Warrior-image next returns in *Cave Birds* he will already have surrendered his aggressive–defensive weapons and ego-armour – and providing a more complete antidote to the experienced illusion of 'The black beast' than even 'Crow's nerve fails'. Our sense of the moral value of the poet's *cyclic* arrangement of poems is confirmed: in this exploratory environment, the image of Crow himself – and those he presents – may be refracted in a number of directions, each with its own ethical potential. It is the reader's own nature that decides the truth of the Crucifixion-image between 'The contender' and 'Crow and the sea', or the location of the Black Beast – Jung's inferior shadow-self – between 'The black beast', 'Crows nerve fails' and 'Crow's account of St. George'. Whatever our interpretative impulse, he faithfully reflects its consequences in the condition of the 'whole' psyche.

'Crow's account of the battle' creates further opportunity for the reader's self-observation *within* the reading experience of the text. The first half of the poem both laments and satirizes the process by which human responsibility for the wartime catalogue of 'unlimited technical violence and absurd death' has been shifted on to 'Theorems', 'Universal Laws' and the justifying 'mishmash of scripture and physics'. The strident tone appears to invite a response of moral outrage, but the second half of the poem suggests that a condemnation of the 'theories' which justify and facilitate mass destruction is not the whole, or even the most important point of the piece:

> When the smoke cleared it became clear
> this had happened too often before
> And was going to happen too often in future
> And happened too easily . . .
> And shooting someone through the midriff
> Was too like striking a match
> Too like potting a snooker ball
> Too like tearing up a bill
> Blasting the whole world to bits
> Was too like slamming a door
> Too like dropping in a chair
> Exhausted with rage
> Too like being blown to bits yourself
> Which happened too easily
> With too like no consequences.

The Logos-illusion runs deeper, it includes not only the belief that humanity can validate or explain war by 'theory', but also the delusion that *it is at all possible* for Man to assume responsibility for his actions given the current 'state of negotiations' within the individual and collective culture – i.e. while he still believes that he can prevent holocausts by a simple shift of conscious attitude. Moral outrage is as superfluous to the reality of the situation as the 'theoretical constructs' it indicts: *both* exemplify the illusion that Man consciously organizes his own world, an illusion defeated by the mechanicalness of 'circumstances', and the 'vicarious' similes in language, narrated in the second half of the poem. The reader who comes to this recognition in the poem is, in Hughes' words, 'thoroughly stripped of any spiritual or mental proprietorship' (Introduction to Popa's *Collected Poems*, p. 4): the poem becomes an educational tool when it demands the seemingly rational, humane response of the first thirty-nine lines in order to demonstrate its irrelevance to the mechanical 'helplessness in the circumstances' – the 'shadow' reading of Reality. At the end of the poem, we get the revealed truth of 'Crow's nerve fails' without its failure of nerve, its *existentialist* conscious addition:

> So the survivors stayed.
> And the earth and the sky stayed.
> Everything took the blame.
> Not a leaf flinched, nobody smiled.

Nothing flinches, the burden of guilt is carried, and the survivors, like Crow, the poet and hopefully the reader stay on, still 'trying to find out what does exist, and what the conditions really are' (Popa Introduction, *ibid.*, p. 4), without premature 'closure' of the world.

Because of its nature as a 'Creative Myth', the Crow-narrative regularly envisages this exploration in its widest metaphysical aspect. Poems such as 'A childish prank', 'A horrible religious error', 'Crow blacker than ever' and 'Apple tragedy' exploit the Genesis story directly, 'negotiating' on the level of the *Imago Dei* rather in the psychological or linguistic dimension. Once it is recognized that all three levels are simply different 'octaves' of the same exploratory 'chord' the usual difficulty with Myth, the suspicion that it constitutes an evasion of the 'contingencies of history', just evaporates: there is no question of escaping historical contingency through the hypnotic powers of Myth, it simply approaches the *conception* of 'history' from a different, internal point of view. For Hughes, the levelling and re-construction of self, language and Creator-image – in which myth participates – *is* a cultural, historical necessity, though its sense of 'history' manifested in the individual and collective *psychology* is scarcely congruent with a Marxist understanding of the term. One cannot imagine, for example, Terry Eagleton acquiescing in Hughes' original contention that 'How things are between man and his idea of the Divinity determines everything in his life, the quality and connectedness of every feeling and thought, and the meaning of every action.'[2]

Myths are in this sense not only 'historical' but also essentially *pragmatic*, concerned with 'Solving little [psychological] problems' ('Ted Hughes and *Gaudete*', in Faas, *Ted Hughes*, p. 213). The little mythic fable or 'visionary anecdote' is a natural extension of the kind of folktale surrealism we observed in *Wodwo*, wiping out the fortifications of the Ego and its language in the dream-flow in order to achieve a register of the objective psyche, direct. 'A childish prank' begins, in fact, by stating the problem to be solved:

> Man's and woman's bodies lay without souls,
> Dully gaping, foolishly staring, inert
> On the flowers of Eden.
> God pondered.
>
> The problem was so great, it dragged him asleep.

The image of the Creator presented is 'corrupt', deficient; having separated himself from Matter as Pure Thought or 'Spirit', he proves quite unable to breathe material life into his creatures. It is left to Crow, whose participation in Matter is undoubted, to finish what God has started:

> Crow laughed.
> He bit the Worm, God's only Son,
> Into two writhing halves.
>
> He stuffed into man the tail half
> With the wounded end hanging out.
>
> He stuffed the head half head first into woman
> And it crept in deeper and up
> To peep out through her eyes
> Calling its tail-half to join up quickly, quickly
> Because O it was painful.

This is, so to speak, Crow's 'compensation' of the incomplete Divine Image. His solution provokes a crisis of readership, equally: the reader immediately finds himself 'writhing' on the mental conjunction of the 'Worm' with 'God's only Son', two concepts he customarily keeps discrete. If he persists in that action, holding the physical–sexual serpent absolutely separate from the spiritual–mental 'Redeemer', he interprets the radically sexual human condition created by Crow's problem-solving impulse as tragic, he *invents* the tragic tone of the next seven lines. *Since then*, every sexual coupling can only appear as a fateful repetition, a mechanistic attempt to soothe the original pains of alienation. The 'tragic' reading is confirmed in the statuesque symmetry of the following stanza:

> Man awoke being dragged across the grass.
> Woman awoke to see him coming.
> Neither knew what had happened.

In this reading, Crow's last-line laughter will only consolidate his status in the reader's eyes as a particularly demonic version of Satan, who has somehow managed to disturb the Creation in a way unintended by God. The poem, likewise, is conceived as a purely negative, moralistic satire of the contemporary lapse of 'spiritual' values.

But the tension of 'He bit the Worm, God's only Son' may still hold in the mind, unresolved, and Crow's dual image gives access to another necessary, though 'potential' reading. In alchemy the serpent was frequently identified with the Spirit Mercurius, who split into two forms, according to an established tradition – his crude or material form (*mercurius crudus*) and his higher, developed form (*mercurius Philosophorum*) in which he appears as a golden lightning snake, hovering in the sky, though at present inactive (see Jung's essay 'A study in the process of individuation', from *The Archetypes of the Collective Unconscious*, pp. 290–354). Two Gnostic sects, the Ophites and the Sethians, venerated the serpent as the cause of Gnosis in mankind, which is the reason why the demiurge Ialdabaôth – severally the 'ramshackle despot' of *Crow*, the God of Genesis and Krogon in Hughes' *Orghast* mythology – cast it out of Heaven in fury. In Sethian mythology, the Invisible Creator beyond the demiurge assumes the form of a snake when he descends into the material world, so that the serpent is received in its aspect of mediator, a symbol connecting Spirit and Matter. In this 'remote' reading the Worm *is* God's only son, but unacknowledged – and thus imprisoned within the 'primitivism' of the image. On closer inspection, we may discover elements within the poem which erode this confinement: the pathos of 'Because O it was painful' is mechanically over-run by the lack of any punctuation, rejecting the luxury of the 'tragic' assessment – i.e. its historically inevitable character. Resistance to the 'orthodox' account of Creation in the first reading, the account of the Logos-God who is fortuitously 'asleep' when Evil in the form of Crow–Satan and the Worm intrude, also entails resistance to the illusion in language, and the sort of ritual music which could close the mind in the encircling spell of Tragedy. Crow's laughter in the final line has the same effect; it is ironic, but fundamentally *moral* laughter, because it annihilates the tragic assessment of human sexuality on which the first reading is founded. The pathos of that assessment, as in 'View of a pig' is 'off the point', irresponsibly obstructing the realization that sexual force at its highest point of refinement opens directly on to 'Spirit', a realization which esoteric teachers like Gurdjieff, Aivanhov and many Sufi Masters all attest. Aivanhov goes so far as to say that

> According to the science of symbols, the Heavenly Father is linked to the brain; Christ is linked to the solar plexus (which is the real heart); the Holy Spirit is linked to love and to the genital organs. For the first time, I reveal this mystery to you: the Holy Spirit is linked to love and to the genital organs. So in order not to commit errors and then be punished, we must learn to have the right attitude to these organs which God has given us. (*Sexual Force or the Winged Dragon*, p. 129)

The force of 'myth' within the poem is lucid and undeflected: the prejudices of the metaphysical concept of the Divine, a psychological attitude towards Matter and their implicit consequences in language are all effectively challenged. The poem starts 'pulling the self together' by giving both Crow's destructive value and hinting at his potentially affirmative contribution. The problems are confronted in their widest aspect, and solved – if we have ears to hear the solution.

The difficulty of a morally positive response to the serpent, which was a problem of readership in 'A childish prank', becomes the explicit subject of 'A horrible religious error'; the snake's appearance magnetically attracts some of the most potent, though materially accurate 'music' in the entire book:

> When the serpent emerged, earth-bowel brown,
> From the hatched atom
> With its alibi self twisted around it
>
> Lifting a long neck
> And balancing that deaf and mineral stare
> The sphinx of the final fact
> And flexing on that double flameflicker tongue
> A syllable like the rustling of the spheres
>
> God's grimace writhed, a leaf in the furnace.

The sinuous audial/visceral/muscular power of such music quite overwhelms the limited authority of God's semantic 'Word'. As in 'Crow on the beach', it emerges only when confident of its secure binding to Matter, by its very nature constraining the flight into a stylistic ideal; the music is in fact all the more impressive for its limited, though morally apposite appearances in the book. The representation of 'the world of final reality' has the important effect of casting into relief the dangers inherent in Crow and the super-simple, super-ugly language associated with him in the last four lines of the poem:

> But Crow only peered.
>   Then took a step or two forward,
> Grabbed this creature by the slackskin nape,
> Beat the hell out of it, and ate it.

If Crow remains fixed on the most primitive level of 'Essence', and the simple–ugly language starts to ossify in its mechanical, purely 'destructive' aspect, the poet's activity becomes as morally culpable as the original impulse to sustain the glamour of the poetry–dance, deprived of its reference to 'humanity', culture and his own condition. For Hughes' ironic, ethical vigilance to be truly embracing, it has to go beyond identification with all its fictions, however 'bracing' and 'purgative', in the interests of exploring the possibilities of *evolution*. The ethically vigilant voice ends up narrating one of the incidents in which Crow misunderstands his relationship with the Creator, and so mismanages the entire encounter. The 'mythic' fable of the poem exploits one of its subdivisions, 'riddle' – the serpent is the 'sphynx of the final fact' – to enforce the ideal of 'serious play' we noted in the surrealism of *Wodwo*: the poet *has* to play, the play-instinct arises from the 'inner necessity' of the riddle's pressure upon him carrying him beyond the 'tragic' conflict of opposites into the 'neutralizing' third position, and the more *human* response demonstrated by 'Your will is our peace' and the *consciousness* of the poem's title. 'The creative mind plays with the object it loves', and the poetic persona more successfully 'tries to become a Man' in his response to the serpent, where Crow for the moment falls short, surrendering consciousness unconditionally to the animal cells.

In the uncollected poem 'A lucky folly', Crow, lacking the usual Ego – 'battlements' – solves the problem of menacing Dragon and screaming maiden with a 'deadpan playful' device of his own, his own body-music providing an outlet for the enraged energies:

> . . . Crow cut holes in his nose. He fingered this flute
> Dancing, with an occasional kick at his drum.
>
> The dragon was dumbfounded – he was manic
> for music. He began to grin.
> He too began to dance. And in horror and awe
> The maiden danced with him incredulous.
> 'O do not stop', she whispered, 'O do not stop'.
> So the three danced – and Crow dared not stop –
>
> To the creaking pipe and the kicked drum.
>
> But, at last, Crow's puff ran out and he stopped.
> The maiden paled.
> But the dragon wept. The dragon licked Crow's foot
> He slobbered Crow's fingers –
> 'More, more' he cried, and 'Be my God'.
>   (Workshop 10, 1970).

The element of ironic laughter threaded through 'A horrible religious error', 'Crow blacker than ever' and 'A childish prank' becomes a

dominant influence in 'Apple tragedy', a witty re-invention of the eating
of the fruit in fable in Genesis: the original sin is traced back to God's
creation of cider out of apple juice, a sin which is first masked, then
denied by its projection onto the 'innocent' serpent:

> Now whenever the snake appears she [Eve] screeches
> 'Here it comes again! Help! Help!'
> Then Adam smashes a chair on its head,
> And God says: 'I am well pleased'
>
> And everything goes to hell.

The laughter generated by this conclusion is also the subject of two other
poems, 'In laughter' and 'Crows's battle fury'. It is not like Beckett's
notion of absurd humour, the hopelessly reflexive, dianoetic 'laugh
laughing at the laugh', but humour attuned to its moral function; in a
sense it is the ultimate form of the Crowish irony which generates a
'fertile chaos', by remorselessly stripping all the illusions of psychologically or culturally fixed 'ideas of the world'. In 'A childish prank' and
'Crow blacker than ever', it guards against the 'heroifying' impulse, the
moral perversity of tragedy. Likewise, in 'Apple tragedy' its energy
over-runs the taboo-solemnity of the Christian myth of original sin.
Tragedy is only *just* when considered as the equal and opposite partner of
annihilating comedy, which reviews the inevitability of the *mechanical*
situation and at the same time prepares for a new direction into the
'matter' presented. Ironic humour keeps space open for an *improvisation*
of the self, resists its premature 'crystallization'. So 'Crow's battle fury'
describes the experience of laughter in terms which draw the psychological development that occurs through a shattering and reconstitution of
self:

> A hair's breadth out of the world
>
>> (With his glared off face glued back into position
>> A dead man's eyes plugged back into his sockets
>> A dead man's heart screwed in under his ribs
>> His tattered guts stitched back into position
>> His shattered brain covered with a steel cowl)
>
> He comes forward a step,
>   and a step,
>   and a step –

It hardly needs to be added that this direct connection between comedy
and moral process rules out any sense of 'comic relief', a temporary
relaxation from the struggle with outer and inner circumstances.

The concentrated focus on the *Imago Dei* naturally invited by myth
powers Crow's repeated efforts to locate his true Creator, God's
'nameless hidden prisoner'. Some of the initial encounters have already

been noted: 'Crow and Mama', 'Revenge fable', and 'Magical dangers' all evidence Crow's (or the protagonist's) attempt to 'get rid of the mother'. In each poem, Crow fails, and is either warned or corrected. But the poems which describe an advance in Crow's consciousness, or a development of the *creative* potential within his double-image, inch him towards a discovery of his own 'higher' value through the objective symbol of the Goddess, to whom Crow addresses the prayer 'Crow's undersong'. As in the background story Hughes details at readings (see Sagar, *The Art of Ted Hughes*, p. 235), Crow's task is to transform the Ogress into a beautiful maiden, and resolve the 'dualistic' riddle presented in 'Fragment of an ancient tablet'. 'Crow's undersong' constitutes a living, poetic bridge built from 'below' to 'above'; it celebrates the God, or Goddess 'of absences and negative attributes' Hughes perceives in Pilinszky's work; more than that, it utilizes the language of negative attributes which is so typical of the *Crow* adventure as the vehicle of its celebration:

> She cannot come all the way
>
> She comes as far as water no further
>
> She comes with the birth push
> Into eyelashes into nipples the fingertips
> She comes as far as blood and to the tips of hair
> She comes to the fringe of voice
> She stays
> Even after life even among the bones.

Language not only strips its lyrical resources down to the mechanical 'bone' – the 'material' repetitive structure which operates in so many of the other poems – it corrects its celebration at the turn of every stanza, and even the expressive rhythm of the single line is subjected to relentless qualification:

> She comes singing/ she cannot manage an instrument
> She comes too cold/ afraid of clothes
> And too slow/ with eyes wincing frightened.

The act of poetic celebration takes place in language which is anti-poetic – in Rozewicz's sense – its very form 'distrusts' the tyranny of aesthetic words or rhythms which have their own idea of how the act of celebration ought to be conducted; if we substitute 'aesthetic surface' for 'Christian Culture', and 'language' for 'the animal', Hughes' perception of Pilinszky's achievement perfectly fits his own poem:

> Though the [Christian Culture] has been stripped off so brutally, and the
> true condition of [the animal] exposed in its ugliness, and words have lost
> their meaning – yet out of that rise the poems, whose words are manifestly

crammed with meaning. Something has been said which belies neither the reality nor the silence. (*Selected Poems*, Introduction, p. 12)

In reality, of course, both versions of Hughes' statement are simultaneous, or interdependent. The song steadfastly resists the specific, 'individualizing' qualities of a poetic false personality, and so pays homage to 'what does not exist', keeping in touch with the truth of Marsyas' undifferentiated 'Aaa' rather than the endless fine-tuning of Apollo's instrumental music. The poem's whole method is at one with the collective, material nature of its subject-matter; the 'She' of 'Crow's undersong' likewise refuses any individualization into the characteristics of the autonomous human world. The 'specifically human' is no more the exact centre of her nature than the personality is the exact centre of the self, or aesthetics the exact centre of language. Throughout the first twenty lines, 'She' continually comes to the fringe of human discourse without entering it fully:

She comes with the birth push . . .

She comes as far as the blood and to the tips of the hair
She comes to the fringe of voice . . .

She comes singing she cannot manage an instrument
She comes too cold afraid of clothes . . .

She comes sluttish she cannot keep house . . .

She comes dumb she cannot manage words.

The reader will only feel 'betrayed' by the progression 'birth push' – 'singing' – 'sluttish' – 'dumb', however, if he has clung too tenaciously to his ego-system and its understanding, neglecting the objective image of the whole which Crow tentatively suggested, and which the Female concretely embodies:

She brings petals in their nectar fruits in their plush
She brings a cloak of feathers an animal rainbow
She brings her favourite furs and these are her speeches.

It is this removal of the *Imago Dei* into the collective or 'invisible' which creates the loving distance Simone Weil spoke of in her essay 'The love of God and affliction'.

Even in its formal climax – the last three lines – Hughes' language continues to make 'audible meanings without disturbing the silence – making no mistakes, but with no hope of finality, continuing to explore' (Introduction to Popa's *Collected Poems*, p. 3), modifying the 'hope' within a double negative, the considered weight of the line-spacing (the 'true' silence) and the final parenthetical realization:

If there had been no hope she would not have come

And there would have been no crying in the city

(There would have been no city).

Lyricism, if it exists at all, has to be based not on the facile optimism often associated with the word 'hope' but on the revealed truth of that final statement which, as Hughes says, 'has the one Almightiness that matters'.

The symbol of the 'terrible' or 'loving' Mother is potent both as an undercurrent tunnelling through *Crow* itself, and as a central element in Hughes' background narrative machinery. She appears in her 'terrible' Ogress-like aspect when the conscious hero's fear of Ego-loss is paramount. When, on the other hand, he allows his arms to be nailed to the cross of the maternal tree ('Crow and the sea'), it is a crushing defeat of the Ego and refinement of his animal nature.

The current status of the Mother-symbol, and its potential for transformation, could really be used to plot the moral position of every poem in *Crow*. The duality of the symbol is explicit in 'Two Eskimo songs', the penultimate poems in the volume. 'Fleeing from eternity', for instance, narrates a tale which helps to explain the origin of the Female's destructive aspect: Man, confronted by the endless natural cycle of death and replacement, suffers the self-torments occasioned by Egoism, his wish to stop the cycle by asserting his own permanent value. He exchanges the individual, or even formal, mechanisms of 'eyes' and 'mouth' in order to possess the women's song which, properly, sings through everything; his action is directly analogous to Krogon's imprisonment of the energies of Sun and Moa in Hughes' *Orghast* mythology, which *prepares* Moa's increasingly frenzied and violent revenges, reducing the value of her image to its most primitive level: at the end of the poem, 'The Woman felt cheated.'

'How water began to play' shows the opposite 'direction' into the same physical reality, whereby the delusion of Ego-hood is snuffed out by the repeated contact with Matter, the individualizing urge of 'Water wanted to live' by an awareness of its objective allegiances, the 'higher' value of the image:

It came weeping back it wanted to die
Till it had no weeping left
It lay at the bottom of all things
Utterly worn out utterly clear.

Only this awareness is capable of the 'serious play' Jung commented upon, and which composes the very title of the poem.

Hughes has said of *Crow*, 'My idea was to reduce my style to the simplest clear cell – then regrow a wholeness and richness organically

from that point'. There can be little doubt concerning the integrity of
that effort, operating in all its various dimensions. The images of poetic
language, the self, and the Creator are all reduced, and from that 'utterly
worn out' base, reconstruction begins. The project is necessarily incomplete within the volume, and several of the questions Crow is asked by
the terrifying Female in Hughes' folktale narrative are only answered in
Cave Birds. That book is the logical continuation of the *Crow* adventure
(its first limited edition appeared in 1975, three years after the publication
of *Crow*). Janos Pilinszky's 'The passion' beautifully describes the moral
logic of that continuity:

> Only the warmth of the slaughter-house,
> its geranium-pungency, its soft shellac,
> only the sun exists.
>
> In the glass-cased silence
> the butcher-boys wash down. Yet what has happened
> somehow cannot even now finish.

CHAPTER 7

———— • ————

GAUDETE

Gaudete, Hughes' first published full-length narrative poem, appeared in 1977, a year before the publication of *Cave Birds*. The germinal seed of the narrative idea – an Anglican minister who suffers mental catastrophe resulting in a torrential release of sexual (i.e. 'elemental') activity – had clearly staked an embryonic claim in Hughes' imagination well before this, as early as 1966 in the dramatized verse of *The Burning of the Brothel*. But the specific contours of *Gaudete* really solidified with 'a series of actual dreams connected with the mythopoeic narrative behind *Crow*' (Faas, *Ted Hughes: The unaccommodated universe*, p. 123), and it is this connection which Hughes re-emphasized in response to ones of Faas' queries:

> *Gaudete* obviously is connected to *Crow*. *Crow*, in full, with big developments, would be the yolk, and *Gaudete* would be the shell. I projected the life of Lumb in the underworld, and it became entangled with *Crow*, and the episodes became like the real events of which the *Gaudete* events are like the shadow on the wall in the cave. (*ibid.*)

The *Crow*-adventure recites the substantial experience of the heroic warrior-self's encounters in the underworld of the psyche, where *Gaudete* attempts to offer a structural overview of that experience; the narrative which Hughes kept in the background of *Crow* is forefronted in *Gaudete* as (most obviously) a Shamanistic dismemberment, flight and return. It is possible to speculate that the synthetic effort of *Cave Birds* is Hughes' attempt to re-align or marry the 'experience' of *Crow* proper with the 'argument' of *Gaudete*. As we shall see, *Gaudete* by itself only intermittently fulfils the function of Joseph Campbell's creative mythmaking: where Joyce and Beckett give us the pathology of symbol or myth as a *fait accompli*, Hughes' poem, striving to restore the broken circle of myth, gives us alternatively glimpses of the self's 'original source' and a painful sense – doubly intensified by the restorative effort – of renewed failure, of the fragmentation and incompleteness of the individual dream unsupported by communal agreement or the contemporary 'spiritual solidarity'.

The two epigraphs which precede the Argument of the poem cast further light on its nature and significance in terms of Hughes' poetic development:

> If it were not Hades, the god of the dead and the underworld, for whom these obscene songs are sung and festivals are made, it would be a shocking thing, but Hades and Dionysos are one. (Heraclitus)

> Their battle had come to the point where I cannot refrain from speaking up. And I mourn for this, for they were the two sons of one man. One could say that 'they' were fighting in this way if one wished to speak of two. These two, however, were me, for 'my brother and I' is one body, like good man and good wife. Contending here from loyalty of heart, one flesh, one blood, was doing itself much harm. *Parzival* (Book xv)

Gifford and Roberts helpfully point out that Hughes' narrative is a more complex, distorted version of Euripides' *The Bacchae*, in which 'King Pentheus rigidly and violently opposes Dionysos but, like Shakespeare's Angelo, is fatally susceptible to that which he suppresses and is seduced by the god into spying on the Bacchae, as a consequence of which he is torn to pieces by his own mother' (*Ted Hughes: A critical study*, p. 151). Both Pentheus and Angelo are what Jung, following Nietzsche, calls 'Apollinian' types: Apollo signifies measure, number, limitation and the subordination of everything wild or animalistic. The protagonist of *Gaudete*, the Reverend Lumb, may be characterized as the same generic type – the Anglican clergyman recapitulates the Socratic rationalist of *Cave Birds* and the earlier dramatized versions of the abstract personality in *The Hawk in the Rain*, *Lupercal* and *Wodwo*. The narrative goes on to describe the disintegration of the Apollinian-self into its opposite, the Dionysian impulse of Lumb's changeling 'double':

> The Dionysian impulse . . . means the liberation of unbounded instinct, the breaking loose of the unbridled dynamism of animal and divine nature; hence in the Dionysian rout man appears as a satyr, god above and goat below. . . . It is therefore comparable to intoxication, which dissolves the individual into his collective instincts and components – an explosion of the isolated ego through the world. (Jung, 'The Apollinian and the Dionysian', *Psychological Types*, p. 138)

From this commentary it should be clear that Lumb's double is nothing less than a paraphrase of Crow himself, identifiable by his completely unfettered instinctual life, his tendency to explode the arbitrarily defined margins of the 'isolated ego' and his potential as mediator of the yawning divide between the animal and divine natures; and the central dramatic climax of *Gaudete* is at once specifically Dionysian and an exploitation of Crow's most explicit feature, his sexuality.

One of the most important and subtle effects of the Dionysian impulse, furthermore, can be observed in the poet–narrator's attitude to his narrative, and its direct consequences upon our readership of *Gaudete*. Jung indicates the impact of the Dionysian impulse on art when he quotes Nietzsche's statement of relations: in the Dionysian rite, man's individuality is entirely extinguished – '*Man is no longer the artist, he has become the work of art*', 'All the artistry of Nature is revealed in the ecstasies of intoxication' (*Psychological Types*, pp. 138–9; my italics). In Dionysian art, therefore, the poet becomes a passive creator, the tool of 'the creative dynamism, [and] libido in instinctive form', which plays through him. Hughes articulates the immediate influence of Dionysos upon his narrative method in the second interview with Ekbert Faas:

> Various people in the book give their opinions, in various tones of voice, which I indicate. *My own opinion I withhold.* It's like a play – it contains no author's comments. As far as interpretation goes – I leave all options open.
> ('Ted Hughes and *Gaudete*' (1977), in Faas, *Ted Hughes*, p. 214; my italics)

Authorial comments – the convictions of the personality – are cut out of the poem as far as possible, in order that the energies of the story may 'take possession of the individual as though he were an object and use him . . . as an expression of itself' (Jung, *Psychological Types*, p. 139); the very construction of the narrative demands of the reader – like the poet in whose footsteps he follows – a Dionysian participation in the literary rite to be performed, in which the security of the judgemental heights, the aesthete's distance, will be denied him. Hughes' absolute refusal to allow the authorial vantage-point that, say, the Victorian novel would encourage its readers to adopt, turns the reader into a 'work of art' – the poem's 'afflicted' subject rather than the 'objective' assessor of its events.

Moreover, the idea of a 'headlong narrative' (Faas, *Ted Hughes*, p. 214) and the dream-basis of the poem recollect the therapeutic torrent of surrealism in *Wodwo*, while the inexorable stripped-down 'monotone' in which it is written is an amplification of the mechanical structures of *Crow*. Both techniques were aimed at breaking down the fortifications of the Ego and more specifically the supremacy of the self-regarding 'artist', focusing Hughes' imaginative re-generation of the figure of Dionysos as an ethical strongpoint in his own poetic development. Hughes, like Nietzsche before him, has to become a humbled 'votary' of Dionysos, rather than 'merely re-experiencing [his] passions at a safe distance, with no danger of becoming involved in them' ('An attempt at self-criticism').

Dionysos is therefore embedded in the actual fabric of the narrative as a principle of its construction. The significance of the epigram from *Parzival* is likewise undoubted: the conflict between Parzival and his Moslem brother is another mythological version of the story of the dualistic self, Hughes' prime imaginative territory. The religious objective, the Grail Castle, is only attained by a *passive hero* who is left defenceless, at the mercy of his perceptually 'black' opposite or double when his blade breaks and confidence in his own powers finally betrays him. *Both* these 'noble sons' were invited to the Castle in Wolfram von Eschenbach's story, a sure sign of the inadequacy of the self-sufficient 'white' intellect or the heroic self-idealization of the Personality. And as Joseph Campbell suggests, Parzival's triumph followed ironically 'rather from his loyalty to Condwiramurs and fearlessness in combat than from his obdurate determination to rediscover the castle' (*Myths to Live By*, p. 165); that is, it proceeded from an innate fidelity to the potentialities of the Essence or the material whole of the psyche, whether in the form of 'inner' fearlessness or the 'outer' mediating shape of the orphaned (i.e. split-off, suppressed) Queen Condwiramurs (Conduire-amour), rather than the egoistic wilfulness of his own independent efforts. Only in this condition is Parzival ready to heal the maimed King Anfortas, or Lumb prepared to cure the wounded baboon-woman in *Gaudete*. There are, however, marked differences in the degrees of dramatic success achieved by the two heroes, which constitute potent sources of irony within Hughes' volume once the similarity of the fundamental psychological pattern is recognized.[1] That irony is in no sense a relaxation from the 'cultural present' *Gaudete* presents, but an intensification of the 'impetus to knowledge' it provides.

The Prologue to the poem proper is preceded by an Argument which summarizes the narrative development, effectively consolidating the suggestion in the two epigraphs that the narrative seeks to 'pull together' the conflicting elements within the psyche by encouraging a therapeutic outflow of elemental–instinctual life which will first wipe out the existing self-construction – as in *Wodwo* and *Crow* – and then re-absorb those unconscious components into an expanded conscious image of the self. Unlike *Wodwo* and *Crow*, however, the psychological process is also observed through its effects in the 'outer', social frame of reference supplied by a village community.

The Prologue projects the reader straight into a narrative bewilderment conspicuously lacking that clear authorial 'control and decision', the lucid overview of events for which Lumb himself is searching:

> He has no idea where he is going. Or where he is.
> Is it dusk or is it eclipse?
> He urges himself, as if towards solid ground . . .
>
> The stillness is every minute more awful
> Like the dusk in a desert.
>
> He walks with deliberate vigour, searching in himself for control
>   and decision.

But the situation is more complex than my initial statement suggested: both Lumb and the reader find themselves immersed in a terrifying chaotic environment, 'All the length of the street, dead bodies/ are piled in heaps and strewn in tangles everywhere between the heaps', in which the possibility of an 'objective' appraisal of events has been denied them, and yet the mechanical signposts of 'objectivity' in the substance of Hughes' prose are all unmistakeably in place; in the first page of the Prologue (p. 11), we are told only the things Lumb experiences, in the order that he experiences them – furthermore experience is equated largely with the discrete reports of the senses. This method of ordering details had, in Hugh Kenner's words, become 'the paradigm of enlightened narrative' or of sophisticated literary presentation by the end of the nineteenth century. Hughes' narrative prose makes every effort to sustain its 'decisive' surface: the ordered clarity of the sense-reports is accentuated by the repetition of the pronoun 'he' as the subject of eight sentences, and in each Lumb is given a lucid, definitive verb ('concentrates . . . turns . . . draws back', etc.), and a simpli-fied, well-clipped syntax. None of these efforts suffice. The empirical goal of 'objective' narrative – its promise to make the collated facts effect their own 'Apollinian' declaration – is never fulfilled in Hughes' Prologue; the clear prose surface is always urging itself '*as if* towards solid ground', frantically gesturing towards the possibility of explaining chaotic events in the face of its own inadequacy, the remoteness of the analogue:

> [Lumb] clambers over corpses, from street to street, turning and turning among the streets, and every street is the same – a trench of fresh corpses. Finally, he simply stands, listening to the unnatural silence. He realises he is lost. The whole town is a maze of mass-graves. (p. 12)

One senses in this realization that Hughes' annihilation of one meaning of the word ' objectivity' is performed in order to open, or rather re-open, its religious or moral semantic: objectivity is not perceived as a technique which simply enables an Apollinian assessment of experience once a certain amount of data has been collected – that assessment will always be unconsciously motivated and predetermined, always open, ironically, to what might be called the Dionysian reproach; in this counter-reaction, objectivity is understood as a deliberate surrender to the 'chaotic' experience of the unconscious elements of the *whole psyche*. This apprehension of the term, in which the hero (poet, reader, dramatic persona) stands, listening in the silence, finally 'realises he is lost', is an objective Hughes has been struggling towards since 'The thought-fox'; the reader's response to the early prose narrative of *Gaudete* is an accurate yardstick of both his ability and willingness to shift from an Apollinian interpretation of 'Objectivity' to a Dionysian understanding of the term.[2]

Four times in the ensuing pages (pp. 13–15) Lumb mistakenly seeks a rational explanation for 'what is happening', unaware that – as the poet found out in *Cave Birds* – the detached scientific-experimentalist attitude to experience must be replaced by the alchemical sense of self-implication in it: the 'outer' by the 'inner' objectivity. Lumb's misappropriation of the term and his consequent ignorance of the psychic landscape in which he is located, lays him open to all sorts of ironies. His plight immediately worsens when he projects the origin of the menace into the apparently external world:

> He begins to run . . .
> As if he might outrun the swift *developing* cunning of this maze,
> Or the *narrowing purpose* of this twilight.
> Or the *multiplying corpses*.
>
> (p. 12)

Expecting to meet a comrade, the terms of a psychological wilderness created by the abstract personality permit him to encounter only opposites, negative prints of that cosmetically unified self:

> A horrible revelation is hurtling towards him.
> That shout is nothing but a mockery of his own shout.
> The blackest clot of the whole nightmare has found a shape and is leaping towards him.
>
> (p. 13)

Confronted by the 'half-animal' woman whom it is his task to heal, Lumb's plea for Apollinian explanation has a consequence similar to that provoked by the hero's Socratic arguments in 'After the first fright':

> the ancient man rocks back on his heels
> And folds his long-boned hands over his skull
> And mourns and cries.
>
> (p. 14)

This woman is clearly a figure for Jung's *anima*, the Female of 'Crow's undersong' and its background narrative, and the three-headed daughter/ mother/bride of 'Bride and groom'; she immediately elicits a poetic range far beyond the prosaic monotone associated with Lumb:

> Lumb bends low
> Over her face half-animal
> And the half-closed animal eyes, clear-dark back to the first creature
> And the animal mane
> The animal cheekbone and jaw, in the fire's flicker
> The animal tendon in the turned throat
> The upper lip lifted, dark and clean as a dark flower.
>
> (p. 14)

The concentration of the poetic 'moment' – epitomized in the suggestive phrase 'clear-dark back to the first creature' – runs counter to the prose machinery used to describe Lumb's illusion of his own 'continuous' consciousness; it is as if the distinction between prose and poetry is in this context representative of the difference between the two rival forms of Objectivity, checking the reader's moral attunement by checking his attunement to a continuous explanatory narrative against his willingness to engage the riddle-like opacity of the mythic *image*. The test is dramatically far too much for Lumb and his Apollinian bias:

> He declares he can do nothing
> He protests there is nothing he can do
> For this beautiful woman who seems to be alive and dead.
> He is not a doctor. He can only pray.

> (p. 15)

As Gifford and Roberts point out, 'Immediately Lumb expresses that division of roles he is struck, as if by a judgement' (*Ted Hughes*, p. 154), and Lumb's decision and its drastic consequences obliquely raise the problem of readership to a critical point. His action expresses the alienating contemporary cultural emphasis on specialization, upon the growth of a mechanical efficiency within narrowly defined, self-enclosed margins. This special emphasis encourages the growth of the Personality, with its own terminology or universe of signs, from which other systems of understanding – embodying other psychic components – are gratuitously excluded. As soon as Lumb separates off the 'spiritual personality' of the priest from his ancient role of *material*/internal healer, the judgement that follows is psychically inevitable – from the psychological–esoteric point of view, doctor and priest are simply two sides of the same coin. In the terms offered by the present discussion, when Lumb's response asserts an Apollinian logic or 'objectivity' (it recalls the parallel reaction of the photographer to the tiger's attack on a woman Hughes recounts in his first 'Myth and education' essay), he is immediately rebuked by the Dionysian version of the term, the whole body's objective lesson to the cerebrum. Unless the reader revises the cultural imprint of the word within his own understanding, he will not be able to establish any connection between Lumb's response and the 'sudden jagged darkness that rends him apart' subsequently. And as in *Crow*, 'understanding' is here associated with a kind of conscious surrender to the blind necessity of narrative experience, a basic sensitivity to the developmental pattern of events in the inner world which anticipates that submission.

Lumb is assaulted by an even more violent set of ironies; his every verb, exhibiting the same narrow mode of perception – 'inspect . . . gazes . . . looks . . . would rather understand' – is savagely undercut by the development of events in which he has no choice at all. 'He is ordered to choose a tree', and then strapped to the young oak, and flogged into unconsciousness by anonymous men 'alike as badgers'. When he regains consciousness, the original Lumb has been supplanted by his double. No sooner has one mythological ritual been consummated than another rite, the *taurabolium* or bull-sacrifice, is enacted. Both Sagar and Gifford and Roberts demonstrate the continuity of the two rituals as purifications or re-births of the sinful body, but the clarity of the mythic meaning in the abstract is intentionally overshadowed by the relentless Dionysian push of the narrative experience; the foreground of the poem is fully occupied by the humiliation and confusion which are central to that experience:

> Curtains of live blood cascade from the open bull above him,
> Wallowing in the greasy pulps, he tries to crawl clear.
> But men in bloody capes are flinging buckets of fresh blood over him. . . .
>
> Lumb scrambles from the swamp.
> He tries to wipe his eyes and to see.
> Men crowd round him, laughing like madmen,
> Emptying more buckets of hot blood over him.
>
> (*Gaudete*, p. 19)

This is the most literal refraction of the 'therapeutic torrent' of *Wodwo*, the suppressed tidal reality of 'The bull Moses' with the interpretative controls of closed door and pushed bolt wiped out. The disintegrative impact of the principle of Dionysos is more than sufficient to sweep away any complacent substitution of the semantic surface of myth for its psychological reality or 'deep structure', just as it engulfed the clear prose surface of the narrative, and the initial inflection of the term 'Objectivity' it seemed to encourage. The literary effects of Dionysos are in their own way as potent as his real effects upon the daughters of Minyas, King of Orchomenus, in the tale.[3] With this in mind, the reader must feel that Lumb's mock ascension into the world of ordinary life at the end of the Prologue will have less than beatific consequences.

The main narrative begins by focusing on the figure of Major Hagen, the original hero of the story. The shift of heroic emphasis from Hagen to Lumb confirms the movement of *Crow*, in which the dualistic predicament is observed for the first time from the vantage-point of the animal–material idea of the self ('Essence') rather than the abstract–rationalistic conception ('Personality') which generally influenced Hughes' first three books: Hagen himself is another version of St George, the puritanical corruption of the Anglo-Saxon warrior-self: watching his wife's intimate rendezvous with Lumb on the Japanese bridge through a pair of voyeuristic binoculars – one of Hughes' emblems of the 'objective' mode of perception – the instinctive response is suppressed:

A nerve is flickering
Under the exemplary scraped steel hair on the bleak skull,
But the artillery target-watching poise of his limbs, stiff-kneed and feet
    apart,
Absorbs the tremor.

(p. 24)

and the facial expression 'Is not moved/ Forty generations from the
freezing salt and the longships' (*ibid.*). Hughes' difficulty deciding the
heroic point of view of the narrative is also translated as a problem of
style. On occasion, he cannot resist exploiting the opportunity to pass
judgement on his characters, the same Apollinian sin of 'objectivity'
which characterized the poet's didactic voice in *The Hawk in the Rain*:
'Hagen's face is graven, lichenous./ . . . Paradeground gravel in the
folded gnarl of his jowls', and on the very next page he is condemned in
titanically extravagant terms which directly recall the earlier volume:

Anaesthetised
For ultimate cancellations
By the scathing alums of King's regulations,
The petrifying nitrates of garrison caste.

(p. 24)

The combination of didacticism and verbal gymnastics, which could
be termed the *masculine* aspect of Hughes' poetic sensibility, reaches a
climax in Hagen's furious assault upon his wife: 'Humiliation of Empire,
a heraldic obligation/ Must have its far-booming say . . ./ A frenzy of
obsolete guns/ Is banging itself to tatters/ And an Abbey of Banners yells
like an exhausted schoolmaster' (p. 34). The Dionysian poet, on the other
hand, concerns himself with 'passive' evocations of the natural world:

The parkland unrolls, lush with the full openness of the last week in May,
under the wet midmorning light. The newly plumped grass shivers and
flees. Giant wheels of light ride into the chestnuts, and the poplars lift and
pour like the tails of horses. Distance blues beyond distance. (p. 23)

The poet, in his non-judgemental *feminine* mode, opens himself to
other, more poignant realizations; having beaten his labrador to death,
Hagen 'Kneels/ Beside the stilled heap of loyal pet/ Hands huge with
baffled gentleness/ As if he had just failed to save it' (p. 35), an ironic
echo of the earlier scene in which he had tossed a dying dove towards
Lumb 'Who catches it/ As if to save it, and clasps it to him/ As if to
protect it' (p. 28). In both cases, the poetic register becomes acutely
sensitive or *receptive* to 'female' psychological states – Lumb and Hagen
are exhibiting their maternal instincts – and does *not* try to 'explain' or
evaluate their origin.

The poet's receptiveness/exposure, which I have termed both 'feminine' and 'Dionysian' (two terms which are closely associated in

mythological tradition) also allows the narrative to be affected by the gravitational pull of Hagen's own idiom, the 'suppressive-of-everything, system of vocal team-calls we know as Queen's English' that characterizes his voice:

> Powerful, age-thickened hands.
> Neglected, the morning's correspondence
> Concerning the sperm of bills . . .
> Coffee on the desk, untasted, now cold . . .
> Major Hagen, motionless at his window,
> As in a machan,
> Shoulders hunched, at a still focus.
>
> (p. 23)

The clipped punctuation and taut delivery suggest that Hagen's idiom is momentarily managing the narrative; like him the prose is 'tight with force'. The poet 'makes of himself a work of art' when he turns over control of his narrative to the competing vocal fragments within the self; when he investigates Hagen-psychology as a serious interior reality rather than an aberration to be accused and ridiculed at an 'objective' distance.

The voluntary dissolution of Hughes' narrative into the dark chaos of its component subjectivisms becomes a general principle of literary conduct. That dissolution may be harmonious, as in the case of Joe Garten, who is much more sharply attuned to his animal nature than the majority of the characters ('A mile away', pp. 29–30). But the disintegrative process usually has far more disturbing consequences: when Pauline Hagen attempts to absorb the 'elementals' numinously revealed in the natural world into her conscious frame of reference, the narrative temporarily threatens collapse, protesting its ignorance of the identifying *word* which could name, and thus comprehend her experience: 'She cannot get far enough down, or near enough' (p. 32).

A second failure to channel Dionysian energies, and a parallel narrative ignorance, is even more painfully conclusive:

> [Mrs Westlake's] brain swoons a little, trying to disengage. The glistening tissues, the sweating gasping life of division and multiplication, the shoving baby urgency of cells. All her pores want to weep. She is gripped by the weird pathos of biochemistry, the hot silken frailties, the giant, gristled power, the archaic sea-fruit inside her, which her girdle bites into, which begins to make her suit too tight.
> She feels the finality of it all, and the nearness and greatness of death.
> (p. 39)

She is 'gripped' by a reality which resists definition in the terms of her own consciousness – 'languages passing from the scientific, through the archetypal, to the everyday' (Gifford and Roberts, *Ted Hughes*, p. 157) prove individually inadequate to the task. Worse still, the narrative itself is gripped by the vagueness and sentimentality of Mrs Westlake's idiom in the last sentence. The methodology of literature – including, for instance, the much-lauded 'omniscient narrator' – can no more 'contain' Dionysian elementals, once released, than any other cultural norm within a puritanical, Externally based society. When Hughes said in his second interview with Faas that Lumb's power to 'bring about the renovation of women and therefore of life in general' (Faas, *Ted Hughes*, p. 215) is critically limited, 'the whole situation being impossibly crystallized in the immovable dead end forms of society and physical life' (*ibid*.), he might well have added the immovable, dead-end forms of poetic narrative to that list, because we are made to experience the disintegrative force of Dionysos as a first principle of reading, of literary and critical construction. When the inaugural Apollinian sense of 'objectivity' crumbles, the reader, like Crow and the other major characters in *Gaudete*, experiences the life of the sympathetic nervous system on its most primitive, unsophisticated – and verbally opaque – level.

The signs of this multi-level dissolution are unmistakeable, and everywhere. Lumb and Pauline Hagen initially complete 'the landscape artist's arrangement' on the Japanese bridge (p. 25), but within thirty lines Hagen's Apollinian arrangement, carefully controlled by the 'objective' lens of his binoculars, has been irrevocably disturbed:

> The vista quivers.
> Decorative and ordered, it tugs at a leash.
> A purplish turbulence
> Boils from the stirred chestnuts, and the spasms of
> the new grass, and the dark nodes of bulls.
>
> (p. 26)

Because the author claims no superiority over his character, the impartial evocation of the landscape – the 'aesthetic' mode of 'To paint a water-lily' – is helpless in its attraction to the magnetic field of Hagen's inner disturbance. The perfection of the lens and the work of art alike yield to 'a tremor/ Like a remote approaching express/ In the roots of his teeth'. In this model of art, the poet is no longer able to create his own aesthetic world, his 'objective' illusion of the object, as in the old Empathy–Abstraction coupling; now the object rounds on him with a savagery akin to Hagen's seemingly docile dog; like a mirror it returns the artist more ruthlessly than before to the chaos of the subject, the self doing the creating (as Eliot, Joyce and Beckett found out), and the Gordian knot of the moral process, the religious function of art.

The reluctance or inability of the author to assert superiority over his characters is also reflected in an overt psychological continuity with earlier volumes. 'Characters' summon, and re-direct, the author's own 'past'. Major Hagen's resemblance to the negative aspect of the German/ Scandinavian warrior-self has already been noted: he fulfils his St George destiny when he confronts his wife in the episode entitled 'Pauline Hagen' (pp. 31–5). His pet labrador springs to her defence, forcing him to enact the archetypal crime of projection narrated in 'Crow's account of St George'; he destroys his perceived enemy

> Till at last he stands, trembling,
> Like somebody pulled from an accident.
> He drops the broken stump of his weapon.
>
> (p. 35)

Hagen's destruction of the dog is a figure for the Ego-Personality's antipathy towards its own unconscious, the real animal nature of nature 'grown cannibal murderous with deprivation'.

Where Hagen confronts Dionysian energies in the person of his wife, Commander Estridge encounters them in his daughters (the second face of the Triple Goddess). His youngest daughter, Jennifer, plays a 'dragonish' Beethoven piano sonata which is 'havocking polished, interior glooms' (p. 41), and the sudden access of sexual force, both sublimated and unsublimated, annihilates his Apollinian idealization of them ('Scherzo', pp. 41–3). Estridge's dream, his own work of art, can no more manage elementals than the authorial voice can exert 'omniscient' influence over his narrative, or the reader apply abstract interpretative, or 'literary' solutions to the psychological problems raised by the story: 'He [Estridge] cannot interpret those atmospherics/ And soundings and cries. It is shouting something impossible, incomprehensible, monstrous' (p. 42). Moreover, he is permitted no respite by the 'terrible engine' of the narrative; the telescope-lens of the 'objective imagination' in which he seeks relief reveals only Lumb's assignation with Mrs Holroyd, crumpling another of Estridge's abstract, puritanical fictions – 'She reminds him of the country love of his youth, who never appeared' (p. 47). Even this, however, is merely a preface to the pitiless Dionysian disclosure which renders him the helpless victim of his own chaotic experience, rather than the creator of fictions about the feminine principle within reality: the suicide of his elder daughter Janet, reported by her younger sister:

> She is running between the shrubs towards him.
> He puts on his spectacles.
> He quickly tries to think what could be the worst possible.
> He finds only helpless fear.

His daughter is screaming something at him
As if in perfect silence.

(p. 48)

This is at once a demonstration of the unity of Hades and Dionysos, the transformation of Estridge from aesthetic artist to chaotic, though *potentially* religious work of art, and a concentration of the options available to the reader: an ego-maintaining distance, the complete separation from narrative events of Dodsworth or Eagleton, or personal commitment to the reality of those events which appears inevitably destructive.

All the central male characters are forced to experience versions of the 'death' Lumb undergoes in the Prologue. We have already examined the shift from the Apollinian to the Dionysian self in Estridge and Hagen, along with the ritual destruction of the 'objective' lens – whether telescope or binoculars – as an adequate perceptual mediator of the double reality (both 'inner' and 'outer') in which they are embedded. The 'Egghead'-personality of both men is shattered to reveal a Crow-like primitive, animal self, a process which ignites 'the whole tree of his [Hagen's] nerves' (p. 33) and for a moment abolishes the grammatical distinction between Hagen and his enraged labrador (p. 35, lines 6–8) which leaps at him with maddened force. The experience of Dr Westlake follows the same pattern: we first encounter his 'professionally baleful stare' during Jennifer's 'explanation' of her sister's suicide (pp. 56–7). The formal situation, its verbal explanatory surface, is confused enough. But the disturbance caused by the narrative's adjustment to the 'helpless uncontrol' of Jennifer's factual record is nothing compared to the explosion of 'objectivity' when it turns to confront Westlake's response:

[He]
Keeps losing Jennifer's words
As he gazes fascinated
Into the turbulence of her body and features . . .
And immersing himself in her voice, which flows so full of thrilling
    touches
And which sobs so nakedly in its narration,
He is scorched by the hard fieriness
A jagged, opposite lightning
Running along the edge of it
Like an insane laughter –

Something in his marrow shrivels with fear.

(pp. 56–7)

The elemental response of the body effortlessly overtakes that of the reflective intellect, as Hughes notes in – among others – his article '*Orghast*: Talking without words'. Westlake's experience of female body-music anticipates the crisis of his own deformed/ suppressed Essence seven episodes later (pp. 71–6). 'Numb-edged with too much noon alcohol', Westlake begins to polarize in the feminine life of instinct and sensation, just as the poetry polarizes in its 'feminine' mode of evocation, its being as a thickly textured, anti-didactic substance:

> some bulky hard-cornered unpleasantness leans on him. He ignores it steadily. He searches for his car-keys, preoccupied, watching the mobs of young starlings struggling and squealing filthily in the clotted may-blossom, like giant blow-flies. (p. 71)

The breakage of Westlake's spectacles, and the rapid adaptation of the narrative voice to his self-suppressive state of awareness ('mobs . . . filthily . . . clotted'), clearly announce entry into the inner world, counterpointing Westlake's urge for rational control – 'He must insist now, on control/ Of every second as it chooses to come' (p. 72) – with the decision which has already been made by his body in its clairvoyant knowledge:

> he has known it all the time,
> And now he only has to look at it, and there it is.
> His wife
> And the Reverend Nicholas Lumb
> Fit together, like a tongue in its mouth.
>   (p. 78)

This double vision persists to the end of the episode, symbolized by Westlake's spectacles, one lens still perfect, Apollinian, observing the artfully 'peeled-back gorges of his rose-blooms, leaning poised in space . . . exactly there, with their strict, fierce edges' (p. 74), the other 'unglassed' and open to the ferocious sexual power of 'the young effortless horses,/ Roistering flamily on the slope opposite', (*ibid.*), a recollection of the Dionysian force he experienced in his imagination of Jennifer Estridge. As he approaches the bedroom door, Westlake creates his own explanation of events, then labels it 'objective':

> He explains to himself yet again, more distinctly, and with a pedantic solemnity of subordinate clauses, that what he hears is indeed the crying of his wife at some bodily extreme, which can have only one explanation. But as his brain mounts its annihilating court-case, which will need only the precise, annihilating words, his body has already moved convulsively, and the door bursts open. (p. 75)

But the 'objectivity' of the situation – his wife's adultery with the vicar – disintegrates, in much the same way as the explanation Lumb is given for a later psychic trauma dissolves, sodden in his hands; it disintegrates in an ironic re-enactment of Lumb's failure in the Prologue, where Mrs Westlake 'is being hysterical in her familiar style. . . . And the Reverend Lumb/ Is sitting at the foot of the bed, considerate as a baffled doctor' (p. 75). Lumb holds up a dramatic mirror-image of Westlake's inner condition: the helpless masculine doctor beside, yet dislocated from the hysterical feminine, unable to heal her because of the split in his own psychic life between Personality and Essence, conscious and unconscious, 'objective' intellectual and 'subjective' instinctual/sexual functions. The sub-text of Westlake's 'objectivity', his obsession with sexuality at its lowest level, dominates his every action, and issues only in destructive effects. At the end of the episode, the doctor spins his gun into the picture-framed roses, for the focus of art is now within: 'Huge hammers of blackness reshape him,/ Huge hammers of alcohol,/ Huge hammers of hellishness and incomprehension' (p. 76).

Dunworth is the other major male victim of Dionysian experience, although the terms of his response to it may indicate an advance upon Westlake's reaction. Dunworth actually catches his wife *in flagrante delicto*, but the experience appears to deliver significantly more 'feminine' and hence positive insights:

> [Dunworth] is helplessly in love.
> He stands there, in his child's helplessness,
> As if he had searched everywhere and at last somehow he had found her.
> An irresponsible joy chatters to be heard, somewhere
>   in the back of his head, as he gazes at her,
> Feeling all his nerves dazzle, with waftings of vertigo,
> As if he were gazing into an open furnace . . .
>
> (p. 87)

Quite unable to isolate the ugliness or ordinariness 'that once bored him so much',

> He feels only a glowing mass.
> He stands there, paralysed by a bliss
> And a most horrible torture –
> Endless sweetness and endless anguish.
>   (*ibid.*, p. 87)

Gifford and Roberts indicate an appropriate parallel to Dunworth's experience in Castaneda's description of what the *brujo* Don Juan calls 'seeing'. In his first experience of 'seeing', Castaneda gazes at Don Juan's face and sees 'a round object which had a luminosity of its own' (*A Separate Reality*, p. 164), an 'amorphous glowing object' (*ibid.*, p. 193).

The reader's response to such an experience tends to split into two possible directions. Pronouncing the final 'endless sweetness and endless anguish' an unequivocal moral positive, he yields to the sentimentalism of the term 'mystic', that caricature of 'religious' experience which typifies the over-correcting rationalist emphasis in the self. Indeed, the ruthless accumulated pressure built up by the Dionysian narrative renders this escapist 'safety-valve' a considerably more attractive option for the reader; the alternative is to recognize the vacuousness embodied

in the 'blind' repetition of 'Endless' – spoken in Dunworth's own idiom –
and the absence of a coherent moral direction within the self which could
make use of that release of energies. The objections put forward in
criticism of the authorial attitude of 'Gnat-psalm' could also be fastened
on to his surrogate 'character' in *Gaudete*. Because the dazzling experience is not accompanied by an 'access of knowledge', 'one has no other
recourse but to use the activities of daily life to take one's mind away
from the fright of the encounter and thus allow one's gap to close'
(*A Separate Reality*, p. 223). For the alternative may be total extinction,
not merely of the Ego, as Don Juan's comments appended to 'Wind'
showed. Dunworth, like the rest of the men, closes the yawning gap by
re-asserting a habitual psychological reflex used in daily life, the
externalization of the evil in a scapegoat (Lumb). More darkly, the
women – for whom no rational/empirical 'return' is possible – act out
the second option, literally blown out of life and into death by the
onslaught of 'inexplicable and unbending forces'; by the end of the main
narrative, Janet Estridge, Mrs Westlake, Felicity and Maud have all
become victims of those energies, and the rest are 'numbed' by the
succession of events. Neither masculine nor feminine principles, working independently, prove adequately 'prepared' for the task set by the
narrative.

Some typical examples of feminine experience in *Gaudete* have already
been discussed. In general, the female exposure to Dionysian energies is
much more complete than in the male response, absolutely free of the
normal rational or interpretative controls. 'Mrs. Holroyd' (pp. 58–62)
gives the positive effects of that exposure, though the most archetypal
incarnation of Female-nature and Female-fate in the narrative is Maud,
Lumb's housekeeper. In his second interview with Faas, Hughes pointed
to her general meaning as 'the representative in this world of the woman
that he [Lumb] is supposed to cure in the other world' (Faas, *Ted Hughes*,
p. 215). This meaning is explicitly confirmed in a mysterious episode in
which Maud follows a woman to the end of the path in the graveyard,
for the woman is the desecrated underworld-female at whose headstone
Maud arranges flowers and to whom she pays homage (see p. 94). In an
earlier episode (pp. 62–4) her clairvoyant powers are presented directly,
as she foresees both Lumb's own end and the principal event of the WI
meeting (Felicity's death); in a later episode (p. 116) she rips a pigeon
apart, and the portentous consequence of her action suggests that her
relationship with Lumb approximates that of puppeteer and puppet, or
witchdoctor and voodoo-doll. All three episodes underline Maud's
Dionysian presence as a 'container' or conductor of elementals, but her
ethical impact is circumscribed by prevailing cultural – and narrative –
conditions, in which 'inner' is absolutely separate from 'outer'; on the

psychological level the Dionysian energies find no expressive outlet in the shell of Apollinian Personality. Her own contact with the 'outer' world has irresistibly comic results; she answers a knock at the door while still in possession of Lumb's magical dagger:

> The breadman wants to know what she wants.
> Nothing.
> He has to take his slight surprise away with him.
>
> (p. 64)

The whole episode begs the question: how can such 'inner' capacities be allowed to play a meaningful role in conscious life, the 'objective' environment of which the breadman is a representative? The narration preserves its silence, its monotone, rendering Maud's ironic incongruity rather than her potential mediative function. The 'clean' narrative thus gives access to one aspect of what I earlier called the broken circle of myth, the pathology of a symbolic character who clearly belongs to that world; unable to fulfil her proper function in a fully assembled mythic world, Maud is finally herself victimized by the energies which have been 'summoned', indistinguishable from the 'senseless' Mrs Westlake, who understood nothing at all. Perhaps she exemplifies the tragic fate of a mythological figure (she has much in common with the witch Medea in the Golden Fleece story) in a world explained by the 'objective imagination'.

Almost every character in *Gaudete* is forced to re-enact the central Dionysian event experienced by Lumb. The episodes that concern him alone, or focus events in his own inner world naturally constitute the firmest indications of the state of negotiations with the Unconscious/ Essence within the main narrative. In an early episode (pp. 49–53), he examines his connection with 'the unalterably strange earth', and the equally remote animal Unconscious. Both that landscape and that self feel 'very like safety' (p. 49),

> But he knows everything he looks at,
> Even the substance of his fingers, and the near-wall of his skin,
> He knows it is vibrant with peril, like a blurred speed-vibration.
> He knows the blood in his veins
> Is like heated petrol, as if it were stirring closer and closer to explosion,
> As if his whole body were a hot engine, growing hotter
> Connected to the world, which is out of control.
>
> (p. 49)

This is a re-statement of Weil's religious paradox: the Crowish realization of the utterly mechanical body as 'a hot engine' – subject to 'Necessity' – is a lens through which Lumb perceives his 'connection to the world', his unity with the natural Creation. Weil's conception of 'Obedience' or 'Voluntary Distance' (the 'third' position), however, which holds out to the imagination the specifically *divine* nature of the relationship with Matter, is lacking; Lumb is totally identified with, and hence at the mercy of his mechanical nature, so that the 'objective' is again murderously obliterated by the 'subjective', the Apollinian by the Dionysian, until the world itself appears to be out of control. This kind of Dionysian subjectivism is not an end in itself; objective–subjective, or Apollo–Dionysos, are simply dualistic axes, opposite sides of the same coin. So Lumb's 'Connection' will have literally destructive – and destructively literal – consequences in daily life. The Kleist-like forceful narrative likewise affords the reader no 'developmental possibility', in the swift and unbroken passage from the right perception 'Connected to the world' to the radical, plummeting subjectivism which achieved it, 'which is out of control'.

When the cost of the achievement is re-affirmed in the 'obscure *convulsions and blunderings* of a music that *lurches* through him' (p. 50), the reader may indeed follow Lumb further in his effort 'to imagine simple freedom':

> His possible freedoms, his other lives, hypothetical and foregone, his lost
>   freedoms . . .
>
> Considering their millions
> All mutually exclusive, all conjunct and co-extensive,
> He sees in among them,
> In among all the tiny millions of worlds of this world
> Millions of yet other, alternative worlds, uninhabited, unnoticed, still
>   empty,
> Each open at every point to every other and yet distinct,
> Each waiting for him to escape into it, to explore it and possess it,
> Each with a bed at the centre.
>
> (p. 50)

The last line completes a conceit initiated thirteen lines earlier ('He looks out across the quilt and embroidery of the landscape'), which distantly echoes the self-delusion of the persona in Donne's 'The sunne rising'. Both that aesthetic pattern, the preponderance of latinate vocabulary and the rhetorical force of the repetitions ('Each', 'Millions') threaten a precipitate return to the Ego, and the reader who allowed his own Apollinian yearning for 'never-used limitless freedom' to blossom is abruptly 'corrected' by the renewed disclosure of the narrative's attraction to personal idiom: 'He yields to *his* favourite meditation./ Forlorn, desperate meditation' (p. 50), and the finality of the tree-image, still primitive and prior to its alchemization in *Cave Birds*:

> Between the root in immovable earth
> And the coming and going leaf

Stands the tree
Of what he cannot alter.
(p. 50)

Character and reader are kept in a state of complete subjection, with
interpretative freedoms cancelled. Both experience an exact replica of the
ironic truth which surprised Crow in 'Glimpse':

His heart surges after his reverie, with lofty cries and lifting wingbeats,
Suddenly he comes against the old trees
And feels the branches in his throat, and the leaves at his lips.

(p. 51)

Moreover, the process is repeated until both are 'emptied': Lumb makes
a second attempt to 'feel his plans steady' (p. 52), and decides to escape
before nightfall, hoping 'To carry his body, with all its belongings,/
Right to the end of its decision.' Within eight lines, a contradictory
image has been unearthed which mocks Lumb's rational control,
demonstrating that his body like 'a giant aircraft out of control, shaking
itself to pieces' has already defined its own fate, regardless of his
'decision'. This ruthless renewal of the episode's irony is one reason why
Hughes can afford to keep the symbolic structure of Lumb's final prayer
'open', or ambiguous:

He tries to make this ash-tree his prayer . . .
Groping to feel the sure return grasp
The sure embrace and return gaze of a listener –

He sinks his prayer into the strong tree and the tree stands as his prayer.
(p. 53)

The reader has two choices: the tree may be used to symbolize Lumb's
(and his own) desire for abstract freedom, his prayer for sure strength to
carry out his 'plan'; or else, it may be construed as a realization of his
double nature (which is *physically* log-like) and particular unalterable–
mechanical fate, requiring the religious attitude of 'obedience' in response. The same possibilities attended Christ, when he prayed in the
Garden of Gethsemane, and characterized our responsive choice to the
Crucifixion-image in 'Crow and the sea'.[4] Only the second response
sustains the integrity of material-*as*-psychological truth, that simultaneous consciousness of 'inner' and 'outer' elements which in
Ouspensky's account involves 'direct attention on oneself without
weakening or obliterating the attention directed on something else.
Moreover this "something else", could as well be within me as outside
me' (*In Search of the Miraculous*, p. 119).

Another facet of the consciousness, that 'one hears one's own voice
and sees and observes oneself from the outside' (*ibid.*), re-appears at the
beginning of a second episode, in which Lumb encounters, and fights

with, his double (pp. 77–83). Listening to the 'babel' of 'outer' voices as he bends low over the on-rushing river 'he recognises voices out of his past', the 'inner' voices of the plural self: 'He manages, as from his deep listening, to answer "I'm here" ' (p. 77). Once this double-sided awareness is established, all the elements of the objective psyche are 'pulled together' in a dream-like scenario: a conscious Lumb, who recollects the original clergyman of the Prologue, is fishing in a manner reminiscent of the persona of 'Pike' ('for what might move, for what eye might move') – the dream-darkness that is watching *him*. 'Pike' prepares a space, somewhat apprehensively, for the experience which is fulfilled in the present episode of *Gaudete*. The unconscious or Dionysian Lumb, 'glistening and joyous', emerges from inner darkness to abduct Felicity, Lumb's intended bride. He recalls the bounding 'blackest clot of the whole nightmare' who leaped threateningly towards the Prologue-Lumb, and who turned out to be the helper and representative of the underworld-Female. And as in the Prologue, the original Lumb is called upon to save the injured Female, and this time he manages it, although the terms of the rescue are again muddied by an interpretative chaos, the product of the narrator's withholding of information. Here is the description of the fight's climax:

> Suddenly under a long electrocuted wriggler of dazzle
> That shudders across the whole sky, for smouldering seconds,
> Their attacker glistening and joyous
> Bounds over the turf bank and on to them.
> Laughing like a maniac, he grabs Felicity's arm.
> With clownish yells and contortions, he starts
>   dragging her again towards the lake.
> Again Lumb knocks him down and the two men wallow pummelling.
> Plastered with peat-mud, under the downpour,
> Finally, gasping and immobilised, they lie face to
>   face, gripping each other's hands,
> One grinning and the other appalled.

(p. 82)

The double is so closely associated – syntactically and imaginatively – with the 'whole' landscape through the phrase 'electrocuted wriggler of dazzle' that Lumb's eventual triumph is rendered equivocal or suspect. He is unquestionably connected to the world but also out of control, and represents that mechanical view of the self against which Lumb's freedom-meditation was directed. Lumb's 'saving of the feminine' thus has something of the tenuousness of that meditation: the resolution is violent and dualistic, the double's hand is torn off in Lumb's struggle to break free of him, Apollo is wrenched apart from Dionysos. (Self-) Recognition does not – in comparison with the meeting of Parzival and his Moslem brother – bring unification or a shared sense of purpose, but confirms Lumb's rational commitment to elope with Felicity 'like an ordinary man/ With his ordinary wife' (p. 147) in opposition to his Dionysian role. The two roles are mutually exclusive, and the reader is exposed to a mythic event which suffers irresistibly from cultural corruption; plunged as he is *in medias res* by the narrative chaos, Hughes' presentation offers the reader the two prevailing – though extreme – cultural options in response to a manifestation of elementals: acceptance of a destructive descent or apparently meaningless 'death', or a suppressive, Movement-like re-emphasis of the routines of ordinary life. Depriving himself of the illusion of authorial (i.e. egoistic) detachment, Hughes makes of his poetic personality an ideal transmitter of those cultural assumptions, despite their negative influence on his 'creative myth' in terms of its power to project an ideal pattern of moral development for the individual. Who would not judge Lumb's action 'sane' or 'natural' in the present episode?

Redemption of the feminine is also the touchstone of the third overtly 'mythic' episode (pp. 98–106), which recapitulates several elements featuring in the first two, and the Prologue. As in the double episode, Lumb is 'initiated' into inner-world events through water:

> What he thought was river is other noises,
> As his head clears, harsh noises din at his head,
> Like an abrupt waking.
>
> (p. 98)

He finds himself among stampeding cattle and men in oilskins who rain blows upon him anonymously, recalling those others 'alike as badgers' in the Prologue. The mass-grave of the Prologue has a correlative, too, in the bodies of the men and women of his parish whom Lumb discovers, buried almost entirely in mud. Moreover, Lumb's conscious voice is recognizably that of the original Lumb, who

> tells them who he is, he asks who they are
> And what is happening.
> What has he done and what do they want?
>
> (p. 100)

The impassioned plea for 'objective' explanation is dealt with peremptorily; a man

> hands Lumb a sodden paper, as if it were some explanation.
> Lumb scrutinises it but can make nothing out of it in the broken rays
> As it disintegrates in his fingers, weak as a birth membrane.
>
> (*ibid.*)

This is not the end of the matter, however, because two pages later Lumb clearly 'improves' his Prologue-understanding. Confronted by the half-alive, half-dead bodies of his parishioners 'his mind dissolves./ He looks at the bodies. No explanation occurs to him./ They are all there is to it.// But now he hears a sharp crying. He looks for it, as for a clue' (p. 102). He is not sidetracked by the 'objectivity' of the situation, but 'listens' for the nature of the action required of him. This shift is critical if he is to perform the central task set within the episode, the healing/rebirth of the woman who first appeared in the Prologue. At first, he repeats his Prologue-error, the specialized perception of functions: 'He calls to her [Pauline Hagen], he speaks to her softly, as to a *patient in a coma*,/ But she continues to scream' (my italics). He is immediately given the opportunity to correct his earlier mistake, nevertheless, when he hears a woman's voice calling him, trapped within a sea of mud. He slides down into a crater 'thinking this one creature he can free', and sees her face to face:

> It is a woman's face,
> A face as if sewn together from several faces.
> A baboon beauty face,
> A crudely-stitched patchwork of faces.
>
> (p. 104)

More clearly even than 'Lumb' (pp. 49–93) with its direct echoes of 'Glimpse' and 'Crow and the sea', Lumb's efforts to climb clear of the pit symbolically project, 'like the shadow on the wall in the cave', one of the skeleton fables of *Crow* – Crow's attempts to cross a river while the Ogress–Female on his back steadily increases in weight: at every step, 'She only clamps tighter, as if she were drowning,/ As if she were already unconscious, as if now her body were fighting to save itself' (p. 104). This is not only a variant of the *Crow*-fable, but also a renewal of Lumb's combat with his double, and thus a barometer of his 'improved' understanding. Her grin and unbreakable grasp are sufficient to identify the woman with Lumb's 'glistening and joyous' attacker; when Lumb tries to break that grip, like the double who disappeared back into the dark lake of the unconscious she clamps him tighter 'as if she were already unconscious', become a suppressed and therefore menacing psychic factor. Lumb is forced to give birth to this woman,

> Flood-sudden, like the disembowelling of a cow
> She gushes from between his legs, a hot splendour
> In a glistening of oils,
> In a radiance like phosphorous he sees her crawl and tremble.
>
> (p. 105)

But the essential change in Lumb's level of consciousness, from 'objectivity' as a primary mode of perception to Gurdjieff's 'Self-remembering' or Hughes' 'Imagination' beyond the subjective–objective polarity, occurred five lines earlier. Lumb's vague effort 'to see what is being done to him' was transformed:

> A swell of pain, building from his throat and piling downwards
> Lifts him suddenly out of himself.
> Somehow he has emerged and is standing over himself.
> He sees himself being delivered of the woman from the pit.
>
> (p. 105)

The difference in modes of perception is explained by Ouspensky in *The Fourth Way*:

> It must be clearly understood that consciousness and functions are quite different things. To move, to *think*, to feel, to have sensations – these are functions; they can work quite independently of whether we are conscious or not; in other words, they can work mechanically. To be conscious is something quite different. But if we are more conscious it immediately increases the sharpness of our functions.
>
> Functions can be compared to machines working in varying degrees of light. These machines are such that they are able to work better with light than in darkness; every moment there is more light the machines work better. *Consciousness is light and machines are functions.* . . .
>
> If you make a serious effort to observe functions for yourself, you will realize that ordinarily, whatever you do, whatever you think, whatever you feel, you do not remember yourself. *You do not realize that you are present, that you are here.*[5] (*The Fourth Way*, p. 55; my italics)

It is only when Lumb experiences his own presence in the world that he is able to deliver the women from the pit, not one moment before. And the clear look at the subject clarifies his perception of the object: 'He sees light./ He sees her face undeformed and perfect' (p. 106). Lumb is delivered from 'objectivity's' heroifying of pure Function as from a sin.

The original Lumb's task in the underworld seems to be successfully accomplished with the end of this chapter. The two episodes I have examined, in addition to the Prologue, resemble hieroglyphic fragments – only partially recovered – of the fabular structure or 'shell' of Crow-experience; they are indeed like 'Shadows on the wall in the cave'. The events of these episodes are similar to Joseph Campbell's account of the mythological hero's inner quest, which he compares to schizophrenic breakdown in contemporary culture: 'A chaotic series of encounters there, darkly terrifying experiences, and presently (if the victim is fortunate) encounters of a centring kind, fulfilling, harmonizing, giving new courage; and then finally, in fortunate cases, a return journey of rebirth to life' (*Myths to Live By*, p. 202). But Lumb's role as mythological hero is crucially compromised; in *The Hero with a Thousand Faces* Campbell identifies three stages in heroic progress, (1) psychic separation, (2) initiation, and (3) return, and it is clear that the second stage (which in Shamanistic practice involves the spiritual instruction of the Initiate) is absent in Lumb's case. The terribly powerful psychological energies released are not supported or controlled by the moral–social order and its forms, and thus turned to good – just as they are given no evolved expression in Lumb's everyday Personality. Lacking cultural validation, their release into the 'outer' world is inevitably destructive. In view of the split condition of *Gaudete*'s 'narrative psyche', Lumb's triumph in the inner region is qualified by his failure in the 'outer' sphere. At this stage, no return from the 'invisible' world of *Crow* to the 'visible' realm of ordinary life seems possible for the poet.

In that realm, Lumb tries ineptly to channel elementals by organizing the women of the parish into a love-coven, and making arrangements for the performance of a fertility rite under cover of the WI meeting. Events rapidly approach a climax when Garten shows copies of a photograph depicting Lumb making love to Mrs Evans to all the husbands: the Male–Female antagonism polarizes ever more distinctly, with all the men congregated at the Bridge Inn bar preparing their revenge, while the women become absorbed in the magico-religious atmosphere of Lumb's ritual. The pressure on Lumb increases proportionately, in his double premonition of a chaotic–destructive fate (pp. 118–19, 121–3) interrupted by the sudden arrival of Felicity, and the temptation of ordinary life:

> Lumb
> Gazes blankly to a re-assessment
> Impossibly beyond him. Two worlds,
> Like two strange dogs circling each other.
> (p. 125)

This is the most explicit statement of Lumb's inability to reconcile his inner crisis with its 'demonized' consequences in the external world. It is as if we are given two alternative histories/fates for Lumb, and maybe for the author as well: (1) The precipitate disintegration of the old personality in the 'visible' world (the Puritan fate of Angelo in *Measure for Measure*), condemned as 'madness'. In this 'outer' environment, no reconciliation of Apollo and Dionysos is feasible (the main narrative). (2) The continuation of the struggle underground, on the 'invisible' level, threaded through the shadow-like experiences of the Prologue, the mythic episodes and the Epilogue. For the author, the destructive descent of *Wodwo*, pushed through the *Crow* adventure towards the self-made mythology of *Cave Birds*, becomes the substance of that struggle – a period of *self-education* which supplies the absence of Campbell's second heroic stage, and prepares for a more regulated release of elementals within the personality, a beneficial 'return' through one of the few cultural norms available, Poetry.

The sequence of episodes focusing on the fertility rite at the WI meeting (pp. 132–3, 139–42, 145–9) mark the final effort to integrate Dionysian elementals, and the ceremonial world of religious activity, or myth, into ordinary life. Hughes' narrative monotone easily adjusts to the music of the ritual, which is 'a tight, shuddering, repetitive machine' (p. 139),

> Which seems bolted into the ground
> And as if they were all its mechanical parts, the women are fastened into it,
> As if the smoke were the noise of it,
> The noise of it raucous with the smoke and the smoke stirred by it.
> A hobbling, nodding, four-square music, a goblin monotony,
> The women in a circle clapping to the tread of it.
>
> (p. 139)

The ritual constitutes perhaps the most significant and damning instance of the narrative's tendency to detect the magnetic field of the nearest experiencing subject, and relegate itself to a function of his/her aware-ness. For the final time, the explanatory apparatus of 'objectivity' dissolves in our hands 'sodden as a birth membrane' fracturing into the 'chaotic subjectivism' of Felicity's consciousness. Her mind has been scrambled by Mrs Davies' magic-mushroom sandwich:

> A tiger
> Is trying to adjust its maniac flame-barred strength to her body . . . She
>   can see Mrs. Davies is infinitely beautiful.
> And Mrs. Garten is a serpentine wreath of glowing light . . .
>
> (p. 140)

> She is already drowning in the deep mightiness of what is about to happen
>   to her.
> She knows she herself is to be the sacramental thing.
> She herself is already holy
> And drifting at a great depth, a great remoteness, like a spark in space.
> She is numbed with the seriousness of it . . .
>
> (p. 141)

> Somehow she has become a goddess.
> She is now the sacred doll of a slow infinite solemnity.
>
> She knows she is burning plasma and infinitely tiny,
> That she and all these women are moving inside the body of an
>   incandescent creature of love,
> That they are brightening, and that the crisis is close,
> They are the cells in the glands of an inconceivably huge and urgent
>   love-animal
> And some final crisis of earth's life is now to be enacted
> Faithfully and selflessly by them all.
>
> (p. 142)

What Felicity 'knows' becomes increasingly ironic with each repetition, as the specificity of the verb splinters into a vague, indiscriminate 'religious' vocabulary; this verbal conscription of elementals numbs the ear ('deep mightiness . . . sacramental . . . holy . . . great depth . . . great remoteness . . . Somehow . . . infinite solemnity . . . infinitely tiny . . . inconceivably huge . . .'), and since 'verbal conscription' – particularly for the poet – means 'conscription for *conscious* use', it becomes evident that Felicity's world-description is completely inadequate to accommodate or focus those energies. She is 'unprepared', to recall Don Juan's commentary on Castaneda's experience of *seeing*. Combining Castaneda with Jung's essay-notes on the Apollo–Dionysos coupling, it is *possible to say* that Felicity fails – and dies for that failure – when she omits to play the role of controlling 'Artist' (Apollo) and that of the 'Work of Art' (Dionysos) equally. But we are prevented by the construction of Hughes' narrative from any precipitate release into a superior critical judgement; *we* simply cannot get past the linguistic barriers to become the two-faced 'artists' of our own experience and re-admit those unleashed energies profitably in the external world, just as the narrator seems incapable of establishing omniscient control of his own narrative. Why, after all should a 'hopeful' or even coherent artistic context to be set up especially for the ritual's performance, when it has no cultural equivalent in the outside world?

> In drug religions what the neophyte finds in the depths of his trance corresponds in detail to the mythology shared by the cult group. In repeating the experience, he deepens his integration into the psychic depth of the shared system of beliefs. So he grows and strengthens. Without a shared mythological framework, the experience of the trance is chaotic – and disintegrative. So repeating the experience destroys the individual. (personal communication, 10 October 1984)

At the height of the ritual, 'the experience destroys the individual', and the initiate – Felicity – is murdered by Maud, who then announces Lumb's intention to run away with her 'like an ordinary man/ with his ordinary wife' (p. 147). The women cling to him like 'one undersea monster' to prevent his escape, forcing him (in the 'outer' world) to re-enact the potential error within the underworld episodes, the cutting away of all ties within the feminine; Lumb breaks free of their 'grip', re-imagines his own illusory freedom.

The final long chapter (pp. 155–70), narrating the man-hunt and death of Lumb, also concentrates his failure in the role of mediator to the elementals: he alternates helplessly between Apollinian meditation: 'He imagines the furious micro-energy and stamina of the blue fly/ But the idea takes no hold' (p. 155); and his biologically determined fate: 'His fuel is burning too fast and smokily. His knees tangle with their chemical limits' (*ibid.*). The fundamental identity of Hades and Dionysos is re-asserted in characteristically Greek terms, as Lumb already tastes the dead man's obol in his mouth: 'The bronze polished light of the lowering sun is without illusion of any sort./ It brings him a poisonous thinness like the taste of pennies' (p. 157). That identity becomes a reality for the pursuers as much as their victim; temporarily numbed by a stone block, Evans' face 'wears a thick mask of drained *woodenness* which he dare not touch' (p. 162; my italics). Even after he has been dealt his death-wound, Lumb 'runs imagining/ Mountains of golden spirit, he springs across their crests. . . . He imagines he is effortless Adam, before weariness entered, leaping for God' (p. 163), but the ritually intense 'exultation' in the powers of the 'spiritual' self break down into a more brutal, mechanical realization, registered in plain speech:

> He runs badly hurt, his blood inadequate,
> Hurling his limbs anyhow
> Lumpen and leaden, and there is no more air . . .
> His precious and only body
> Is nothing more than some radio-transmitter, a standard structure.
>
> (p. 164)

To the very end of the narrative, Lumb finds no 'direction' which satisfactorily bridges the distance between the material and the spiritual, the Apollinian and the Dionysian, or recognizes the evolutionary continuity between the two terms. No trace of his effort remains, either: the bodies of Maud, the Reverend and Felicity are burned all together, on a funeral pyre: 'All evidence goes up.'

THE EPILOGUE

The main narrative is not, however, the end of the story. In the Epilogue, the original Lumb turns up again, 'in a straggly sparse village on the West Coast of Ireland' (p. 173). Three small girls report their encounter with him to the local priest, in which he whistles up an otter out of the nearby lough. This harmonious summoning of unconscious elementals is not only a consolidation of Lumb's advance from his previous experience with a creature of the lake (the double episode), but also in marked contrast to the priest's sentimental response, which conspicuously fails to translate the released emotions into conscious profit: he compares Lumb's miracle to 'this giant, shining beauty that God whistled up out of the waters of chaos' (p. 175), but the speech he delivers is presented through its negative effect on the girls ('[they] became dull, and the moment his words paused they vanished through the doorway' (*ibid.*), and his own mistaken response, interpreting the violent shifts of a dualistic awareness as a supernatural experience: 'The priest hardly noticed, he was so astonished by his own emotion. He sat down, trembling and faint, as in a fever. He thought something supernatural had happened' (*ibid.*). The main narrative fails to consolidate, or consecrate, the private fantasy of Lumb's adventures in the 'inner' underworld into the religious and ceremonial structure of the community. In the public world, Lumb is 'insane', his actions in the 'outer' realm have disastrous consequences. So here the roles of poet and priest are kept tragically separate, the artist is denied the support of the 'spiritual solidarity' which confirms the validity of his adventure and gives it a solid purpose.

The priest then copies out the 'densely-corrected' verses which Lumb had left behind with the children: these are the immediate fruits of his 'return', and it is with them that the volume, and the account of the original Lumb's fate concludes. They were originally conceived as a sequence of little prayers or *vacanas* in response to Hughes' fear that he might have throat cancer; their inspiration was A. K. Ramanujan's collection of free-verse lyrics written in praise of the deity Śiva (*Speaking of Śiva*):

> I began to write these *vacanas* as little prayers – about a hundred of them, some of which will be published in *Orts*. And then, when I was shaping up *Gaudete*, I realised there should be something at the end and that this sort of poem would be ideal if I could write it in the right context. (Hughes in conversation with Faas, quoted in Faas, *Ted Hughes*, p. 138)

The ideal nature of this short devotional form lies in its explicit alliance of 'Poetry' and 'Religion': the Bhakti saints who wrote the verses in Ramanujan's book composed what he calls an 'anti-structure' of devotion, an 'ideological rejection of the idea of structure itself' (Introduction, p. 35) as it was embodied in the 'public' face of Hinduism (i.e. texts, ritual and mythology). The Sufic idea of 'truth without form' – or with minimal concessions to form – is one we have encountered before, and it could be described as the conscience of organized religion, its essential regenerator. The subject intentionally distances himself from the Establishment, which concerns itself with the Cosmic Creator and his Creation as *objects*, in order to re-discover the self imprisoned in its own illusions, for which death is the ultimate reality. It is this act of 'compensation' which creates the conditions for Religion's subsistence, in the same way as the Central European post-war anti-poetry enabled the survival of literary art on a morally defensible basis after the Holocaust. One of the meanings of *vacana* is 'what is said', as opposed to what is imitated or received second-hand. And like those poets, the Vīraśaiva saints abjure all formal satisfactions absolutely – *vacana* also means 'prose', a built-in defence against the seductive glamour of 'Poetry'. 'The instrument is not what is "made", but what one "is" '

(*Speaking of Śiva*, Introduction, p. 38), as indicated by the following two
lyrics by Basavaṇṇa:

> 494
> I don't know anything like time-beats and metre
> nor the arithmetic of strings and drums;
> I don't know the count of iamb and dactyl.
>
> My lord of the meeting rivers,
> as nothing will hurt you
> I'll sing as I love.
>
> 500
> Make of my body the beam of a lute
> of my head the sounding gourd
> of my nerves the strings
> of my fingers the plucking rods.
>
> Clutch me close
> and play your thirty-two songs
> O lord of the meeting rivers!
>
> (*ibid.*, pp. 82–3)

But where the Bhakti saints' profession of anti-structure and the
unmediated religious encounter becomes *complementary* to the 'public'
aspect of organized religion,[6] Hughes' reaction against form is *imposed*
rather than voluntary, and does not even inadvertently consolidate that
'continuity with an older ideal'; rather, it composes a lament for the
apparent impossibility of religious negotiation on the communal and
individual level alike, given the circumstances of the main narrative:

> *I hear your congregations at their rapture*
>
> Cries from the birds, long ago perfect
> And from the awkward gullets of beasts
> That will not chill into syntax.
>
> And I hear speech, the bossed Neanderthal brow-ridge
> Gone into beetling talk
> The Java man's bone grinders sublimed into chat.
>
> Words buckle the voice in tighter, closer
> Under the midriff
> Till the cry rots, and speech
>
> Is a fistula.
>
> (*Gaudete*, p. 176)

Elementals do not willingly 'chill' into the available verbal forms,
syntactical and metrical, but that 'universal' reluctance is not the major
point of the poem. In the passage from the first to the second stanza the
cultural premise is driven like a spike between contemporary discourse
and 'original' or elemental speech, and the possibility of their integration.

The antipathy between the verbal and the real is expressed in the shuddering transition from the Anglo-Saxon 'grinders' to the Romanesque 'sublimed' and the empirical abbreviation 'chat'. The cultural premise – observable in the sudden division of vocabularies and the disturbing dualism of the word 'fistula', where the medical or 'objective' meaning of the term thinly conceals its ferocious audial/visceral/ muscular energy – brings that antipathy into focus and sharpens it, because the religious context which should be renewed by the un-mediated experience – and which gives it public assent – seems absent, or unavailable to the artist. As in the main narrative, the 'truth' of that experience stands in jeopardy of remaining chaotic–destructive, exclusively Dionysian.

The *controlled* utterance of the whole psyche, which was beyond every character in the narrative proper, is crucially compromised for the 'new' Lumb, too:

> *Waving goodbye, from your banked hospital bed,*
> Waving, weeping, smiling, flushed
> It happened
> You knocked the world off, like a flower-vase.
>
> It was the third time. And it smashed.
>
> I turned
> I bowed
> In the morgue I kissed
> Your temple's refrigerated glazed
> As rained-on graveyard marble, my
> Lips queasy, heart non-existent
>
> And straightened
> Into sun-darkness
>
> Like a pillar over Athens
>
> Defunct
>
> In the glaring metropolis of cameras.
>
> (pp. 185–6)

The whole poem is an elegy for the 'state of negotiations' perceived between masculine and feminine, 'My brother and I', Personality and Essence in a world ruled by the 'objective imagination'. If the protagonist makes the attempt to articulate the paradigmatic action required by the main narrative – the saving of the feminine principle in nature – that cultural premise crucially intervenes between him and the object of his 'devotion'. He petrifies 'like a pillar over Athens' into an arcane religious relic, clinically pronounced dead by the finality of the latinate 'Defunct' and the all-pervasive 'objective' lens, tragically elevated to the status of cultural norm in the single word 'metropolis'.

The hero's dramatic experience runs up against the riddle rehearsed throughout the main narrative: the anachronism of religious devotion, performed in a world where its conscious/structural 'shell' is either defunct, or itself exposed to the disintegrative impact of the Dionysian energies it purports to contain. Again, the paper Lumb was offered as an explanation of events dissolved in his hands, 'weak as a birth-membrane'. Disintegration, structurelessness, the hero's 'absence' are indeed keywords in the experience of the Epilogue poems:

> *The Swallow – rebuilding –*
> Collects the lot
> From the sow's wallow.
>
> But what I did only shifted the dust about.
> And what crossed my mind
> Crossed into outer space.
> And for all rumours of me read obituary.
> What there truly remains of me
> Is that very thing – my absence.
>
> (p. 187)

Here is the self's anti-structure, its natural moral conclusion; and yet the admirable effort to get rid of false structural 'rumours' of the self now has to be reversed, in order to give that conclusion a stable conscious context. The poet–hero's final self-addressed query becomes mortally urgent, because the fate of the changeling is already threatening:

> So how will you gather me?
>
> I saw my keeper
> Sitting in the sun –
>
> If you can catch that, you are the falcon of falcons.
>
> (p. 187)

The hero's difficulty is fully pointed: Hughes is renewing the imaginative campaign of *Crow* to liberate himself from structural tyrannies, but the Epilogue poems seem much more conscious of the dangers of their own 'invisibility', the dangers of the 'subjective' descent Hughes detects in his second 'Myth and education' essay ('So *how* will you gather me?'); the emergency self of the Epilogue is so completely deluged by the onrush of elementals (its 'Dionysian intoxication') that the provision of an appropriate conscious context becomes an absolute priority. But just as the changeling failed to create suitable structural channels for those forces in the existing social order, so the relationship between the half-buried intermittent 'structure' of Lumb's underworld experience and the 'anti-structural' dramatic monologue of the poems is incomplete or disjoined. The divisive border between the narrative and the Epilogue begins to look ever more implacable, as if it were a mirror to the disjunction of the two terms 'Religious' and 'Poetic', and the collective realization of individual experience.

This problem finds a concrete manifestation in the disturbing lack of assimilation of many of the abstract elements within the poems themselves. 'I skin the skin', 'A doctor extracted', 'The sun, like a cold kiss in the street' and 'Having first given away pleasure' are typical examples; in 'Calves harshly parted from their mamas', the concrete description of the calves 'stupor sadness' is only apparently resolved by the presence of the tiger, and its caricature of psychic balance: 'He is roaming the earth light, unseen./ He is safe,/ Heaven and hell have both adopted him' (p. 197). The explicit or didactic conjunction of opposites co-exists uneasily with, for example, the complete surrender to dream-flow imagery that characterizes 'The viper fell from the sun.' The favours of the Goddess are sought from the point of view of Apollo, and that of Dionysos independently; their mutually 'repelling' images of the poet and their modes of worship have to be kept discrete, in separate poems.

The distance between the absent/unavailable structure and the anti-structure of the subject's chaotic experience may be covered by *nostalgia* – that 'nostalgia for the religious temperament' Hughes observed in himself in his letter to me of 10 October 1984, and which characterizes the ending of 'I see the oak's bride in the oak's grasp' in the persona's admiration of the remote or buried symbol of the cruciform oak; but more fundamentally than nostalgia, prayer covers the distance and offers to answer the seminal question of the very first poem:

> How will you correct
> The veteran of negatives
> And the survivor of cease?
> (p. 176)

It is prayer which envisages the re-birth of the self's 'absence' when the old self closes its 'objective' eye for the last time:

> *When the still-soft eyelid sank again*
> Over the stare
> Still bright as if alive
> The chiselled threshold
> Without a murmur
> Ground the soul's kernel
>
> Till blood welled.
>
> And your granite –
> Anointed –
> Woke.
>
> Stirred.

The poem bears a particular resemblance to another *vacana* by Basavaṇṇa:

> 686.
> He'll grind till you're fine and small.
> He'll file till your colour shows
>
> If your grain grows fine
> in the grinding,
> if you show colour
> in the filing,
>
> then our lord of the meeting rivers
> will love you
> and look after you.
>   (*Speaking of Śiva*, p. 86)

Basavaṇṇa's conditional is the conditional of prayer, which holds open rival possibilities for the subject: the potential for reduction and a meaningless 'death' – if the condition is not fulfilled – and the potential for reduction and refinement, if it is fulfilled. The animal-level elementals unleashed in *Gaudete* must be channelled carefully; the beautiful, integrated woman has to be re-configured out of the patchwork of her primitive 'masks'. This precipitation of 'her' whole image out of the welter of phenomenal appearances is the task of several poems: 'Who are you?', 'The lark sizzles in my ear', 'I watched a wise beetle', 'A primrose petal's edge', 'The grass blade is not without', 'Sometimes it comes, a gloomy flap of lightning' and 'Hearing your moan echo, I chill, I shiver' all evince the same effort. Even Hughes' use of the *vacana*-like prayer form is none the less afflicted by division; that division in the semantic of 'prayer' Gurdjieff singles out:

> it must be understood that there are different prayers and their results are different. . . . When we speak of prayer or of the results of prayer we always imply only one kind of prayer – petition. . . . Most prayers have nothing in common with petitions. I speak of ancient prayers; many of them are much older than Christianity. These prayers are, so to speak, *recapitulations*; by repeating them aloud or to himself a man endeavours to experience what is in them, their whole content, with his mind and feeling.
> (in Ouspensky, *In Search of the Miraculous*, p. 300)

Not all of Hughes' poems are recapitulations of the dramatic act of understanding; 'I watched a wise beetle', 'The grass-blade is not without' and 'This is the maneater's skull' are definitely *petitions* for that dramatic moment, they prescribe the present distance from it – the same distance between the subject and the religious object of his devotion. The petitionary version is a grim reminder of the horrendous dualisms which inhabit *Gaudete*, where the recapitulations open the possibility – if the poet or reader have ears to hear – of re-experiencing an ultimate moral revelation:

The saviour
From these veils of wrinkle and shawls of ache

Like the sun
Which is itself cloudless and leafless

Was always here, is always as she was.

(p. 192)

or re-affirming the collective self outside mechanical functions which derives its terms of importance from 'death':

Looking for her form
I find only a fern.

Where she should be waiting in the flesh
Stands a sycamore with weeping letters.

I have a memorial too.

Where I lay in space
Is the print of the earth which trampled me

Like a bunch of grapes.

Now I am being drunk
By a singing drunkard.

(pp. 192–3)

The poem is written from the point of view of the refined 'I', whose expression is damaged by the absence of an appropriate formal personality; that personality is 'intoxicated' or overwhelmed by its Dionysian experience, it is 'out of control'. In this condition, *recapitulation* is only intermittently possible, and prayer finds itself repeatedly descending to the level of *petition*, the appeal of the disunified self.

Keith Sagar is surely right when he claims that the most recognizable progenitor of *Gaudete* in modern English literature is *The Wasteland*. Like Hughes, Eliot too suffered the second-hand futility of the prevailing cultural and literary models for the 'poetic' self, fully dramatized. The chaos was covered poignantly by the terminology of oriental mysticism, supplying the 'false resolution' with which the poem ended. In *Gaudete*, the disintegrative force of elementals is released fully, confirming the direction of Hughes' effort in previous books, but no context seems adequate to 'contain' that power. All the characters, including the poet and the reader, are made to submit to the Dionysian annihilation of 'controls'. In consequence, the changeling fails utterly to incorporate those energies in a significant social form, and for the poet of the Epilogue their organization by the 'shell' of Gaudete's underworld episodes – i.e. their *conscious* absorption – is incomplete or problematic. The mythic blueprint itself is only completed technically in *Cave Birds*. Furthermore, it is not until *Remains of Elmet, Moortown* and *River* that a successful return to the 'outer' – social, cultural and Natural – world is engineered, and the benefits of the invisible quest begin to be registered in everyday life.

———————— • ————————

CHAPTER 8

CAVE BIRDS: AN ALCHEMICAL CAVE DRAMA

> In my own country, people do not like poetry. I have long searched for
> people who want action, but all they want is words. I am ready to show
> you action; but none will patronize this action. So I present you with –
> words. (Jalaludin Rumi, in Shah, *The Way of the Sufi*, p. 117)

Cave Birds is the natural development of the process of 'pulling yourself
together' which Hughes inaugurated in *Crow*. As a consequence, the
mythic structure of the book is etched even more definitively, so that
none of the poems included in the sequence acquire an individual life
beyond the transformative purpose of the narrative nor are they made
available for consideration as separate literary objects. Hughes' summary
of the basic narrative, which concerns 'the psychological crime,
punishment and compensation of Socrates', was originally a subtitle to
the volume:

> *The Death of Socrates and his Resurrection in Egypt* – with some idea of
> suggesting that aspect of it which is a critique of sorts of the Socratic
> abstraction and its consequences through Christianity to us. His resurrec-
> tion in Egypt, in that case, would imply his correction, his re-absorption
> into the magical–religious archaic source of intellectual life in the East
> Mediterranean, and his re-emergence as Horus – beloved child and spouse
> of the Goddess. (Letter to Gifford and Roberts, *Ted Hughes: A critical study*,
> p. 260; my italics)

The vibration of that single word 'correction' immediately stitches the
psychological seam between *Crow* and *Cave Birds*, before we ever reach
the identity of aims – Crow's potential destiny was 'union with his bride'
– in the last statement. Crow as a 'shadow-man' enacted, or occasionally
observed, the 'inferior' characteristics of an animal nature which had
been cut off and hence depraved by abstracted consciousness, with a
savage clarity. The images of the condition of 'Essence', or the contents
of the Unconscious that he proposed were primitive, child-like, and
often violent. Because an outright antagonism between 'Personality' and
'Essence' dominated large expanses of the volume – normally in the form

of the Genesis God's opposition to Crow himself – its moral activity was essentially ironic, reductive; Crow's potential image remained just that, a subterranean possibility; and the symbol of the Triple Goddess onto which it opened remained an underswell, barely audible. But once the shadow-truths exposed by Crow have begun to be accepted into consciousness, all the paradigms of spiritual transformation come into play with full force: the death–re-birth matrix universal to the Religious response, the shamanic dream of dismemberment, flight and return, most concisely the alchemical transformation of 'coarse' material into 'fine', of 'below' into 'above'. The high profile of such esoteric structures and a narrative which is 'thinking for itself' above and below the impulses of consciousness could be seen as a coming antidote to the authoritarian personality which was given charge of whole poems in the early poetry, establishing its own autonomous voices within a plural self. On the other hand, more darkly, the problematic nature of *Gaudete* seems to have been partially inherited, in the form of a painful rift between 'structural' and 'dramatic' elements and the heuristic compositional process of the book; one begins to sense that the dramatic accounts of the Body struggle consistently to keep pace with the new, 'corrected' structural narrative adopted by the Mind. And this difficulty in turn finds a reflection in the unease of the critic who discovers that his own 'critical story' – so easily attracted by the intellectual completeness of esoteric 'theory' – is continually in danger of *fabricating* the book's triumph; the isolated cell of scholarly cross-referencing and synthesis outruns dramatic achievement, germinating its own fictional success.

Alchemy, or the alchemical nature of the drama enacted in *Cave Birds*, is the keystone to any structural appreciation of the sequence. Jung compresses the objectives of alchemy admirably:

> The alchemical operation consisted essentially in separating the prima materia, the so-called chaos, into the active principle, the soul, and the passive principle, the body, which were then reunited in personified form in the *coniunctio* or 'chymical marriage'. In other words, the *coniunctio* was allegorized as the hierosgamos, the ritual cohabitation of Sol [Sun/Masculine] and Luna [Moon/Feminine]. From this union sprang the *filius sapientiae* or *filius philosophorum*, the transformed Mercurius, who was thought of as hermaphroditic in token of his rounded perfection. ('Paracelsus as a spiritual phenomenon', *Alchemical Studies*, pp. 122–3)

Jung's use of the terms 'soul' and 'body' is initially open to dualistic misinterpretation, but the central point remains the same: the aim is to unify the opposites, whether they are screened as masculine–feminine, Unconscious–Conscious, or Essence–Personality. This 'chymical marriage' consolidates the image of 'the transformed Mercurius', who is actually a figure for Crow himself, raised to a higher power. Mercurius is Crow's own 'developed image':[1]

'What is below is like what is above, that the miracle of the one thing may be accomplished.' This one thing is the lapis or *filius philosophorum.* As the definitions and names of the prima materia make abundantly plain, matter in alchemy is material and spiritual, and spirit spiritual and material. Only, in the first case matter is *cruda, confusa, grossa, crassa, densa,* and in the second it is *subtilis. (Alchemical Studies,* p. 140)

The hermaphroditic image is a refinement of Crow's often 'gross' and 'chaotic' efforts to locate his true Creator, in accordance with Paracelsus' revelation that God created man 'from below upwards'. That the image of the Redeemer should break the literary surface in precisely these terms could not be called either a cultural accident or a cultural irrelevance. The notion that it originates in Matter may be understood as unconscious nature's 'compensation' of the dangerously aloof image of Christ himself, which appears to be open to misinterpretation as a radical rejection of the body and physical nature, particularly in a book like Revelation. It is clear from this commentary that the visible, 'chemical' face of alchemy – recognition of which provides the ground for the modern ridicule of the alchemist's art – is its least significant aspect, totally subordinate to the psychological experiment it symbolizes, and the 'spiritual' product which it – hopefully – precipitates. Shah quotes from the *De augumentis scientarum* of the alchemist Roger Bacon: 'Alchemy is like the man who told his sons that he had buried gold for them in his vineyards. They dug and found no gold, but this turned the mold for the vine roots and caused an abundant harvest' (*The Sufis*). From this point of view, it might be said that *Cave Birds* embodies Hughes' endeavour to become a 'complete scientist', witnessing, yet fully implicated in his experience rather than conducting an 'objective' experiment outside it.

The alchemical operation is performed on more than one level. In *Crow* we were given a language 'afflicted' – in Simone Weil's sense of the word – by a knowledge of its own mechanical procedures, a language which refused to move too far from Matter, or Silence, for fear of falsifying them. 'Poetry' itself was reduced to the lowest level, at the bottom of all things, intensely wary of any 're-birth' which might occur in the purely verbal dimension. Even at first glance, however, it is evident that the poetic texture of *Cave Birds* is denser, richer, that the words have regained much of their suggestive depth and many of their semantic 'freedoms'. This renewal of poetic language, which Graham Bradshaw in a footnote to his essay on *Crow* finds so reassuring, is due entirely to the change in the moral environment effected by *Crow*: once the 'material' obligations of language have been realized, the 'air of trial-

and-error exploration' – Popa's discursive model of poetry – can be projected into a wider, more ambitious field, and words can begin to refine their expressive abilities as a direct register of the protagonist's own psychological movement 'upward'. It is the expressiveness of the self which finally decides the nature and extent of language's alchemical refinement. So much of Hughes' earlier 'ritual intensity of music' returns, but within the terms of this new, ethically comprehensive framework. The first and last couplets of the second poem, 'The summoner' give a simple example:

> Spectral, gigantified,
> Protozoic, blood-eating . . .
>
> Sooner or later
> The grip.

The verbally dense texture of those latinate adjectives would find no place in the primitive world of *Crow*; but the crucial point is that the 'poetic' thickness of the diction, which has its culmination in 'Protozoic', is only rehearsing the Summoner's material origin more and more accurately (a protozoa is one of the most primitive, simply structured organisms); and when, in the final rotation of vocabulary, the 'refine-ment' suddenly precipitates 'blood-eating' and the Anglo-Saxon 'grip', the effects of Hughes' alchemization are clear – a trap snaps shut with 'grip', and the old self (with its language) is made to acquiesce passively in the awesome transformative process which is already eating away at its very foundations.

The principle of alchemy also played a significant role in the 'layered' compositional process of the volume, almost by accident: at first Leonard Baskin produced only nine drawings, which Hughes converted into a complete cycle of poems ('The summoner', 'The advocate' [absent from the 1978 edition], 'The interrogator', 'The judge', 'The plaintiff', 'The executioner', 'The accused', 'The risen' and 'Finale'); then he drew another ten birds, and, as Sagar indicates 'To accommodate them Hughes had to invent a whole series of further stages between execution and resurrection' (*The Art of Ted Hughes*, p. 243). These poems include 'The knight', 'The gatekeeper', 'A flayed crow in the hall of judgement', 'The baptist', 'A green mother', 'A riddle', 'The scapegoat', 'The guide', 'Walking bare', and 'An owlflower'. Finally, Hughes added twelve more poems of his own volition: 'The scream', 'After the first fright', 'She seemed so considerate', 'Your mother's bones wanted to speak', 'In these fading moments', 'First, the doubtful charts of skin', 'Something was happening', 'Only a little sleep', 'As I came, I saw a wood', 'After there was nothing there was a woman', 'His legs ran about', 'Bride and groom'. As we shall see, there are some important refinements which occur in the open space between the three groups of poems, and indeed in the space between the initial statements of various words/images and their subsequent 'revision' at later stages of the sequence. Each aspect of the alchemical process is devoted to the same end, the self-integration to be achieved within the Crucible or 'cave' of the protagonist's being: 'Break nature's frame, be resolute and brave,/ Then rest at peace in Unity's black cave' (Attar, *The Conference of the Birds*, p. 30). The sequence opens with 'The scream', which Hughes introduced as follows in the broadcast of *Cave Birds*: 'The hero's cockerel innocence, it turns out, becomes his guilt. His own self, finally, the innate nature of his flesh and blood, brings him to court.' Within the poem itself, the self's guilt is observed in some haunting echoes of Hughes' own literary 'past':

> There was the sun on the wall – my childhood's
> Nursery picture. And there was my gravestone
> Which shared my dreams, and ate and drank with me happily.
>
> All day the hawk perfected its craftsmanship
> And even through the night the miracle persisted.
>
> Mountains lazed in their smoky camp.
> Worms in the ground were doing a good job.
>
> Flesh of bronze, stirred with a bronze thirst,
> Like a newborn baby at the breast,
> Slept in the sun's mercy.
>
> And the inane weights of iron
> That come suddenly crashing into people, out of nowhere,
> Only made me feel brave and creaturely.
>
> When I saw little rabbits with their heads crushed on roads
> I knew I rode the wheel of the galaxy.
>
> Calves' heads all dew-bristled with blood on counters
> Grinned like masks, and sun and moon danced.

Before the experience of *Crow*, the portents of death in, for example, 'Relic' from *Lupercal* or 'The green wolf' from *Wodwo* did indeed co-exist more or less harmoniously with the prevailing 'I'-fiction of those volumes – they never pressurized the formal structures of those poems to the point of disintegration, and the 'death of poetry' we encountered in *Crow*; in 'The hawk in the rain' the poet practised his craftsmanship through the 'perfected' hawk-image, all in the interests of preserving his 'empathizing' personality. A certain ritually excessive complacency also characterized 'Mountains' (*Wodwo*), which had

> no need to labour, only to possess the days,
> only to possess their power and their presence,
>
> Smiling on the distance, their faces lit with the peace
> Of the father's will and testament.

Likewise, the phrase 'worms in the ground were doing a good job' exploits a potential within some of the responses to Nature in *Season Songs* (1976), which evidenced a kind of self-conceit when considered in isolation, aside from the often brutal life of their dramatic contexts. Even the 'brave and creaturely' responses of lines 11–27 summon the ghosts of Hughes' previous sentimentalizations of the animal self, Dick Straightup from *Lupercal* and Billy Red from the story 'Sunday', included in *Wodwo*. The abstracted falsity of self is not derided from a superior, 'objective' position, as in 'Egghead' and 'A man seeking experience', but observed on the most intimate level, in the elements of Hughes' own poetic personality. The failure of the first three volumes to counter-attack upon the mass of false or fragmentary poetic selves with the sustained commitment and urgency one imagines Hughes wanted, ensured the surrealistic desperation of *Wodwo*, and the 'shadow'-eruption of *Crow*, casting aside all the individual elegances and exclusive vocal purities once and for all. It is revealing to keep this appreciation in mind during the reading of the last six lines of the poem:

> Then I, too, opened my mouth to praise –
>
> But a silence wedged my gullet.
>
> Like an obsidian dagger, dry, jag-edged,
> A silent lump of volcanic glass,
>
> The scream
> Vomited itself.

This works well as a description of *Crow*'s appearance, with all the shock of an autonomous psychic complex, after the 'personality-poetry' of *The Hawk in the Rain*, *Lupercal* and to a slightly lesser extent *Wodwo*. The 'old self' is only rendered totally passive by the destructiveness of such an experience *in literature*, stopping its 'poetic' machineries as well as its psychological bias. The passivity of the old self automatically creates the conditions in which alchemical transformation can take place: the 'flesh of bronze, stirred with a bronze thirst' recalls the base substance – either copper or bronze – which was to be transformed first into silver, and finally the gold of the objective psyche. In one of the Visions of Zosimos, for instance, the meaning of 'priest' is defined as the man who is no longer the 'brazen man, for he has changed the colour of his nature and become the silver man; and if you will, you will soon have him [as] the golden man' (*Alchemical Studies*, p. 64). And in Andreae's *The Chymical Wedding of Christian Rosencreutz* – which Hughes sees as a seminal 'tribal dream' – the hero is led into a three-cornered, underground tomb supported by a 'lower' trinity of animals (eagle, ox and lion); the tomb belongs to Venus, destroyer of many questing heroes, and the door opening on to it is engraved with a secret, riddling copper inscription –

the riddle of our lower nature, which harbours the creative image of the Goddess within it.

The basic material 'bronze image' of the self recurs in 'The summoner', and its alchemical potential, Crow's own 'silent' possibility of development is glimpsed, emerging from the destructive 'shadows':

> Among crinkling of oak-leaves – an *effulgence*,
> Occasionally glimpsed . . .
>
> . . . You grow to recognize the identity
> Of your *protector*.
>   (my italics)

The challenge for the reader is the paradoxical – and in this context paradox should be considered as a kind of verbal equivalent of the alchemical *coniunctio oppositorum* – realization that the hero's 'protection' (and his final spiritual 'effulgence') entails his own death, and that further progress can only be achieved in terms of the seemingly 'grotesque' whole Body, not the abstract Mind. The reader's response to paradox, to the 'Conjunction' of the body's lethal grip *as* its saving grace determines the possibility of his own refinement, and his willingness to broaden the completeness of the narrative through his own experience of it. The paradox is at the centre of the trap I examined earlier, which closes with the shift of vocabularies between the first six lines and the final couplet.

'After the first fright', like 'The scream', belongs to the third group of poems Hughes produced; the effect of these two pieces, flanking 'The summoner', is to reverse a tendency which first appeared in *The Hawk in the Rain*. Where, in the earlier book, the *arguments* against hubris of poems like 'Egghead' and 'A man seeking experience' remained alarmingly unconscious, unsupported by any dramatic discovery of the same inclination 'within' – so that language even began to exhibit its own rhetorical egoism 'unconsciously' – in *Cave Birds* the 'structural' account ('The summoner') is validated by the material *experience* of the first and third poems.

The reclamation of argument by inner experience is actually the subject of 'After the first fright':

> I sat up and took stock of my options.
> I argued my way out of every thought anybody could think
> But not out of the stopping and starting
> Catherine wheel in my belly.

In *The Conference of the Birds* Zulnoon experiences a similar plea: 'Don't chatter about loss – be lost! Repent,/ And give up vain, self-centred argument' (p. 131). The hero's conceptual strongholds – first 'Civilization', then 'Sanity and again Sanity and above all Sanity' – are undermined by responses culled from different cultural environments:

the loss of fingers by the bereaved is one of the requirements of mourning in primitive societies, and the disembowelling 'cross-shaped cut' is a social requirement in Japanese culture, under certain circumstances. For Hughes, both responses evince '*the* symbolic act of the acceptance of the *reality* of what hurts. It is part of the reverence – in that case not short of worship – for the actuality of inner experience' (Gifford and Roberts, *Ted Hughes*, p. 260). Such an attitude not only echoes the Sufi demand to 'detach from fixed ideas and preconceptions. And face what is to be your lot' (*The Sufis*, p. 182), it necessitates a temporary return to a *Crow*-ish, machine-like structure in the poem – a movement Gifford and Roberts regret, finding it 'redundant in this sequence' (*Ted Hughes*, p. 207). It is difficult to see, none the less, how else the inescapability of the message from the material 'whole' could be translated into poetry, and also difficult not to suspect that the critical reluctance stems not so much from a 'purely literary' dissatisfaction (which is a delusion anyway) as a psychological discomfort with the evident helplessness of all the civilized and sane human arguments in the circumstances. The 'grip' of the poem's mechanical patterning and the material process undergone either force the reader's acknowledgement of his own helplessness in the requirements of the narrative or his rational–humane rebellion against it. As in *Crow*, this polarization of the reader's response becomes the traumatic occasion for self-knowledge, so that it appears to decide his fate, or the nature of the world he wants to inhabit. From the psychological–esoteric point of view, 'After the first fright' is absolutely *functional*, not redundant: 'its declaration to the "I" in the poem is immediate and complete, totally understood. But at the same time (perhaps this too influences the tone and style of the piece) it is a language that excludes concepts and words' (*ibid.*, p. 260). At the end of the poem, 'The guilt came./ And when they covered his face I went cold.' It is the rigidity of the protagonist's conscious attitude which ensures the transformation of the summoner into the more active, accusatory figure of 'The interrogator', who is represented in Leonard Baskin's drawing as a vulture:

> Small hope now for the stare-boned mule of man
> Lumped on the badlands, at his Concrete Shadow.

> This bird is the Sun's key-hole.
> The Sun spies through her.

We have already observed how the earliest phase of the dissolution of Egoism was narrated by a seismic vocabulary shift, the latinized crust allowing a transparent view down on to the volcanic reality beneath; this was part of Hughes' linguistic return to origin, to the Germanic–Norse heritage and dialect instinct he associated with his real self in the *London*

Magazine interview, 'Ted Hughes and Crow'. In *Cave Birds*, the high incidence of substantive and adjectival compounds – of which 'stare-boned' is the earliest conspicuous example – offers a further verbal indication that the deeper levels of the psyche have been fully engaged in dramatic form. Compounding is a dominant technique in *Beowulf*, and it involves the qualification or 'refinement' of a literal base-word by a conceptual element, retaining the real force of both concreteness and abstraction. Compounds participate in the world of 'heroic' action by exhibiting their own tension between the two warring elements, which are in a state of 'negotiation' continuous with the *outward* aspect of the narrative, the hero in conflict with the monstrous shapes of the unknown – or as in Hughes' improvisatory discourse, concepts are 'tried out' on the root-word with varying results. The compound in 'The interrogator', 'stare-boned', shows a harmonious state of negotiation: the concept 'stare', because it is held in check by the 'matter' of the base-element 'boned', never threatens to turn into the concentrated rational stare which Hughes, in his two 'Myth and education' essays, and Alan Watts in *The Way of Zen*, are at pains to condemn. This is the kind of perceptual gaze which strips to the bone (a version of the shamanistic experience of 'seeing one's skeleton'), and burns away all the ego-pretensions in the ray cast by death, rather than consolidating them.

In the present context, the compound also has an alchemical effect, condensing an 'outer' and an 'inner' meaning so that the hero is simultaneously being stripped by the vulture's stare and the helpless staring witness to the material process which is correcting him. Both meanings are confirmed by the reference to the '*mule* of man', a common Sufi image for the self in its mechanical or unconscious state, customarily disguising its true nature with the freedom of an arbitrary Personality; we might recall Gurdjieff's analogy of horse and driver (see Ch. 4, p. 86) or the more immediately relevant introduction to Attar's main narrative:

> Since love has spoken in your soul, reject
> The Self, that whirlpool where our lives are wrecked;
> As Jesus rode his donkey, ride on it;
> Your stubborn Self must bear you and submit –
> Then burn this Self and purify your soul.
> (*The Conference of the Birds*, p. 30)

Furthermore, the image from Sufi esoteric teaching is conflated with one from the world of Jungian psychology in the phrase 'at his concrete *shadow*', implying that the principle of alchemization is absolutely central to the experience of both poet and reader.

Another variant on an alchemical operation takes place in the third line. The perception of the ominously black vulture shadowing the

brightness of the Sun is really a moral test for the reader: it summarizes
the ethical challenge of Crow and the animals of Hughes' earlier poetry
to transform our dualistic response to oppositional pairings (Good/Evil,
Light/Darkness, Creation/Destruction, etc.) into something closer to
what Jung terms the alchemist's 'antinomian thinking'. Here Spirit is
nothing more than transformed Matter, Light a production of Darkness
and the descent 'Below' a necessary induction to the ascent 'Above' –
even as we saw in the title poem of Hughes' first volume. In the present
case, the alchemical Sun – which Dorn equates with gold, and in which
'the seminal and formal virtue of all things whatsoever lies hid' (Jung,
Mysterium coniunctionis, p. 94) – is *obscured at its birth*. And this
denigration is the beginning of the work, the sign of putrefaction, and
the sure beginning of the commixture' (Jung, quoting from the *De
chemia, ibid.*, p. 118). The notion of the 'black sun' as a *coniunctio
oppositorum* essential to further development is actually true on the most
elementary material level; as Graham Bradshaw in his intelligent
commentary 'Creative mythology in *Cave Birds*' (in Sagar (ed.), *The
Achievement of Ted Hughes*, pp. 210–38) points out, black sun-spots are
actually more than usually intense concentrations of energy (see p. 230),
so that Hughes' lines achieve a compression of Spirit and Matter which is
above all a triumph of the unifying moral intelligence, and only
secondarily a triumph of linguistic resource: 'You must go through the
gate of the blackness if you would gain the light of Paradise in the
whiteness' (Jung, quoting Ripley's *Chymische Schrifften*, in *Mysterium
Coniunctionis*, p. 98). In the concreteness of the resemblance one senses
that Hughes' ambition to uncover the Ur-language, or language-behind-
language, 'to which all men might attain' is no longer Utopian wish-
fulfilment but becomes a real thing. That sense is reinforced by lines 5–9
(examined in Chapter 1), in which the 'spiritual' realization is
consolidated as a transformation of the poem's aesthetic surface: the
musical or audial–visceral impact of the Norse–Germanic vocabulary
fleshes out the 'semantic' understanding, appealing directly to the body
rather than the mind exclusively. The poet's knitting-together of two
'alienated' worlds of language – they tend to work autonomously in
English cultural life – is the surest 'poetic' sign of his own returning
psychic balance, a coming reconciliation of his own 'inner system of
stresses'.

'She seemed so considerate' subsists in the same relationship to 'The
interrogator' as 'The scream' and 'After the first fright' do to 'The
summoner', deepening the structural outline in the language of 'ordinary
talk' and straightforward confession, suggesting an Imagination freed of
its dependence on words:

I felt life had decided to cancel me
As if it saw better hope for itself elsewhere.

Then this bird-being embraced me, saying:
'Look up at the Sun. I am the one creature
Who never harmed any living thing.'

I was glad to shut my eyes, and be held.
Whether dead or unborn, I did not care.

If anything, the Imagination takes its cue from Baskin's drawing rather than an 'expressive' verbal idea, in the sudden fusion of the death of the hero's 'pet fern' in the poem – 'the one fellow creature I still cherished' – with the drawing's visual suggestion, that dying cock and decayed fern are one and the same thing. The eye is drawn from the words on the page to the ambiguity of the picture and back again, in a pendulum-movement which shows that the true flight of the moral Imagination cannot be confined to the immediate text, it is fundamentally extra-literary. The co-presence of word and picture – and the Pilinsky-like 'lack of language' within the poem itself – recall the epigraph at the beginning of the chapter, which accurately represented the difficulties which besiege the poet and reader of *Cave Birds* at every turn.

Cave Birds is the first sequence to discover a context in which the deity of 'Hawk roosting' and 'Gog' can acquire a controlling influence. 'The judge', for instance, is a reincarnation of Gog but invested with his proper material authority. The poem embodies a paradox, in which diction like 'Pondering', 'Law', 'geometry', 'Cosmic equipoise' cumulatively appears to invite the 'pure' image of Judgement conventionally filled out by the Logos-God. It soon becomes obvious, however, that judgement derives not from the 'objective' standards of that 'Absolute' historical image of the Creator but from everything it shuts out; it comes not from a set of abstract principles but from the material level of the psyche itself. The protagonist is his own judge, just as the reader is given an explicit opportunity for self-assessment: he is required to perform a similar operation to that in 'Hawk roosting', sending a conceptual vocabulary back to its root in Matter ('teeters', 'web-glistening', 'Lolling', 'garbage-sack', 'buttocks'). But the savage irony of the reader's failure to straddle the distance between words and things was an isolated instance in the earlier poem; any weakness in the present context will effectively terminate any further possibility of 'negotiation' within the volume for the reader. It will indeed become an 'invisible book' to him, confirming the potential for the sort of responsive exile Hughes noted in *Crow*.

The pressure on the reader is increased *unconsciously* by the next poem, in which interrogator hardens into plaintiff, and the claustrophobic 'alchemical' concentration of images intensifies to match the 'humbling weight' of the accuser's glare. The painful difficulty of the self-unifying process is dramatized as a compositional problem, with its own negative effects on the reading experience of the poem; up until the last four lines, 'The plaintiff's' appeal for unity scarcely budges from the 'structural' level – sampled as a scholarly search for correspondence provoked by lines 1–8, with their oblique reference to the alchemist's 'Luna', Jung's 'shadow' and the 'inverted tree' image of Christian mysticism. The same is true of 'The accused' and 'An owlflower', which also open the door back on to Aesthetic Criticism by inviting the application of one of its characteristic methods, the mechanical–intellectual sifting and correlation of 'interesting' allusions.

Only towards the end of the poem the schematic 'argument' begins to be translated into the language of everyday 'experience', a momentum which is carried forward wholesale in the following poem 'In these fading moments'; the reader is left in no doubt none the less, that the 'pulling together' that the large narrative structure of *Cave Birds* performs involves a real pain, a pain which inhabits the deathly though diminishing space between structural and dramatic accounts within the sequence.

The worst aspect of the 'structural' impulse – the protagonist's superior imagination of his own 'imbecile innocence' – is annihilated in 'In these fading moments', as all his reactions are registered only in their most severe inner consequences: a damning self-neglect. The whole shift is expressed through a sudden switch to prosaic monologue, and the almost Hardyesque simplicity of the last three lines, in which the 'I' has been literally supplanted, so that it is no longer visible in even the grammar of the poem:

The whole earth
Had turned in its bed
To the wall.

That visibility is crushingly confirmed in 'The executioner', where the intonations of argument and experience coalesce with devastating effect:

The executioner

Fills up
Sun, moon, stars, he fills them up

With his hemlock –
They darken

He fills up the evening and the morning, they darken
He fills up the sea

He comes in under the blind filled-up heaven
Across the lightless filled-up face of water

He fills up the rivers he fills up the roads, like tentacles
He fills up the streams and the paths, like veins

The tap drips darkness darkness
Sticks to the soles of your feet

He fills up the mirror, he fills up the cup
He fills up your thoughts to the brims of your eyes

You just see he is filling the eyes of your friends
And now lifting your hand you touch at your eyes

Which he has completely filled up
You touch him

You have no idea what has happened
To what is no longer yours

It feels like the world
Before your eyes ever opened.

This poem is the most explicit narration of the death of Socrates within
the sequence, even down to the incidental detail of his death by hemlock
in the third line, and may be considered as a dramatic amplification of his
death-induced realization in Attar's poem that 'throughout my life not
one small particle/ Had any knowledge of itself at all!' *Crow* first
introduced the sense of poetry as an 'afflicted' production of the
mechanically inevitable, and that anti-poetry has its ultimate triumph in
'The executioner'. The repetition of the 'ugly' compound verb fills up
the entire poem with the most fundamental reality of Matter, but it is just
at this point that the Sufi 'requirement' – to pre-empt one's own physical
death by an act of moral intention – is satisfied, and the conditions for
poetry's future subsistence are established. The Sufi axiom 'Aesthetics is
only the lowest form of perception of the Real' (Barqi, in Shah, *The Way
of the Sufi*, p. 164) is re-affirmed and all opportunities for 'poetic'
expansion are spurned: in the fourth couplet, for example, the adjectival
possibilities of 'heaven' and 'water' find their way home to the single
phrase and the unalterable reality it presents ('blind *filled-up* heaven',
'lightless *filled-up* face of water'). The latent danger of 'The plaintiff',
that the preoccupation with fusing the schematic strands of the 'argument' might overwhelm the plain–intimate account of 'experience' and
the poet turn impersonal experimenter with language, is defused: 'The
executioner' is indeed a pivotal poem in the narrative structure of *Cave
Birds*, and localized tokens of the 'argument' are in evidence ('Sun' and
'moon' in the second line), but they are tuned to the particular
wavelength and language of 'experience', in which the poet is not
experimenter but sufferer and self-transformer:

And now lifting your hand you touch at your eyes

Which he has completely filled up
You touch him.

Lines like this comprise a denial of the indulgence of scholarly procedures openly invited by 'The plaintiff', hinting at their inadequacy, or the necessity of initiating 'objective' criticism into the disproportionately more monstrous world of experience.

'The executioner' is really Hughes' final revision of 'View of a pig', invoking the same 'death of poetry' and abandonment of outer familiarities, social personality, thoughts, narcissistic self, etc. as the earlier poem, but in a dramatic context in which the poem's potential can be fulfilled. It gives Hughes' clarification of the rationale behind Zbigniew Herbert's 'Study of the object': as in the fifth part of Herbert's poem, he obeys 'the counsels of the inner eye' to admit no-one, returning the world and the self to its uncreated silence, and waits for the revelation from its 'depths', from 'the iris of necessity/ the pupil of death'.

The whole poem concentrates a developing problem of readership in Hughes' work, in the terms in which I have been discussing it. It focuses the issue of *Death* on all its levels (psychological, linguistic, metaphysical), its central verb exposing the decision made by the reader's nature in response to that reality; his interpretation creates either the sense of an 'empty conclusion' on the one hand, or of 'ful-fillment' on the other. The predicament is unavoidable in the last couplet: 'It feels like the world/ Before your eyes ever opened.' The statement is not only close in spirit to the Buddhist use of the *Koan*, it mimics one such Koan quite specifically: 'Show me your original face before you were born.' Here is D. T. Suzuki's commentary on the purpose and experience of Koans:

> The *Koan* . . . has a most definite objective, the arousing of doubt and pushing it to its furthest limits. A statement built upon a logical basis is approachable through its rationality; whatever doubt or difficulty we may have had about it dissolves itself by pursuing the natural current of ideas. All rivers are sure to pour into the ocean; but the *Koan* is an iron wall standing in the way and threatening to overcome one's every intellectual effort to pass. . . . When [the] climax is reached, your whole personality, your inmost will, your deepest nature, determined to bring the situation to an issue, throws itself with no thought . . . of this or that, directly and unreservedly against the iron wall of the *Koan*. This throwing your entire being against the *Koan* unexpectedly opens up a hitherto unknown region of the mind. Intellectually, this is the transcending of the limits of logical dualism, but at the same time it is a regeneration, the awakening of an inner sense which enables one to look into the actual working of things. For the first time the meaning of the *Koan* becomes clear, and in the same way that one knows that ice is cold and freezing. (*An Introduction to Zen Buddhism*, pp. 108–9)

The act of reading poetry entails more than either admiring or harshly judgemental appreciation; it involves the reader in a certain commitment to the moral process poetry enacts in words; it is the kind of poetry which changes the nature of criticism. In Jung's psychiatric model, the patient has to change with the doctor, and here the reader must 'die' to his intellectual appreciation – what Suzuki calls 'logical dualism' – and throw the weight of his whole nature into Hughes' paradox and the search for self-knowledge, if the narrative is to survive as a meaningful event in his imagination. The 'I's of poet, his dramatic protagonist and the reader all alike reach the limit and discover their impotence, so that they 'give up the ghost'.

'The executioner' is followed by two poems which narrate the hero's 'confession' of his old self, 'The accused' and 'The knight'. But where the former labours under the same schematic afflictions as 'The plaintiff', as the 'conscious' mind (of both poet and reader!) struggles to fix its awareness of the material process undergone by the whole psyche, the latter functions successfully to resolve the image of the warrior-self which was present from Hughes' first books. The negative tendency of the warrior in 'Gog' 'for dealing with unpleasant or irrational experience, the complete suppression of the terror' ('Myth and education', 1, p. 66), was ironically reduced by the advance in consciousness of 'Crow's account of St. George', and it is annihilated utterly in 'The knight', which confirms Hughes' account of the initial state of his hero in the children's story *The Iron Man*:

> The story opens at the moment of complete crisis, when the defences of my hero have been shattered. He's finished. My hero is completely exposed. He's without any outer defences whatsoever. His Iron Man, his St. George armour, has been completely scattered off him. I begin right at the centre of his difficulty and then I piece him together, I bring him out of it. It's a way of starting at the bottommost point simply. ('Myth and education', 1, p. 68)

This commentary predicts just as ably the conclusion of the *Cave Birds* adventure in its last two sentences. Here is the protagonist's voluntary exposure at the beginning of 'The knight':

The knight

Has conquered. He has surrendered everything.
Now he kneels. He is offering up his victory
And unlacing his steel.
In front of him are the common wild stones of the earth –
The first and last altar
Onto which he lowers his spoils

The hero achieves Simone Weil's desired objective of conscious obedience to the Necessity represented by Matter. And as soon as the poetic persona fulfils Pilinszky's imperative, the approach to Reality 'with eyes downcast', the components of Hughes' own ideal language are pulled together: the exclusively Graeco-Roman external film of language – which we still live out as a cultural norm – is broken, along with the world of will-ful Egoism, in the phrase 'The quaint courtly language/ Of wing bones and talons', enabling the 'deep structure' of English language, in which the Latin–French pole is re-combined with its Norse–Celtic 'opposite', to emerge again. One might say that once the 'helplessness in the circumstances' of the hero's conscious personality has been fully established by the violent, Anglo-Saxon grip of the previous poems, the acknowledgement of what is happening in his 'deepest life' can now be expressed in the language of the 'ordinary mind':

> His *submission* is flawless.
>
> Blueflies lift off his beauty.
> Beatles and ants *officiate*
>
> Pestering him with *instructions*.
> His *patience* grows only more vast.

The use of latinate diction is not an irony here, as it is in 'Hawk roosting'; it is a sign of the completeness of the Personality's surrender to the lesson of the whole psyche. In the same way, the emphasis on 'ritual intensity of music' is re-combined with the accent on a 'colloquial prose readiness':

> 'His eyes darken bolder in their vigil
> As the chapel crumbles'.
>
>   . . .
>
> An unearthly cry goes up.
> The Universes squabble over him –
>
> Here a bone, there a rag.
> His sacrifice is perfect. He reserves nothing.

The directness of the visionary statement also has important consequences in the readership of the poem: the typical modernist anxiety associated with dual or multiple interpretations (a consequence of the plural nature of the self), simply vanishes; his conquest is *stated* as his surrender, his allegiances are beyond doubt ('in earth's name'), we are even given the benefit of an authorial intrusion ('And that is right') to ensure that we make no mistakes. If we are capable of the same submission as the poem's hero, we may find a *certainty* – simultaneously earthen and spiritual – which permanently eclipses the multiplicity of the old self. All Hughes' worlds overlap to the point of identity, and the opportunity for 're-combination', to regain our lost wealth, exists on all levels.

The sequence goes on converting itself from the 'static mystery-play' of its original form (the first group of poems) to personal human drama (the second and third group of poems), furthering its alchemical process. 'Something was happening' first recapitulates the conclusion of 'In these fading moments' and then moves beyond it, spotlighting Attar's demand that the 'grosser self' be separated from the 'aspiring heart'; the echo of 'In these fading moments' – 'The earth, right to its far rims, ignored me' – refines towards the psychic possibility opened by 'the knight' in the last five lines:

> Only the eagle-hunter
> Beating himself to keep warm
> And bowing towards his trap
> Started singing
>
> (Two, three, four thousand years off key.)

The eagle-hunter begins to sing, significantly, just one poem after the poet himself successfully hauled together the root-elements of his own voice in an act of celebration. He recalls the paradoxical nature of the poetic protagonist in 'The thought-fox' as both hunter and victim ('Bowing towards the trap'), and the image of control provided by 'The dove breeder'. Two images Hughes intuited at the earliest stage of his published development recur, but here the obstacles to their development have been cleared away, because they are embedded in the morally enhancing environment of the present narrative sequence, rather than the volatile, 'alienated' context of *The Hawk in the Rain*. The image is still primitive – '(Two, three, four thousand years off key)' – but the line of its future progress via the narrative, is clear, unimpeded.

It comes as no surprise when, in 'A flayed crow in the hall of judgement', the double-headed figure of Crow starts to 'condense' in his higher form, which the alchemists called the Spirit Mercurius, as acceptance of the shadow-reality of the psyche promises a re-birth:

> Darkness has all come together, making an egg.
> Darkness in which there is now nothing.
>
> A blót has knócked me dòwn. It clógs me.
> A glóbe of blót, a dróp of unbeing.
>
> Nothingness came close and breathed on me – a frost
> A shawl of annihilation has curled me up like a new foetus.

Even these six lines, considered alongside 'The executioner', are enough to suggest that the summit of Hughes' endeavour to reverse the effects of the theological dualism of the Light–Darkness opposition (applied metaphysically, psychologically or stylistically) has been reached. Jung demonstrates in *Mysterium coniunctionis* that great importance was attached to the blackness as the starting-point of the work, and adds that this blackness was often termed the 'Raven's head' or 'black sun' in alchemical practice; as in Hughes' poem, this is the condition of the incubation or pregnancy of the self. In the second couplet, the 'blackness' is interpreted in language as a renewed – though inverted or 'dark' – vision of the Old English line, which has acquired a moral distinction it neglected in 'The hawk in the rain': where in the earlier poem the use of dominant alliterating consonants invested the poem's 'I' with a kind of heroic prestige, here the vowelling music of the long 'o' sounds, strengthened by their coincidence with the stress and rhythm, totally envelop the self and its consonants in an 'audial' blackness, an ocean of sound. The line, by dramatizing the process of self-loss, gives us its own re-birth, raised to a higher power. In the same way, details from further back in the sequence are 'illuminated', the leaves of the plaintiff's body are re-interpreted not in their accusatory aspect, but in their transformative aspect – the protagonist is curled by a lethal frost like a leaf, a leaf which is also a foetus.

Jung recounts a revealing commentary from the 'Aurelia Occulta' which summarizes the transformation of Crow into Mercurius, of lower in to higher value – and which includes details of specific relevance to the poem. Mercurius is speaking in the first person:

> If you do not have exact knowledge of me, you will destroy your five senses with my fire. . . . Therefore you should skilfully separate the coarse from the fine, if you do not wish to suffer utter poverty. I bestow on you the powers of the male and the female, and also those of heaven and earth. . . . I am the *egg of nature*, known only to the wise, who in piety and modesty bring forth from me the microcosm. . . . I am the old dragon found everywhere on the globe of the earth, father and mother . . . death and resurrection, visible and invisible, hard and soft; I descend into the earth and ascend to the heavens, I am the highest and the lowest . . . I am dark and light . . . I am the carbuncle of the sun [cf. 'The interrogator'], the most noble purified earth, through which you may change copper, iron, tin and lead into gold. (*Alchemical Studies*, p. 218)

The black Osiris who is eventually resurrected in his son Horus is pictured as simultaneously 'heaven' and the 'scum of the sea' in the alchemical interpretation of Egyptian mythic characters. And Dorn speaks of the Cross as another 'black' preparation for resurrection in terms strikingly similar to Simone Weil's understanding of the purposive effect of Affliction.[2] Finally, we should note that in Sufi practice black is associated with wisdom, to the extent that the words are homonyms in Arabic, thus achieving one of the ideals of language Hughes sought in Orghast: the 'redeeming' connection of concepts with Matter. In the dramatic context of the poem, the catalogue of questions in stanzas 6–8 are a direct reminder of the Crow-past of 'Crow's nerve fails': confrontation with his own blackness prompted Crow to close the world into an existentialist caricature ('He cannot be forgiven'), and that was his own failure of nerve, his 'false conclusion' to the poetic problem. Returning as the Mercurius-like hero, that closure is exchanged for the openness of the subject–object relation, the truthful 'vast inner exposure' of the self:

A great fear rests
On the thing I am, as a feather on a hand.

I shall not fight
Against whatever is allotted to me.

My soul skinned, and the soul-skin laid out
A mat for my judges.

The persistent deployment of ironic, emergency selves yields this result: the old self is rendered entirely passive, its interpretative impulses have been disconnected. By now, Hughes' affinity with Janos Pilinszky (his translation of Pilinszky's *Selected Poems* appeared in 1976) is quite effortless, as the perspective of the religious artist offers to resolve the *Crow*-like predicaments of writers like Herbert, or Rozewicz:

Sadness trickles searching
Past my orphaned lips.
What happened to my mother's milk?
I smudge my coat.

I am like the stone –
No matter what comes, let it come.
I shall be so obedient and good
I shall lie down full length.
('Under the winter sky', *Selected Poems*, p. 19)

Two poems that follow, 'A green mother' and 'As I came, I saw a wood' narrate the hero's encounter with two 'false paradises', suggesting that even at this relatively late stage of his adventure, the protagonist may still be prone to error. The poems – especially 'A green mother' – are equally a test of the reader's vulnerability to his own 'religious' expectation, reflections of his own world-description. A precipitate release from the fear of 'A flayed crow' is readily available:

Why are you afraid?
In the house of the dead are many cradles.
The earth is a busy hive of heavens.
This is one lottery that cannot be lost.

The poem takes its cue from the narrative method of *Gaudete*; in this stanza and the three that succeed it, the reader is given no 'objective' or ironic vantage-point from which he can comfortably evaluate the heavens the poem offers. He is even given the opportunity to imprint his own idea of paradise on the transformative experience, and the negative consequences of that choice – 'The City of Religions/ Is like a city of hotels, a holiday city' – are only briefly indicated before a conclusion in which the irony is almost impossible to detect:

> This earth is heaven's sweetness.
> It is heaven's mother.
> The grave is her breast
> And her milk is endless life.
>   You shall see
> How tenderly she has wiped her child's face clean
> Of the bitumen of blood and the smoke of tears.

The reader has to enter his own illusion fully, follow it even into the heart of the blissful–ecstatic natural environment in the next poem, before the shattering truth descends,

> a voice, a bell of cracked iron
> Jarred in my skull
> Summoning me to prayer
> To eat flesh and to drink blood.

The 'everlasting' static tableaux of paradise presented were premature falsifications of Matter; or they embodied states of 'ecstasy' which were delusory in the same way that 'Gnat-psalm' was delusory: they 'resemble a dream in which a wish is fulfilled, thus enabling the disturbed dreamer to continue with his sleep' (Shah *The Sufis*, p. 298). In this case, further knowledge is prevented, as we shall see in *Moortown*. Perhaps we should have been alert to the hint in 'The baptist', where the 'blissful' potential of the 'swathing balm' of the waters and its tissue of illusion was cut away by the Anglo-Saxon edge of 'carrying you blindfold and *gagged*'.

It is the concreteness of knowledge, not the 'sensation' of it, which is demanded by 'A riddle':

> Who am I?
>
> Just as you are my father
> I am your bride . . .
>
> Now as you face your death
> I offer you your life
>
> Just as surely as you are my father
> I shall deliver you
>
> My firstborn
> Into a changed, unchangeable world
> Of wind and of sun, of rock and water
> To cry.

The poem condenses the meanings of the Triune Goddess: she is daughter, bride and mother to the hero simultaneously. In her aspect as mother, she is the Old Testament Sophia who 'was set up from everlasting, from the beginning, or ever the earth was' (Proverbs, 8:23), before God 'set a compass on the face of the deep' (*ibid.*, 8:27), creating the multiplicity of phenomena and the plural mechanisms of the Personality. The hero thus encounters and dies to her 'lower' value – in which she gives birth willingly into the multiple forms of Matter or mechanisms of the psyche – in order to find his way home to her 'higher' value, in which she is the 'spotless' female aspect of the Godhead, the Queen of Heaven or the single centre of psychic gravity outside those mechanisms. In the great Hebrew love-poem The Song of Songs she is thus both 'black' and 'comely', both 'fair as the moon, clear as the sun, and terrible as an army with banners' (Canticles 6:10). What I have called her higher value is the meaning of the virgin mother who is such a prominent influence in Christian mythology, and of figures as diverse as Maya-Shakti in Buddhism, Isis in Egyptian mythology, and Ceres/Astarte in the Roman/Mesopotamian versions. In her aspect as the hero's bride, she is personified as his shadow-self, awaiting illumination in a *unio mystica* – his most immediate challenge. We might add that her aspect as daughter brought to birth by the protagonist embodies simply the realization that it is the hero's own *conscious work* which enables her purest form, and his psychic wholeness, to emerge fully. At the end of the poem, the mechanically structured 'idea of style' of *Crow* has midwifed a 'spiritual' re-birth out of Matter, scarcely imaginable given the psychological and linguistic darkness of that book. Like the material world itself, the root of language is 'unchangeable', although the awareness perceiving it has been irrevocably, even miraculously 'changed'.

The miraculous renewal of Matter and language alike is the subject of 'After there was nothing there was a woman', which is the first of a final group of poems which explicitly confirm Jung's summary of alchemical – and Sufic – objectives: 'The substance that harbours the divine secret is everywhere, including the human body. It can be had for the asking and can be found anywhere even in the most loathsome filth' (*Psychology and Alchemy*, pp. 299–300). So in the poem the woman

> . . . had found her belly
> In a clockwork pool, wound by the winding and unwinding sea.
> First it was her toy, then she found its use
> And curtained it with a flowered skirt.
> It made her eyes shine.

The woman's origin is both materially 'lowest down' and collective, and thus true to both halves of the Goddess's double image. Furthermore, she is in a meaningful sense *derived* from the language Hughes projected as a desirable model in his commentaries on Vasko Popa, Shakespeare and Keith Douglas. She originates, so to speak, in versatile-exploratory casual speech: '[Her] breasts had come about . . ./ After many failures, but they were here now', the frequently super-ugly 'homely spur-of-the-moment improvisation out of whatever verbal scrap happens to be lying around' (*A Choice of Shakespeare's Verse*, p. 11),

Via the vulture's gullet . . .
. . . and she remembers it . . .
. . . come about . . .
. . . but they were here now . . .
. . . She had made it but only just, just –

Celebration takes place dramatically in speech that is, finally nothing more than a refinement of *Crow*'s 'idea of style', which itself 'lay at the bottom of all things/ Utterly worn out utterly clear'. The poetic structure is still afflicted by repetition, the remorseless hammering pattern of glances and revised glances at Matter, just as the united self no longer flinches from its mechanical 'lot':

Her bones
Lay as they did because they could not escape anything
They hung as it were in space
The targets of every bombardment.

The open-ended exposure of such language encourages the contours of the abstract schema of *Cave Birds* to vanish into the palpitating life of its experience. The reality of that experience could hardly be more pointed than in the last line 'She had made it but only just, just –', where the celebration is not fixed by a formally satisfying conclusion, or even a full-stop; even the most basic elements of 'masculine' self-sufficiency are denied in the interests of pursuing the continuity of the process – which exists outside any single poem in the sequence – set in motion by the original imperative 'Know thyself.' The concrete spiritual product of the poem resides in the description of the re-born female:

Having about as much comprehension as a lamb
Who stares around at everything simultaneously
With ant-like head and soldierly bearing.

She regains a kind of perception which takes account of every psychological impulse or 'I' at the same time, and which closely resembles the vision in which Don Juan educates Castaneda (he is forced to 'shift his gaze' or 'blink' to avoid fixed vision), or that which Alan Watts describes in *The Way of Zen*:

We have two types of vision – central and peripheral, not unlike the spotlight and the floodlight. Central vision is used for accurate work like reading, in which our eyes are focused on one small area after another like spotlights. Peripheral vision is less conscious, less bright than the intense ray of the spotlight. We use it for seeing at night, and for taking 'subconscious' notice of objects and movements not in the direct line of central vision. Unlike the spotlight, it can take in very many things at a time. (p. 28)

The idea of union with this re-constituted woman is taken up again in 'His legs ran about', itself a preface to the fuller realization of the marriage in 'Bride and groom'. Before we reach that point, however, the re-assembling self is dramatized individually in two other poems, 'The guide' and 'Walking bare'. The guide is the last antidote to the delusions fostered by 'A green mother', emptying the hero with a red wind – a colour synonymous in Sufi practice with Spirit – and scouring him with a black wind (Intuition in Sufism); that is to say, the hero is cleared of his attachment to dualistic opposites, leaving him in the 'third' position of inspired equilibrium:

> I am the needle
>
> Magnetic
> A tremor
>
> The searcher
> The finder

Once again, the direct connection between 'The guide' and 'His legs ran about' and Attar's poem is registered on the 'lowest' most intimate level, in the most basic elements of vocabulary:

> When you are worn out by love's fierce despair
> And in your weakness tremble like a hair,
> You will become the hair and take your place
> In curls that cluster round the loved one's face.
> . . . You will not waste away, your soul
> Has made the seven gates of hell its goal.
> (Attar, *The Conference of the Birds*, p. 204)

Only when the hero is reduced to a tremoring needle or hair, 'magnetic' in the sense of Gurdjieff's 'magnetic centre', which promoted the growth of Essence, do the twin – and fundamentally identical – aims of Love and Conscious Individuality become possible. So in 'Walking bare', the 'progress beyond assay' continues 'breath by breath', breath being the literal meaning of the Sufi term *nafs*, or consciousness. As in Attar's poem, the protagonist has to lose himself repeatedly – 'A one gravity keeps touching me' – 'before his gain is finally consolidated in his union with his bride', which was of course the primary objective of *Crow*.

The hero's union with his intended bride is consolidated in 'Bride and groom lie hidden for three days', which comes from a story in which 'supernatural beings' first claim responsibility for the creation of Man and Woman, then argue for the relative importance of each principle ('Did he give most, or did she give most?'). This metaphysical quarrel of

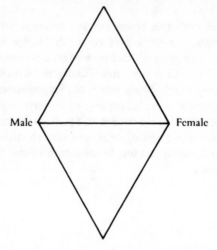

Knowledgeable narrator of 'Bride and groom' 'Higher' Crow (Mercurius)

Male ◄────────────────► Female

'Lower' Crow – primitive narrator of 'Lovesong'

Figure 8.1

opposites – on a purely supernatural or 'spiritual' level – is resolved by a knowledgeable 'third' person, who returns the problem to a more basic material level, and the world of 'inner' human responsibility. He declares that 'they had no part in it, man and woman had done it on their own' (Ted Hughes and Paul Muldoon, Faber poetry cassette). The knowledgeable one is none other than Crow himself, for, as Sagar points out (see *The Art of Ted Hughes*, p. 235), the question is one of those the Ogress–Female asks Crow while they are crossing the river. But this is Crow transformed into man, or the image of the hermaphroditic Mercurius, who is 'also called husband and wife, bridegroom and bride, or lover and beloved' (*Alchemical Studies*, p. 219). The 'invisible' narrative voice, or emergency self, has been gradually firming up into a permanent 'I' in the dramatic course of the sequence, so that it is possible to reproduce a diagram similar to that in Chapter 1 (see Introduction, note 3) to describe the advance from *Crow* and 'Lovesong', to *Cave Birds* and 'Bride and groom' (see Figure 8.1).

In Ouspensky's visualization (see Introduction, note 2), the consciousness of a multiple, changing self (Jung's shadow) shattered the False Personality, establishing a 'magnetic centre'/'single I' which in turn enabled the development of the Body/Essence and its natural, dramatic expressiveness, Love. When Essence was allowed to grow in this consciously prepared space, the opposites which defined the lower forms of the self fell away, to be replaced by their conscious higher values: Crow's endeavour to 'become a man' was achieved.

Furthermore, one might tentatively replace the male–female axis in the pictured diagram with a structural–dramatic axis to explain the importance of 'Bride and groom' in the verbal dimension of *Cave Birds*: where earlier poems in the sequence demonstrated a perceptible split between the abstract appreciation of the transformative process, often entailing extreme compression of alchemical/esoteric/mythological material and the plain-style apprehension of it as an immediate, or bodily experience, 'Bride and groom' heals the linguistic 'opposition' at a higher level, completely satisfying both structural and dramatic requirements. Apart from presenting an image of the re-generated Mercurius, it fuses lines from Attar's poem,

> The man who's kindled by love's radiance
> Will give birth to a woman; when love's fire
> Quickens within a woman this desire,
> She gives birth to a man; is it denied
> That Adam bore a woman from his side,
> That Mary bore a man?
>
> (p. 183)

with the final marriage of the royal pair in *The Chymical Wedding*, and the individuation of its protagonist, with the union of Sol and Luna in Alchemy, and the general necessity of the *coniunctio oppositorium* on all levels. It even raises a distant echo of the later theological interpretation of Christ as *sponsus* to the Church's bride. At the same time, the marriage takes place in the 'utility general-purpose style' which is Hughes' ideal, improvising the union out of a language which is not only characterized by its functionality, but additionally pays homage to Matter by describing that union in mechanical terms: both language and the 'world' it contours are pure mechanism, neutral media dependent on the user–perceiver's moral status for fulfilment of their higher values. In this sense, the poem's language and approach to its subject-matter comprise a final test of the reader's willingness to revolutionize his perception of material nature, the 'World of final Reality' itself. 'Bride and groom' is a poetic antidote to the misperception triggered by the Petrarchan love-sonnet, and the abstract perfection of its form and its idealization of love. In Sidney's *Astrophel and Stella*, for example, the exalted act of 'spiritual' or rational praise foundered on the unmanageability of material desire, which ended by decisively breaking the form of the Italian sonnet itself. Even the Metaphysicals' resolutions of love depended too exclusively on verbal ingenuity and the intellectual force of the conceit or syllogism. Hughes' love-poem is a corrective to that literary past, celebrating the

'Matter' of love on its own terms, and the 'spiritual' product coming from that:

> He is polishing every part,
>   he himself can hardly believe it
> They keep on taking each other to the sun,
>   they find they can easily.

And of course they bring each other 'to perfection' out of the mud, a 'collective' triumph which is the reverse of the impulse to make one little room an everywhere:

> The Sufi doctrine of a continuum or refinement of Matter will here be seen to be quite different from that of other systems. . . . In actual fact, every degree of materiality has its own function; and materiality extends in successive refinement until it becomes what has been generally considered to be separate – spirit.

> According to Sufism, what is generally referred to in religious terminology as the Spirit is a substance, with physical characteristics, a subtle body.
> (Shah, *The Sufis*, pp. 160, 395)

'The risen' is the most explicit account of the resurrection of Horus from the dismembered remains – the 'offal' of the abstract personality – of the 'black' Osiris. The poem is the concluding piece in Hughes' original group of nine poems, attempting to resolve the creative difficulties which beset 'The plaintiff': the poet is clearly striving to establish vocal continuity amid a welter of images, yoking together some images from further back in the sequence with others from Hughes' more distant literary past:

> His each wingbeat – a Convict's release.
> What he carries will be plenty.
>
> He slips behind the world's brow
> As music escapes its skull, its clock and its skyline.
>
> Under his sudden shadow flames cry out among thickets.
> When he soars, his shape
>
> Is a cross, eaten by light,
> On the Creator's face.

The 'full presence' of Hughes' subject, the resurrected body or psychic whole, here contextualizes the need for poetic music to escape its confinement to formal horizons – 'its clock and its skyline' – and literally illuminates the earlier image of 'The plaintiff', which was first perceived as the 'heavy-fruited, burning tree/ Of your darkness'. It gives us the higher potential of the Crucifixion-image which came to prominence in *Crow* with poems such as 'The contender' and 'Crow and the sea'. Here the image does not represent a negative 'senseless trial of strength' nor is it simply a material reprimand to Crow's responsive 'freedoms', its spread wings actually define the 'Creator's face' in terms of Matter by throwing a cross-like shadow over the sun. The religious symbol, it turns out, comprehensively amplifies the vulture–interrogator's being as 'the sun's key-hole' in the fourth poem. Within an even wider frame of reference, the falcon of 'The risen' is an 'exaltation' – to borrow a word from alchemy – of the hawk in 'Hawk roosting'. Particularly with the marriage of 'Bride and groom' in mind, it focuses the Brhadaranyaka–Upanishad meanings associated with the bird noted in Chapter 4: the egoistic appearance of the claim 'I am this, I am all' – the hawk as its own best world – is revised and transformed by the moral environment of *Cave Birds*, so that we only observe its 'higher' value, its ability to dissolve the distinction between Other and Self 'as a man embraced fully by a loving woman knows no distinction of other and self'. And this perception of course consolidates the lesson of 'Bride and groom'.

This kind of rehearsal and synthesis of the recent and more distant literary past is one way of re-discovering vocal continuity within the 'I', at least on the level of the narrative's abstract schema. But that rehearsal and synthesis fails to take us to the dramatic core of the poem; the reading experience of the poem fails utterly to afford the reader the security that the word 'synthesis' implies. The completeness or hermetic self-sufficiency of each couplet image, enhanced by the almost reverential solemnity of the typographic spacing, never succeeds in fixing a conceptual definition of the elusive falcon-self. In fact, elusiveness is the falcon's principal characteristic: he is invisible behind the 'world's brow', an indistinguishable black shape on the sun's face, both the shadow which draws attention to the flaming thicket and the burning tree itself. Each image – aesthetically satisfying in isolation – is in turn levelled and transformed in the incredibly rapid, protean shifts of lines 5–20. The reader is allowed to fix his gaze on no single 'aesthetic' point, or particular *verbal* triumph within the poem. The whole movement is epitomized by the last four lines:

> In the wind-fondled crucible of his splendour
> The dirt becomes God.
>
> But when will he land
> On a man's wrist.

All the elements of an aesthetically or structurally just conclusion are contained in the penultimate couplet: the 'scouring' or 'emptying' wind of 'The guide' has been harmonized as 'fondled', and the self recognized as the crucible of the alchemical experiment in which Matter is transformed into Spirit, and Essence into Individuality. But neither the formal brilliance of the image nor our critical appreciation of its suggestive subtleties would provide a truly dramatic finale, one which unifies itself with the reader's present 'state of being' and necessary moral direction. The final couplet is essential as an 'impetus to Knowledge', challenging the reader to convert the abstract–structural pronoun 'he' into the dramatic pronoun 'I', to fill out the schematic frame of Hughes' creative myth with the substance of his own experience. 'When will he land/ On a man's wrist' is a question directed at the reader in the everlasting present, a permanent moral barometer of his condition. Moreover, the absence of any equivalent to 'The risen' in the Hughes' third compositional group indicates that the question is reflexive too. The extent to which the dense 'bronze' mass of esoteric 'theory' and imagism has been successfully refined in the dramatic experience of poet and reader remains an open question; overweening 'creative' and 'critical' reconciliations of that predicament now have to exist – if they exist at all – in the full knowledge of their frailty as aesthetic or conceptual strongholds. Attar's poem ends with exactly the same distinction between aesthetic perception of the real (*appreciation* through form) and the moral or religious perception of it, which always provokes *action*:

> If it were lawful for me to relate
> Such truths to those who have not reached this state,
> Those gone before us would have made some sign;
> But no sign comes, and silence must be mine.
> Here eloquence can find no jewel but one,
> That silence when the longed-for goal is won.
> The greatest orator would here be made
> In love with silence and forget his trade,
> And I too cease: I have described the Way –
> Now, you must act – there is no more to say.
> (*The Conference of the Birds*, p. 229)

The push towards this productive Silence is a significant advance for the poet, away from the hubristic conclusion of 'The dove breeder' and the authoritarian poetic stylism of the book which contains it. As if the conclusion of 'The risen' were not enough, the same idea is re-emphasized in 'Finale': 'At the end of the ritual/ up comes a goblin.' The sequence points beyond its own sufficiency towards the poet's, and the reader's, future action. The moral process is always unfinished; it never releases the self from its responsibilities and continually resists the possibility of petrification into a false personality. In these circumstances, poetry remains a provisional, open-ended venture:

> You choose a subject because it serves, because you need it. We go on writing poems because one poem never gets the whole account right. There is always something missed. At the end of the ritual up comes a goblin. Anyway within a week the whole thing has changed, one needs a fresh bulletin. And works go dead, fishing has to be abandoned. While we

struggle with a fragmentary Orestes some complete Bacchae moves past too deep down to hear. We get news of it later . . . too late. In the end, one's poems are ragged dirty undated letters from remote battles and weddings and one thing and another. ('Ted Hughes and Crow', *London Magazine*, p. 15)

In Hughes' own work from *Gaudete*, and more particularly from *Remains of Elmet* onwards, the endeavour to 'get the whole account' of the self right increasingly entails a re-emergence into the outer human world, and the world of nature to balance the 'inner' descent of *Wodwo*, *Crow* and *Cave Birds*; and this return is part of both traditional Sufi practice and the 'ideal aspect' of poetic development that Hughes identified in W. B. Yeats, a moment before the above statement:

he managed to develop his poetry both outwardly into history and the common imagery of everyday life at the same time as he developed it inwardly in a sort of close parallel so that he could speak of both simultaneously. His mythology is history, pretty well, and his history is as he said 'the story of a soul'. (*ibid.*)

CHAPTER 9

———————— • ————————

REMAINS OF ELMET AND MOORTOWN

REMAINS OF ELMET (1979)

Remains of Elmet: A Pennine sequence defines most clearly the poet's 'return' to the outer world of the physical landscape and human history. It is Hughes' first fulfilment of the developmental pattern he divined in W. B. Yeats:

> The ideal aspect of Yeats' development is that he managed to develop his poetry both outwardly into history and the common imagery of everyday life at the same time as he developed it inwardly in a sort of close parallel . . . so that he could speak of both simultaneously. His mythology is history, pretty well, and history is as he said 'the story of a soul'. ('Ted Hughes and Crow', *London Magazine* Interview, pp. 14–15)

The passage from *Crow* through *Gaudete* to *Cave Birds* gradually but explicitly opened up the religious or holy foundation of poetry, and now *Remains of Elmet* begins the consolidation of that mythology as a communal history, or the history as an amplified image of Hughes' own soul-story. Where the three books cumulatively strove to re-colonize the uninhabitable wilderness of the primitive unconscious – symbolized in the poet's imagination as the *Celtic* root-self whose linguistic deposits composed the origin of the English language – and render it 'workable' once more, *Remains of Elmet* chronicles the death of the kingdom of the whole psyche in historical terms. Like *Gaudete* it laments the absence of a framing religious context – the chapels have died – and it registers the alienation of the community 'so rooted for so long' as surely as *Cave Birds* dramatized the alienation of its individual hero; it dismantles human fictions of the Natural as ruthlessly as *Crow* stripped away the ego's fictions of the whole self, or the Logos–God's fictions about the Creator.

The detection and dispersal of these human fictions about the natural environment is really the starting-point of *Remains of Elmet*:

These grasses of light

Which think they are alone in the world

These stones of darkness
Which have a world to themselves

This water of light and darkness
Which hardly savours creation

And this wind
Which has just enough to exist

Are not

A poor family huddled at a poor gleam
Or words in any phrase
Or wolf-beings in a hungry waiting
Or neighbours in a constellation

They are
The armour of bric-a-brac
To which your soul's caddis
Clings with all its courage.

(p. 16)

Here is one of the central lessons of *Gaudete*, recapitulated: the 'objectivity' of the landscape embodied in lines 1–8 is a poetic delusion unconscious of its origin and its 'motivation'. The corrupt or fallen body of images in those lines comprises a version of the Empathetic instinct at work in Hughes' earliest poems, with the crucial difference that here the impulse is not put blindly into mechanical operation, but becomes conscious of itself, and therefore an occasion for self-knowledge; then four endings, each a 'fanciful' though rootless completion of the metaphoric world of the first eight lines, are 'tried out' and rejected as Hughes' open-ended discourse improvises towards a conclusion validated by the moral imagination. That imagination becomes active in the collision of 'objective' and 'subjective', 'outer' and 'inner' environments in those last four lines. It is upon this imaginative axis – the imagination which faces double, towards both 'objective' and 'subjective' simultaneously – that both the pathos (appealing to Gurdjieff's 'emotional centre') and the revelation ('intellectual centre') of *Remains of Elmet* are hinged. Those elements which would preserve an ignorance of the 'subjective' motivation of 'the world' are disposed of peremptorily: the possible variants of an Empathetic conclusion (lines 10, 12 and 13) are scattered, and the futile irony of literary self-reflexivity (line 11) cancelled. The 'objectivity' of the text vanishes utterly for the reader, too; if he has failed to absorb the lesson of a poem like 'Owl's song', for example, the sin of projection will be exposed in the final stanza with a sort of religious intensity. In other terms, acquiescence in a set of 'unconscious' literary devices (personification, the Pathetic Fallacy, etc.)

has traumatic consequences once their underpinning psychological attitude is realized. The entire poem reads like an ethical answer to 'Pilbroch' (from *Wodwo*), and the temptation to stamp its *attitude* of self-enclosed alienation a 'universal' condition.

> A tree struggles to make leaves –
> An old woman fallen from space
> Unprepared for these conditions.
> She hangs on, because her mind's gone completely.
>
> (*Wodwo*, p. 177)

What the reader might see in retrospect is the Empathetic impulse at work, the dismantling of Ego-fortifications *causing* the external Dark–Empty Void, the inner process still pathetically unconscious, or only half-conscious.

Several poems pursue the moral end of 'These grasses of light', purging the natural environment of polluting human fictions: 'Moors', for instance, 'Are a stage for the performance of heaven./ Any audience is incidental' (p. 19). In 'The trance of light',

> The light, opening younger, fresher wings
> Holds this land up again like an offering
>
> Heavy with the dream of people.
>
> (p. 20)

Often, the same task seems to be set dramatically for the reader, the successful disentangling of 'human' and 'natural' elements: in 'Hardcastle crags' the task is embodied in the need to sift the 'human' 'name-lists of cenotaphs' from the 'natural' voice of the river, and interpret the ambiguity of the phrase 'a grave of echoes': the *reader* may find in the landscape an echo of the human tragedy, or else make it a 'grave' of that imprisoning past. Where one reading infects the natural environment, the other cleanses it. The infection is one Hughes noted in his radio talk 'The rock', later reprinted in *The Listener*: 'Everything in West Yorkshire is slightly unpleasant . . . . A disaster seems to hang around in the air there for a long time. I can never escape the impression that the whole region is in mourning for the First World War' (*The Listener*, 19 September 1963). Both the specific source of the disease (the First World War) and the collective potential of Nature to repair the human rent in the fabric are evidenced in the final stanza:

> And beech-roots repair a population
> Of fox and badger. And the air-stir releases
> The love-murmurs of a generation of slaves
> Whose bones melted in Asia Minor.

From another point of view – 'far above' – the natural environment 'escape[s] like wings' from the disastrous human 'history', the collective extra-human world carries forward the positive values ('love-murmurs') which were suppressed or distorted in the purely human context. *We* are part of, and subordinate to the earth's evolution, and not vice versa, as in the usual cultural assumption. And this liberation of the 'Other' is equivalent on the macrocosmic level to the 'inner' release of the unconscious from the tyranny of the conscious Personality which was the poet's first subject.

The contest between 'human' and 'natural' perspectives dominates 'Lumb chimneys' as well; for the first nine lines of the poem, the 'slogging world' could easily be the human world, subsisting in the modern industrial myth of the impoverished present and an always-remote, infinitely rewarding future. It is only in the second half of the poem that, in a shattering reversal of expectation, the human world starts providing metaphors for its natural counterpart, and the semantic of the word 'progress' comes full circle, from its *materialist* to its *material* sense: 'Before these chimneys can flower again/ They must fall into the only future, into earth.' The specifically 'human' perspective is a sort of interpretative hologram through which we advance to the 'natural' perspective, which is both human and 'everything else that lives'.

The most damning and explicit assault on the negative effect of human fictions, however, occurs in the poem 'Churn-milk Joan', in which a legend is transcribed, then subverted. A stone column supposedly marks the place where Joan was killed by foxes:

> You take the coins of the hollow in the top of it.
> Put your own in. Foxes killed her here.
> Why just here? Why not five yards that way?
> A squared column, planted by careful labour.
>
> Sun cannot ease it, though the moors grow warm.
>
> Foxes killed her, and her milk spilled.
>
> Or they did not. And it did not.   (p. 59)

All momentary doubts about the veracity of the legend are quelled, until the tenth line, by the repeated assurance 'Foxes killed her.' Before that line – and barring the brusque interruption in line 6 – the poem sustains its 'objective' recital of the legend admirably, the first narrative voice sustains its own 'internal talk' through that mesmeric repetition. But the recital comes to an end with the prosaic tenth line, itself 'a squared column' planted in the world of the poem by careful labour. Its 'objectivity' is defeated by an even more prosaic explanation:

> Farmers brought their milk this far, and cottagers
> From the top of Luddenden Valley left cash
> In the stone's crown, probably in vinegar,
> And the farmers left their change.

The reader does not receive the promised aesthetic satisfaction of a story fully completed, finished, but the irony of a superstition exposed, the story told at one remove:

> Churn-milk *jamb*. And Joan did not come trudging
> Through the long swoon of moorland
> With her sodden feet, her nipped face.
> Neither snow nor foxes made her lie down
> While they did whatever they wanted.
>
> The negative of the skylines is blank.
> The legendary terror was not suffered.
>
> Only a word wrenched, and the pain came,
> And her mouth opened.

Beneath the 'objectivity' of the text is the 'motivated' text, a legend created by the wrenching of the word '*jamb*' (French for 'leg' or 'limb') and the perception of an unyieldingly hostile Nature. As in 'These grasses' a secondary Imagination provokes consciousness of the 'subject-ive' interpretative grid being imposed on the poem's contents. It is that Imagination, devoted equally to the 'subjective' origin of the story and its 'objective' veracity, which repudiates the Empathetic 'long *swoon* of moorland' and the power of verbal fancy to help realize fictions about the surrounding world. It 'wipes the landscape clean': 'The negative of the skylines is blank.' The real pain of the story derives not from its apparent *contents* – the fictive story about Man's victimization by Nature – but from the psychological *attitude* which produced it in the first instance;

> And now all of us,
> Even this stone, have to be memorials
> Of her futile stumblings and screams
> And awful little death.

We invent our own pain when we wrench, via a word, our biological connection with the world into its fictional hostility towards us. Hughes animates the legend by presenting it as responsive choice: the reader dramatizes himself as a stone-like 'memorial' when he agrees to the world-idea of the original story, and this may be unavoidable, since the story is culturally implanted, and reaction against it would entail direct descent into the horrific ordeals recited in Hughes' previous books. Meanwhile the poet's anti-story is present but remote to the understand-ing, the bottomless cry 'beat[s] itself numb against Wesley's foundation stone' here as in the later poem 'The sluttiest sheep in England', in which the animals appear as natural symbols of a demonized wilderness; they collectively resemble the primitive warrior-self,

                                    tossing
Their ancient Briton draggle-tassle sheepskins
Or pose, in the rain-smoke, like warriors,
                                    (p. 104)

possessing an unfulfilled potential image, cloaked by material form:

This god-of-what-nobody-wants
In his magnetic heaven
Has sent his angels to stare at you
In the likeness of beggars.

The ghostly recollection of Hughes' previous practice, hinted at in 'Mount Zion', is drawn more forcefully in two poems which renew the tree-image that featured in *Crow, Gaudete* and *Cave Birds*. The dramatic core of the poems already examined – the human versus material dichotomy – is substantialized in the single emblem, and the midpoint division of 'Tree' (p. 47). In the course of the poem the tree proclaims the human fiction of hostile Nature, is 'emptied' and converted into a conductor or medium of the material whole. As in its usage in 'These grasses', personification is a *conscious* device, resisting the Abstraction–Empathy polarity – here the abstractive attitude of lines 1–9 rather than the Empathetic version of 'These grasses' – until it realizes the complete story of the psyche through the second half of the poem. Literary devices, like everything else, are 'inert' or neutral, depend entirely upon the subject–user's level of consciousness. 'A tree' (p. 63) likewise embodies a conscious personification of the moral process chronicled in Hughes' previous, 'invisible' work. The tree 'stripped to its root letter, cruciform/ contorted/ Tried to tell all', but like Crow is humbled into silence:

Finally
Resigned
To be dumb.

Lets what happens to it happen.
                                    (p. 63)

Throughout thirteen lines the poem remains faithful to the 'world of spirits' and the tree's subterranean psychic story without distorting the 'world of things', and its realist nature. Sheep, trees, even the tomb of an Ancient Briton, all are transformed into symbols of the possibilities of the self in such a context. In 'The Ancient Briton lay under his rock' (p. 84), this 'Mighty Hunter' is 'a whorl in our ignorance'; as the eager archaeologists dig deeper, the rock recedes further from them, the ideal of the self represented by the Ancient Briton shrinks from the communal grasp with it, 'Labouring in the prison/ Of our eyes, our sun, our Sunday bells.'

Whenever the characteristic imagination of *Remains of Elmet* exercises its influence, moving simultaneously inwards and outwards, even the largest units of the natural environment may be *consciously personified* as histories of the collective psyche. In 'Hill walls', for example, the land itself is imaged as a single body or vessel, colonizing uninhabited space:

> It set out –
> Splendour burst against its brow
> Broke over its shoulders.
> The hills heeled, meeting the blast of space.
>
> The stone rigging was strong.
> Exhilarated men
> Cupped hands and shouted to each other
> And grew stronger riding the first winters.
>
> The great adventure had begun –
> Even the grass
> Agreed and came with them,
> And crops and cattle –
>
> No survivors.
> There is the hulk, every rib shattered.
>
> A few crazed sheep
> Pulling its weeds
> On a shore of cloud.[1]
>
> (p. 30)

The initially vigorous state of negotiations between the colonizing, organizational effort and the wild 'blast of space' was broken up, leaving a stranded body, a 'hulk, every rib shattered'. The description of the physical environment has a mirror-image in Hughes' psychological assessment of British cultural history: a vigorous state of negotiations between Ego-Personality and Unconscious was finally broken up by the Reformation, leaving a contemporary malaise – the stranded post-war Ego, barely surviving, but 'crazed' and disorganized. Morever, Hughes' intuition about Yeats re-writing personal history as 'outer' social history is confirmed in his own work: the microscale events in the drama of the self are now being observed in their widest context. Imagine 'Hill walls' as a commentary upon the psychological passage between the adventurous vigour of *The Hawk in the Rain* and the splintered hulk of *Gaudete*, its failure of 'colonization'.

But once poems like 'Hill walls' and 'Top withens' have finished their task of 'swabbing the human shape from the freed stones', reducing the illusion that 'the earth is a heap of raw materials given to man by God for his exclusive profit and use' (the semantic of the Industrial Revolution), a vision of radiant Nature 'excellent as the first day' slowly starts to re-assemble itself. The process of re-construction begins with Hughes' creation of his own legend, an antidote to the fictions recounted in 'Churn-milk Joan':

Heptonstall old church

A great bird landed here.

Its song drew men out of rock,
Living men out of bog and heather.

Its song put a light in the valleys
And harness on the long moors.

Its song brought a crystal from space
And set in men's heads.

Then the bird died.

Its giant bones
Blackened and became a mystery.

The crystal in men's heads
Blackened and fell to pieces.

The valleys went out.
The moorland broke loose.

Hughes' legend, replacing the imperfect superstition of 'Churn-milk Joan', possesses the genuine attributes of a symbolic story noted by Gurdjieff; Hughes' exposure of the superstition tended to prescribe the reader's own posture as a 'memorial' of 'her futile stumbling and screams/ And awful little death', as an ironic victim of a merciless 'reader-trap'. His own legend, in contrast, invites the reader to complete the process unironically (that is, the poem is not ironically *constructed*) in an open reading situation: he is given the opportunity to unearth the motivation of the legend for himself, to re-discover the double-edged imagination dramatically by penetrating the paradoxical, tricksterish form of the legend. For as long as the narrative certainty of the legend (its 'objectivity') remains intact – 'Then the bird died.// Its giant bones/ Blackened and became a mystery' – it is 'history' in its most negative aspect, the 'remote' account of an unalterable past flatly disconnected from the understanding. The reader has to cultivate intentionally the invisible 'inner' story in order for the legend to operate fully in all its dimensions, in an active, changeful present: the 'objective' statement has a 'subjective' corollary, 'The crystal in men's heads/ Blackened and fell to pieces.' *Since then*, 'The valleys went out./ The moorland broke loose.' The poem really begs its unspoken sub-text: the plural self is in the ascendant, and 'unconscious' mechanical functions assume control of the organism, when the 'crystal' or single centre of gravity within the psyche is absent. And that permanent 'I' stands in the same relation to mechanical functions as the great bird's 'song' to the phenomenal items of the natural world (valleys, moors, bog, heather etc.). The individual's quest aims to restore that central point, renewing 'its song' as the dominant grammatical subject of the whole poem, not merely the first half of it. In this sense, it is the reader's responsibility to renew the 'innocent' situation of the psyche/ natural world described in lines 1–7, he has to bridge the midpoint divide of the poem's experience. The poem is transformed into a moral paradigm, and the mystery resolved from the interior outwards. 'Heptonstall old church' distils the educative force of 'Churn-milk Joan' as a free responsive choice, and the (reasonable) didactic tendency as a dramatic measure of the understanding. We are asked to heal the wound signified by the superstition of the earlier poem, the misperception of a radically hostile Nature and the inferior life of Instinct, Emotion, Sensation, etc. alike. But the act of healing is only possible if the reader absorbed the lesson of *Gaudete*, reading 'outer' events as 'inner' events, and vice versa.

The act of healing comes forward a step in the poem 'In April', where the landscape is perceived as 'a soft animal of peace', and achieves its major epiphany in 'Heptonstall cemetery':

Wind slams across the tops.
The spray cuts upwards.

You claw your way
Over a giant beating wing.

And Thomas and Walter and Edith
Are living feathers

Esther and Sylvia
Living feathers

Where all the horizons lift wings
A family of dark swans

And go beating low through storm-silver
Toward the Atlantic.

(p. 122)

The protagonist is exposed to the same *Grenzsituation* as the heroic 'I' of 'Wind', in the first four lines. But the violence of the elements is not, as in the earlier poem, interpreted as a mortal threat to the hero's abstract psychological fixture. The semantic of the natural scene is not 'hostility' to Man. The impulse to 'claw', resolving the contact with elementals negatively in favour of a St George-type aggressive–defensive attachment to the conscious Personality, is momentarily entertained, then rejected. The poetic reception of elementals (lines 5–8) turns 'fluid' and the dead, buried in the cemetery, have no option but passively to follow the rise-and-fall movement of the 'giant beating wing'. The imagination becomes moral as its grip relaxes, rather than tightens, and when the metaphor it produces is no longer 'accidental' or temporary – as in the

Movement usage – but extended, a permanent identity; the instability of the wind-blown landscape becomes an occasion not for self-fortification, but a 'prepared' flight away from the arbitrary fixity of the Ego. The poet himself is transformed into an obedient living feather, belonging to the collective centre beyond human fictions reviving the song-animated landscape of 'Heptonstall old church' before it was fractured into dark oblivion. He achieves that revival by re-illuminating the crystal in his own head, by the psychological action of 'keeping space open' in the silent passage between the fourth and fifth lines. The sense of a harmonization of the multiple 'dogfight of voices – all falsehoods, but all ringingly sincere' ('Orghast: talking without words', *Vogue*, December 1971) is pronounced:

> this other rarely speaks or stirs at all, in the sort of lives we do not lead. We have so totally lost touch, that we hardly realize he is absent. All we know is that somehow or other the great, precious thing is missing. And the real distress of our world begins there. The luminous spirit (maybe he is a crowd of spirits) that takes account of everything and gives everything its meaning, is missing. Not missing, just incommunicado. . . . It is human, of course, but it is also everything else that lives. (*ibid.*)

It is this voice which speaks sparely enough – but enough – for a dozen lines in 'Heptonstall cemetery'.

The 'collective' imagination also assumes control of 'Football at slack', in a more playful vein – though it is in Jung's sense of 'play' which is simultaneously comic and deadpan-serious/purposive:

> Between plunging valleys, or a bareback of hill
> Men in bunting colours
> Bounced, and their blown ball bounced.
>
> (p. 68)

The playful verb 'bounced' will only appear purely comic if the reader is ignorant of the ethical function of 'play'; it prescribes (literally) an 'elastic' state of negotiations between the human and the natural, the ego and the unconscious. The men 'bounce' in a series of instinctive, provisional adjustments to the exhilarating instability of their surroundings. Wind is again the characteristic feature of those surroundings, but the human inhabitants neither 'claw' nor 'grip' themselves deep within distinctively human fictions. Gurdjieff's model of co-operation between Personality and Essence, horse and rider, is vindicated in the single reference to 'a bareback of hill', and the long Anglo-Saxon line (lines 2–3) is renovated, observed in its most positive aspect: the vigorous interaction of consonants and vowels mirrors the joint vigour of men and wind, and there is no temptation – as at the beginning of 'The hawk in the rain' – to stiffen the poetic/'human' control of the situation,

separating off consonants and vowels, and thus the terms 'human' and
'natural', in a kind of lethal linguistic Civil War. The 'natural' perspective
is dominant, so that even human activity is analogized by a metaphor
which seems to derive from a collective or extra-human vantage-point:
'The blown ball jumped, and the merry-coloured men/ *Spouted like water*
to head it.' Gifford and Roberts also note the dominance of this
perspective, though they find it at least partially 'absurd':

> The danger of any discussion of the poem is that its gently mocking,
> quietly admiring humour might be overwhelmed. In fact the humour
> derives not only from the slight exaggeration of 'rubbery men' and 'the
> goalie flew horizontal' but also from the absurdity that results from *viewing
> the players as a group at a distance, as the landscape is viewed.* (Ted Hughes: *A
> critical study*, pp. 238–9; my italics)

The point is, surely, that the 'collective imagination' which achieves this
perspective is *not* absurd at all, but something for which the poet has been
striving all along. As Hughes suggested in his *Vogue* article, the centre
lies outside the exclusively 'human' circle, or the artificial circle drawn by
a false personality – the heroifying of mechanical functions. The material
'whole' – as outer, physical Nature or the collective psyche – is the truly
creative force: given full expression, it recreates Man as a 'Work of Art'
in the religious sense of the phrase:

> Winds from fiery holes in heaven
> Piled the hills darkening around them
> To awe them. The glare light
> *Mixed its mad oils and threw glooms.*
> Then the rain lowered a steel press.
> (my italics)

When the relationship between the two terms ('human' and 'natural') is
described by self-conscious art, religious 'awe' does not deteriorate into
'hostility', and the unconscious construction of lies about the natural
world; the 'collective imagination' persists until the very end of the
poem: 'And once again a golden holocaust/ Lifted the cloud's edge, to
watch them.' The material whole 'paints' through the poet, reversing the
angle of vision in 'To paint a water lily', and we are invited to adopt the
same point of view 'to watch them'. Only this imagination renders 'play'
possible, defying the gravity of self-importance: 'But the wingers leapt,
they bicycled in air/ And the goalie flew horizontal', and modifying the
destructive, engulfing effect of Lumb's Dionysian experiences in the
Prologue so that consciousness can bob up 'washed and happy' on the
surface of the unconscious:

> Hair plastered, they all just trod water
> To puddle glitter. And their shouts bobbed up
> Coming fine and thin, washed and happy.

Hughes is performing the seminal action, plucking the 'human' from its self-enclosed 'jam-jar' and lobbing it back into the 'material'-collective like loach into canal-water, 'Back into their Paradise and mine' ('The canal's drowning black').

MOORTOWN

At first glance, *Moortown* appears to be Hughes' least integrated collection to date, defying any simple statement of its place within his overall poetic development. Poems from a much earlier phase of Hughes' career are included: 'A motorbike' ('Earth-numb') first appeared twelve years before the publication of *Moortown*, in *The Listener* (30 November 1967), and the whole of 'Prometheus on his crag' was conceived and written at the time of the *Orghast* project in Persia (1971), to give two examples. Moreover, these two sequences – 'Earth-numb' and 'Prometheus on his crag' – are not obviously related either to each other or to a third group of poems which first appeared in 1978 under the title *Moortown Elegies* (Rainbow Press edition) and which comprised a 'verse journal about the author's experiences farming in Devon' (Note, dust-jacket of *Moortown Elegies*). On deeper consideration, however, it is possible to discern a continuity of interests between the present volume and *Remains of Elmet*, and a broadening rather than a fracturing of imaginative focus: the elements of the 'inner' descent are present in their purest form, particularly in the sequences 'Adam and the sacred nine', 'Seven dungeon songs' and 'Four tales told by an idiot', though in determined alliance with the 'outer' record of the verse-journal, within the same volume. The imagination reaches in both directions at once, applying the same principles of cause and effect to both worlds; it is for the first time at home, comfortable in the 'collision' of 'subjective' and 'objective' factors, in an improvement on the state of negotiations dramatized by *Gaudete*. The sole of the human foot is comfortable 'pressed to the world-rock' of its material surroundings

> With even, gentle squeeze
> Grateful
> To the rock, saying
>
> I am no wing
> To tread emptiness
> I was made
> For you.
>   ('The sole of a foot')

The verse-journal poems, composing the first third of the book, envisage Hughes' confident re-emergence into the external world anticipated by *Remains of Elmet*. In his introduction to a reading on Radio 3, Hughes indicated his desire for an imaginative record which was neither 'subjective synthesis' – and thus susceptible to Empathetic–Abstractive delusion – nor a completely 'objective' reduction of the 'fresh simple presence of the experience':

> If I let the event go past, four or five days, and then I made my note, even though I remembered every detail perfectly, those details no longer seemed important. . . . I'd no wish to make a subjective synthesis of these external details, all I wanted was the record, the externals neat. But only a very few details seemed worth setting down. The rest hadn't gone, but their charge of importance had gone. (Broadcast, 10 May 1980)

The 'third' imagination is as necessary to the process of getting 'the externals neat' as it was to the process of striking down false selves. It is this imagination which also affects the form of the poems themselves organically, at their most intimate mechanical level. Hughes discovered that the formal disciplining of line and stanza imposed a 'subjective synthesis' of its own, weighting the experience with an unconscious bias, while 'ordinary journal prose, a shorthand sort of jotted details' ('Ted Hughes and R. S. Thomas read and discuss selections from their own poems', The Critical Forum, Norwich tapes, 1978) tended to entrap the living event as an 'objective' memory deprived of dramatic attributes; only in the mediative form of 'rough verse' did the poet 'move deeper and more steadily into reliving the experience' (*ibid.*), find a 'third' language for the ideal imagination.

With this in mind, the formal conflict between the poles of ritually intense music and colloquial prose readiness which so accurately reflected the persona's psychological struggle in Hughes' early work is finally abolished. And the critical response to styles which so accurately measured the reader's moral status vanishes with it. More so even than *Remains of Elmet*, the success of the *Moortown Elegies* depends upon the reader's ability to pick up signals that are fundamentally infra-linguistic, rather than *ultra-linguistic* in nature. In the very first poem 'Rain', for example, the pared-down but well-sinewed verbal economy that is so typical of these poems resists any possible linguistic apotheosis of the natural scene:

> Rain, Floods, Frost. And after frost, rain.
> Dull roof-drumming. Wraith-rain pulsing across purple-bare woods
> Like light across heaved water. Sleet in it.

The abruptness of the sentences suggests that language is only responsible to the 'natural' event; it remains steadfastly uninterested in furthering its own independent rhythms, the equivalent of the autonomous 'human' contribution. In the course of the whole poem, rain as a 'poetic occasion' only submits to imperceptible refinements, from 'wraith-rain' to 'mist-rain' to 'rain-mist', no further. The real occasion is poetic in the moral sense of the word, as the flexible passivity of rough verse admits both the 'externals neat' and the 'subjective' shadow of the landscape, its precise inner echo:

> The fox corpses lie beaten to the bare bones,
> Skin beaten off, brain and bowels beaten out.
> Nothing but blueprint bones last in the rain . . .
>
> Nowhere they can go
> Is less uncomfortable. . . .
>
> Magpies
> Shake themselves hopelessly, hop in the spatter. Misery.

In the fullest re-living of the experience, natural description is transformed into a dramatic rehearsal of the required, humbling shamanistic 'death' of *Cave Birds* and the inescapable mechanical conditions of psyche and world alike. In the last two lines even snipe, though 'invisible', are notably amenable to the synthesis of the 'third' imagination: 'Snipe go over, invisible in the dusk,/ With their *squelching* cries' (my italics).[2]

Several of the poems in this section of *Moortown* approach fulfilment – within given cultural restraints – of the criteria for *objective art* set down by Gurdjieff and transmitted by A. R. Orage in his commentary on *Beelzebub's Tales to his Grandson*, developing the renewal of the term 'objectivity' which was a major concern in *Gaudete*:

1. There are two categories of art, subjective and objective – unconscious and conscious. (p. 143)

2. Art evokes a range of emotions that nature would, but cannot, produce. The degree to which the artist is conscious in this defines his importance from our point of view. The artist must be in the spirit of Nature, in the laws of Nature. . . . True artists are the antennae of Nature; coming Nature casts its artists before it. (pp. 143–4)

3. Minor art is concerned with self-expression. Major art is an effort at conveying certain ideas for the benefit of the beholder; not necessarily for the advantage of the artist. In speaking of ordinary subjective art, we say that a perfect work of art completely satisfies our sense of harmony – every part of our sensory, emotional, and intellectual being. From Gurdjieff's point of view . . . to wake us out of sleep, the said satisfaction of harmony (which is not real tranquillity but a form of higher sleep) is the last thing to be desired. Aesthetic contemplation is sublime sleep; consciousness is in abeyance.

   The object of the Adherents of Legominism was to cause people to 'remember'. They introduced lawful inexactitudes into works of all kinds so that people would ask 'Why is it so?' This idea was found in the ancient Zen Buddhist schools, which were responsible for the flowering

of great Japanese art; among the traditions which grew out of it was that
in a perfect work of art something should be left unfinished. (p. 187)

4. Objective art brings about a state of non-identification. The one great
   art, so far as this work is concerned, is that of making a complete
   human being of oneself. (C. S. Nott, 'Orage's commentary on
   "Beelzebub" ', in *Teachings of Gurdjieff*, p. 144)

The increase of consciousness (1 and 4) of the poetry has already been
suggested by the presence of the characteristic imagination which strives
to get both internals and externals 'neat', bringing about the state of
'non-identification' that is psychologically ideal. Likewise, the artist's
posture (2) as a collective mouthpiece for the material whole or inaudible
Natural 'emotions' is something even Hughes' earliest practice established as an aim – his elevation of the 'Natural' perspective in *Remains of
Elmet* was merely the latest step towards its achievement. The preference
(3) for the education of self and beholder and the deliberately unfinished
work of art over against artificially produced aesthetic emotion is also
familiar: the reader finds himself continually asking the question 'Why is
it so?', as even the aesthetic assurance of a poem like 'The thought-fox' –
'The page is printed' – is broken:

> The fox
> Hangs his silver tongue in the world of noise
> Over his splattering paws. Will he run
> Till his muscles suddenly turn to iron,
> Till blood froths his mouth as his lungs tatter,
> Till his feet are raw blood-sticks and his tail
> Trails thin as a rat's? Or will he
> Make a mistake, jump the wrong way, jump right
> Into the hound's mouth? As I write this down
> He runs still fresh, with all his chances before him.
>   ('Foxhunt')

In the 'lawful inexactitude' of these lines the fox's symbolic progress is
entirely a matter for the reader's imagination: the fresh, undeformed
Essence may be 'ground' and refined in an exhausted death, or overtaken
and decimated by the formal machinery of the 'civilized' foxhunt.

Orage's statements provide a useful organizational model for the first
section of *Moortown*. We find the poet confidently projecting himself into
the range of 'Natural' emotions, or functioning as the antennae of
'coming Nature', without imposing his own state of feeling upon it. In
'Feeding out-wintering cattle at twilight', for example, the persona picks
up the signals of coming Nature – the cattle are 'knee deep in porage of
earth . . . on their steep, hurtling brink' – in *his own* 'half dissolved'
floundering, and here, unlike 'The hawk in the rain', there is no further
resistance to the prospect of dissolution. The happy flexibility of his

mental grasp ('what do they care') recalls Don Juan's definition of a 'hunter':

> A hunter uses his world sparingly and with tenderness, regardless of whether the world might be things, or plants, or animals, or people, or power . . . he's not squeezing his world out of shape. He taps it lightly, stays for as long as he needs to, and then swiftly moves away leaving hardly a mark. (Castaneda, *Journey to Ixtlan*, p. 86)

A similar lightness of touch characterizes 'Couples under cover', and the more complex account of 'Struggle', where the necessity of paying attention to Nature and its externals actually suppresses the momentary possibility of a 'subjective descent'. The poem describes the birth of a calf from its distressed mother:

> The walk towards her was like a walk into danger,
> Caught by her first calf, the small-boned black and white heifer
> Having a bad time.

Twenty years before, that first line would be an open invitation to explore internal dangers, but here the self is expansive enough to ignore any perceived threat to its well-being and give the other its full consideration. This denial of any possible fixation with the 'subjective' actually expands our sense of the poet's role, too: his chief function in the present poem is clearly *extra-linguistic*, *extra-literary*, that of an active assistant in the calf's birth rather than an abstract framer of an artistic picture. The poet reclaims his religious role when he resists the specialization of the term 'poet' and becomes a practical healing agent in communal life, closing the fissure opened by Lumb's tragic division of functions (priest and doctor) in the Prologue to *Gaudete*, advancing another step towards the unity of 'Poet' and 'Shaman'.

What I called the 'full consideration of the other' and the de-emphasis of the purely 'subjective' filters down even to the most basic syntactical constructions, like the formation of a simile: 'He mooed feebly and lay like a pieta Christ/ in the cold easterly daylight.' The 'inner' suggestiveness of the symbol – pieta Christ – is subordinated to the animal it analogizes; the use of the human symbol to consecrate animal life may appear shocking, but it is consonant with Hughes' general endeavour to establish a collective 'Natural' perspective, and it does realize the animal base of the Cross-symbol, which Crow also discovered. As Janos Pilinszky knew, the transfigurative force of the Crucifix and the attainment of the 'fully human' depends on the acknowledgement of a 'wholly animal' origin, lowest down:

> *We and they*
>
> That we are damned is all right,
> but that barefoot animals are

is even more so. Because
they bear, they suckle, they raise
the helpless God,
and the Son taken down from the Cross
they hide even from Mary,
and carry him everywhere with them.

        (*Crater: Poems 1974–5*, p. 49)

Within four lines, the poet's creation of an open space and his submission
to 'coming Nature' is complete: '*We stood back*, letting the strength flow
towards them.' Moreover, the poem draws attention to itself as an act of
consciousness in the last four lines, detecting 'affliction' as a principle of
the natural world as it was a principle of the operation of the psyche:

But his eye just lay suffering the monstrous weight of his head,
The impossible job of his marvellous huge limbs.
He could not make it. He died called Struggle.
Son of Patience.

The poem ends not with aesthetic harmony but the disturbing unans-
wered question 'why is it so?'; the first three of Orage's criteria for
objective art are satisfied, and the reader completes the process by
assimilating – if he is able – the 'third' imagination dramatized within it,
and 'remembering' the inner understanding of both mechanical nature
and the fact of death which comprehends it in a meaningful pattern.

    This imagination consistently attracts the same landscape in different
versions throughout *Moortown*: on the one hand, an environment which
is all machine, all function, on the other, an environment which is lashed
by a permanent, collective, animating wind outside the mechanical; the
landscape draws itself up in an identical set of relations to those of the
ideal psychic inscape:

Pressure
Climbing and the hard blue sky
Slowed by gales. The world's being
Swept clean. Twigs that can't cling
Go flying, last leaves ripped off
Bowl along roads like daring mice. . . .
Exhilaration
Lashes everything. . . .

The powers of hills
Hold their bright faces in the wind-shine.
The hills are being honed. The river
Thunders like a factory, its weirs
Are tremendous engines.

        ('New year exhilaration')

The machinery is 'honed' by the wind-centre outside it, guaranteeing the
happy instability of the conclusion:

People
Walk precariously, the whole landscape
Is imperilled, like a tarpaulin
With the wind under it. 'It nearly
Blew me up the chymbley!' And a laugh
Blows away like a hat.

In this poem as in others, wind is freed from its earlier semantic in the eponymous poem from *The Hawk and the Rain*, where it existed primarily as the trigger of an unconscious fear crossing into consciousness. It is more 'materially' and 'spiritually' itself, the Pneuma 'that blows all living things on this earth'. This shift in the reception of 'Wind' is another example of Hughes' undoing of the hypnosis of unconscious idea or mood which at times held the early poet in its subjectivist grip, the fear which in *Lupercal* very nearly paralysed any further moral progress. The psychological condition which facilitates this undoing is exactly the state of the 'non–identification' that Orage mentions as essential to the objective artist; in one poem, 'Surprise', the purging of hypnotic thoughts is dramatically re-enacted: the poet is trying to decide the function of a plastic apron apparently hitched beneath the tail of one of the cows:

I thought
Of aprons over ewes' back-ends
To keep the ram out till it's timely. I thought
Of surgical aprons to keep cleanliness
Under the shit-fall. Crazily far thoughts
Proposed themselves as natural, and I almost
Looked away.

Both thoughts are puritanical in origin, but the concealment or suppression of the 'material' they represent becomes conscious with 'Crazily far thoughts', and the potential compromise of the poet's wholeness of attention is crucially restrained by 'almost'; no thought identification actually occurs, the possibility of 'hypnosis' is shattered, and the act of consciousness materializes as a real birth, where the 'apron' is in fact the calf's natural birth-sac, not a puritanical obsession at all!

Two poems in particular, 'Ravens' and 'February 17th', concentrate the poet's new-found obligation to the objective world of Nature, his duties as farmer. The farm becomes a kind of 'working laboratory' (Craig Robinson), a provisional point of collision for the 'human' and the 'natural' which ideally locates in the outside world the emergency self which proved such an accurate barometer of 'inner' negotiations between Ego and Unconscious, Abstract Personality and Material Essence. As in the psychological scenario – where the aim was the *irrigation* of the conscious Personality by the Essence/Unconscious, not the elimination of one and the sentimentalizing of the other – there is no invitation to elevate the rural above the urban as a pastoral idyll; the objective is rather to render the urban mentality receptive to the real nature of Nature, that educative force which a rural community cannot either ignore or suppress.[3]

Nature certainly gives an implacable lesson in 'Ravens', which Hughes has called the 'record of a disaster' ('Ted Hughes and R. S. Thomas', Norwich tape) partly induced by the farmer's failure to attend, and thus assist in, the birth of a new lamb at the height of the lambing season. Up until the last eight lines the poem is a dialogue between the poet/ persona and a three-year-old child he has brought to the field with him. The child's 'attention' is complete in Simone Weil's sense of the word; 'empty and ready to be penetrated by the object', first by the presence of a new-born lamb, then by that of a dead one, preyed on by Ravens. The child is pure Essence, unrefined and waiting to be educated. But the natural 'lesson' is not enforced by the imposition of conscious interpretative controls on the part of the poet, and his 'explanation' of the lamb's death is nothing more than a statement of the 'externals neat', swept clean of 'subjective' bias:

> I explain
> That it died being born. We should have been here, to
> help it.
> So it died being born.

Pushed further by the child's subsequent question, the poet's objectivity only deepens; in Weil's 'silence' he holds the dead lamp up materially *as its own interpreter*:

> 'And did it cry?' you cry.
> I pick up the dangling greasy weight by the hooves
> Soft as dogs' pads
> That had trodden only womb-water
> And its raven-drawn strings dangle and trail,
> Its loose head joggles, and 'Did it cry?' you cry again.

This explanatory delay is repeated in the next eight lines, as the child's cry, 'in a three-year-old field-wide/ Piercing persistence', merges first with that of another living new-born lamb, 'testing the note it finds in its mouth', and finally with the dead lamb's imagined cry, concretized by the poet's answer: ' "Oh yes" I say "it cried".' In these intervals it is once again left to the reader to finish the poem's process, deprived as he is by the persona's state of 'non-identification', of any clearly mapped responsive attitude towards the matter the poem presents. In one reading, there is a dualistic temptation, in the passage between the first and second 'intervals', to retreat before the physical reality of death into a divisive concentration on the new-born lamb, as evidence of the heroic triumph of 'life' over 'death'; the two terms are split in their usual state of culturally sanctioned warfare. This reading is ironically undercut by Hughes' eventual affirmative answer, with its denial of any precipitate consolation. The reader has to substitute a second reading, a consciousness based upon the 'Knowledge of affliction' and the blending of cries, human and animal, living and dead. The commonality of the 'cry', and the literal proximity of the dead lamb to life ('it died being born') establish the unity of the two terms, and 'affliction' as a centre pin in the organization of the poem's reading experience and the structure of material existence alike. ' "Oh yes" I say "it cried" ' comes with the certainty of the tolling bell, and constitutes the 'steady attention' which is, according to Simone Weil, necessary to face affliction, the knowledge that the soul 'is a dead thing, something analogous to matter' ('Additional pages on the love of God and affliction', *Gateway to God*, p. 93). 'To philosophize is to learn to die' said Plato, and the poet submits to death as a first principle of coming Nature. He dies to the ephemeral self and its consolations in order to divulge the collective roots of his own real voice:

> Though this one was lucky insofar
> As it made the attempt into a warm wind
> And its first day of death was blue and warm
> The magpies gone quiet with domestic happiness
> And skylarks not worrying about anything
> And the blackthorn budding confidently
> And the skyline of hills, after millions of hard years
> Sitting soft.

The separate paragraph might be called Hughes' fully conscious 'addition' to the material experience, framing it but wary of unconscious interpretative distortion. The child's 'open', attentive Essence was educated or organ-ized by a 'clean' Personality, and left to draw its own conclusions through a careful juxtaposition of all the evidence. Out of that debate, a third voice emerged which was not recognizably either the poet–farmer's or the child's, a voice which could determine the lamb as 'lucky', which had learned to love affliction:

> it is not enough to be aware of this possibility; one must love it. One must tenderly love the harshness of that necessity which is like a coin with two faces, the one turned towards us being domination, the one turned towards God, obedience. ('Additional pages on the love of God and affliction', *Gateway to God*, p. 88)[4]

The poet fulfils the active extension of his literary role more directly in the very next poem, 'February 17th', describing the 'birth' of a lamb which has already grown too large for its mother's womb, and cannot be delivered alive into the world. Here is Hughes' introduction to the poem:

> The birth of a lamb can usually be left to a lamb and its mother. Occasionally, things go wrong. . . . It's unlucky for the lamb if he's conceived inside a small mother. It's unluckier if he then proceeds to grow too well inside her, and unluckiest of all if at the moment of birth he fails to get his front feet up beside his nose for a proper, graceful dive out into the world. (Ted Hughes and Paul Muldoon, Faber poetry cassette, 1983)

Hughes' emphasis on 'luck' again recalls Weil's reference to the 'mechanical brutality of circumstances', and it was presumably a revulsion against this notion which provoked critical protest in the audience at one of Hughes' readings:

> Once I read this in a hall full of university students, and one member of the audience rebuked me for reading what he called a disgusting piece of horror writing. Well, we either have a will to examine what happens, or we have a will to evade it. . . . Throughout [the piece], I might say, I was concerned not at all with the style of writing, simply to get the details and steps of the event for the record. ('Ted Hughes and R. S. Thomas', Norwich tapes)

An abstract emotionalist sympathy with the dead/semi-born lamb outweighs the practical or 'collective' need to save the mother only in this dualistic view. In fact, it is that purely aesthetic emotion which resists the expansion of poetic function beyond the literary which the *Moortown Elegies* as a whole attest, and the posture of obedience to Necessity which is a positive in Weil's religious vocabulary. In this case the reader finds himself trapped within an aesthetic range which cannot promote *action*, as in Hughes' story of the photographer's impotence as a tiger suddenly starts mauling a model to death (he took pictures of the event). Moreover, the same aesthetic confinement threatens to suppress as 'horrible' an important symbolic statement by the 'collective imagination':

> I went
> Two miles for the injection and a razor.
> Sliced the lamb's throat-strings, levered with a knife
> Between the vertebrae and brought the head off
> To stare at its mother, its pipes sitting in the mud
> With all earth for a body.

The style of the piece is itself purely functional – a resistance to the aesthetic preoccupation with verbal resource – and the reader fulfils the ethical role of 'critic' only by realizing the symbolic force of the decapitated head 'with all earth for a body' as the *original* religious situation of the psyche: the individual body as 'simply carbon' at bottom, with a collective centre outside the body's functions. The reader completes the process by revivifying the symbol inside his own experience, and the symbol materializes *only* as a consequence of both poet and reader's willingness to push poetic *function* beyond the realm of pure aesthetics.

A simultaneous rejection and expansion of aesthetic emotion also characterizes 'Coming down through Somerset', in which the poet, 'driving through England', stops to pick up a recently slain badger. Initially, each individual concentration on the badger's beauty seems to be reprimanded more strongly – the aesthetic verb within the phrase 'Flies, drumming,/ Bejewel his transit' is rebuked by the material imperative 'Get rid of that badger'; but this rebuke only exists as long as the reader assumes that the poet wants to preserve an abstract picture of the badger's beauty. On second consideration, it becomes evident that the act of preservation 'blocks time' by observing the object *in the process* of decay, keeping faith with the individual beauty and the collective origin opened by death alike. *Both* 'His rankness, his bristling wildness', *and* 'His thrillingly painted face' are equally worthy of praise, in Hughes' resolution of the tragic Shakespearean dichotomy of artifact pitted against material flux (which dominates his *Sonnets*). The poet blocks time by consciously submitting everything to its changeful 'moment', paradoxically; in such circumstances the 'individual' is hammered like a nail into the 'collective':

> I stand
> Watching his stillness, like an iron nail
> Driven, flush to the head,
> Into a yew post. Something
> Has to stay.

The image unavoidably draws to itself the particular resonance or vibration of the Crucifixion-symbol, as the aesthetic/individual is pinned on to the Necessity which governs all material life. In the ambiguity of the simile, the object of the comparative – whether poetic 'I' or the badger's stillness – is momentarily uncertain, suggesting the presence of Gurdjieff's perceptual paradigm which looks towards the subject and the object simultaneously. The conclusion becomes an exact copy of 'February 17th' in its essentials: the unalterability of the given situation on the mechanical level, the confrontation of death as a door to the 'collective imagination' or objective consciousness, the sense that what 'stays' will be outside the exclusively human range and the evolution of aesthetic emotion depending on its localized 'death', are elements common to both poems, and to the broad spectrum of verse-journals in general.

The 'Prometheus on his crag' sequence belongs to a much earlier phase of Hughes' development (it was written in 1971); it exists in the present context as in 'limbo . . . a numb poem about numbness'. *Earth-numb*, by contrast, presents a much wider variety of external subject-matter, gathering up languages characteristic of Hughes' preceding volumes. 'Old age gets up', for example, uses the device of personification in a manner recalling 'Heptonstall' from *Remains of Elmet*; 'The lovepet' and 'Actaeon', are recognizably *Crow*-poems, whilst the title poem itself derives from the linguistic foundation of *Season Songs*. The sequences, such as 'Four tales told by an idiot' and 'Seven dungeon songs' appear as developments out of the *Gaudete* Epilogue-style. It is as if Hughes is summoning all the stylistic ghosts of his own literary past in order to discover their point of unity, the point at which the multiplicity of styles and the variety of 'accidental' external situations 'roll into one', to use Tadeusz Rozewicz's phrase. To this end, a scrutiny of the two sequences, 'Earth-numb', 'Actaeon' and 'The lovepet', and the poem 'Deaf school' – with its variant of the journal-prose style of *Moortown Elegies* – will prove representative. Taken together, they demonstrate a unity of moral purpose, embodying a concerted assault on the Personality and its unconscious reduction of the self.

'The lovepet' and 'Actaeon' are the most immediately accessible poems within this frame of reference. 'The lovepet' is really a seminal acknowledgement, a full consciousness of the destructive effects of the Personality: Crow's clear-sighted song – and it is surely Crow who sings – is a definite consummation of his effort to 'become a man', harmonizing the expression of Hughes' earliest didactic tendency by funnelling it through the 'open' fabular form of a mythic anecdeote. Man and woman surrender everything, including their humanity, to what should be servant to them; the poem reads like some horrendous involution of Crow's own progress, which entails the shattering of Personality, though it is left to the reader to unriddle the lovepet's nature – the answer to the question 'Was it an animal was it a bird?' depends utterly upon the evolution of a certain attitude within the critic-initiate, and his capacity dramatically to fulfil a 'concealed' sub-text in the complete absence of extraneous explanatory data. The appeal to the discursive mind is entirely suppressed by this withholding of information, testing our familiarity with the culturally informed wars and weddings in 'inner' space. The sub-text is exactly diagrammed by a psychological 'reader' like Omraam Mikhail Aivanhov:

> It is the personality which wants, thinks, suffers, demands, and when you do not know this, you do everything to satisfy it. People who have never analysed themselves do not know the true nature of the human being, the

different planes and stages of evolution, and they identify with the personality, the physical body. (p. 35)

The personality has no morals, no ethics, no generosity, no compassion, nothing. The personality wants everything, and, as it never has enough, it remains ungrateful, perpetually irritated not to receive more attention. . . .
 The personality has become inflated over the years because of the way man has been brought up, he has been taught to develop the lower nature, the personality and its cravings, until it has become a giant tumour inside him. (*Man's Two Natures: Human and divine*, pp. 48–9)

So the ending of 'The lovepet' illustrates the cultural tragedy like this:

They wept they called it back it could have everything
It stripped at their nerves chewed flavourless
It bit at their numb bodies they did not resist
It bit into their blank brains they hardly knew

It moved bellowing
Through a ruin of starlight and crockery

It drew slowly off they could not move

It went far away they could not speak.

Moreover, 'Actaeon' is a sort of sister-poem to 'The lovepet', in which the 'he' of the piece is the personality itself, glimpsed in the action of misinterpreting the feminine 'her' (the Essence/Anima): 'He looked at her but he could not see her face.' As in the earlier poem, the absence of punctuation seems to shape language as the helpless witness of an 'unalterable' animal–mechanical situation, with only the invisible narrative voice remaining outside the voice of the last few lines:

And still his face-blank went on
Staring, seeing nothing, feeling nothing

And still his voice went on, decorating the floor

Even though life had ceased.

Gurdjieff prescribes the psychological situation as accurately as Aivanhov penetrated the scenario of 'The lovepet' when he reveals that

it happens fairly often that essence dies in a man while his personality and body are still alive. A considerable percentage of the people we meet in the streets of great towns are people who are dead inside, that is, they are actually *already dead*.
 It is fortunate for us that we do not see and do not know it. If we knew what a number of people are actually dead and what a number of those dead people govern our lives, we should go mad with horror. (Ouspensky, *In Search of the Miraculous*, p. 164)

Where 'Actaeon' offers a mythic narration of the over-developed Personality, 'Deaf school' envisages precisely the opposite condition, a condition in which the deaf children are almost painfully deprived of any elements that could be called 'not their own': 'Their selves were not woven into a voice/ Which was woven into a face/ Hearing itself, its own public and audience.' In fact, the poem's greatest reading-danger is the assumption of comfortable superiority to the deaf which is apparently invited by individual phrases – 'They lacked a dimension/ They lacked a subtle wavering aura of sound and responses to sound', and principally

> What they spoke with was a machine,
> A manipulation of fingers, a control-panel of gestures
> Out there in the alien space
> Separated from them.

In both quotations, the 'unconscious' judgement of the deaf as deficient or inadequate is an active possibility, although a counterview is simultaneously made available in 'they lived through the eyes,/ The clear simple look, the instant full attention', and 'Their unused faces were simple lenses of watchfulness/ Simple pools of earnest watchfulness.' That is, we are given the option to assess the children from the point of view of the *Personality*, or that of the *individuality*, to re-cycle Aivanhov's terms. Far from judging them inferior, the second response recognizes spiritually instructive features: the knowledge of the 'public' Personality as simply a *machine*, the fullness of attention guaranteed by an un-obstructed Essence, the silencing of the Personality's 'internal talk', all these elements show the educative force of *deafness*, perhaps explaining part of the moral origin of Pilinszky's reasoning that 'in art the deaf can hear, the blind can see, the cripple can walk, *each deficiency may become a creative force of high quality*' (from Hughes' introduction to Pilinszky's *Selected Poems*, p. 8; my italics). The two rival centres of judgement alternate to the very end of the poem:

> the self looked through, out of the face of simple concealment
> A face not merely deaf, a face in darkness, a face unaware,
> A face that was simply the front skin of the self concealed and separate.

Any assessment from the physical 'objectivity' of the situation, however, damningly forecloses on our possibility of 'negotiating' in the silent region *between* the 'unaware face' and the living *self* 'concealed and separate', we crystallize as abstract judges and lose our being as provisional mediators, living witnesses.

'Earth-numb' thrusts the assault on the Personality, and the realization of the living self 'concealed and separate', into a dynamic pattern of development, straddling the distance between *Season Songs* and *River*. The poem reaches even further back into Hughes' history than that, beginning at the point where an 'outer' event (the hunting of salmon) shows its 'inner' correlative, the open-ended searching or religious prayer of 'Pike':

> The lure is a prayer. And my searching –
> Like the slow sun.
> A prayer, like a flower opening.
> A surgeon operating
> On an open heart, with needles

What is initially perceived as 'an electrocuting malice/ Like a trap', is then experienced as simply energetic rather than hostile, in a significant adjustment by the poetic consciousness: 'A piling voltage hums, jamming [him] stiff – ', and the protagonist becomes a 'third' conductor outside the opposites of river and sky, heaven and earth, inner and outer, renewing our sense of the *permanent* or material metaphor which is *always* valid in both worlds. As the ghost of the divine nature grows solid within the supra-ordinate imagination in one huge, 'whole' sentence of fifteen lines, the 'Personality' – also incredulous – fixes its own death-exposure of the apparently discrete items of the natural world:

> And a ghost grows solid, a hoverer,
> A lizard green slither, banner heavy –
>
> Then the wagging stone pebble head
> Trying to think on shallows – . . .
>
> As the eyes of incredulity
> Fix their death-exposure on the celandine and the cloud.

By now it should be evident that, even in the selection of poems examined so far, the summoning of Hughes' vast range of poetic styles is directed towards, and united by, a single *conscious aim*; every voice and its attendant language is thrown into the breach, asked by the supra-ordinate imagination to focus Hughes' central fable through its own particular lens.[5] And as Hughes noted of Shakespeare, 'whenever Shakespeare wrote at top intensity, at unusual length, in a burst of unusually self-contained completeness, he was almost unvariably hammering at the same thing – a particular knot of obsessions' (*A Choice of Shakespeare's Verse*, p. 181), so his own particular knot of obsessions received its most concentrated attention in the completeness of self-contained sequences. One of the smaller sequences, 'Four tales told by an idiot', begins the recital of that fable: as the title subliminally indicates, it is based upon an 'intentional stupidity', that deliberate deafness to Personality which was the ethical positive of 'Deaf school'. It is 'intentional stupidity' which attracts some of the seminal events of Hughes' fable. The Personality's 'racket' stops, and the Feminine principle in nature is immediately transformed into a creative 'hinge',

'Who so *focussed* the sun, with her *glassy* body,/ She roasted my inmost marrow, my inmost ghost' (p. 2; my italics). She devours the assumed backbone of the self, its abstract solidity ('dragged the spinal cord out of me downward/ Like a white hot wire – // This she swallowed and became incandescent'), and the poem concludes with an explicit Jungian coalition of shadow and Anima: '[she] lay down in front of me with my shadow./ The sun set, and they vanished together.'

The third and fourth poems make a return to the repetitive formulas of *Crow*, representing language's intentional stupidity in the face of its own expressive verbal potential; that anti-style is again appropriate to a situation recognized as unchangeable on the mechanical level, but unlike the majority of poems in the earlier volume the pressure of that knowledge creates a new conscious attitude which finds its expression within the poem:

> That star
> Will scorch everything dead to its blueprint
>
> That star
> Will make the earth melt
>
> That star . . . and so on.

As soon as the poet becomes conscious of mechanical structure – on both the formal and real levels – with the phrase 'and so on', he automatically *prepares* himself for the encounter with death, extending that opportunity to the reader:

> There is no escape.
> Not one of them is good, or friendly, or corruptible.
> One chance remains: KEEP ON DIGGING THAT HOLE
> KEEP ON DIGGING AWAY AT THAT HOLE.

The imperative 'Keep on digging that hole' may constitute *conscious preparation* for death, creating a space in which the subject learns to 'die' to the individualizing Personality before his physical death takes it from him, still poignantly 'unprepared' – for embedded within the ambivalence of the phrase, is the suggestion of endless, futile labour played out in ignorance of death. Both meanings, the fullness of the moral opportunity in those two lines, are beautifully caught in one of the symbolic events in *Tales of Power*: Castaneda narrates a story to Don Juan in which two cats are being taken by car to the animal hospital to be put down; one cat goes 'to his death trustingly, filled with his cat's judgements' (p. 111), the other, overtaken by 'cat spirit', accepts the chance to escape offered by Castaneda. Castaneda's understanding of the symbol rotates around the escaped cat, he believes that the 'spirit of man' will overtake his own cosmetically unified life in the same way. Don

Juan, however, castigates his student for failing to 'use all the event' (p. 111):

> You think you're like Max [the escaped cat], therefore you have forgotten about the other cat. You don't even know his name. *Having to believe* means that you must consider everything, and before deciding that you are like Max you must consider that you may be like the other cat; instead of running for your life and taking your chances, you may be going to your doom happily, filled with your judgements. (pp. 111–12)

> Death is the indispensable ingredient in *having* to believe. Without the awareness of death everything is ordinary, trivial. (p. 114)

Like Castaneda the reader must keep the entirety of the event intact, in the ambivalence of the imperative; for he may be like the man who goes on digging his senseless hole all his life, pathetically split off from the 'mechanical' knowledge of death, or those 'whose death will encircle them while they are alone, unaware, staring at the walls and ceiling of an ugly barren room' (*ibid.*, p. 115). The structure of Hughes' poem asks the reader to consider all the possibilities, and to 'believe' only in the face of death after he has dug a grave for the personality and his trust in its 'independent' judgements.

Other sequences do indeed contain poems which dig this grave for the Personality, transforming it into an object of observation, not a point of attachment. Poem 3 of 'Seven dungeon songs', for instance, opens with a lucid recollection of the plural self, healing slowly in the light of the sun or collective centre of gravity 'outside' mechanisms:

> Face was necessary – I found face.
> Hands – I found hands.
>
> I found shoulders, I found legs
> I found all bits and pieces.
>
> We were me, and lay quiet.
> I got us all of a piece, and we lay quiet.
>
> We just lay.
> Sunlight had prepared a wide place.
>
> And we lay there.
> Air nursed us.

and concludes with a similarly clear image of the abstract Personality which obstructs the full recuperation of the whole psyche:

> Only still something
> Stared at me and screamed
>
> Stood over me, black across the sun,
> And mourned me, and would not help me get up.

The description is a precise reminder of Hughes' original notion of Krogon in *Orghast at Persepolis*: 'he imprisons his father Sun. Now all that the world can see of the natural order and authority which Krogon has invented to perpetuate his own power' (p. 93). It is this act of inner separation which prepares to substantialize man's importance through the 'natural', not the exclusively 'human' perspective, through the body's collective materiality rather than its abstract Ego-hood:

> . . . If head of lakewater and weather
> If body of horizon
> If whole body and balancing head
>
> If skin of grass could take messages
> And do its job properly
>
> If spine of earth-foetus
> Could unfurl
>
> If man-shadow out there moved to my moves
>
> The speech that works air
> Might speak me.

The prayerful conditional of this, the final poem in 'Seven dungeon songs' is the real point of departure for 'Adam and the sacred nine' and its re-assembly of the 'innocent' body, the 'first Man'; the sequence properly includes five additional poems which appeared as part of the sequence in the Rainbow Press edition (200 signed copies, 1979). These poems embody collectively a re-definition of the Genesis Creation myth in the terms of Hughes' own 'religious' development; to start with, the conception of the Fall is removed from its abstract *historical* context promoted by theology, and shifted towards an understanding in which man must – to use Don Juan's phrase – *assume responsibility* for its re-enactment in the present tense. This shift of emphasis has, of course, been evident in the readership of Hughes' poetry – in which the reader constantly stood in danger of 'missing the mark' – from the very beginning. In the second poem, Adam 'falls' when his abstract–specialized 'dream' moves too far ahead of his own materially undeve-loped status, and when the passion for 'objective' achievement forgets his 'subjective' exposure and origin: 'Too little lifted from mud/ He dreamed the tower of light.' In psychological terms, the Fall is an ever-present possibility attendant upon the creation of an abstract Personality split off from the real condition of the animal. All the following birds encourage Adam, the first man, to awake from this delusion or 'sleep', culminating in the familiar figure of Crow and the riddle of Matter he embodies:

> 10   The Crow came to Adam
>
>   And lifted his eyelid

And whispered in his ear

Who had understood the Crow's love-whisper?
Or the Crow's news?

Adam woke.

The five extra poems in the Rainbow Press edition prefaced 'The sole of a foot', the final poem in the published edition of *Moortown*, re-modelling our sense of the term 'innocence', the condition to which Adam wakes, in accord with the revelation of *Crow* and *Cave Birds* and *Gaudete*:

Light

Eased eyes open, showed leaves.

Eyes laughing and childish
Ran among the flowers of leaves
And looked at light's bridge
Which led from leaf, upward, and back down to leaf.

Eyes, uncertain
Tested each semblance,
Light seemed to smile.

Eyes ran to the limit
To the last leaf
To the least vein of the least flower-leaf.

Light smiled
And smiled and smiled.

Eyes
Darkened

Afraid suddenly
That this was all there was to it.

The whole poem, apart from the last four lines, is written from the point of view of the 'higher' Individuality, from what in *Remains of Elmet* I called the 'natural perspective'. Up until those lines, Light – the true subject, grammatically and symbolically – frames in lines 1–2 and 13–14 the responsive activity of 'eyes' so that the organs of perception appear just that, purely functional transmitters of 'the world speaking'; the eyes are a mechanism by which *the world observes itself*, they correct the earlier sin of *re-making* the world in their own image of it, the unconscious and hence futile labour of the 'objective imagination'. Aivanhov compares the light cast by the Individuality or divine nature to that of the sun:

> The fundamental virtue of the higher Nature is to give. That is what virtue is: a radiance, a projection of the self from the centre to the periphery, a need for sacrifice, for the giving of the self, like the sun which gives and gives. The personality is like the earth in that it does nothing but take . . . egoism does not project light! (*Man's Two Natures: Human and divine*, pp. 62–3)

The poem articulates perfectly the displacement of what Aivanhov terms the 'law of acquisition' by the 'law of radiation'; moreover, the projection of the self from its permanent centre rather than its periphery runs a close parallel to the projection of language from its moral centre, not its aesthetic periphery in the lines 'Light smiled/ And smiled and smiled.' The critical suspicion that language is failing to fulfil its obligations to itself in the spareness of the repetition is accurately anticipated in the last four lines, and its 'motivation' exposed: 'Eyes/ Darkened// Afraid suddenly/ That this was all there was to it.' The eyes darken, and the fear comes, when man starts peopling the world with his own superfluous constructions, linguistic or otherwise, the 'interesting' *obligations* the Personality is always ready to heap upon his intelligence:

> Nothing has contributed more towards weakening faith and encouraging unbelief than the mistaken conception of an obligation on the part of the intelligence. All obligations other than that of the attention which itself is imposed on the intelligence in the exercise of its function stifle the soul – the whole soul, and not the intelligence only. (Weil, 'Letter to a priest', in *Gateway to God*, p. 133)

The poem dramatizes the state of innocence whilst defining the 'inner' origin of dualistic error (the eyes *darken*) and offering up both to the reader's responsive choice, itself determined by the aesthetic expectations he imposes on the first fourteen lines. Hughes' mythic anecdote is reminiscent of those *mandalas* of the Creation-myth (the most famous is probably the thirteenth-century mosaic in the atrium of St Mark's, Venice) whose circular form has the effect of rendering alll possible moral 'directions' (innocence, fallen vision) *simultaneously available* to the onlooker.

The poem that follows, 'Skin', takes up where 'Light' leaves off:

Skin

Made out the company of grass.

Grass pricked it
In its language
Smelling fellow earth, but nervous.

Skin tightened
Suppressing its reflex
Shudder of dawn

Thinking, it is beginning – first fingerings
At my knots
Then will come renderings, and drenchings of world-light

And my naked joy
Will be lifted out, with shouts of joy –

And if that is the end of me
Let it be the end of me.

The dualistic reflex, shuddering with fear at the contiguity of the 'human' and the 'natural', is suppressed by the open-ended 'conscious addition' of 'Thinking, it is beginning'; the *tonal* (see p. 67) simply keeps its fluidity and wholeness of attention, so that even death is foreseen and integrated as part of a moral requirement in the final couplet. As in 'Light', the truest poetic obligation is not to language or aestheticism but to a certain attitude of consciousness to 'whatever comes'. That attitude characterizes the ending of 'Bud-tipped twig' as well, in which 'Breast', like 'skin', has to find its way home to a central point or axis of spiritual orientation. The *conscious personification* of Breast has the effect – as it does for skin and eyes – of reducing human attributes to exactly the same functional–material level of grass or leaves or clouds; one might go so far as to assert that the conscious usage of the device in itself deliberately represses any possibility of *identification* with the mechanical elements belonging to both human and natural contexts. For example,

> The sea, preoccupied with moon and sun
> With earth's centre, with its own substance and the laws of waves
> Made the breast feel lost.

There is no mutual re-assurance between the 'human' and the 'natural' on the horizontal (i.e. animal) level of the opposition; on that level the 'law of acquisition' is fully empowered – the sea is preoccupied with its *own* substance and laws. The unification of contraries occurs only with the appeal to a 'third' point, the sun equivalent of Light in 'Skin' and the eponymous poem:

> Breast lifted its simple face
> To the sun.
> The first beggar.
>
> Unable to see
> Or to hear
> Or to cry.

'Wiped clean' of egoism, the component parts of the body look upward, 'and God descends', in dramatic proof of Simone Weil's insight.

Guided by the elemental force of such prayers, the final poem, 'The sole of a foot' provides proof, if any further proof were needed, that symbolic perception is not an arbitrary literary habit but a comprehensive religious act, a wholly distinct way of experiencing the world. Once Gurdjieff's paradigm of perception – which observes both subject and object at once – is in full command, Hughes' long-term objective of the renovation of Metaphor is achieved: the reader comes to a seamless unity of the poised 'outer'/physical act (treading on earth) and the 'inner' reciprocal balance of subject and object, individual and collective, Personality and Essence. As above, so below, we appreciate a permanent identity, an effortless 'innocent' reading of natural signs as it was in the beginning before a multiplicity of languages – all 'knowing' their own truths – cast a Krogon-like shadow across the sun at the Tower of Babel. Even the repressive language of social convention ('acquaintance . . . host') is renewed in collective terms, beyond the merely 'human' range, or the range of the personality which demands wine and colour, conversation and light. Affection is being returned to its proper object, which is neither the Personality which is only interested in acquisition and self-gratification, nor even simply 'other people', but rather the world itself, and the material whole of the psyche.[6] The deformed condition of Metaphor and of a 'closed' language is restored, and any possible flight into as melodramatic a caricature of the religious objective as *Asceticism* is is foreseen and proscribed:

> *I am no wing*
> *To tread emptiness.*
> I was made
>
> For you.
>   (my italics)

That language 'devoid of all interesting qualities' has become perfectly transparent to the act of celebration – 'agreeing to come with it' unreservedly – scarcely seems to require independent or 'specialized' comment. The nature of criticism has been changed, too, by the poetic act of self-transformation, so that it is no longer appropriate to discuss the poem's achievement in terms of a stylistic intelligence working through it or the interplay of its verbal mechanisms.

The function of that changed criticism may be summarized, in conclusion, by analysis of a poem which, although it stands outside the sequences, provides the most apposite point of culmination for Hughes' book, 'The stone'.

> *The stone*
>
> Has not yet been cut.
> It is too heavy already
> For consideration. Its edges
> Are so super-real, already
> And at this distance,
> They cut real cuts in the unreal
> Stuff of just thinking. So I leave it.
> Somewhere it is.
> Soon it will come.
> I shall not carry it.

The absolute lack of verbal poetry does not in any wise diminish the dramatic force of the poem. The first seven lines, for example, set up immediately friction between the stone's alleged *super-reality* and its resistance to rationalistic definition or explanation; even in line 1 the stone's literal non-existence is contradicted by its 'material' embodiment in the audial properties of those consonantal 't' sounds which *do* configure the stone's brutal edges in the reader's imagination, and the smallest, least visible lexical unit ('it') goes on to dominate the four short sentences between lines 7 and 10. The reader is invited to contemplate the split in his own understanding between the 'thinking-stuff' of the Personality, which receives no satisfactory empirical data about the nature of the stone, and the archaic instinctual response which absorbs the 'unfathomable' but definite musical shock of its phonetic presence. In the circumstances, his rationalistic frustration may be such that he, like the protagonist, 'leaves' it or refuses to carry it further in the imagination; at just this point, when the Personality's abstracted intelligence is ready to 'march away' in disgust,

> With horrible life
> It will transport its face, with sure strength,
> To sit over mine, wherever I look,
> Instead of hers.

The reader's implicit association with the 'I'-consciousness of lines 7 and 10 has severe consequences: it ensures his 'unpreparedness' for the super-reality of the headstone, the fact of death, and it permanently blocks out the view of *her* face, the Goddess 'un-deformed and perfect'. But if the musical–material impact of the stone's super-reality has cured the reader of precipitate identification with that consciousness, the poem begins to open out, flower-like, on to another reading-potential; in this case, the ambivalent 'Instead of hers' is conjugated with 'over mine' rather than 'its face', the existing 'I'-consciousness is necessarily sacrificed in the interests of preserving a clear vision of *her* face. And the next sentence keeps the two readings intact: 'It will even have across its brow/ Her name.' Again, the headstone may either be (1) the museum-type memorial of her death, or (2) the paradoxical doorway ('He who loses his life shall find it', etc.) to 'her' full realization in the drama of the self. The reader is being challenged to transform his readership, from a 'lower' to a 'higher' interpretation, and that challenge becomes acute in the following six lines:

> Somewhere it is coming to the end
> Of its million million years –
> Which have worn her out.
> It is coming to the beginning

Of her million million million years
Which will wear it out.

From the point of view of 'lower' consciousness the erosion of death occurs in linear time, in some remote future; from the point of view of the 'higher' self those unspecific 'millions' are irrelevant to the moral endeavour to 'wear out' the hologram of death and see through to her undeformed image beyond it, which always occurs in the present tense, without stopping or starting-points. The true location of 'Somewhere' is not 'out there' but within man's 'sense of himself', his level of consciousness. 'The beauty of the world is not an attribute of matter in itself. It is a relationship of the world to our sensibility, the sensibility which depends on the structure of our body and our soul' (Weil, 'Forms of the implicit love of God'). 'She will not move now/ Till everything is worn out', and the text is a designed opportunity for the reader to wear out a redundant point of view and re-animate 'her' image from a different perspective, in exact mimicry of the 'designed opportunity' offered by the world itself.

'The stone' is indeed characterized by that refusal of aesthetic emotion and the change-provoking 'lawful inexactitude' belonging generically to Gurdjieff's objective art, though it is perhaps only in *River* (1983), that the poet fulfils the early obligation of the artist of *Moortown Elegies* to function as the antennae of 'Coming nature' with irreproachable consistency. It is to that much-desired denouement that we must now turn our attention.

———————— • ————————

CHAPTER 10

RIVER

River, alongside *Remains of Elmet*, is Hughes' most closely unified collection of poems to date. There is a real sense of a completed re-emergence into the 'outer' world of Nature, of the recovery of 'the Other', on all possible levels. And like the earlier volume, it constitutes the most astringent test of the critic's ability to follow the continuity of Hughes' work through against the likely grain of this own culturally enforced psychological bias. Thomas West, for example, detects a simple reversal in Hughes' development, a shift away from 'inner drama' and the struggle against Personality towards a 'poetry of description', in which

> Nature becomes radiant before it becomes symbolic. The threat of the brain god Logos of old is simply overwhelmed by the evidence of the surface of things . . . a world without shadows and without depth – all light, all surface. *River* is a naturalist Psalter. (*Ted Hughes*, p. 116)

The romantic myth of 'Naturalism' could scarcely be said to stimulate a more dynamic state of negotiations between ego-self and other, Personality and Essence – rather it strengthens the suppressive instinct, which thrives on that horizontal axis, it invites the story of the 'sensual life of the Body' as it is told in *Crow*, the savage excesses without the potential advances in consciousness. Here natural description obtains no connection with 'inner drama', precarious surface-light splits off from shadow-depth, symbol becomes a kind of special technical addition to the 'Naturalist' view of radiant Nature. But West's Naturalist fallacy pays no attention to the necessity of a collective or supra-ordinate imagination and its object of self-integration, and it repeats the Movement's 'alienating' reduction of symbolic language; in the terms offered by Hughes' own creative myth, it is difficult to avoid the conclusion that the critic is re-enacting Agoluz's misunderstanding, suffering from its confinement to the 'lower' level of dualistic conflicts.

More concretely, it is difficult to see why West adjudges a priority of
'natural description' over dramatic 'inner' elements'; the poetic imagination seems, rather, equally preoccupied with the world of things and the
world of spirits. If the poem 'New Year' has a recognizable progenitor,
for instance, it is surely 'Waving goodbye' from the *Gaudete* Epilogue:
the poet, searching for a way to describe the relationship between the
river and the dead or dying salmon it contains, imagines 'a Caesarian'
and the details of a surgical operation;

> And walking in the morning in the blue glare of the ward
> I shall feel in my head the anaesthetic,
> The stiff gauze, the congealments. I shall see
> The gouged patient sunk in her trough of coma –
>
> The lank, dying fish. But not the ticking egg.

Nature becomes dramatic as it aligns itself with the patterns already
unearthed in the 'inner world', as the 'lank, dying fish' is conflated with
the self which has suffered the frightful operation, and the barely alive
female archetype of the psyche 'sunk in her trough of coma'. Such
description belongs neither to the senses nor to the flat surface of things –
the Naturalistic imagination is displaced critically by the moral imagination, which is as interested in depth and shadow as it is in surface and
light. Nature becomes radiant or meaningful *as* it becomes symbolic, i.e.
as in *Remains of Elmet*, the symbolic dimension is not the result of
unconscious Empathy but of the consciousness of the two-pronged
imagination. The 'third' position afforded by that imagination springs its
own improvement on the *Gaudete* version out of the collision of 'outer'
and 'inner' circumstances. The high-profile 'I', 'defunct' and immured in
its own Ego-inertia, which sees only 'the lank, dying fish', has to give
ground to an unstressed or 'silent' consciousness which manifestly *is*
aware of the possibility of an explosive death–re-birth in the last line.
Hughes exorcizes the earlier *Gaudete*-personality and the fiction of
Nature it threatens to create – the poem thus attuning itself to one of the
main lines of effort in *Remains of Elmet* – replacing it with a 'freed' view
of Nature–nature's double potential: two rival possibilities sitting side-
by-side, each in its own half-line.

The 'silent' imagination manages to make its presence felt with greater
clarity and assurance than it does in *Moortown*. In 'August evening', the
poet literally comes clear to 'make a silent third' at the end of the poem –
he is watching sea-trout as

> . . . Their procession kneels, in God-hush.
> Robed in the still flow of their Creator
> They inhale unending. I share it a little.
>
> Slowly their white pathway sinks from the world.

The river becomes terrible.

Climbing out, I make a silent third
With two owls reassuring each other.

If there are some signs of a stubborn–resistant Personality in the phrase 'I share it a *little*', it is perhaps more important to distinguish a healthy improvement upon the state of negotiations disclosed by 'Gnat-psalm' and the fertility rite in *Gaudete*. There is no impulsive surrender to ecstatic experience and its 'dazzle' without either structure or control; as soon as the persona detects the danger of an escapist release, shadowed by 'unending' and more explicit in the very next line, he detaches himself from the possibility in the final couplet. And this is not the dualistic detachment which merely re-emphasizes the ego's abstraction from its own experience of elementals – i.e. as 'the river becomes terrible' – but a climbing out of Nature *into* Nature; the 'silent' subject – cleansed of his own judgements – keeps the humility of his collective point of view intact, re-affirming a 'religious' attitude long after the dazzle of the specific religious occasion has vanished. And this is Nature's 'higher' point of orientation, rather than its 'lower' centre, Schopenhauer's *principium individuationis*..

River habitually attempts to examine Nature from its own point of view, in an elevation of the narrative practice of *Gaudete*, its Dionysian readiness to speak in the idiom of the nearest dramatic presence, human or natural, in all situations. It is this angle of vision, if anything, which saves the poet from direct re-enactment of the tragic past. Here is the ending of 'Strangers', which like 'August evening' attests the 'religious purpose' of trout:

The sea-trout, upstaring, in trance,
Absorb everything and forget it
Into a blank of bliss.

And this is the real samadhi – worldless, levitated.
Till, bulging, a man-shape
Wobbles their firmament.

   Now see the holy ones
Shrink their auras, slim, sink, focus, prepare
To scram like trout.

The bulging man-shape which interposes between worldless samadhi ('ecstatic equilibrium' according to Evans-Wentz) and its free physical expression recalls Krogon's shadow, which wilfully held apart the sun and Moa, obstructing their natural unity. We are also reminded of the 'man-shadow' which 'screamed, and would not help me get up' in 'Seven dungeon songs'. That shadow splits up the two elements of the Natural firmament, 'higher' and 'lower', and resists the translation of one into the other even in the literal arrangement of the poem. Likewise, it stands between the re-combination of latinate discourse ('levitated') and the Norse–Celtic inheritance ('scram') which Hughes foresees as a linguistic barometer of the attempt at psychological re-combination in poetry. As in the conclusion of 'Seven dungeon songs', only the act of non-identification with the obtrusive Personality begins to save the poet from a renewal of inner trauma, easing the reduction of the fishes' divinity to their most basic animal instinct – fear – by seeing the disturbing event momentarily through their eyes. The poet is function-ing as the antennae of 'Coming Nature', and the full significance of his action is made explicit in 'The kingfisher': first the bird erupts through the self-admiring mirror of the Personality in 'a shower of prisms', then he triggers the reversal of perspective that goes with that shattering:

> Through him, God, whizzing in the sun,
> Glimpses the angler.
>
> Through him, God
> Marries a pit
> Of fishy mire.

As soon as the 'lower' self is made an object of perception like any other object, God descends; once more 'available' as the cardinal point of orientation within the psyche, even the 'fishy mire', the grossest material proves capable of refinement.

'God glimpses the angler' at greater length in 'A cormorant', where the archaic fishing-machinery of 'Pike' is finally abandoned; Hughes, standing awkward in the river and overwhelmed by equipment, hopes that 'some fish, telepathically overpowered,// Will attach its incomprehension/ To the bauble I offer to space in general.' Meanwhile,

> The Cormorant eyes me, beak uptilted,
> Body – snake low – sea-serpentish.
>
> He's thinking, 'Will that stump
> Stay a stump just while I dive?' He dives.
>
> He sheds everything from his tail-end
> Except fish-action, becomes fish.
>
> Disappears from bird,
> Dissolving himself
>
> Into fish, so dissolving fish naturally
> Into himself. Re-emerges, gorged,
>
> Himself as he was, and escapes me.
> Leaves me high and dry in my space-armour,
>
> A deep-sea diver in two inches of water.

The provisional persona within the poem readily deserts the old self and its machinery and effects its own 'dissolution' into the cormorant-self,

the more efficient hunter. It happily sheds the stolid, earth-bound
Personality in its 'space-armour' for the duration of its 'flight', comically
reducing its self-importance in the second quoted couplet and the last
three lines. The poet's divine nature glimpses the early authoritarian
angler as merely a 'stump', or 'a deep-sea diver in two inches of water',
his scope for exploration fatally limited by the lack of a truly 'collective'
frame of reference, or contentment in that frame.

'That morning' offers a more complex presentation, complete with its
own false conclusion; Hughes and his companions stand waist-deep
amongst massed, wild salmon, and – as in 'August evening' – the fish
invoke the 'dazzle' of an ecstatic experience which proves dangerously
susceptible to interpretive delusion: the idea of 'imperishable fish// That
had let the world pass away' – 'as if the fallen/ world and salmon were
over' – is the poem's 'darkening thought', dramatically embodied; it
actually darkens of its own volition, committed to the preservation of the
Individual on its own terms, in a self-perpetuating eternity. A true
commitment to the Collective is contrastingly demonstrated only within
the last eight lines:

> Then for a sign that we were where we were
> Two gold bears came down and swam like men
>
> Beside us. And dived like children.
> And stood in deep water as on a throne
> Eating pierced salmon off their talons.
>
> So we found the end of our journey.
>
> So we stood, alive in the river of light
> Among the creatures of light, creatures of light.

Here the salmon are materially perishable like everything else, but the
'direction' into Matter – and the fact of death especially – has been
transformed completely; *the world speaks* through all its creatures,
resisting attachment to any individually appealing form – likewise the
poem resists its own identification with the individually appealing,
Ascetic/Reformed Protestant 'interpretative container': the material
range of evidence is infinitely broader than the limits of that response
allow. As soon as the poem hooks itself up to the material range in the
last eight lines, 'Matter' effects its own 'Spiritual' declaration – true, as it
were, from the bottom-most point upwards – and the result is a renewal,
not an abolition of Lyricism:

> *So we found* the end of our journey.
>
> *So we stood*, alive in the river of *light*
> Among the *creatures of light, creatures of light.*
>   (my italics)

After much trial-and-error exploration, the ritually intense elements of Hughes' poetic language reach this finale; a whole history of false lyricism, of lyric potential manipulated by the Personality towards its own ends, is recapitulated in the ritual threefold repetition of 'As if . . .' between lines 13 and 18. Those lines and the next four as well, indeed, represent the fractured unity of lyricism, its immoral or unconsciously motivated 'rootless fancy'. But then dramatic exemplification is super-seded by dramatic restoration in lines 23–30, as ritual-musical intensity finds its way home *in the course of* the poem. Lyricism becomes viable as it pays attention to Matter and thus starts to 'sing' from its proper collective base. We might call it Conscious Lyricism, to distinguish from the Unconscious type exhibited in a poem like 'To paint a water-lily'. As in the moral process of the self, Lyricism 'dies' – voluntarily abandons its first picture of things – in order to re-establish itself on more solid ground.

The most clear-cut, and certainly the longest achievement of the collective imagination in *River* is the four-page poem 'Gulkana', which narrates another of Hughes' fishing expeditions in Canada. The task of the poem is first interpreted as the unravelling of the strange word itself, its hieroglyphic solidity:

> What did it mean?
> A pre-Columbian glyph.
> A pale, blue line, scrawled with a childish hand
> Through our crumpled map.

Already in the phrase 'scrawled with a childish hand' there is a warning about the primitive or undeveloped state of the glyph, the ancient semantic of Material nature. If the individual's map is crumpled, however, the social dimension exhibits something akin to total sterility; the Indian settlement is described as 'comatose', victim of 'a cultural vasectomy'. In the fusion of 'outer' and 'inner' levels, the natural landscape goes on willingly to draw Hughes' characteristic psychological scenario, where

> (The whole land was in perpetual seismic tremor).
> And the Gulkana
> Biblical, a deranging cry
> From the wilderness, burst past us – . . .
>
>   nearly a fear,
> Something I kept trying to deny
> With deliberate steps.

A seismic tremor in the terrain of the psyche is also induced, in which the 'I'-fiction finds itself clinging, as in 'Pike' and 'Wind', to an unstable world-description, menaced by the 'deranging cry from the wilderness'.

In the present poem – in sharp contrast to the others – fear becomes the occasion for the protagonist's conscious transformation of his explanatory structuring of Nature–nature. His *tonal*, to pick up Don Juan's phrase, becomes fluid, flexible to the fullest impact of the experience:

> I explained it
> To my quietly arguing, lucid panic
> As my fear of one inside me,
> A bodiless twin, some disinherited being
> And doppelganger other, unliving,
> Everliving, a larva from prehistory
> Whose journey this was,
> Whose gaze I could feel, who now exulted
> Recognizing his home, and who watched me
> Fiddling with my fear – the interloper.
> The fool he had always hated.

The explanation helps to engineer an almost imperceptible shift in narrative control, whereby the disinherited being/doppelganger other is both acknowledged and momentarily permitted to 'accuse' the previous commanding self as an 'interloper – The fool he [has] always hated': the I's last-gasp resurgence (line 8) is first swallowed by the prehistoric self's increasingly powerful effort to break out of the encasing relative clause, then it is grammatically obliterated in lines 9–11 as the new subject is invisibly prescribed. From the vantage-point of the 'third' imagination, the Personality is weakened sufficiently to afford a glimpse of Essence in its retarded condition, the 'larva from prehistory' which corresponds to the Gulkana's own 'deranged' wildness.

After this revelation, it is hardly a surprise to find the returning 'I', coming back to the 'outer' world of salmon fishing, 'underpowered', unable to capture anything: 'Even when we got one ashore/ It was too big to eat.' The egoistic prestige of the capture, which Hughes elevates even as late as 1967 (see *Poetry in the Making*, p. 21), is firmly denied, as is the principle of *acquisition* belonging to the lower nature. If Hughes' first 'explanation' kept space open, by a deliberate effort, for the prehistoric self to 'exult' in its return to origin, his activity in the 'outer' world demonstrates a similar sensitivity to collective life, the life of the material whole:

> We relaunched the mulberry-dark torsos,
> the gulping, sooted mouths, the glassy faces,
>
> Arks of undelivered promise,
> Egg-sacs of their own Eden —
>
> Heavily-veiled, seraphs of heavy ore
> They surged away, magnetized
> Into the furnace boom of the Gulkana.

The salmon are intentionally freed to re-enact a fundamental event –
magnetically imprinted – in the 'journey' of the natural world and the
psyche alike. The possibility of 'human' interference in the 'Natural'
process is curbed by the insertion of a salvo of questions as preface to this
passage – 'What had I come for?', the danger of seeking merely a
'camera-flash' or an 'objective' capture is consciously exorcised by the
presence of the collective imagination, which for a second time succeeds
in shifting the narrative viewpoint beyond the range of the Personality:

> They were possessed
> By that voice in the river,
> By the drums and flutes of its volume. We watched them
> Move like drugged victims as they melted
> Toward their sacrament – a consummation
> Where only one thing was certain:
> The actual, sundering death. The rebirth
> Unknown, uncertain. Only that death
> In the mercy of water, at the star of the source –
>
> Devoured by revelation,
> Every molecule seized, and tasted, and drained
> Into the amethyst of emptiness –
> I came back to myself.

All the signs of a religious understanding of Matter present themselves:
the possession by voices or specimens of the 'life outside one's own', the
necessity of death and reduction to nothing, the potential for re-birth at a
higher level. But the language used to point at the *goal* of religious
'consummation' also contains its own deformities, proves somewhat
shrunken or dwarf-like in terms of both poetic scope and accuracy – the
ambiguous 'drugged' recalls the dreadfully uncontrolled invocations of
Essence in *Gaudete*, and the possibility of re-birth is clouded by its
vagueness, 'unknown, uncertain'. Only in the last three lines does the
'disinherited being' within the protagonist sway to its full stature, find its
true weight and proportion, 'exulting' memorably *through* language:
'Every molecule seized, and tested, and drained/ Into the amethyst of
emptiness.' It is at this point that the protagonist 'comes back to himself'
in the fullest sense – returned to his Essence, not to the Personality, 'a
spectre of fragments' which 'Lifted my quivering coffee, in the aircraft,/
And sipped at it' – always present, but no longer an object of
identification. The function of the Personality – and of the language-
machine – is that of a super-sensitive recording device, ready to register
the slightest disturbance or alteration within the psyche:

> Word by word
> The burden of the river, beyond waking,
> Numbed back into my marrow. While I recorded
> The King Salmon's eye. And the blood-mote mosquito.

And the stilt-legged, one-rose rose
With its mock aperture, tilting toward me
In our tent-doorway, its needle-tremor.

And the old Indian, in his tatty jeans and socks, who smiled.

Adjusting to our incomprehension – his face
A whole bat that glistened and stirred.

The triumphant *capture* of the King Salmon, the expected aesthetic climax never materialized. Instead, the 'third' imagination conducts an exploration of the prehistoric self 'whose journey this was', playfully examining it from both its own point of view and that of Personality in a rapid alternation. This imagination not only recognizes Essential deformities when it sees them, it embodies the potential for development/correction of those flaws by its own dramatic presence within the poem. It cannot avoid confronting Essence, the human material whole, at every point – under its influence, even the final emblem the poem offers is a figure for the primitive Essence, a haunting remnant awaiting refinement: the old Indian headman, 'his face/ A whole bat that glistened and stirred.'

The 'third' imagination also achieves some triumphant improvements on Hughes' literary past. 'Visitation', for instance, shows a clear improvement on the state of negotiations at the beginning of the *Gaudete* Epilogue. There, the response to the miracle performed by Lumb – the summoning of the otter from the lough – was split between the children's 'innocent' reception and the priest's precipitate *naming*, and reduction of the emerging animal. It is the task of 'Visitation', on the contrary, to reverse that diminishing of the Natural which characterized the priest's attitude, and to amplify the *collectivity* of the children's response; they were quite unable to distinguish the *individual* identity of the creature, separate from everything else, as it broke the water's surface:

All night the river's twists
Bit each other's tails in happy play.

Suddenly a dark other
Twisted in among them.

And a cry, half sky, half bird,
Slithered over roots.

At this stage of the poem, the text's innocent openness is such that the 'dark other' could even be a cormorant rather than an otter; and of course the open-endedness naturally points in another direction, keeping space open for the 'inner' or psychic interpretation of the light/shadow's happy interplay. The natural environment either stays silent, refusing conscious addition, or asks the respondent/student to preserve its 'harmony of innocence' of his own accord, without the destructive naming of *Gaudete*:

Dawn
Puzzles a sunk branch under deep tremblings.

Nettles will not tell.
  Who shall say
That the river
Crawled out of the river, and whistled,
And was answered by another river?

'The morning before Christmas' contains Hughes' most recent improvement represented in *River*: here the poet is playing the role of practical, fully active assistant which first came to prominence in the *Moortown Elegies*, and his presence proves an unqualified success, surpassing his efforts in poems like 'Ravens' and 'February 17th'. The poet rescues a dead or dying cock-salmon and a live hen-fish, and mixes their sperm with her eggs in plastic kitchenware. His artful re-combination of male and female on the realist–Natural level is again the principal focus, rather than an aesthetic re-combination subsisting *solely* in language. At the end of the poem, the results of the poet's endeavour are stamped into future natural possibilities just as the exterior events have been 'dazzle-stamped' into his own body; he occupies the same 'third' position in giving a helping hand to the union of the sexes in the outer world as he did when assisting the 'alchemization' of male and female within the self, in his earlier work.

All events in the inner realm may be coaxed into revealing a Natural context, and in 'Go fishing' the physical act eases into moral process; the poet wades in water and 'underbeing', obedient to a succession of imperatives:

Lose words
Cease . . .

. . . Become translucent – one untangling drift
Of water-mesh, and a weight of earth-taste light . . .
Let the world come back, like a white hospital
Busy with urgency words

Try to speak and nearly succeed
Heal into time and other people.

The personal pronoun is absolutely eliminated from the poem as the protagonist becomes 'translucent' to the processes of both the entire surrounding river-scape and those of the explored inner world: those last six lines, taken in isolation, could easily be seen as a confident development *out of* 'Waving goodbye' (*Gaudete*) and 'Seven dungeon songs' (*Moortown*), their obverse 're-assembled' face. It is this healing into the other on all levels which also characterizes the explicitly religious final poem in the book, 'Salmon eggs'. Once again 'the piled flow supplants me' as the protagonist effaces the ordinary self, and an unironic Christianized vocabulary becomes viable for the first time:

> Sanctus Sanctus
> Swathes the blessed issue.
>
> Perpetual mass
> Of the waters
> Wells from the cleft . . .
>
> It is the font, brimming with touch and whisper
> Swaddling the egg.
>
> *only birth matters*
> Say the river's whorls.

For a moment the individualized poetic exploration appropriates its ideal religious context and terminology, where *birth* appears to be nothing less than the principle of transformation existing above the dualism of 'raptures and rendings', within the self and in external Nature:

> Freedom, liberation, this must be the aim of man. To become free, to be liberated from slavery; this is what a man ought to strive for when he has become even a little conscious of his position . . . in order to become free, man must gain inner freedom.
>
> The first reason for man's slavery is his ignorance, and above all, his ignorance of himself. Without self-knowledge, without understanding the working and functions of his machine, Man cannot be free, he cannot govern himself and he will always remain a slave, and the plaything of the forces acting upon him.
>
> This is why in all ancient teachings the first demand at the beginning of the way to liberation was '*Know thyself.*' (Ouspensky, *In Search of the Miraculous*, p. 104)

Only the collective imagination can reach up towards this ideal of the term 'birth', the imagination which has eased itself into the re-discovered unity of the two vocabularies, Frenchified/Romanesque and Anglo-Saxon/Celtic:

> And the river
> Silences everything in a leaf-mouldering hush
> Where sun rolls bare, and earth rolls,
>
> *And mind condenses on old haws.*
>
> (my italics)

In the silence, the obtrusive mind voluntarily crystallizes – via the latinate verb – in its material or collective origin, the hawthorn branch, and the Old English root-word for hawthorn hedge, *haga*. In this imaginative environment, there is no question of ideational or dualistic development of Hughes' aphorism 'only birth matters', or of any self-glorification of the 'human'. Man grows *out of* the world, *out of* his collective psychic origin, he was not dropped into it self-sufficiently, with the freedom to do as he – or rather his lower self – pleases. He had better be centred in that origin, and in the higher region of negotiation, if he wants to survive the crash of a collapsing culture:

> Popa, and several other writers one can think of, have in a way cut their losses and cut the whole hopelessness of that civilization off, have somehow managed to invest their hopes in something deeper than what you lose if civilization disappears completely and in a way it's obviously a pervasive and deep feeling that civilization has now disappeared completely. If it's still here it's still here by grace of pure inertia and chance and if the whole thing has essentially vanished one had better vanish. And this is a shifting of your foundation to completely new Holy Ground, a new divinity, one that won't be under the rubble when the churches collapse. ('Ted Hughes and Crow', *London Magazine*, p. 19)

Only when the distinctively 'human' or 'conscious' contribution disappears does a view of man's real allegiances become available. Such a view is that of the collective imagination, free of all its mechanical prejudices:

> The infinite terrible circumstances that seem to destroy man's importance, appear as the very terms of his importance. *Man is the face, arms, legs, etc., grown over the infinite, terrible All.* Popa's poems work in the sanity and fundamental simplicity of this fact, *as it might appear to a man sitting in a chair.* (Introduction to Popa's *Collected Poems*, p. 8; my italics)

The sanity of this fact alone re-establishes the value of the 'felicitous moment' of literary creation in its true proportion; every poem, every conscious/aesthetic 'attempt' on that awful reality is little more than a shiver, a mechanical reaction in language to the downdraught of silent, collective Nature. Only the poet's (and critic's) voluntary obedience to this realization paradoxically allows the imagination to follow its moral trajectory 'upwards', clarifying the nature and usage of poetic language (criticism) beyond the walls of its aesthetic prison.

One senses that the momentary – though strengthening – availability of such a perspective is enough to give the lie to Roland Barthes' assertion that 'life never does more than imitate the book, and the book itself is only a tissue of signs, an imitation that is lost, infinitely deferred' ('The death of the author', from *Image–Music–Text*, p. 147), right at the heart of the contemporary literary appreciation:

> it is occasionally possible, just for brief moments, to find the words that will unlock the doors of all those many mansions inside the head and express something – perhaps not much, just something – of the crush of information that presses in on us. . . . Words that will express something of the deep complexity that makes us precisely the way we are, from the momentary effect of the barometer to the force that created men distinct

from trees. Something of the inaudible music that moves us along in our bodies from moment to moment like water in a river. Something of the spirit of the snowflake in the water of the river. . . . And when words can manage something of this, and manage it in a moment of time, and in that same moment make out of it all the vital signature of a human being – not of an atom, or of a geometrical diagram, or of a heap of lenses – but a human being, we call it poetry. (*Poetry in the Making*, p. 124)

And when the overarching 'third' imagination unlocks these moments of consciousness, beyond the book's obsession with itself as a 'tissue of signs', with its own immense dictionary, and simultaneously beyond the Personality's *penchant* for ventriloquism – when this happens, it is an act of love. The true nature of the act may be finally clarified within the following poem by the Czech poet Vladimir Holan:

No, don't go yet

No, don't go yet, don't be afraid of all the excitement,
it's the bear opening beehives in the orchard.
He'll soon be quiet. I too will hold back
words that rush like the serpent's sperm
to the woman in Eden.

No, don't go yet, don't lower your veil.
The fuel of crocuses has lit up the meadows.
That's what you are then, life, although you say:
– By desire, we add something. But love
remains love.

(*Selected Poems*, p. 20)

By the all-eclipsing *desire* for consciousness of the 'lower' self in Hughes' early work, its harrowing fervour, something was added. But love remains love. And the act of consciousness remains itself, where the poet becomes – as if for the first time –not merely a word-arranger but a complete human being, with his own vital signature.

NOTES

CHAPTER 1 INTRODUCTION

1. Hughes has commented, in a letter to Ekbert Faas (Faas, *Ted Hughes* p. 37), that he has read all of Jung's translated volumes. He calls Jung 'The philosopher of the next hundred years'. In a letter of 8 November 1982 he also first drew my attention to the close relationship between Gurdjieff's system and Sufism, and indeed Castaneda also. Idries Shah in his book *The Way of the Sufi* confirms this connection:

   > G. I. Gurdjieff left abundant clues to the Sufic origins of virtually every point in his 'system'; though it obviously belongs more specifically to the Khagjagan (Naqshbandi) form of dervish teaching. . . . Both the Naqshbandi Sufis and the Gurdjieff–Ouspenskians call their studies 'The Fourth Way'. (p. 43)

2. The diagram shows Ouspensky's visual schema of human development within the understanding of three forces (*The Fourth Way*, p. 181). The top triangle shows the Body/Essence deprived of its possibility of refinement by the domineering influence of the False Personality, preventing any simultaneous view of all the multiple I's, many of which are consequently repressed into the unconscious. The second trinity demonstrates the beginning of moral growth, when a 'provisional' magnetic centre – overseeing the whole of the plural self – starts to grow at the expense of the imaginary picture of oneself. In the latter stages of development, one approaches the final trinity in which a permanent 'I' controls all the other 'I's, and allows the full transformation of all aspects of Essence (the intellectual, emotional, intuitive aspects, etc.) into their higher values.

3. A spatialized schema of the situation might look like the diagram on p. 254. From the point of view of the Light, the opposites on the horizontal axis – Spirit and Matter – are morally neutral, having this point of unification 'above', in which their exchange of energies flows freely. From the vantage-point of the subject contaminated by Krogon's illusion, wherever he looks, he sees the irreconcilable pair of opposites always at war with each other – because he is unconscious of his centring in the region 'below', which is the first cause of deluded perception. This is simultaneously true of the situation in the self and that in the idea of the Creator.

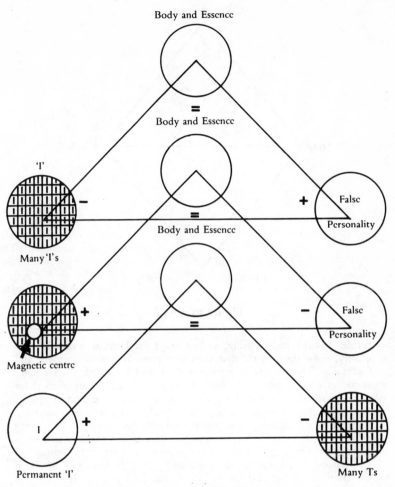

Figure to note 2: *The Fourth Way*, p. 181.

4. In Beckett's view, that authentic self has been obscured by what he calls 'the mess', a chaos which must be 'let in' if any progress is to be made:

> The confusion is not my invention. We cannot listen to a conversation for five minutes without being acutely aware of the confusion. It is all around us and our only chance now is to let it in. The only chance of renovation is to open our eyes and see the mess. It is not a mess you can make sense of. . . . One can only speak of what is in front of him, and that now is simply the mess. (Tom Driver, 'Beckett by the Madeleine')

5. Sagar quotes an unpublished essay by A. S. Crehan:

> It is a return to an alliterative poetry that, pounding, brutal and earthbound, challenges the Latinate politeness of artificial society with

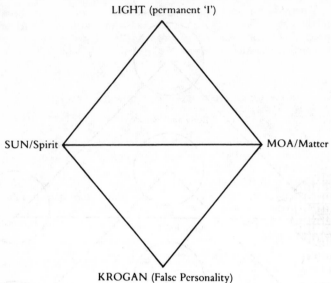

Figure to note 3

ruthless energy and cunning, and so drags the Latinate words into its unruly, self-ruling world that even *they* come to sound northern and Germanic. The pummelling trochees and lead-weighted, bludgeoning spondees have a mesmeric effect, beating and rooting out of us those once apparently safe underlying rhythms of rhetorical and philosophical discourse, mental scene-painting and nostalgic or evocative reflection, with which the iambic pentameter is so closely associated. . . . Yet such a bold counter-revolution necessarily involves, for Hughes at least, a ferocious reaction against nine hundred years of Christianity, humanism and rationalism, a reaction that, because it must be ferocious, acts as if the trunk, branches and leaves of nine hundred years of humane and literary culture had borne little but rotten fruit. (' "Natural" rhythms and poetic metre', from *The Art of Ted Hughes*, p. 229)

6. This symbiotic relationship between writer and reader, in which the self-education of the educator guarantees the integrity of his effects on the subject, was already unearthed by Jung in his paradoxical view of the doctor–patient relationship in analytical psychology:

> we have learned to place in the foreground the personality of the doctor himself as a curative or harmful factor . . . we have begun to demand his own transformation – the self-education of the educator. Everything that happened in the patient must now happen to the doctor, and he must pass through the stages of confession, explanation and education so that his personality will not react unfavourably on the patient. The physician may no longer slip out of his own difficulties by treating the difficulties of others . . . .

What was formerly a method of medical treatment now becomes a method of self-education, and therewith the horizon of our modern psychology is immeasurably widened. ('Problems of modern psychotherapy', from *Modern Man in Search of a Soul*, p. 60)

CHAPTER 2 THE POST-WAR POETIC ENVIRONMENTS: THE MOVEMENT AND CENTRAL/EAST EUROPEAN POETRY

1. The resemblance to Eliot comes through Prufrock, who spends his life not on imprecisions, but rather 'a hundred indecisions,/ . . . a hundred visions and revisions'.
2. Hughes has read Rozewicz's work widely: although he was originally more conscious of Zbigniew Herbert, Vasko Popa and Miroslav Holub, he recognizes that 'it was the wavelength – that flight in that particular dimension' (Personal communication, 22 November 1983).
3. *Head in a void*

> If you think you are
> a beautiful head
> set up
> on high
>
> if you think you are
> the quick head
> of a motionless trunk
> which sinks in earth
> blood and cow-dung
>
> if you think you circle
> upon pure orbits of the intellect
> where from below you can hear only
> the grunting bustling
> and lip-smacking mob
>
> if you think this
> you are a head
> which sways gently
> in depopulated air
>
> you are a head
> which will be taken down
> and cast aside
> (*Conversation with the Prince*, p. 46)

4. It is this development which concerns Vasko Popa's poem 'A conceited mistake':

> Once upon a time there was a mistake
> So silly so small
> That no one would even have noticed it
>
> It couldn't bear
> To see itself to hear of itself

It invented all manner of things
Just to prove
That it didn't really exist

It invented space
To put its proofs in
And time to keep its proofs
And the world to keep its proofs

All it invented
Was not so silly
Nor so small
But was of course mistaken

Could it have been otherwise

5. 'Study of the object' (Parts 5 & 6)

5. obey the counsels
    of the inner eye

    do not yield
    to murmurs mutterings smackings

    it is the uncreated world
    crowding before the gates of your canvas

    angels are offering
    the rosy wadding of clouds

    trees are inserting everywhere
    slovenly green hair

    kings are praising purple
    and commanding their trumpeteers
    to gild

    even the whale asks for a portrait

    obey the counsels of the inner eye
    admit no-one

6. extract

    from the shadow of the object
    which does not exist
    from polar space
    from the stern reveries of the inner eye
    a chain
    beautiful and useless
    like a cathedral in the wilderness

    place on the chair
    a crumpled tablecloth
    add to the idea of order
    the idea of adventure

    let it be a confession of faith
    before the vertical struggling with the horizontal

let it be
quieter than angels
prouder than kings
more substantial than a whale
let it have the face of the last things
we ask reveal o chair
the depths of the inner eye
the iris of necessity
the pupil of death

CHAPTER 3 *THE HAWK IN THE RAIN*

1. The first stanza exhibits what we might call the masculine dimension of
   language: words are self-conscious shapers, organizers, and the raw materials
   of the poem are set under the commanding authority of grammatical and
   syntactical structures – in contrast to the feminine pole, which gives priority
   to musical texture and evocation.
2. We could judge Hughes by his own standards: 'So the comparative religion/
   mythology background was irrelevant to me, except as I could forget it. If I
   couldn't . . . I find it again original in *Crow*, I wasn't interested to make a
   trophy of it' (Letter to Keith Sagar, *The Art of Ted Hughes*, p. 107). If we
   substitute 'literary' for 'religion/mythology', the criterion of judgement is
   disclosed as the *original* rediscovery of literary images etc., in the exploration
   of the self, rather than formal, trophy-making repetition in the abstract.
3.   The descent into the depths always seems to precede the ascent. Thus [a]
   theologian dreamed that 'he saw on a mountain a kind of Castle of the
   Grail. He went along a road that seemed to lead straight to the foot of
   the mountain and up it. But as he drew nearer he discovered to his great
   disappointment that a chasm separated him from the mountain, a deep
   darksome gorge with underworldly water along the bottom. A steep
   path led downwards and toilsomely climbed up again on the other side.
   But the prospect looked uninviting', and the dreamer awoke. Here
   again the dreamer, thirsting for the shining heights, had first to descend
   into the dark depths, and this proves to be the indispensable condition
   for climbing any higher. . . .

      The statement made by the dream meets with violent resistance from
   the conscious mind, which knows 'spirit' only as something to be found
   in the heights. 'Spirit' always seems to come from above, while from
   below comes everything that is sordid and worthless. For people who
   think in this way, Spirit means highest freedom, a *soaring over the depths*,
   deliverance from the poison of the Chthonic world, and hence a refuge
   for all those timorous souls who do not want to become anything
   different. . . .

      The unconscious is the psyche that reaches down from the daylight of
   mentally and morally lucid consciousness into the nervous system that
   for ages has been known as 'sympathetic' . . . [which] not only gives us
   knowledge of the innermost life of other beings but also has an inner
   effect upon them. In this sense it is an extremely collective system, the
   operative basis of all *participation mystique*, whereas the cerebrospinal

function reaches its high point in separating off the specific qualities of the ego, and only apprehends surfaces and externals – always through the medium of space. It experiences everything as an outside, whereas the sympathetic system experiences everything as an inside. (*The Archetypes of the Collective Unconscious*, pp. 19–20)

4. The pressure on the reader's response often splits into two possible readings, realized even in the smallest units of the poem, its verbal ambiguities:

1. 'That maybe *in his own time* meets the weather . . .' can mean (a) that 'by relaxing his (i.e. the hawk's) will, he has let the earth fall upon his head', as Keith Sagar points out in *The Art of Ted Hughes*, (p. 16), putting the accent on hawkish control, so that it appears able to choose the moment of its death. But (b) it can mean that the hawk must inevitably submit, like everything else, to the laws of natural process and the loss of individual identity. Which of these responses is more dangerous as a human psychological reflex hardly needs pointing out.

2. 'Hallucination' (line 7) may signify either 'visionary' in a quasi-Romantic sense (a), or simply an 'illusory image' (b).

In both cases, the reader's choice of responses could be said to measure his own level of 'predilection' (Castaneda). A good example of the abstract reading is to be found in Gifford and Robert's commentary in *Ted Hughes: A critical study* (pp. 35–6), which notes the aesthetic superiority of lines 4–5 to lines 13–14, omitting any discussion of the dramatic context of the idea of style in the poem.

5. The Greek word for 'wind', *pneuma*, also means 'spirit'. This is quite an important point, because Early Christianity – including the Gnostic Sethian sect – upheld a threefold conception of human nature: man consisted of body (*soma*), soul (*psyche*), and spirit (*pneuma*), in which spirit was of a divine nature, transcending – and mediating – the potential conflict of 'soul' and 'body'. The development of Christian theology tended to equate 'spirit' with 'soul', however, leaving no alternative to a dualistic understanding.

CHAPTER 4 *LUPERCAL*

1. Jung makes some revealing comments about aestheticism (that is Jung's phrase for the 'aesthetic view of the world') in relation to the German philosopher Schiller:

Aestheticism is not fitted to solve the exceedingly difficult and serious task of educating man, for it always presupposes the very thing it should create – the capacity to love beauty. It actually hinders a deeper investigation of the problem, because it always averts its face from anything evil, ugly, and difficult, and aims at pleasure, even though it be of an edifying kind. Aestheticism therefore lacks all moral force, because *au fond* it is only refined hedonism. (Schiller's ideas on the Type-problem, *Psychological Types*, p. 121)

2. In the seventh and eighth stanzas, the poem even stages its own empty digression, in a sequence of anecdotes and 'interesting' information about pigs which acquire meaning only as an intentionally superfluous context that

wilfully cuts itself off from the basic realization of the poem as a whole: 'Distinctions and admirations such/ As this one was long finished with.'

CHAPTER 5 *WODWO*

1. Within this framework, the group of poems clustered around the voice of 'Wings' approximates model (A), and the group including 'You drive in a circle' and 'Mountains' (C). The more complex 'Gnat-psalm' enacts the desperate attempt of the conscious version (A) to accommodate the unconscious version (B), and again ends up as (C). 'Gog' (I) gives (B) suppressed by the 'controlling' third part (A)/(C).

CHAPTER 6 *CROW*

1. That the psychological conditions which engineered the existence of the earlier poem could not be sustained (and it was a 'one-off' achievement in the overall context of *The Hawk in the Rain*, its multiple organization), and that the complete dispersal of the old self and its poetic machinery was imperative in order to re-discover those conditions on a more permanent basis, neither recognition appears to concern Bradshaw.

2. Graham Bradshaw, meanwhile, seems to demand that Hughes follow Eliot's demand for a 'mythological method' which gives a shape and significance to 'an immense panorama of futility and anarchy' ('Ted Hughes' Crow as Trickster–Hero', p. 104–5). Again, it is not part of *Crow*'s ironic programme to give voice to 'primordial images', or access to the original 'meanings' which rendered legends 'powerful and moving' (p. 105), and criticism's craving for immediate, unequivocal answers is a conscious impulse whose origin ought to be acknowledged, and itself submitted to rigorous scrutiny. It almost seems to constitute a Cartesian resentment that the 'whole' body's understanding of its own experience cannot keep pace with the quicksilver assimilations – and, of course, misinterpretations – of it made by the Mind.

CHAPTER 7 *GAUDETE*

1. Once again, any attempt to use the *Parzival–Gaudete* analogy as an ironic escape from the chaotic, authorless experience of the book's events should be resisted: the *availability* of the moral triumph of *Parzival* is corrupted, in that case, into a false literary remedy to the reading difficulties which necessarily beset *Gaudete*, and which prescribe its capability as an ethical instrument of change.

2. This semantic shift is utilized by Gurdjieff:

Gurdjieff used the expressions 'objective' and 'subjective' in a special sense, taking as the basis the divisions of 'subjective' and 'objective' states of consciousness. All our ordinary knowledge which is based on ordinary methods of observation and verification of observations, all scientific theories deduced from the observation of facts accessible to us

in subjective states of consciousness, he called *subjective*. Knowledge
based upon ancient methods and principles of observation, knowledge
of things in themselves, knowledge accompanying 'an objective state of
consciousness' . . . was for him *objective* knowledge. (Ouspensky, *In
Search of the Miraculous*, p. 278)   \

3.   Among the chastisements which Dionysos inflicted, one of the most
     famous concerned the daughters of Minyas, King of Orchomenus.
     There were three sisters: Alcithoe, Leucippe and Arsippe. Since they
     refused to take part in the festivals of Dionysos, he visited them in the
     guise of a young maiden and tried to persuade them by gentleness. Being
     unsuccessful, he turned himself successively into a bull, a lion and a
     panther. Terrified by these prodigies, the daughters of Minyas lost their
     reason and one of them, Leucippe, tore her son Hippasus to pieces with
     her own hands. (*New Larousse Encyclopaedia of Mythology*, p. 159)

4. Christ was obedient even to the point of his own death by crucifixion:

   38   Then saith he unto them, My soul is exceeding sorrowful, even
   unto death: tarry ye here, and watch with me.
   39   And he went a little further, and fell on his face, and prayed, saying,
   O my Father, if it be possible, let this cup pass from me: nevertheless not
   as I will, but as thou *wilt*. (Matthew 26:38, 39)

5. It may be necessary to point out that Gurdjieff/Ouspensky's usage of
   Consciousness–Unconsciousness is the reverse of Jung's, and our everyday
   usage. They consider our ordinary state of awareness as 'unconscious', and
   'consciousness' as a state achieved by the creation of a permanent 'I' above
   functions; in Jung's terms, the integration of the Ego and shadow/*Anima* on
   the 'third' level.

6.   Like European Protestants, the Virasaivas returned to what they felt was
     the original inspiration of the ancient traditions no different from true
     and present experience.
       Defiance is not discontinuity. Alienation from the immediate environ-
     ment can mean continuity with an older idea. Protest can take place in
     the very name of one's opponent's ideals. (Introduction, *Speaking of
     Śiva*, p. 33)

CHAPTER 8   *CAVE BIRDS: AN ALCHEMICAL CAVE DRAMA*

1. Crow has much in common with Mercurius: both present images which
   include every conceivable pair of opposites, and suffer the initial contra-
   dictions of that situation (Crow's right hand has an alarming tendency to fight
   with his left hand, for instance); both are devils, redeeming psychopomps,
   and evasive tricksters, in alternation; both define God's image in Material
   nature, and contain within themselves the 'Spiritual' potential of Matter (cf.
   Alchemical Studies, p. 237).
2. The following two passages may be conjoined:

   In the furnace of the cross man, like the earthly gold, attains to the true
   black Raven's head; that is, he is utterly disfigured and is held in derision
   by the world, and this is not only for forty days and nights, or years, but

often for the whole duration of his life; so much so that he often experiences more heartache in his life than comfort and joy, and more sadness than pleasure. . . . Through this spiritual death his Soul is entirely freed. (Dorn, quoted by Jung, in *Mysterium coniunctionis*, p. 354)

When thought is obliged by an attack of physical pain, however slight, to recognize the presence of affliction, a state of mind is brought about which is as acute as that of a condemned man who is forced to look for hours at the guillotine which is going to cut off his head. Human beings can live for twenty or fifty years in this acute state. We pass quite close to them without realising it. What man is capable of discerning such souls unless Christ himself looks through his eyes . . . (Weil, 'The love of God and Affliction' *Waiting on God*, p. 78)

CHAPTER 9 *REMAINS OF ELMET AND MOORTOWN*

1. The poem brings to mind R. S. Thomas' 'Schoonermen', in which Welsh sea-faring representatives of the Celtic self are likewise in direct, pioneering contact with elementals:

> Great in this,
> They made small ships do
> Big things, leaping hurdles
> Of the stiff sea, horse against horses
> in the tide race.
>   What has Rio
> To do with Pwllheli? Ask winds
> Bitter as ever
> With their black shag. Ask the quays
> Stained with spittle.
>   Four days out
> With bad cargo
> Fever took the crew;
> The mate and the boatswain,
> Peering in turn
> Through the spray's window,
> Brought her home. Memory aches
> In the bones' rigging. If tales were tall,
> Wavers were taller.
>   From long years
> In a salt school, caned by brine,
> They came landward
> With the eyes of boys,
> The Welsh accent
> Thick in their sails.

2. Only rarely is a poem unhappily distracted into the purely 'objective' imagination, and converted into an inanimate, factual catalogue; 'Last night' is the clearest example of this tendency. On the other hand, a debilitating 'subjective synthesis' occurs in 'Orf', written 'about two weeks' (*Moortown Diary*, p. 64) after the event it describes.

3. At a graduation ceremony at Seale Hayne Agriculture College (Summer 1986), Hughes stunned his farming audience into complete silence by cataloguing the pollution of the 'rural' produced by the techniques of modern industrial farming, which is squarely-based on 'urban' technology and its palpable disrespect for the environmental whole. More recently, he has been personally involved in a project aiming to give City children access to the countryside, thus bringing the 'urban' and the 'rural' into a hopeful co-operation in the minds of those upon whom our cultural growth depends.

4. It might be added that the poem as a whole acts as an objectification of Hughes' compositional model introduced in Chapter 5, in which the (A) conscious and (B) unconscious versions ideally 'work as one' (Z).

5. It is notable that even those poems, like 'Song of longsight' and 'Life is trying to be life', which threaten to diminish that fable by over-intellectualizing it – i.e. subjecting it to the abstractive tendency – are recognizably governed by the same urge to unify the opposites.

6. On the psychological level, it is necessary to love – at Simone Weil's unattached distance – the whole of oneself, *not* just the 'positive' self-image with which West European cultures invite us to identify, in order for the self to be able to give out light.

   On the external level, it is necessary to spread love over the widest area possible, human and non-human, in order that the 'whole' environment of the earth may be regenerated.

   Love directed at the Personality or exclusively 'human' produces that contempt for the Material world, and the appalling misuse/ exploitation of it, which characterizes our own contemporary 'state of negotiations'.

BIBLIOGRAPHY

Both Sagar, in *The Art of Ted Hughes*, and Stephen Tabor, in *Ted Hughes: A Bibliography 1957–75*, provide comprehensive bibliographies about Hughes. What follows is thus a selective listing of works by and about Hughes.

SELECTION OF WORKS BY TED HUGHES

The Hawk in the Rain, London, Faber, 1957.
Lupercal, London, Faber, 1960.
The Burning of the Brothel, London, Turret Books, 1966; limited edition (300 copies).
Recklings, London, Turret Books, 1966; limited edition (150 copies).
Wodwo, London, Faber, 1967.
Poetry in the Making, London, Faber, 1967.
The Iron Man (children's story), London, Faber, 1968.
Seneca's *Oedipus* (adaptation), London, Faber, 1969.
The Life and Songs of Crow, London, Faber, 1970.
Eat Crow (radio play), London, Rainbow Press, 1971; limited edition (150 copies).
Season Songs, London, Faber, 1976.
Gaudete, London, Faber, 1977.
Orts, London, Rainbow Press, 1978; limited edition (200 copies).
Cave Birds: an alchemical cave drama, London, Faber, 1978.
Remains of Elmet: A Pennine sequence, London, Faber, 1979.
Moortown, London, Faber, 1979.
River, London, Faber, 1983.
Flowers and Insects, London, Faber, 1986.

ESSAYS, REVIEWS, INTERVIEWS AND OTHER PROSE WRITINGS BY TED HUGHES

'Ted Hughes writes', *Poetry Book Society Bulletin* 15 (September 1957).
'The poetry of Keith Douglas', *Listener* 67 (21 June 1962), pp. 1069–71.
'The poetry of Keith Douglas', *Critical Quarterly* 5 (1963), pp. 43–8.

Review of *Vagrancy* by Philip O'Connor, *New Statesman* 66 (9 August 1963), pp. 293–4.
'The rock' (radio talk), *Listener*, (19 September 1963).
Introduction to *Selected Poems* of Keith Douglas, London, Faber, 1964.
Review of *Myth and Religion of the North* by E. O. G. Turbeville Petre, *Listener* 71 (19 March 1964), pp. 484–5.
Review of *Astrology* by Louis MacNeice, *New Statesman* 68 (2 October 1964), p. 500.
Review of *Shamanism* by Mircea Eliade and *The Sufis* by Idries Shah, *Listener* 72 (29 October 1964), pp. 677–8.
'The genius of Isaac Bashevis Singer', *New York Review of Books* 4, 6, (22 April 1965), pp. 8–10.
'Notes on the chronological order of Sylvia Plath's poems', *Tri-Quarterly* 7 (Autumn 1966), pp. 81–8.
Review of *The Selected Letters of Dylan Thomas*, ed. C. Fitzgibbon, *New Statesman* 72 (25 November 1966), p. 783.
Introduction to *A Choice of Emily Dickinson's Verse*, London, Faber, 1968.
Introduction to *Selected Poems* of Vasko Popa, Harmondsworth, Penguin, 1969.
'Myth and education' (1), *Children's Literature in Education* 1 (1970), pp. 55–70.
Review of *The Environmental Revolution* by Max Nicholson, *Spectator* (21 March 1970).
'Ted Hughes' *Crow*', *Listener*, (30 July 1970), p. 149.
'Ted Hughes and Crow', an interview with Ekbert Faas, *London Magazine* 10 (10 January 1971), pp. 5–20.
Introduction and note to *A Choice of Shakespeare's Verse*, London, Faber, 1971.
Interview with Tom Stoppard reported in 'Orghast': *Times Literary Supplement* (1 October 1971), p. 1174.
'Orghast: talking without words', *Vogue* (December 1971).
Edition of *Modern Poetry in Translation* (1–10), 1965–71, with Daniel Weissbort.
Review of *A Separate Reality*, by Carlos Castaneda, *Observer* (5 March 1972).
Introduction to *Children as Writers* 2, London, Heinemann, 1975.
'Myth and education' (2), *Writers, Critics and Children*, ed. Geoffrey Fox, London, Heinemann Educational, 1976, pp. 79–94.
Introduction to *Selected Poems* of Janos Pilinszky, Manchester, Carcanet, 1976.
'Janos Pilinszky', *Critical Quarterly* 18, 2, pp. 75–86.
Introduction to *Collected Poems* of Vasko Popa, Manchester, Carcanet, 1977.
Introduction to *Amen* by Yehuda Amichai, Oxford University Press, 1977.
Introduction to *Collected Poems* of Sylvia Plath, London, Faber, 1981.

RECORDINGS BY TED HUGHES

'The poet speaks', XVI, Tape 527, British Council, 1963.
'*Crow*', Claddagh CCT9–10, 1973.
'Ted Hughes and R. S. Thomas read and discuss selections from their own poems', The Critical Forum, Norwich Tapes, 1978.
'Ted Hughes and Paul Muldoon', Faber poetry cassette 1983.

CRITICISM OF TED HUGHES

Alvarez, A., Introduction to *The New Poetry*, Harmondsworth, Penguin, 1962.
Bedient, Calvin, 'On Ted Hughes', *Critical Quarterly*, (Summer 1972).

Bold, Alan, *Thom Gunn and Ted Hughes*, Edinburgh, Oliver and Boyd, 1976.
Bradshaw, Graham, 'Ted Hughes' Crow as Trickster–Hero', in P. Williams (ed.) *The Fool and the Trickster: A Festschrift for Enid Welsford*, Ipswich, Boydell Press, 1978.
Conquest, Robert, 'The hawk in the rain', *Spectator* (11 October 1957).
Cox, C. B., and Dyson, A. E., *Modern Poetry*, London, Arnold, 1963.
Dodsworth, Martin, 'Gaudete', *Guardian* (19 May 1977).
Eagleton, Terry, 'Gaudete', *Stand* 19, 2 (1978).
Faas, Ekbert, *Ted Hughes: The unaccommodated universe*, Santa Barbara, Calif., Black Sparrow Press, 1980.
Gifford, Terry and Roberts, Neil, *Ted Hughes: A critical study*, London, Faber, 1981.
Hainsworth, J. D., 'Ted Hughes and violence', *Essays in Criticism*, (July 1965).
Hamilton, Ian, 'Ted Hughes' *Crow*', *A Poetry Chronicle*, London, Faber, 1973.
Holbrook, David, 'From "vitalism" to a dead crow: Ted Hughes' failure of confidence', in *Lost Bearings in English Poetry*, London, Vision, 1977.
Lodge, David, '*Crow* and the Cartoons', *Critical Quarterly* 13, 1 (Spring 1971), pp. 37–42.
May, Derwent, 'Ted Hughes' in M. Dodsworth (ed.), *The Survival of Poetry*, London, Faber, 1970.
Newton, J. M., 'Some notes on Ted Hughes' *Crow*', *Cambridge Quarterly* 5, 4 (1971), pp. 376–82.
Probyn, Hugh, *Ted Hughes' Gaudete*, Preston, Harris, 1977.
Rawson, Claud, 'Ted Hughes: A re-appraisal', *Essays in Criticism* 15, 1 (January 1965), pp. 77–94.
Robinson, Ian, and Sims, David, 'Ted Hughes' *Crow*', *Human World*, 9 (November 1972), pp. 31–40.
Sagar, Keith, *Ted Hughes*, Manchester, Longman for the British Council, 1972.
Sagar, Keith, *The Art of Ted Hughes*, 2nd edn, Cambridge University Press, 1978.
Sagar, Keith, ed. *The Achievement of Ted Hughes*, Manchester University Press, 1983.
Taylor, Stephen, *Ted Hughes: A bibliography 1957–75*, Los Angeles, University of California Press, 1977.
Thurley, Geoffrey, 'Beyond positive values: Ted Hughes', in *The Ironic Harvest*, London, Arnold, 1974, pp. 163–89.
Uroff, Margaret D., *Sylvia Plath and Ted Hughes*, University of Illinois, 1979.
Walder, Dennis, *Ted Hughes, Sylvia Plath*, Milton Keynes, Open University Press, 1976.
West, Thomas, *Ted Hughes* (Contemporary Writers), London, Methuen, 1985.

GENERAL

Aivanhov, Omraam Mikhael, *The Tree of the Knowledge of Good and Evil*, Frejus, Prosveta, 1984.
Aivanhov, Omraam Mikhael, *Sexual Force or the Winged Dragon*, Frejus, Prosveta, 1984.
Aivanhov, Omraam Mikhael, *Man's Two Natures: Human and Divine*, Frejus, Prosveta, 1985.

Aivanhov, Omraam Mikhael, *Spiritual Alchemy, Complete Works II*, Frejus, Prosveta, 1986.

Alvarez, A., *The New Poetry*, Harmondsworth, Penguin, 1962.

Amis, K., *Collected Poems 1944–1979*, London, Hutchinson, 1979.

Andreae, Johann Valentin, *The Chymical Wedding of Christian Rosencreutz*, trans. Foxcroft; reprinted in *Cross and Crucible*, The Hague, John Montgomery, 1973.

Attar, Farid ud-din, *The Conference of the Birds*, trans. Afkham Darbandi and Dick Davis, Harmondsworth, Penguin, 1984.

Augustine, *Confessions*, trans. R. Pine-Coffin, Harmondsworth, Penguin, 1961.

Barthes, Roland, *Writing Degree Zero*, trans. A Lavers and C. Smith, New York, 1968.

Barthes, Roland, 'Science versus literature', in M. Lane (ed.), *Structuralism: A reader*, London, 1970.

Barthes, Roland, *Image–Music–Text*, London, Fontana, 1977.

Beckett, Samuel, *Molloy*, London, Calder, 1955.

Beckett, Samuel, *Malone Dies*, London, Calder, 1958.

Beckett, Samuel, *The Unnameable*, London, Calder, 1959.

Beckett, Samuel, *Proust and Three Dialogues*, London, Chatto and Windus, 1961.

Beckett, Samuel, *Watt*, London, Calder, 1963.

Beckett, Samuel, *How it is*, London, Calder, 1964.

Berger, Peter, *Invitation to Sociology*, London, Pelican, 1966.

Blake, William, *The Complete Poems*, Harmondsworth, Penguin, 1977.

Borowski, Tadeusz, *This Way for the Gas, Ladies and Gentlemen*, Harmondsworth, Penguin, 1976.

Brodeur, A. G., *The Art of Beowulf*, University of California, Berkeley, 1959.

Bruns, Gerald, *Modern Poetry and the Idea of Language*, New Haven and London, Yale University Press, 1974.

Buckley, Vincent, *Poetry and the Sacred*, London, Chatto and Windus, 1968.

Campbell, Joseph, *The Hero with a Thousand Faces*, New York, Pantheon, 1949.

Campbell, Joseph, *The Masks of God: Creative mythology*, London, Secker and Warburg, 1968.

Campbell, Joseph, *Myths to Live By*, Souvenir Press, 1973.

Castaneda, Carlos, *The Teachings of Don Juan*, Harmondsworth, Penguin, 1970.

Castaneda, Carlos, *A Separate Reality*, Harmondsworth, Penguin, 1973.

Castaneda, Carlos, *Journey to Ixtlan*, Harmondsworth, Penguin, 1974.

Castaneda, Carlos, *Tales of Power*, Harmondsworth, Penguin, 1976.

Castaneda, Carlos, *The Second Ring of Power*, Harmondsworth, Penguin, 1979.

Castaneda, Carlos, *The Eagle's Gift*, Harmondsworth, Penguin, 1982.

Castaneda, Carlos, *The Fire from Within*, Harmondsworth, Penguin, 1985.

Conquest, Robert, *New Lines*, London, Macmillan, 1956.

Davie, Donald, *Articulate Energy: An enquiry into the syntax of English poetry*, London, Routledge and Kegan Paul, 1955.

Davie, Donald, *The Purity of Diction in English Verse*, London, Routledge and Kegan Paul, 1967.

Davie, Donald, *Collected Poems 1950–70*, London, Routledge and Kegan Paul, 1972.

Davie, Donald, *The Poet in the Imaginary Museum: Essays of two decades*, Manchester, Carcanet, 1977.

Doresse, Jean, *The Secret Books of the Egyptian Gnostics*, Vermont, Hollis and Carter, 1960.

Douglas, Keith, *Selected Poems*, London, Faber, 1964.
Driver, Tom, 'Beckett by the Madeleine', Columbia University Forum, IV, 1961.
Eliade, Mircea, *Patterns of Comparative Religion*, London, Sheed and Ward, 1958.
Eliade, Mircea, *The Sacred and the Profane*, Harcourt Brace Jovanovich, 1959.
Eliade, Mircea, *Myth and Reality*, New York, 1963.
Eliade, Mircea, *Shamanism*, London, Routledge and Kegan Paul, 1964.
Eliot, T. S., *Selected Poems*, London, Faber, 1954.
von Eschenbach, Wolfram, *Parzival*, New York, Random House, 1961.
Evans-Wentz, W. (ed.) *The Tibetan Book of the Dead*, Oxford University Press, 1960.
Feder, Lilian, *Ancient Myth and Modern Poetry*, Princeton University Press, 1971.
Fish, Stanley, *Self-Consuming Artifacts*, University of California, Berkeley, 1972.
Gombrowicz, Witold, *Dziennik 1953–1956*, Paris, 1957.
Graves, Robert, *The White Goddess*, London, Faber, 1961.
Gurdjieff, G. I., *Views from the Real World*, London, Arkana, Routledge and Kegan Paul, 1984.
Gurdjieff, G. I., *A Further Record*, London, Arkana, Routledge and Kegan Paul, 1986.
Hamburger, Michael (ed. and trans.), *East German Poetry*, Oxford, Carcanet, 1972.
Harner, Michael (ed.), *Hallucinogens and Shamanism*, Oxford University Press, 1973.
Heaney, Seamus, *Preoccupations: Selected prose 1968–78*, London, Faber, 1980.
Herbert, Zbigniew, *Selected Poems*, trans. C. Milosz and P. Dale Scott, Harmondsworth, Penguin, 1968.
Herbert, Zbigniew, *Selected Poems*, trans. John and Bogdana Carpenter, Oxford University Press, 1977.
Holan, Vladimir, *Selected Poems*, trans. Ian and Jarmila Milner, Harmondsworth, Penguin, 1971.
Holub, Miroslav, *Selected Poems*, trans. Ian Milner and George Theiner, Harmondsworth, Penguin, 1967.
Holub, Miroslav, *From Notes of a Clay Pigeon*, trans. Ian and Jarmila Milner, London, Secker and Warburg, 1977.
Jung, Carl Gustav, *Psychological Types* (Collected Works, vol. 6), London, Routledge and Kegan Paul, 1921.
Jung, Carl Gustav, *Modern Man in Search of a Soul*, London, Ark, Routledge and Kegan Paul, 1933.
Jung, Carl Gustav, *Psychology and Religion*, Oxford University Press, 1938.
Jung, Carl Gustav, *Psychology and Alchemy*, (Collected Works, vol. 12), London, Routledge and Kegan Paul, 1953.
Jung, Carl Gustav, *Symbols of Transformation* (Collected Works, vol. 5), London, Routledge and Kegan Paul, 1956.
Jung, Carl Gustav, *The Undiscovered Self*, London, Routledge and Kegan Paul, 1958.
Jung, Carl Gustav, *The Archetypes of the Collective Unconscious* (Collected Works, vol. 9, (I)), London, Routledge and Kegan Paul, 1959.
Jung, Karl Gustav, *Aion* (Collected Works, vol. 9, (II)), London, Routledge and Kegan Paul, 1959.
Jung, Carl Gustav, *Mysterium Coniunctionis* (Collected Works, vol. 14), London, Routledge and Kegan Paul, 1963.

Jung, Carl Gustav, *Alchemical Studies* (Collected Works, vol. 13), London, Routledge and Kegan Paul, 1968.

Jung, Carl Gustav, 'On the psychology of the Trickster-figure', in Radin, *The Trickster*, pp. 195–211.

Jung, Carl Gustav, Foreword to D. T. Suzuki's *Introduction to Zen Buddhism*, pp. 9–29.

Laing, R. D., *The Politics of Experience and the Bird of Paradise*, Harmondsworth, Penguin, 1967.

Larkin, Philip, *The Less Deceived*, London, Marvell Press, 1955.

Larkin, Philip, *The Whitsun Weddings*, London, Faber, 1964.

Mann, Thomas (ed.), *The Living Thoughts of Schopenhauer*, London, Cassell, 1949.

Merton, Thomas, 'Symbolism – communication or communion?', *New Directions* 20 (1948), pp. 1–2.

Merton, Thomas, *Mystics and Zen*, New York, 1967.

Milosz, Czeslaw (ed.), *Post-War Polish Poetry*, University of California, Los Angeles, 1983.

Morrison, Blake, *The Movement*, Oxford University Press, 1980.

New Larousse Encyclopaedia of Mythology, London, Hamlyn, 1968.

Nietzsche, Friedrich, *The Birth of Tragedy*, London, Haussmann, 1909.

Nott, C. S., *The Teachings of Gurdjieff*, London, Routledge and Kegan Paul, 1961.

Ouspensky, P. D., *In Search of the Miraculous*, London, Routledge and Kegan Paul, 1950.

Ouspensky, P. D., *The Fourth Way*, London, Routledge and Kegan Paul, 1957.

Ouspenksy, P. D., *Conscious: The search for truth*, London, Routledge and Kegan Paul, 1979.

Picard, Max, *Man and Language*, Chicago, 1963.

Pilinszky, Janos, *Selected Poems*, Manchester, Carcanet, 1976.

Pilinszky, Janos, *Krater* (Collected Writings in the Hungarian), Budapest, Szepirodalmi Konyvkiado, 1976.

Pilinszky, Janos, *Crater: Poems 1974–5*, trans. Peter Jay, London, Anvil, 1978.

Plath, Aurelia, S. (ed.), *Letters Home*, London, Faber, 1976.

Plath, Sylvia, *Collected Poems*, London, Faber, 1981.

Popa, Vasko, *Selected Poems*, Harmondsworth, Penguin, 1969.

Popa, Vasko, *Collected Poems*, Manchester, Carcanet, 1977.

Radin, Paul, *Primitive Man as Philosopher*, New York, 1957.

Radin, Paul, *The Trickster*, New York, 1972.

Ramanujan, A. K., *Speaking of Śiva*, Harmondsworth, Penguin, 1973.

Robins, R. H., *A Short History of Linguistics*, London, Longman, 1967.

Ross, M. M., *Poetry and Dogma*, New Jersey, Rutgers University Press, 1954.

Rozewicz, Tadeusz, *Faces of Anxiety* (Europe 12), London, Rapp and Whiting, 1969.

Rozewicz, Tadeusz, 'Tadeuz Rozewicz in conversation with Adam Czerniawski', *The New Review*, 25, (London 1976).

Rozewicz, Tadeusz, *Conversations with the Prince and Other Poems*, trans. Adam Czerniawski, London, Anvil, 1982.

Santa, Ferenc, Interview in *Life and Literature*, (6 May 1967).

Sartre, Jean-Paul, *Nausea*, Harmondsworth, Penguin, 1965.

Shah, Idries, *The Sufis*, London, Octagon Press, 1964.

Shah, Idries, *The Way of the Sufi*, Harmondsworth, Penguin, 1974.

Smith, A. C. H., *Orghast at Persepolis*, London, Eyre Methuen, 1972.

Staff, Leopold, *An Empty Room*, trans. A. Czerniawski, Newcastle, Bloodaxe, 1983.

Stanford, W. B., *Greek Metaphor: Studies in theory and practice*, London, 1936.

Stevens and Mandel (ed.), *Old English Literature*, University of Nebraska Press, 1968.

Suzuki, D. T., *The Essentials of Zen Buddhism*, ed. B. Phillips, New York, 1962.

Suzuki, D. T., *An Introduction to Zen Buddhism*, London, Rider, 1969.

Swami, Shree Purohit and Yeats, W. B., *The Ten Principal Upanishads*, London, Faber, 1937.

Tezla, Albert (ed.), *Ocean at the Window: Hungarian prose and poetry since 1945*, University of Minnesota Press, 1980.

Thomas, Dylan, *The Poems*, ed. Daniel Jones, London, Everyman/Dent, 1981.

Todorov, Tzvetan, *Theories of the Symbol*, trans. C. Porter, Oxford, Blackwell, 1982.

Wain, John (ed.), *Anthology of Modern Poetry*, London, Hutchinson, 1963.

Watts, Alan, *The Supreme Identity*, London, Faber, 1950.

Watts, Alan, *The Way of Zen*, London, Pelican, 1962.

Watts, Alan, *Beyond Theology*, Wildwood House, 1974.

Watts, Alan, *Myth and Ritual in Christianity*, London, Thames and Hudson, 1983.

Weil, Simone, *Intimations of Christianity among the Ancient Greeks*, London, Routledge and Kegan Paul, 1957.

Weil, Simone, *The Notebooks of Simone Weil*, London, Routledge and Kegan Paul, 1958.

Weil, Simone, *Waiting on God*, London, Fontana Collins, 1959.

Weil, Simone, *On Science, Necessity and the Love of God*, Oxford University Press, 1965.

Weil, Simone, *First and Last Notebooks*, Oxford University Press, 1970.

Weil, Simone, *Gateway to God*, London, Fontana Collins, 1974.

Williams, P. (ed.), *The Fool and the Trickster, a Festschrift for Enid Welsford*, Ipswich, Boydell Press, 1979.

Wimsatt, W. K. and Beardsley, W., *The Verbal Icon*, Lexington, Ky, 1954.

Worringer, Wilhelm, *Abstraction and Empathy*, trans. M. Bullock, London, 1953.

Yeats, W. B., *Collected Poe,s*, London, Macmillan, 1982.

INDEX